Reality Exploration and Discovery

In honor of

K.P. Mohanan

on the occasion of
his 60th birthday

Reality Exploration and Discovery

Pattern Interaction in Language & Life

edited by

Linda Uyechi &
Lian-Hee Wee

CSLI PUBLICATIONS
Center for the Study of
Language and Information
Stanford University

Center for the Study of Language and Information
Leland Stanford Junior University
Printed in the United States
13 12 11 10 09 1 2 3 4 5

Library of Congress Cataloging-in-Publication Data

Reality exploration and discovery : pattern interaction in language and life / edited by Linda Uyechi and Lian-Hee Wee.

p. cm. – (CSLI lecture notes ; no. 197)

Includes bibliographical references and index.
ISBN-13: 978-1-57586-588-1 (pbk. : alk. paper)
ISBN-10: 1-57586-588-2 (pbk. : alk. paper)
ISBN-13: 978-1-57586-589-8 (cloth : alk. paper)
ISBN-10: 1-57586-589-0 (cloth : alk. paper)
1. Lexical phonology. 2. Mohanan, Karuvannur Puthanveettil.
I. Uyechi, Linda, 1957– II. Wee, Lian-Hee, 1973–

P26.M58R43 2009
414 –dc22 2009025595
CIP

∞ The acid-free paper used in this book meets the minimum requirements of the American National Standard for Information Sciences—Permanence of Paper for Printed Library Materials, ANSI Z39.48 -1984.

CSLI was founded in 1983 by researchers from Stanford University, SRI International, and Xerox PARC to further the research and development of integrated theories of language, information, and computation. CSLI headquarters and CSLI Publications are located on the campus of Stanford University.

CSLI Publications reports new developments in the study of language, information, and computation. Please visit our web site at
http://cslipublications.stanford.edu/
for comments on this and other titles, as well as for changes and corrections by the authors, editors, and publisher.

Contents

Contributors

FIRMIN AHOUA: Department of Linguistics/ILA, Université de Cocody, 08 BP 887, Abidjan 08, Côte D'Ivoire.
Fahoua2003@yahoo.fr

ALEX ALSINA: Departament de Traducció i Filologia, Universitat Pompeu Fabra, La Rambla 30-32, 08002 Barcelona, Spain.
alex.alsina@upf.edu

NORHAIDA AMAN: National Institute of Education, Nanyang Technology University, 1 Nanyang Walk, Singapore 637616. Singapore.
norhaida.aman@nie.edu.sg

JEAN ANN: Department of Curriculum and Instruction, 119 Wilber Hall, School of Education, State University of New York, Oswego, NY 13126, USA.
jean.ann@oswego.edu

ARTO ANTTILA: Department of Linguistics, Stanford University, Margaret Jacks Hall, Stanford, CA 94305-2150, USA.
anttila@stanford.edu

DIANA ARCHANGELI: Department of Linguistics, Douglass 200E University of Arizona, Tucson, AZ 85721, USA.
dba@u.arizona.edu

BAO ZHIMING: National University of Singapore, Block AS5, 7 Arts Link, Singapore 117570. Singapore.
ellbaozm@nus.edu.sg

JOAN BRESNAN: Department of Linguistics, Stanford University, Margaret Jacks Hall, Stanford, CA 94305-2150, USA.
bresnan@stanford.edu

MIRIAM BUTT: Universität Konstanz, FB Sprachwissenschaft, Fach D 186, D-78457 Konstanz, Germany.
miriam.butt@uni-konstanz.de

PETER COLE: University of Delaware, Department of Linguistics, Newark, DE 19716. USA.
pcole@udel.edu

MARY DALRYMPLE: Centre for Linguistics and Philology, Walton Street, Oxford OX1 2HG UK.
mary.dalrymple@ling-phil.ox.ac.uk

MARK DONOHUE: Centre for Research on Language Change, Australian National University, Australia.
mark@donohue.cc

VIVIENNE FONG: Undergraduate Advising and Research, Stanford University, Sweet Hall, 590 Escondido Mall, Stanford, CA 94305-3094, USA.
vivienne@stanford.edu

GABRIELA HERMON: University of Delaware, Department of Linguistics, Newark, DE 19716. USA.
gaby@udel.edu

TONY T.N. HUNG: Language Centre, Hong Kong Baptist University, Kowloon Tong, Hong Kong SAR.
tonyhung@hkbu.edu.hk

TRACY HOLLOWAY KING: Microsoft Corporation, 475 Brannan St., San Francisco, CA 94107, USA.
Tracy.King@microsoft.com

PAUL KIPARSKY: Department of Linguistics, Stanford University, Margaret Jacks Hall, Stanford, CA 94305-2150, USA.
kiparsky@csli.stanford.edu

PAUL KROEGER: Graduate Institute of Applied Linguistics (GIAL), 7500 W. Camp Wisdom Rd., Dallas, TX 75236. USA.
paul_kroeger@gial.edu

WILLIAM R. LEBEN: Department of Linguistics, Stanford University, Margaret Jacks Hall, Stanford, CA 94305-2150, USA.
leben@stanford.edu

BETH LEVIN: Department of Linguistics, Stanford University, Margaret Jacks Hall, Stanford, CA 94305-2150, USA.
beth.levin@stanford.edu

YO MATSUMOTO: Kobe University, 1-1 Rokkoodai-cho, Nadaku, Kobe Japan.
yomatsum@lit.kobe-u.ac.jp

K.P. MOHANAN: National University of Singapore, Block AS5, 7 Arts Link, Singapore 117570. Singapore.
ellkpmoh@nus.edu.sg

MALAVIKA TARA MOHANAN: 'Anangan', Panamanna PO, Kerala 679501, India
redpill42@gmail.com

CAROL NEIDLE: Linguistics Program, Department of Romance Studies, Boston University, 621 Commonwealth Avenue, Room 101, Boston, MA 02215, USA.
carol@bu.edu

TATIANA NIKITINA: Department of Linguistics, Stanford University, Margaret Jacks Hall, Stanford, CA 94305-2150, USA.
tann@stanford.edu

EUNJEONG OH: Department of Chinese, Translation and Linguistics, City University of Hong Kong, Tat Chee Avenue, Kowloon Tong, Hong Kong SAR.
ilto:eunjeooh@cityu.edu.hk

JOHN C. PAOLILLO: School of Informatics and School of Library and Information Science, Indiana University, 901 E Tenth St, Bloomington, IN 47408, USA.
paolillo@indiana.edu

LONG PENG: Department of Curriculum and Instruction, 111 Wilber Hall, School of Education, State University of New York, Oswego, NY 13126, USA.
long.peng@oswego.edu

DOUGLAS PULLEYBLANK: Department of Linguistics, University of British Columbia, E270-1866 Main Mall, Vancouver, B.C. V6T1Z1, Canada.
douglas.pulleyblank@ubc.ca

GILLIAN RAMCHAND: Institute for Linguistic, Humanities Faculty, University of Tromsoe, Tromsoe, N-9037. Norway.
gillian.ramchand@hum.uit.no

PETER SELLS: Department of Linguistics, School of Oriental and African Studies, 10 Thornhaugh Street, London WC1H 0 XG, UK.
sells@soas.ac.uk

SHIAOWEI THAM: Department of East Asian Languages and Literatures, Wellesley College, 230 Green Hall, Wellesley, MA 02482, USA.
stham@wellesley.edu

K.G. VIJAYAKRISHNAN: Centre for Linguistics and Contemporary English, School of Language Sciences, The English and Foreign Languages University, Hyderabad 500007, India.
kgvijayakrishnan@gmail.com

LIAN-HEE WEE: Department of English Language and Literature, Hong Kong Baptist University, Kowloon Tong, Hong Kong SAR.
lianhee@hkbu.edu.hk

SHÛICHI YATABE: Department of Language and Information Sciences, University of Tokyo, 3-8-1 Komaba, Meguro-ku, Tokyo, 153-8902, Japan.
yatabe@phiz.c.u-tokyo.ac.jp

MARIA LUISA ZUBIZARRETA: Department of Linguistics, University of Southern California, GFS 301, LA, CA 90089-1693, USA.
zubizarr@usc.edu

Intellectual Restlessness: Inquiry and Analysis

LIAN-HEE WEE AND LINDA UYECHI

Reality Exploration

Exploring reality is the enterprise that drives the inquiring mind. Regardless of the domain of inquiry – be it biology for the biologist, chemistry for the chemist, physics for the physicist, society for the sociologist, or language for the linguist – if we take a giant step back, we discover shared building blocks across domains of inquiry. We share motivations for exploring reality revealed through puzzles, problems, and questions, common approaches to analysis, and a desire to analyze reality in the service of understanding puzzles, solving problems, and answering questions.

True riches, measured in the depth of understanding reality that one's analysis provides and the ability to communicate those new insights to others, are available to those who not only recognize the building blocks of the process they use to explore reality but who also apply an understanding of that process to communicate their ideas both within their own field and across disciplines. Indeed, an improved understanding of the process of reality exploration leads not only to a deeper understanding of reality, but also to an ability to reconstruct our path of discovery – the latter of which leads to more effective communication of our ideas to others and, if we are truly successful, an improvement in our ability to understand others.

No one understands this better than K.P. Mohanan who, when pressed by a student (see Ann, this volume) to describe what he meant by "analysis", was at a loss for a simple explanation. In the exploration of reality, one is confronted with one's observations and a desire to analyze them. But what

Reality Exploration and Discovery: Pattern Interaction in Language and Life.
Linda Uyechi and Lian-Hee Wee (eds.).

does analysis mean? Mohanan (1996) responds that there must at least be four possible kinds of analysis:

(1) a. Analysis as break-up and labeling
  b. Analysis as the crystallization and articulation of an intuitively apprehended pattern
  c. Analysis as mechanical procedure
  d. Analysis as an explanation to a puzzle

It is hard to find examples in real life (academic or otherwise) where only one of the four modes in (1) is used, though different enterprises may rely on a particular mode more heavily than others. In linguistics one does a little bit of everything.

When analyzing the constituents of a sentence, there is a lot of break-up and labeling, (1a). Depending on one's pet theory, a sentence may be broken up into NPs and VPs; or into subject, predicate and object; or themes and rhemes, topics and comments. Sometimes such breaking up and labeling is done rigorously, requiring empirical motivation for each constituent and its category, and at other times it may be applied more intuitively. For example in qualitative analysis in chemistry, breaking-up and labeling is a careful and rigorous procedure so that one can determine, without risk of poisoning, if a sample of blue crystals is $CuSO_4$ (Copper Sulphate) or sugar crystals from a serving of Blue Curaçao. In biology, when labeling parts of an animal's body as head, neck, torso, and the like, boundaries are less obvious since it may be hard to determine, for example, where a head ends and a neck begins. This is also true of linguistics when one tries to decompose phrases into words, morphemes or phonemes. The boundaries are not always clear, and the linguist must exercise rigor in establishing the labels and their corresponding parts.

Thus given the intricacies of natural language, for the linguist, intuition, (1b), is a valuable tool that helps one grapple with complexities that, if approached systematically, would require the analyst to address infinite possibilities. Consider, for example, the five-word sentence *the boy pinched the elephant* (see cover design). By relying on intuition, an observer, let's call him Moe, would probably suggest the following constituency: [[the boy] [pinched [the elephant]]]. Moe's proposal is likely to have come from an intuitively apprehended pattern observable from other sentences such as *Joey kissed a cow, The frog tickled her*, and *Raccoons wear dark glasses*. If asked to articulate his intuition, Moe might point out a do-er, an action and a victim in each sentence. This may, on closer examination, be inadequate, but Moe's intuition has provided him with a head start because he can now examine his intuition against more carefully related examples until he arrives at a rigorously tested theory. Had Moe not appealed to his intuitions at all, he would have had to try any of the more than twenty possible groupings of the five-word sentence before arriving at the grouping best supported by empirical evidence.[1]

Mechanical procedures, (1c), are also of great value in linguistics. There are at least two ways of thinking about mechanical procedures. In Mohanan (1996), it is understood as taking a sample of something to be analyzed and then running a series of operations to uncover properties of that sample. This is typically done in DNA testing where a sample is put through a standard series of operations to reveal the DNA coding. In linguistics, this approach is particularly useful in statistical analyses of corpora, where tagged items are counted and then subject to a series of statistical procedures to yield generalizations. Additionally, a mechanical procedure can be one in which a set of procedures are applied to produce a desired result. This is best exemplified in engineering where, let's say, the civil engineer must figure out the procedure for building a bridge (e.g. to build a suspension bridge such as the Brooklyn Bridge requires a series of steps: sink caissons, build bridge towers, run wires and cables over and across the bridge towers and, finally, lay the bridge surface).

The latter approach to analysis is prevalent in the rewrite rules and derivations of linear grammars. Consider, for example, Tianjin, a Northern Mandarin language, where syllables undergo tone sandhi. Among the many sandhi rules, when two syllables both carrying rising tones, R, are adjacent, the initial R surfaces as H, i.e. R → H/__R (e.g. *haoR jiuR* → *laoH jiuR* 'good wine'). Also, when an R syllable precedes a syllable with a high flat tone H, then the R surfaces as H, i.e. R → L/__H (e.g. *haoR renH* → *laoL renH* 'good person').[2] Now, consider an input of /RRH/. The attested surface form turns out to be [HLH] regardless of morphosyntactic configuration. To get the attested form, one has to mechanically apply the R →H rule before the R → L rule. The mechanical procedure produces the right results but it brings into question why the procedures are the way they are.[3]

Finally, explaining puzzling phenomena, (1d), is also a type of analysis applied by linguists. For example, if sentences are made up of words, why do arbitrary strings of words not form grammatical sentences? In other words, why can we say *The child pinched the elephant*, but not **Elephant the the*

[1]Use of intuition is common in literary, music and art appreciation where a pattern has to be intuitively apprehended, crystallized and then articulated. For example, listen to Rachmaninov's "Rhapsody on a Theme of Paganini", Bach's "Goldberg Variations" or any music that is a variation on a theme. One's intuition might quickly identify the presence of a pattern but extricating and articulating that pattern requires considerably more effort.

[2]For detailed analyses, see Chen (2000) and Wee (2004) and references cited therein.

[3]It is important to note that the proposal and/or application of a procedure does not entail/require an explanation or understanding of any more substantive principles at work. For example, one can calculate the standard deviation of a set of values without knowing what standard deviation means.

pinch child ? Both strings are made up of the same words, and the meaning is not obscure: because elephants cannot pinch, the only sensible interpretation is one where the child is doing the pinching. So it is puzzling that one sequence should be unacceptable. In fact, many other unacceptable sequences can be as easily constructed. Likewise, if words are made up of sequences of phones, why can't any arbitrary sequence of sounds be a potential word? For example [sput] is possible in English but *[zbut] is not; [sut] and [put] are possible words in Cantonese, but *[sput] is not. Physiologically, all of these sequences can be uttered, so physical limitations do not provide an explanation, and semantics plays no role in this puzzle because we are only exploring sound sequences that make up possible words.

Those who are intrigued when presented with data like that above experience one of the main motivations that drive linguists: linguists delight in solving puzzles. In simple terms, a puzzle is a situation where our expectations of randomness or regularity are not met by empirical observation. When confronted with a puzzle, there is a strong urge to figure out how the situation came to be the way it is. Are there rules and laws governing how all the elements in the situation interact? Did the situation come to be the way it is because of a chain of related events? In the example involving *The child pinched the elephant*, an explanation (i.e. analysis in the sense of (1d)) for the unacceptability of **Elephant the the pinch child* might be a set of statements on English syntax. For example, an English declarative sentence must have the order NP followed by VP (i.e. S → NP VP), where NP is made up of a Det N (NP → Det N) sequence and VP → V NP. Violations to these laws, such as those found in **Elephant the the pinch child* produce unacceptable sentences.

Despite our attempts in the above paragraphs to exemplify each notion of analysis in (1), as illustrated by the example just presented, the reality is that it is the rare situation that can be approached with only a single mode of analysis. In this most recent case, the solution to the puzzle, (1d), was enhanced by the application of a mechanical procedure, (1c). Instinctively, the inquiring mind is likely to employ a combination of analytical modes. Taking that instinct, evaluating our process for exploring reality, and being able to articulate those processes in terms like (1) takes us one step closer to truly mining the riches of intellectual inquiry.

We take another step towards intellectual riches by simply asking: What triggers us to engage in analysis in the first place? We suggest that there are three situations, described in (2), which motivate inquiry.

(2) a. *Puzzle* A situation where one's expectations of regularity or randomness is not met

b. *Problem* A situation where there is a mismatch between the current situation and an ideal situation

c. *Question* A situation where the characteristics of some X is not known

Language poses many puzzles for the linguist, so it is unsurprising that many examples of puzzles, (2a), have been given above. But in other domains, problems, (2b), are just as likely to trigger analysis. Consider, for example, deciding on the best course of action for next Valentine's Day. The problem is a situation in which you currently have no sweetheart, but ideally would win one. The problem triggers more than one type of analysis: you label and identify your beloved person's likes and dislikes (1a), calculate the cost of chocolates and flowers within the parameters of a budget (1c), and apply intuition (1b) to arrive at the best combination of timing and mode of delivery.

In medicine it is common to know a result without knowing the characteristics of its cause. So analysis here is often triggered by questions, (2c). For example, cancer is an insidious disease in which tumors appear, a person weakens and, without treatment, will eventually die. Years ago, the simple question "What is (are) the cause(s) of cancer?" triggered a line of inquiry which (when appropriately funded) continues to lead scientists to apply the entire arsenal of analyses. Thankfully, the question has been partially answered – but, as in many explorations of reality, a simple question triggers an entire industry of analyses.

And though inquiries into love and disease seem somewhat removed from inquiries into language, we include them here because they illustrate the depth of understanding we can gain from dissecting how we explore reality – and, more to the point, how that informs our examination of language in this volume. Having been exposed first-hand to the thought processes that characterize Mohanan-the-restless-intellectual, the presentations in this volume reflect, in various ways, a continuing conversation with him – not only about linguistic content and details of analysis but also a meta-conversation about one's approach to reality exploration.

Discovery

As noted above, puzzles in language are easy to find. Recall the puzzle mentioned earlier, that utterances are made up of units of sounds. If this is all that is known, one would expect that any combination of sounds would be acceptable. But the null hypothesis is quickly dispelled. Consider, for example, the sequence [lcc] which is an acceptable pre-pausal consonant cluster in Malayalam as in [a.ka.lcca] *distance*. Given this, it is mysterious that [lcc] is not allowed word-initially (Mohanan 1986:73). This asymmetry is a puzzle which demands an explanation and motivates further inquiry (which in this case was taken up in T. Mohanan (1989)).

Answering such questions in linguistics provides insight as to how natural human languages work and generates building blocks for developing an architecture of mental grammar. Most of the contributions in this volume have a strong puzzle-solving flavor, though are by no means restricted to only puzzle-solving. In the area of phonology, Kiparsky's contribution explains how puzzling phenomena related to reduplication can be addressed by a layering of constraints, an insight inherited from his earlier models of lexical phonology. Peng's contribution is an analysis of very intricate puzzles in Kikuyu that can be addressed by ranking a small and simple set of universal constraints. This shows that explanations to puzzles may have simple postulates, but are certainly not simplistic.

Simplistic answers are all too common in explorations of reality where explanations are attributed to singular causes, curiosity is satisfied, and careful observations are abandoned. In contrast, Donohue's presentation of the competition between breathiness and nasality in Palu'e exemplifies the value of obtaining a full picture of data before jumping to conclusions. In the same careful spirit, Kroeger presents not only the rule for accounting for Kimaragang's vowel harmony patterns, but argues that the rule must be a lexical one. On a more diachronic front, Leben and Ahoua's contribution explains the patterns of tone change in the Kwa languages of Côte d'Ivoire by the addition and deletion of tonal links in adjacency. Shifts can also take place when languages come into contact. In this volume, Bao explains how, when two languages come into contact and produce a third language, the influence of one of the languages, though no longer visible in terms of surface elements, may persist in the form of rules and constraints, Another case of language contact is given in Wee's squib on split-gemination in Hong Kong English, where the puzzle is really a paradox that he believes is addressable if linguistic representations are allowed to have information correspond unfaithfully across nodes.

As one can see, it appears that the natural laws of human languages themselves form patterns of their own, often revolving around central sets of phenomena, synchronically or diachronically. This triggers the need for deeper explanations as to why natural linguistic laws pattern the way they do. An attempt to answer such questions in the area of phonology is made in the contribution by Mohanan, Archangeli and Pulleyblank.

In the domain of syntax, Oh and Zubizarreta's contribution compares the double object constructions in English and Korean to reveal that both languages may share similar structures or have differing ones depending on whether the double object construction is one that pertains to a goal or to a benefactive. Likewise in Matsumoto's contribution, a comparison of Malayalam, Yoruba and Japanese reveals that logophoric pronouns tend to respect the perspective of the first-person (P-PIVOT) rather than other possible deictic centers.

Theoretical understanding does not just come from relating similar phenomenon across languages, as exemplified by Alsina in his theory of structure sharing that allows for raising and long-distance dependencies to be captured under one analytical umbrella. And Dalrymple shows how a review of earlier analyses can bring about new ones with new insights as she shows how what was invisible to the Path Containment Condition (Mohanan 1984) can now be captured in an LFG setting for gap relatives and correlative binding. The multi-dimensional approach to the study of grammar is also found in Levin and Sells' contribution where puzzles appear inseparable in terms of syntax and semantics. In their study, the unpredicated use of particles with surface contact and change of state verbs is possible only if telicity can be determined solely from the properties of the expressed location object. Tham extends that multi-dimensional view (crucially for her, the separation of categorical and relational properties) to even bigger domains of discourse, and shows how strategies useful for puzzle solving is really not domain specific. It would be narrow-minded to think that language must be audible, and in this volume, Neidle provides agreement puzzles in ASL that likewise require the analyst to look at complex interactions between different levels/dimensions of grammar ranging across phonology, morphology, semantics and syntax. However, structures in the mind extend beyond language, and here, Vijayakrishnan demonstrates how strategies used in the study of grammar may be applicable to the study of music.

Pattern Interaction in Life and Language

Good answers to puzzles are often tested by some kind of modeling, so that one can better see if they reflect empirical observations. In this area, we have contributions from Bresnan and Nikitina, Yatabe, Paolillo, and Fong and Anttila. Drawing upon corpora (Switchboard corpus and Treebank corpus in particular), Bresnan and Nikitina show, with the help of stochastic OT, how the theoretical machinery of LFG match corpora, thus predicting gradience in dative alternation as well as categoricity. Despite their extensiveness, corpora do not provide negative data, and Yatabe takes care of that by employing questionnaires, with responses which argue for a linearization-based theory of syntax. Like Bresnan and Nikitina's work, Paolillo's contribution and that by Fong and Anttila center around a similar fascination with variation in the surface manifestation of mental grammars. Paolillo's main idea is to put weights in grammars (see also Mohanan 1993) so that probabilities may be calculated. Fong and Anttila's approach is to create typological orders (T-orders).

Distinct though the above models are, they are successful in capturing the complicated patterns of variation that exist in reality. While improving on explanations given to puzzles, these works also point in the direction of how theoretical developments may be brought to bear on problem solving. Since problems are defined in (2b) with respect to some ideal, they exist only when one has a particular goal in mind. In the case of linguistics, goals may range from the desire to have a naturally communicating robot, to a way of recreating the human brain with respect to language acquisition and production, and to simulating a human community. Precise models such as those given by Bresnan and Nikitina, Yatabe, Paolillo, and Fong and Anttila allow us to find ways to narrow the gap between goals like those and our current understanding of language in real life. This bridging of modeling and real life is best seen in the treatment of complex predicates by Butt, King and Ramchand. In their contribution, a debate takes place in the lively setting of a pub where arguments for computational implementation are pitched against calls for sound grammatical architecture through rigorous theorizing. The outcome of their discussion requires the serious researcher to understand fundamental assumptions across frameworks, unsurprisingly by now calling to mind Mohanan's analysis of inquiry and reiterating the value of not only exploring reality but also understanding how we explore it. The work by Butt, King and Ramchand puts an exclamation point on the theme of this volume, and provides apt tribute to their teacher.

Inquiry After All

In short, this volume is primarily an exploration of puzzles in the linguistic domain and proposals for how to capture the patterns revealed through those examinations. From one perspective, the value of such an enterprise would be to identify and apply solutions to problems. Yet, from our Mohanan-influenced perspective the enterprise is valuable for the insights it provides, because – more important than simply providing an answer – solutions generate deeper questions, as suggested by (2c). Such questions are typically of the kind "What is X?" Given our understanding of phonological patterning, for example, can we state what "opacity" is in theory-neutral terms (i.e. in terms that makes as few theoretical assumptions as possible)? Or, what is "logophoricity"?

Take the notion of "grammaticality": What is "grammaticality"? To the lay speaker, often steeped in prescriptivism, an utterance must conform to a rule in a grammar book to be "grammatical". To some linguists, a specific theory of grammar may color their interpretation of "grammaticality" such that, for an analyst steeped in a pre-OT model of language, "grammaticality" may mean that an utterance, S, perfectly obeys the rules of a language, L. And to an analyst working within the OT framework, "grammaticality" is not accounted for in terms of absolutes, but rather in terms of what is optimal, that is, the best form in terms of the conflict resolution given by L's grammar. But, as Alsina (p.c.) points out, linguists are better served by treating "grammaticality" as a theory-independent meta-feature of data that captures the acceptability (or not) of an utterance. This leads us back to our source of data, namely, the lay speaker and her community, which raises the question of which acceptability judgment to consider in the analysis of a language – that of the speaker's or her community's (notions Chomsky (1965, 1985) carefully teased apart as I-language and E-language) and how to conduct that study? The contributions in this volume present data from careful studies of a small set of informants in some papers and rigorous studies of corpora in others. How does one's interpretation of "grammaticality" impact the authors' results? We leave the final word in the hands of the reader.

The point here is to observe the benefit of taking a step back and dedicating time and effort to question the patently "obvious" building blocks of analysis. Sometimes the labels we rely on to communicate our ideas take on realities of their own. Recall the path of inquiry initiated for Mohanan when faced by the need to explain "analysis". Indeed, such questions lead us to situations which challenge one's basic philosophy of inquiry, something that Mohanan is mindful of when he looks at data, methods, ideas and concepts in linguistic research. Mohanan, our prime example of intellectual restlessness, allows his philosophy to evolve by actively solving puzzles of all kinds – for him they lie in the realm of phonology, syntax, and semantics (and often in areas as close at hand as the crispness of banana chips). He regards specific frameworks in those sub-fields as useful only so far as they provide the means to express and capture insights (see this volume, Part IV, A Bibliography of K.P. Mohanan's Work, for the range of subjects that characterize his intellectual pursuits). As a result, Mohanan is framework-agnostic and can express his ideas about syntax within frameworks as diverse as Government and Binding and Lexical Functional Grammar. And when he finds frameworks overly restrictive for expressing insights, he creates new ones, as in Grammatical Semantics (T. Mohanan and Wee 1999, also taken up in Levin and Sells, this volume). This spirit of open-minded inquiry is also manifest in his critique of phonological models regardless of the model of the day; he was at it during pre-OT days (Mohanan 1993), and continues even now when OT is prevalent (Mohanan 2000 and Mohanan, Archangeli and Pulleyblank, this volume).

Simply put, questioning reality is invigorating, no matter one's motivation or mode of analysis. Mohanan spreads that excitement to those around him, and to areas beyond linguistics. It takes little prompting (especially over a cup of tea in the morning, or a glass of beer on a muggy afternoon) to coax a story or two from those who have worked with Mohanan about the influence of his passion on their ideas and ways of approaching their own work. Ann and Hung capture their stories in this volume, and M.T. Mohanan punctuates that section with her prolegomena – really, a field guide to a life in linguistics.

In this collection of papers, Mohanan's teachers (Paul Kiparsky and Joan Bresnan), his friends, colleagues and students come together to honor his enthusiasm for and significant contributions to exploring various realities in linguistics and the patterns that surface from such explorations. The preceding paragraphs provide only a glimpse of the papers collected here, and in so doing, may seem to imply that they fit into neat little categories. In reality, the papers are richer than we could do justice to in a few words, so it is the collection of papers that celebrates a spirit of inquiry infused with the courage and desire to uncover and face realities – not unlike that depicted in the Matrix movie trilogy[4] inspiring Mohanan's fascination with the REDPILL – here interpreted as REALITY EXPLORATION AND DISCOVERY: PATTERN INTERACTION IN LANGUAGE AND LIFE.

Acknowledgements

Thanks to our gurus Miriam Butt, Tracy King and Tara Mohanan for practical advice, moral support, technical tools, and unbounded friendship. The ensemble of authors here have enriched this volume not only with the words and ideas they've contributed but also with the kindness, understanding, cooperation, and patience they've shown us. The preface has benefited specifically from feedback from Alex Alsina, Long Peng, Jane Simpson, Tracy King, and Peter Sells. The entire volume has been enhanced by the thorough work of the reviewers: Akinbiyi Akinlabi, Alex Alsina, Arto Antilla, Ash Asudeh, Ashwini Deo, Beth Levin, Bruce Long Peng, Chee Yam San, Chin Seok Koon, Diana Archangeli, Donca Steriade, Doug Pulleyblank, Graham Horwood, Gillian Ramchand, Peter Hurst, Jane Simpson, Jean Ann, Joe Pater, John Paolillo, Louisa Sadler, Mark Donohue, Nick Clements, Paul Fallon, Paul Kiparsky, Paul Kroeger, Peter Cole, Peter Sells, Rajesh Bhatt, Shuichi Yatabe, Soh Hooi Ling, Tara Mohanan, Tham Shiao Wei, Tibor Kiss, Tony Hung, Tracy King, Tsuneko Nakazawa, Vivienne Fong and Will Leben. We wish also to register our thanks to Christian Werkmeister, Katrin Schuhman, and Daniela Valeva for their painstaking work in helping us out on various horrifying editorial duties. Special kudos to Lauri Kanerva whose patience and technical expertise ensured that the volume could take its final steps to

[4]A set of science-fiction-adventure films written and directed by Larry and Andy Wachowski, and starring Keanu Reeves: *The Matrix* (1999), *The Matrix Reloaded* (2003), *The Matrix Revolutions (2003)*.

the printer. For his support from inception to production, we are grateful to Dikran Karagueuzian. We, the editors, are really just basking in their glory.

For so much more that it will have to wait for the right words and an appropriate moment over hot tea, flamingly spicy pickles, or a particularly heated discussion, we simply acknowledge here, on behalf of everyone involved, the teacher, mentor, colleague and friend formally known as Karavannur Puthanveettil Mohanan. Without him there would have been no volume and no reason for us, the editors, to have enjoyed each other's long distance company, enabled and enhanced by the matrix of the internet. To all who dare, join us in raising a glass and downing the REDPILL!

References

Chomsky, Noam. 1965. *Aspects of the Theory of Syntax*. Cambridge: MIT Press.

Chomsky, Noam. 1985. *Knowledge of Language: Its Nature, Origin and Use*. Greenwood Publishing Group.

Mohanan, K.P. 1993. Fields of attraction in phonological theory. In J. Goldsmith, ed., *The Last Phonological Rule*, pages 61–116. University of Chicago Press.

Mohanan, K.P. 1996. Analytical skills in language studies. National University of Singapore.

Mohanan, K. P. 1984. Operator binding and the path containment condition. *Natural Language and Linguistic Theory* 2(4):357–396.

Mohanan, K. P. 2000. The theoretical substance of the optimality formalism. *Linguistic Review* 17(2-4):143–166.

Mohanan, Tara and Lian-Hee Wee. 1999. *Grammatical Semantics: Evidence for Structure in Meaning*. Stanford and Singapore: CSLI and NUS.

Pinker, Steven. 1997. *How the Mind Works*. Penguin Books.

Wachowski, Larry and Andy Wachowski. 1999. *The Matrix*. Warner Brothers and Village Roadshow Pictures.

Wachowski, Larry and Andy Wachowski. 2003a. *The Matrix Reloaded*. Warner Brothers and Village Roadshow Pictures.

Wachowski, Larry and Andy Wachowski. 2003b. *The Matrix Revolutions*. Warner Brothers and Village Roadshow Pictures.

Part I

Realities and Life

1

"He Who Can, Does" – and Teaches, and Teaches Teachers

TONY T. N. HUNG

It was George Bernard Shaw who once said, "He who can, does. He who cannot, teaches"[1], thereby casting a (not wholly deserved) slur on teachers for all time. Some wit augmented this by adding, "He who cannot teach, teaches teachers" – again with a grain of truth which must be taken with an even larger pinch of salt.

Whatever the merits of this classic put-down, the supposed dichotomy between 'doing' and 'teaching' is more true of the creative and performing arts[2] than of academia in general. In fact, in a discipline like linguistics, it would be hard to think of a 'doer' who is not also a 'teacher', from Chomsky to Halliday to the linguist sitting in your chair right now. Therefore, instead of "He who cannot, teaches", a variation on Shaw's aphorism which would seem more pertinent to our profession would be: "He who does, cannot teach, or doesn't want to."

Those of us who have been in the teaching profession long enough will know how much truth there is in this. Like other academics, most linguists are simply too busy doing research and publishing and trying to make an impact on the academic world to want to bother too much about teaching, which is something they tend to regard as a mere distraction if not a downright nuisance (albeit a necessary one, to make a living). What's more, most of

[1] Actually, it would have been more true to say "...He who cannot, *criticises*" especially music critics!

[2] One has only to think of such singers as Maria Callas and Elisabeth Schwarzkopf, who turned to teaching only when they could no longer perform in public.

Reality Exploration and Discovery: Pattern Interaction in Language and Life.
Linda Uyechi and Lian-Hee Wee (eds.).

them tacitly assume that any academic worth his salt would know how to teach, and that there is surely no more to teaching than transmitting what you know to your students. Any attempt to talk about one's philosophy of teaching would evoke either a yawn or a look of despair and pain.

When I first got to know Mohanan when he re-joined the National University of Singapore (NUS) around 1990, I had of course known about his work on Lexical Phonology and in Generative Linguistics in general – as well as his tireless efforts to proselytize it in the unregenerate linguistic community at NUS during his first sojourn there in the mid 1980s. He had something of the reputation of a crusader then. In the early 1990s, we co-taught a third-year course on Phonology. It was the beginning of a fruitful teaching partnership that lasted until my departure in 1997, including the period when he headed the new but short-lived Linguistics program at NUS.[3]

This brings me back to the title of this squib: "He who can, does – *and* teaches, *and* teaches teachers", which pretty well sums up Mohanan's work in NUS in the years since 1990, *pace* Shaw and the rest. In his case, far from being incidental to or even in conflict with each other, linguistics and the teaching of it have always been closely intertwined – a 'pattern interaction' of a kind.

From its very inception, the Linguistics program at NUS was very much a product of Mohanan's thinking. Two of his major concerns were these: *Why* do we teach Linguistics, and *how* should we teach it? His approach was very much in the spirit of General Education, which was at that time only beginning to make itself felt in a (then) rather traditional and conservative university like NUS. How many of our students who major in Linguistics (he asked) actually end up making it their profession? No more than a handful. What is the most valuable and enduring legacy that they can possibly gain from studying Linguistics – or for that matter, any other liberal arts subject? Surely not the knowledge content of the subject as such, which most of them are going to forget almost as soon as they graduate, and which in any case has little relevance to what they will eventually be doing for the rest of their lives. Rather, what will be of infinitely greater benefit to them are the (transferable) intellectual skills acquired in studying the subject.[4] Hence, Mohanan's objective in designing the Linguistics program was not to stuff the students with as much linguistic knowledge as possible, or even to provide a comprehensive survey of the field (which they could get from books anyway), but to inculcate in them the ability to think critically, analytically and creatively about language,

[3]For reasons too convoluted to go into here, the Linguistics program was closed down after only a few years of existence. It is a sad reminder that, in this world, excellence and innovativeness does not always prevail over mediocrity and conformity.

[4]One is reminded of the saying, "Education is what survives when what has been learnt has been forgotten".

and by extension about other important things in life.

It follows then that Mohanan would never lecture in the conventional sense to his classes, nor concern himself with transmitting to them a ready-made body of knowledge in the field of linguistics. To him it was much more important for the students to understand the nature of knowledge in the discipline how it is arrived at, evaluated, and accepted or rejected or revised. Thus, rather than learning how to define *subject* and *object* and mechanically tag the constituents of a sentence with these labels, it is much more important for the students to question the justification for the concepts *subject* and *object* in the first place, and to examine the evidence for and against them.

The extent to which Mohanan's teaching has left its mark on his students may be gauged from the following anecdote. During a conference (on teaching and learning) held in NUS at the end of 2006, a former colleague of mine, on listening to one of the presenters – an ex-NUS student[5] whom she did not know personally – declared without hesitation, "He must have been a Mohanan student," just from the way he questioned established notions and proposed logical solutions.

Mohanan carries about him a passion and commitment to teaching which inspires some of his colleagues as much as it discomforts others. He is one of the most generous colleagues I have ever known, from the way he unstintingly shares what he knows and thinks about linguistics and about teaching, to the extent of taking the time and trouble to sit in on colleagues' classes and discussing their lessons with them afterwards. I know that not everyone (in the Linguistics programme) appreciated this, and in a way it was typical of Mohanan that, because he himself welcomed others visiting and discussing his lessons with him, he assumed that the feeling was reciprocated. As a teacher, I could not but agree with Mohanan's assumption. After all, by the very nature of their profession, teachers are supposed to be – more so than anyone else – 'reflective practitioners', and the most effective and illuminating kind of reflection is *interactive* rather than merely introspective (cf. Kumaravadivelu 2003).

Since the mid-1990s, Mohanan has been devoting more and more of his time and energy to the teaching and learning enterprise in general, and not just the teaching of linguistics. His pioneering work for the Center for the Development of Teaching and Learning (CDTL) at NUS has been instrumental in raising the academic community's consciousness to key issues in teaching and learning, and establishing a robust culture of sharing and discussion among colleagues there. To date, the CDTL has developed into perhaps the best and most comprehensive support unit on teaching and learning of any university in the region (cf. http://www.cdtl.nus.edu.sg/ and the articles by

[5]He is in fact one of the editors of this volume – no prizes for guessing!

Mohanan cited in the References section below).

In the remainder of this squib, I briefly mention some of the most important and lasting contributions that Mohanan has made to teaching and learning at NUS through CDTL. One was his efforts to define what makes an excellent teacher – a difficult and nebulous concept which is too often relegated to the realm of popular acclaim, or to the mechanical computation of teaching evaluation (TE) scores based on questionnaires which are themselves questionable and open to misinterpretation. Mohanan has always harboured a healthy skepticism about popular or charismatic teachers whose appeal may often lie in other things than teaching excellence, and about TE scores taken too literally at face value. He has always insisted that any evaluation of teaching quality ought to focus on the process of learning rather than on the teacher, and that it should therefore take into account far more than a teacher's performance in front of a class, and include all the available evidence of effective teaching/learning, such as course objectives and syllabuses, handouts and readings, classroom activities, assignments and projects, exams and other modes of assessment, and student feedback together with a reasonable estimate of the learning outcome that they facilitate, in terms of critical thinking, knowledge application, independent learning, etc. (cf. Mohanan 2005a). His characterization of good teaching has in turn shaped the selection criteria for NUS' Teaching Excellence awards, and led also to his being invited to serve as a consultant on teaching excellence by other universities (such as the City University of Hong Kong).

In contrast with most other universities, where fledgling teachers are left to sink or swim, Mohanan has done a great service in initiating new, inexperienced teachers at NUS into the fundamental principles and concepts in teaching and learning, through CDTL's Professional Development Programme which provides them with a rich variety of core and elective modules (cf. www.cdtl.nus.edu.sg/pdp/). The core modules focus on such fundamental issues as 'the values and desired outcomes of a higher education', while the elective modules deal with practical, down-to-earth problems in teaching (such as 'Spoonfeeding: How do we wean university students from the dependence on spoon-feeding?'). For the academic community at large, he and his colleagues initiated a series of seminars and workshops under the Continuing Professional Development Programme in the belief that even seasoned teachers need to constantly keep abreast of new ideas in teaching and learning as well as reflect critically on established ones.

When Mohanan first joined NUS there were hardly any courses with open book examinations. Teachers were more comfortable with traditional closed-book exams which put a premium on rote-learning and recall and were easy to set and grade. This was in contrast to the much more demanding task of writing a good open-book exam to truly test the students' understanding, critical thinking and problem-solving skills. Mohanan was a pioneer not only in getting open-book exams accepted at NUS, but in starting a trend among other teachers to prefer the open-book exam – one which continues to this day.

In sum, his work for CDTL is likely to remain Mohanan's most enduring contribution to NUS – and the most striking example of how 'doing', 'teaching' and 'teaching others how to teach' are all integral parts of the same enterprise called 'education'.

References

CDTL-NUS. 2009. Center for the Development of Teaching and Learning website. http://www.cdtl.nus.edu.sg/.

Kumaravadivelu, B. 2003. *Beyond Methods: Macrostrategies for Language Teaching*. Yale University Press.

Mohanan, K. P. 2003. Critical thinking and pedagogy. CDTL-NUS website.

Mohanan, K. P. 2005a. Assessing quality of teaching in higher education. CDTL-NUS website.

Mohanan, K. P. 2005b. The place of student feedback in teaching evaluation. CDTL-NUS website.

Mohanan, K. P. 2005c. University education for career advancement. CDTL-NUS website.

Mohanan, K. P. 2005d. Who is an educated person? CDTL-NUS website.

Mohanan, K. P. 2006. Open book examinations. CDTL-NUS website.

2

Educating a Linguist

JEAN ANN

2.1 Introduction

If I were asked to describe K.P. Mohanan as a scholar and a teacher, and explain why his particular set of virtues means something to me, I would say that Mohanan is a textbook loathing, Powerbook schlepping, handout writing, comment giving, academic boundary disrespecting, theory deconstructing, assumption unearthing, teaching-obsession nursing, way-too-early rising Malayalee linguist with inexhaustible energy for talking, listening, reading and writing about a range of topics which lie at the core of our lives.[1] I attribute the fact that I'm still trying to make sense of linguistics and sharing the fun with undergraduate students, in part, to Mohanan. In this chapter I explain the insights I've gained from a journey that began with something Mohanan said many years ago. My struggle with it has helped me learn to teach my undergraduate students (most of whom will not become linguists) joyfully, while still doing my own research and writing. In telling this story, I hope to add my voice to Mohanan's and others who insist that we get better at teaching our subjects and that we do it for our own good (Spring 1997, Feynman, Leighton and Hutchings 1985, Bain 2004, Mohanan 1999, Mohanan 2007, Mohanan and Mohanan 2006).

Let's begin at the beginning, when, as a freshly minted Ph.D., I met Mohanan and Tara. I was the new kid on the block at the National University of Singapore (N.U.S.) and, like all new kids, I juggled my insecurities and my excitement. Almost everything was terrifying and somewhat unsettling, yet

[1]Little that Mohanan loves is peripheral, though I don't understand the commotion about chilis, cooking, horror movies ... maybe it's me.

Reality Exploration and Discovery: Pattern Interaction in Language and Life.
Linda Uyechi and Lian-Hee Wee (eds.).

beckoning were all the possibilities that come with discoveries to be made, and a ready made collection of linguists and students from different intellectual backgrounds with whom to make discoveries.

By the time I left N.U.S., I had participated with a community of linguists who were talking about issues the field as a whole was only just beginning to grapple with: What was the job of a linguist? If we said we 'analyzed' or 'explained' problems in language, what did we mean by 'analysis,' by 'explanation'? What kinds of 'problems' needed 'analysis'? How did we know when we had explained something that needed explaining? How did we know when an explanation really explained something? What did our explanations offer that an examination of the data itself did not? What did it mean that there were researchers who asked very different kinds of questions and sought very different kinds of solutions and yet all called themselves 'linguists'? Were we all in one field? If so, what did it mean that our field was so diverse?

Not only had I participated in stimulating conversations about linguistics, which might not seem terribly surprising when one is part of a community of linguists, after all, but I also observed that the linguistic conversations had a strange genesis. They arose, at least partly as a result of trying to resolve the difficult problems in how to teach linguistics to undergraduates who, if we let them, often push us up against our intellectual borders[2]. So there we were, a community of linguists grappling with how to teach our somewhat eccentric subject (which, in some ways, we ourselves had barely begun to understand) to unsuspecting undergraduates. Mohanan functioned as a ringleader in this environment (see also Hung, this volume) in which the flow of ideas and thoughts and hypotheses was always intriguing but sometimes the cause of disequilibrium, as everything we thought we knew suddenly was called into question and scrutinized. This uncharted and sometimes grueling terrain provided me a welcome and needed space to make significant strides in thinking about linguistics and how to teach linguistics.

Years have passed and I no longer feel like the new kid on the block as I had at N.U.S. For around ten years I've been teaching linguistics to students, many of whom will become teachers of English to speakers of other languages in elementary and secondary school settings. My tenure home is in a school of education, not a college of arts and sciences. As a result, my closest colleagues sincerely think that how we teach and what we teach in our college classes is critically important (unlike what Hung, this volume, suggests is true in many cases). Therefore, each day I am subject to a certain level of their scrutiny. Even if I wanted to, I could not get away with not thinking through my pedagogy and my curriculum in my linguistics courses,

[2]I suggest that one reason for this is that (thankfully) undergraduates simply don't know not to.

as one often can (and I did) in circumstances under which my teaching was an object of only passing interest to my colleagues.

Much about the conversations at N.U.S. still echoes in my mind, and some of what we said has lent itself to expansion and revision as I've tried to understand what use linguistics is to anyone, particularly language teachers, particularly teachers of English to speakers of other languages (E.S.O.L.). In fact, asking these questions resulted in Ann and Peng (2005), which argued that although some of the content of linguistics can be useful to E.S.O.L. teachers, more useful is knowledge of the way linguists take data and try to understand it. This brings me to a claim I first heard Mohanan make in many conversations over the course of three years in the mid 1990s. My ensuing struggle with it has guided much of what I've done since. This claim appears in (1).

(1) A linguistics professor cannot accept the idea that her needs and her students' needs are mutually exclusive, so that to attend to one entails ignoring the other. Research and teaching are two sides of the same endeavor. They do not pull against each other, and, in fact, to engage in one feeds and nurtures the other.

On the face of it, (1) has to be wrong, as I daresay anyone who is learning to be a professor will attest. There is far too much to learn when one begins, from how to fit one's intellectual passions into the daily workings of an academic department to how to talk to colleagues and students about passions they may not share. Teaching and all it entails looms frighteningly large; research begins to wane. So, when Mohanan said (1), it certainly sounded absurd (even if it was sort of a nice thought).

The clearest glimpse I ever got of teaching and research existing in harmony in a professor's world was from a story Mohanan told me. I had been in Singapore about fifteen minutes when Mohanan started to talk to me about the idea of what 'analysis' is. His clarity amazed me. I eventually asked Mo how he started on this path of thinking. He attributed it to an extraordinary encounter with a graduate student named John Paolillo some years before. John had handed in an assignment, and Mo told John that he didn't have an analysis. John asked, "If this isn't an 'analysis,' then what is?" As Mo began to explain, he realized he had to unpack what he and other linguists meant by 'analysis,' since it was not clear even to linguists themselves. This started years of thinking in writing – handouts, chapters, papers, and finally book drafts (Mohanan and Mohanan 2006, Mohanan 1999, Mohanan 2007). I loved the story. I think it is highly significant that John Paolillo had the curiosity to ask the question, and that he asked it of a linguist who could not only *really hear* its merits, but who also had the curiosity and persistence to begin to answer it. The many pieces of work borne of this exchange raise the question of what might have happened if it had never occurred. What if John hadn't cared about Mohanan's 'analysis' comment? What if he took the grade he got and forgot about it? What if Mohanan let John slide and didn't bother raising the issue of 'analysis' in favor of writing his own papers? This potential for loss happens every day. As I took the story to heart and began to consider what it might mean for me, I contemplated the possibility that someday I would be able to say that I paid close enough attention to what my students were wondering about that it changed what *I* was doing in linguistics. Such an occurrence seemed a sort of pinnacle.

So if the claim in (1) was ever going to be true in my life teaching linguistics, it had to start being true on a day-to-day basis. In what follows, I explain two (alas, probably artificially separated) areas of thinking I have done on this matter. Section 2 addresses the needs of students. Section 3 addresses the needs of professors in general, and specifically, my needs as a professor.

2.2 Some Thinking About the Needs of Students of Linguistics

As I've often heard Mohanan and Tara lament, linguistics is usually presented in textbooks as a set of conclusions that linguists have arrived at about various aspects of grammar. To teach students the set of conclusions takes the fun out of linguistics, since it denies students the chance to actually participate. If students have nothing to do while they are learning linguistics except to consume (that is, believe, accept) the things the professor thinks are knowledge, it's hard for them to make an intellectual investment. In this scenario, the student knows she isn't really necessary. She is there almost as decoration for the important thing: the professor. This can't help students become educated linguists. And why would a professor want to surround herself with students who are not reaching their potential?

No, if research and teaching were ever going to go together at all, I figured I had to do a fantastic job of teaching. Then my students could become my research/thinking partners, excellent writers and scholars that I couldn't help but respect. So I began to make decisions about how to teach so that students[3] would be able to make an investment in themselves by learning about linguistics. I try to encapsulate these in (2)-(5).

First, I discuss readings. Readings are often an issue for students, who don't like to read them for various reasons. Often students cannot explain their misgivings about reading, but their misgivings should alarm us. Thinking about this and watching students semester after semester, I finally came to the realization in (2).

(2) Students of linguistics need and deserve to be introduced to academia and to our field with good materials to read (by 'the field,' I mean, at least partly the field we envision, not necessarily the field we have).

[3]Except where noted, 'students' means students in introductory linguistics.

I confess to using a popular textbook for years. Though not perfect, it presents some ideas reasonably well. In places where it fails, I write my own handouts to help students unearth things they haven't thought about with respect to language, in hopes of awakening their curiosity[4]. The students use my readings and the textbook. As the years go by, and I get more clear about what is important about linguistics, and what students find interesting, I add more to my readings, and take more of the text away. The students' reactions to my readings, both positive and negative, encourage me to keep improving them.

Another issue involves the complex and demanding tasks of asking students to do written work and grading it. It seems clear that they don't pick up just from my modeling what they need to do. Every semester I watch the students and try to figure out what I need to say and do to get them to accomplish what I want them to accomplish in their writing. I realized that:

(3) Students of linguistics need my attention for what they are thinking and writing.

Therefore, a huge part of my course is designed to help students with their thinking and writing. The better we can get their thinking and their writing, the more I'll be able to read their work and sincerely focus on the content. The only hope I have of enjoying reading their work is if the quality is good. The only hope I have of that is if I invest in that work. I do this by writing handouts in which I try to be excruciatingly clear about what they have to do, having meetings with them, giving demonstrations, and getting the students who have made sense of the content and internalized the skills of thinking like a linguist to act as teaching assistants for the new students. They serve as models that prove that what I am asking students to do really can be done.

The point here is that I realize my students and I are struggling with the same issues. We all need help becoming whatever we are becoming. Just as learning what it takes to become a professor was not obvious to me, and was sometimes scary and overwhelming, learning what it takes to become a thoughtful student of linguistics is not obvious to them. I notice that in areas in which I got help when I was trying to think things through, I am often reasonably clear about how to give help to students now. I have to work the hardest in areas in which I did *not* get the help I need in order to offer help to my students.

My course fulfills a general education requirement, so some students begin their work with me with a desire to 'get their tickets punched' more than out

[4]At N.U.S., both Mohanan and Tara wrote handout after handout and tried them out on students. I watched what I saw then as their time-consuming labor of love mostly in agony, trying to emulate it as best I could. Only later did I come to more fully internalize the value – to students but more importantly to myself – of fully working through the assumptions and processes we use to come to conclusions.

of any great curiosity about language. It may seem that a student in that state cannot invest in linguistics. But this thinking doesn't get me anywhere. It serves my purposes to believe that every student is interested in linguistics, because of the observations in (4).

(4) Students of linguistics bring rich resources to their study such as the language/s they speak or sign and the innate curiosity they have about the world.

If a professor really believed that students arrive in her class ready to offer the contributions in (4), it would make sense to accept these contributions. For me this has meant embracing the students' native languages and using them to demonstrate particular points about language or linguistics.

This was easier when I taught in places with linguistic diversity. These days my students are mostly Americans, mostly monolingual native English speakers. Still, in every class in my central New York college, there is at least one person from the New York City area. The "upstaters" and "downstaters" have slightly different vowels, syntactic constructions and the like, which students have often noticed, but either ignored or made fun of[5]. It is only after really listening to each other, and learning a bit about prescriptive and descriptive views of language, that we move into any technical details in linguistics. In other words, it is only after they've come to understand that when they talk, others think what they say is interesting or different, and only after they've heard someone whose speech they think is interesting or different, that we begin to think about what the interesting, different bits might be.

Sometimes, native speakers of Mandarin Chinese, Spanish, African American Vernacular English, Japanese, Hindi or Ukrainian take introductory linguistics and consent to answering questions about their languages in class. We always try to use the languages of the people in the class to learn about aspects of linguistics. Sometimes we find ourselves curious about something and our class starts to head in directions I didn't anticipate. Although I write a detailed syllabus each semester (in advance of knowing who speaks what, and whether they'll be willing to answer questions about it), I tell the students we can replace what's on the syllabus with things we find more fun (if they are willing to do some work, and enough people like the idea)[6].

[5]Of course geographic dialects are only one piece of the complexity in ways people talk, but it is one that is accessible to students.

[6]My usual m.o. is to ask a student to say something in their language in order to make a point about linguistics. However, on more than one occasion, students have asked if other students would mind just speaking their language so that they can listen even though they don't understand. When I ask why, they simply say it sounds cool, fascinating. This puzzled me. Later it occurred to me that in our extremely monolingual environment, most students don't have a lot of contact with languages besides English. As a result, English is a sort of background noise that they don't even 'hear.' Through our work in introductory linguistics, students discover that they actually want to know more about English, and the extension to other languages is then quite natural.

Finally, I have the sense that students are actually looking for academic places in which to invest. I try to help them see that linguistics is a good place to do so by embracing the idea in (5).

(5) Students of linguistics need to know that linguistics is not all worked out. There is much that we have not begun to understand about language. Consequently there are questions we do not even know to ask.

I remember fearing that if I let undergraduates see that there are many contradictions in linguistics and that linguistics doesn't deal with every conceivable question about language, they would believe that linguistics wasn't as legitimate as 'real' sciences, or that nobody in linguistics really has a handle on how to do it. This forced me to teach the least controversial things. When I would think about my teaching, I would wonder whether students thought that all the problems in linguistics are solved, and if they did, did they question what the point of studying it could be? How could they interact with a body of knowledge that could not be extended? On the other hand, the areas of linguistics that I find most absorbing are murky – second language acquisition, language contact, and the structure of sign languages, for example – and, if right answers are important, horrible to teach.

These days, I explain that although linguists have some impressive reasons, methods and tools for analysis, there is much that isn't completely understood. I invite students to think about what they would want to know about language, and what their own possibilities might be for finding out more about linguistics. I ask them what kind of interest might lie inside of them that could result in their using linguistics in some way in their lives. Can they see themselves contributing to linguistics or an allied field later?

Of course, not every student who takes introductory linguistics continues. I had a bilingual student who'd gotten a good workout in his first course because we often asked for Spanish data and for his native intuitions about Spanish. Sometimes he would check his intuitions with his mother's in New York City and report insights back to us. He was engaged, enthusiastic, and even seemed to indulge a certain internal struggle with theoretical ideas like "phoneme" and "syllable." (What were they good for? Why did we need them?) These attributes would have served him well as a linguistics major. So when we said goodbye at the end of the course, I asked him if he would be joining me for more linguistics the next semester.

I can still hear his answer. "You know," he said, "I think linguistics was invented by some really smart people who wanted to teach people other languages or something like that. I bet people would find linguistics pretty helpful if they wanted to use ideas from it to learn another language." But though he appreciated what linguistics could do, he wouldn't be joining us for more. We wished each other well, and he disappeared.

I was a little puzzled by what he said. I hadn't thought much about the origins of linguistics; my vision extended only as far back as Chomsky's Syntactic Structures (1957). So I catalogued his remarks in my mental file of 'things students say that I don't know what to do with.' Years later I discovered a passage in Seuren (1998:22) from a chapter entitled "Linguistics from Antiquity till the Seventeenth Century" in which he discusses the origin of the study of the structure of languages and observes that:

> The work done by the Alexandrines marked the beginning of what we now call 'linguistics.' And if we are right in linking this with a widespread demand for the teaching of Greek it began, strictly speaking, as applied linguistics, the teaching of Greek as a foreign language. It is clear that from then on, the study and analysis of language was no longer the exclusive province of philosophers. Professional linguists began to be heard as well.

Thunderstruck, I remembered what my student had intuited about the origins of linguistics. It taught me that there is great potential for students (even the ones who slip away after only one course) and professors to help each other make sense of the subjects they think and talk about together.

To conclude, I would say that when I am at my best with respect to following the thinking in (2) – (5), everyone learns more, including me, and students turn into colleagues that I respect and admire. When students feel like they will be contributing to a body of knowledge, they can invest – and when they invest, they learn, and when they learn, they are interesting and fun. By the time our students get to advanced linguistics, many have become creative, systematic, hard-working risk-takers who write well. Although to some extent they want to get right answers, they also want to be free to play, to ask questions and to try out some crazy ideas.

2.3 Some Thinking About the Needs of Linguistics Professors

The second set of ideas that my struggle with (1) set in motion concern the linguistics professor. In a setting like mine, in which professors have heavy teaching loads and many other time-consuming duties, I have discovered that the linguistics professor must take care of her needs as a scholar or else she will not be able to offer much to her students. A professor is relied upon by many to be a teacher, but a professor also must be committed to nurturing her own brain and getting smarter, even if there were no students to face each day. Therefore the linguistics professor has to come to know what it is about scholarship that is most valuable to her and make sure that she gets those things regularly and often. My first discovery appears in (6):

(6) The linguistics professor has to have time to read the work that helps her thinking progress.

Mohanan has made enormous efforts in reading and synthesizing a great deal about scientific inquiry from the 'hard' sciences, and, in so doing, he has brought much to his students. Observing this, it became clear to me that I couldn't just read the articles I was used to reading. Over the years, my reading not across disciplines but within different schools of thought in linguistics has helped me immeasurably in my writing and thinking. Two of the chapters in Ann (2006) are my attempt to help linguists think about how we approach sign language data. My final note here concerns writing.

(7) The linguistics professor has to have time to write.

More than anything else about being a professor, I love writing. It makes me happy. Apart from being a form of exercise in logical thinking, writing is the means through which I get a chance to create something beautiful, orderly, and meaningful out of words on paper. If I write a lot each week, I help myself in my thinking, and I potentially get help from others because I have a draft to share. If I don't write a lot each week, I resent the students because they are in my way; they are getting more of my attention than I am. Therefore, to the best of my ability I make the commitment that even when I'm busy, there has to be time for me to write. If I'm too stressed to do linguistics writing, I write something easier.

I've learned a lot about how to pay abundant attention both to students and to myself (see Paolillo, this volume, for a memory of Mohanan). I've come to understand that my students are watching me to learn what famous linguists think about problems in language, and how linguistic theories move our field ahead. But they are watching me to learn something more. They want to learn something about themselves, their brains, their thinking. They want to learn about their power as thinkers, analysts, scientists, artists and writers. I strive to be able to hear their questions, and risk an answer, as Mohanan did with John Paolillo. And just as my students look to me, I've learned that I watch students too, to see what questions bother them, and what they wonder about fuels my inquiry as well. I watch them to see where they think linguistics is boring or trivial, surely a sign of something important.

What I have noticed is that the better I get at thinking and writing about linguistics, the better I get at teaching. And since I have been teaching courses like introductory linguistics in a serious manner, I have been more curious, wondered more and published more than before. I have more to learn in all areas of linguistics and teaching, and I am completely enjoying doing so. I was lucky to have a few years working beside Mohanan to learn about language, and learning, and teaching. I remember him saying that the best teachers make themselves useless to their students as quickly as possible (see Wee, this volume). And I still wish I could talk to him once a week to get his responses to my latest understandings and see what he's writing and thinking about. If Mo is supposed to be useless to me, I'd say that it's going slowly, at best.

Acknowledgments

I gratefully acknowledge Bobbi Schnorr, Barbara Beyerbach, Chris Walsh, Mary Harrell, Tania Ramalho, Bonita Hampton, Sharon Kane, Pam Michel, Oscar Fernandez, and two anonymous reviewers for assistance in thinking through and writing parts of this paper. I acknowledge Bruce Long Peng with respect and gratitude for his solid dedication to both teaching and research and his clear thinking on (1) all these years.

References

Ann, Jean. 2006. *Frequency of Occurrence and Ease of Articulation in Sign Language Handshapes: The Taiwanese Example*. Washington, DC: Gallaudet University Press.

Ann, Jean and Long Peng. 2005. The relevance of linguistic analysis to the role of teachers as decision makers. In K. Denham and A. Lobeck, eds., *Language in the Schools: Integrating Linguistic Knowledge into K-12 Teaching*, pages 71–86. Mahwah, NJ: Lawrence Erlbaum Associates.

Bain, Ken. 2004. *What the Best College Teachers Do*. Cambridge, MA: Harvard University Press.

Chomsky, Noam. 1957. *Syntactic Structures*, vol. 4 of *Janua Linguarum*. The Hague: Mouton.

Feynman, Richard P., Ralph Leighton, and Edward Hutchings. 1985. *"Surely You're Joking, Mr. Feynman!": Adventures of a Curious Character*. New York, NY: W.W. Norton.

Mohanan, K. P. 1999. Foundations of linguistic theory. Ms., National University of Singapore.

Mohanan, K. P. 2007. Academic knowledge and inquiry. Ms., National University of Singapore.

Mohanan, Tara and K. P. Mohanan. 2006. Exploring patterns of language structure. Ms., National University of Singapore.

Seuren, Peter A. M. 1998. *Western Linguistics: An Historical Introduction*. Malden, MA: Blackwell.

Spring, Cari L. 1997. *Linguistics for Humans: Field-based Learning Exercises*. Catalina, AZ: Real Grammar.

3

A Prolegomenon to Linguistology

MALAVIKA TARA MOHANAN

When I was little I joked that nobody came to see us because we had headless relatives (the kind described in Aman et al., this volume), our trees were all upside down (as illustrated in Alsina, Aman et al., Bresnan and Nikitina, Dalrymple, Levin and Sells, and so on, this volume), and kids were always pinching elephants (see Butt et al., this volume). This was unfair and untrue; we've always had streams of visitors.

Most of the people floating through our home, especially during our Stanford years (1986-90), were linguists – unsurprising, because both my parents are linguists.[1] People often asked if I would become one too, and I always replied, Hell-no-anything-but, or some polite version of it. In some ways I'm still anything-but, yet somehow I find I haven't strayed (or rather, warp-speeded) as far as I thought. In a room full of linguists I feel like Mowgli with the wolves: very different, but perfectly at home. I may not be one, but I know what linguists are and what they do; maybe I even am and do some of those things myself.

What follows is a cursory attempt at a characterization of this strange species of academics. The principles are loosely binding, with a large statistical variance, and shed little light on the field of linguistics itself, but the overall picture may be useful for any linguistologist out there who despairs of ever understanding their subject.

1. **Linguists are weird.** They dress weird, talk weird, make weird noises (which they give weird names like implosives and ejectives), and play

[1]Of the 'generative' tradition, to be exact, that traces its ancestry to Noam Chomsky, and Morris Halle; this is the tradition I refer to when I say linguist/linguistics from here on.

Reality Exploration and Discovery: Pattern Interaction in Language and Life.
Linda Uyechi and Lian-Hee Wee (eds.).

weird music (in groups with weird names like Dead Tongues).

2. **Linguists are crazy.** This principle is related to but not entirely covered by P1. It refers to a certain unpredictability, a mild volatility, and a disregard for conventional behavior.
3. **Linguists are politically left-leaning.** This characteristic is often accompanied by a distinct anti-authoritarian streak, and a penchant for peace, justice, democracy, freedom, and other such elusive concepts[2] None of this is surprising, given their evolutionary history (see fn 1).
4. **Linguists are loud.** A lone specimen might seem quiet, but the decibel level of a gathering of linguists is distinctly higher than an equivalent group of, say, microbiologists, computer scientists, or medieval historians. This might be partially attributed to P2, P3, and P10, and has a synergistic effect when combined with P5.
5. **Linguists like beer.** If the sampling were limited to the subjects in my household the hypothesis would meet an inconclusive statistic of 50 percent. Rest assured, however, that the larger the sample size, the more conclusive the result. It is safe to say that there is a definite predilection for fermented malt beverages, particularly when accompanied by pizza.
6. **Linguists like food.** Except Chomsky. They like eating their normal food, trying out new food, making food, talking about food, using food as teaching examples, everything to do with food. That is to say, linguists who follow Chomsky (fn 1) like food. Chomsky doesn't follow himself (*following* being a non-reflexive relation), so isn't actually a counterexample.
7. **Linguists like the outdoors.** While the itinerary for international gatherings of psychiatrists, economists, or literary critics might include wine and caviar on a cruise ship, the equivalent event for linguists would more likely be a forest trek or a mountain hike, though of course, preferably with evening access to a bar or a pub.
8. **Linguists are not necessarily multilingual.** Contrary to the popular confusion between 'linguist' and 'polyglot', not all linguists speak several languages. They are, however, always on the lookout for language data. This means they are ever vigilant and eager for exposure to as many languages as possible.
9. **Linguists listen well**, but not always to what one expects. As mentioned above, they are always looking for data, so during a conversation

[2]There are various eyewitness accounts of MIT linguists breaking off from heated debate (see Principle 10 to understand the significance of such interruption) and sprinting down the stairs in Building 20 (which used to house the Linguistics Department through the second half of the twentieth century) to pull down the newly posted ROTC (Reserve Officers' Training Corps in the Army) fliers from the notice boards. A combination of principles 2 and 3 might explain such behavior.

about the Matrix or banana fritters or underspecification, the specimen might have hitherto been making a remarkable pretense at conventionality, but a moment comes when an observant conversing partner will notice a shift in the specimen's eye, for which the explanation emerges only months or years later as an example or counterexample for such-and-such linguistic theory. (Linguistologists would do well to note the irony of the observed specimen becoming the observer.)

10. **Linguists like to argue**, discuss, ask questions, and generally get down to the bottom of things. (If this is accompanied by getting down to the bottom of a pitcher of lager, all the better. See P5). This instinctive curiosity and thirst for truth is not limited to just their field of study; it extends to the world at large. It is sometimes sadly mistaken for belligerence and obsessiveness, but can be rather entertaining and fruitful if taken in the right spirit.
11. **Linguists like drawing diagrams.** Writing implements are essential for pictorial representations (such as upside down trees) that are, in turn, essential for making the various points in the arguments referred to in P10. The previous generations were weaned on, and often still show a preference for, blackboard and chalk. The more recent specimens are amenable to technological developments such as whiteboards, and more recently, PowerPoint. These tools, however, are not always accessible, since P5 is often the most weighted for deciding where to carry out P10. The diagrams are often drawn, therefore, on napkins decorated with pizza sauce and soggy with beer (see also Butt et al. this volume).
12. **Linguists love patterns.** There is little that thrills a linguist so much as when the processes involved in P9, P10, and P11 lead to the discovery of a pattern in which all the relevant pieces fall into place. The more complex the pattern the better, and if there are interactions between patterns that demand a description of a meta-pattern, even better. When starved for intellectual stimulation they can go so far as to complexify reality just to find a simple explanation, scouring roadside signs, for instance, for their inconsistent spelling of names of towns.[3]

I reiterate that these principles are merely a loose guide. They are not exhaustive, and no one specimen will fit neatly into the box.

There is, however, one specimen who exhibits at least 11 of these 12 properties. The logic is circular, perhaps, since this specimen was a key sample in postulating the principles in the first place. Nevertheless, this method is not entirely unfounded since the specimen is widely recognized as representative of the species. The specimen, K.P. Mohanan, is weird, crazy, leftist, loud,

[3] For a telling example, consult Tracy Holloway King or Miriam Butt.

likes beer (especially with pizza, but he doesn't drink it as much anymore because of the various social-political implications of beer as a commercial product), likes food, likes languages but speaks only two, listens constantly for data, argues about everything (see also the acknowledgements in Aman et al., this volume), draws diagrams at every opportunity, and obsessively explores patterns and reality. (See also Ann, this volume, and Hung, this volume.) He doesn't like trekking, climbing or sweating, but he is by no means unaffected by the power and beauty of the Wild.

So, O weary but charmed linguistologist, despair not; in time the mystery will unravel. Meanwhile, drink, be merry, keep your head on, your trees upside down, and your principles optimized.

Part II

Exploration of Interaction in Sound Patterns

4

Persistent Substratum Contrasts

BAO ZHIMING

4.1 A Thought Experiment

It is well-known among people who know K.P. Mohanan that he likes ideas, including apparently crazy ideas. So one day during an official 'chat' between Mohanan and me the conversation took a curious turn – to the outcome of competition between two non-isomorphic subsystems from typologically distant languages. The problem can be formulated as follows. In an idealized contact ecology, two languages, A and B, compete to provide linguistic materials to a third language, C. Let's say A contributes a grammatical construction or subsystem to C, to be exponenced – or 'fleshed out' – by suitable morphosyntactic materials from B. In the contact linguistics literature, A is identified as the substratum language, B the superstratum, or lexifier, and C the emerging contact language. Both of us are trained as phonologists, so for evidence the conversation naturally turned to phonological subsystems, specifically the obstruent system. An interesting case is this: if the substratum and superstratum obstruent systems are not isomorphic, and the substratum system contains more contrasts than the superstratum obstruent system,[1] what happens to the 'surplus' substratum contrasts in the obstruent system of the emerging contact language? Mohanan argued that the surplus contrasts will

[1]The superstratum system may contain more contrasts than the substratum system. Hong Kong English is an example. In Cantonese, stops contrast for aspiration, and neither stops nor fricatives contrast for voicing. This pattern is found in the obstruent system of Hong Kong English, with Cantonese aspiration taking the contrastive role of English voicing; see Hung (2000) for details. Incidentally, in Southern Min, the main substratum language in early stages of Singapore English, voicing is contrastive among obstruents (Bodman 1955). In present-day Singapore English voicing is contrastive among obstruents. I thank the referee whose comment lead to this clarification.

Reality Exploration and Discovery: Pattern Interaction in Language and Life.
Linda Uyechi and Lian-Hee Wee (eds.).

find a way to surface—this is the empirical content of PERSISTENCE proposed by Mohanan and Mohanan (2003). I tried a different tack. Prima facie, one would expect the surplus substratum contrasts to have no chance of emerging in the contact language for lack of suitable exponencing materials from the superstratum language, and for lack of a need in the contact language. But the debate ended when we realized that our meeting had veered off-track, and we reluctantly returned to the more serious business of the day.

Lexical and structural borrowing is, of course, long known to modern scholars. After half a century the analysis of lexical borrowing in Haugen (1950) is still relevant today, as is Weinreich's (1964) analysis of the structural consequences of borrowing. From the point of view of systemic transfer, when an entire system of contrasts is transferred from the substratum to the contact language, the 'fate' of the surplus substratum phonological contrasts is a matter of considerable analytical significance, although curiously it has not received much attention from students of language contact. Here I follow up on the conversation with Mohanan by exploring the possibility that the surplus contrasts do not persist, as Mohanan and Mohanan (2003) argued. On the contrary, they are filtered out of the contact language. The substratum contrasts (from Language A) that 'persist' in the contact language (Language C) are those which are sanctioned by the grammar of the superstratum language (Language B) which contributes the exponencing materials.

4.2 The Facts, and the Appearance of Persistence

Mohanan and Mohanan's (2003) insight about the persistent substratum feature is based on an analysis of the sound system of Malayalee English, a non-native variety with a Malayalam substratum. The Mohanans' persistence argument can be illustrated with the obstruent system, the focus here. The 'surface' obstruent systems of Malayalam, English and Malayalee English are summarized in (1).[2]

The data are collated from Mohanan and Mohanan (1984, 2003), notated with standard IPA symbols. Aspirated stops, not discussed in Mohanan and Mohanan (2003), are included in (1) from Mohanan and Mohanan (1984). Note that aspiration does not persist in Malayalee English, a fact which is important for the argument I present in the next section. Stops in Malayalam contrast in aspiration and voicing in all places of articulation except the alve-

[2]Following Mohanan (1982, 1986), Mohanan and Mohanan (1984, 2003) recognize three levels of representation, underlying, lexical and phonetic, in their analysis of the lexical phonology of Malayalam. The Malayalam consonants in (1) are found at the lexical level, which are subject to postlexical rules to be mapped onto the phonetic level of presentation. For our purpose, the surface level includes the lexical and phonetic levels, and the phonemic level corresponds to their underlying representation. The palatalized alveolar fricative s^j and the palatal stops are not found at the underlying level; in other words, they are not phonemic in our terms.

olar, where we only find the voiceless stop *t*. In Malayalee English, the alveolar stops, in italics in (1), are allophones of the retroflex stops, as we shall see shortly.

(1)		*Malayalam*	*English*	*Malayalee English*
a.	Labial	p, p^h, b, b^h	p, b	p, b
			f, v	f
b.	Dental	t̪, t̪^{h}, d̪, d̪^{h}	θ, ð	t̪, d̪
c.	Alveolar	t	t,d	*t, d*
		s, s^j	s, z	s
d.	Palato-alveolar	c, c^h, ɟ, $ɟ^h$	tʃ, dʒ	c, ɟ
			ʃ, ʒ	-
e.	Retroflex	ʈ, $ʈ^h$, ɖ, $ɖ^h$	-	ʈ, ɖ
		ʂ	-	ʂ
f.	Palatal	k^j, k^{jh}, g^j, g^{jh}	-	-
g.	Velar	k, k^h, g, g^h	k, g	k, g

The correspondence between the Malayalee English obstruents and their English counterparts is displayed in (2), which establishes the sources of the obstruents we see in the contact vernacular.

(2)		*English*	*Malayalee English*
a.	Labial	p, b	p, b
		f, v	f
b.	Dental	θ, ð	t̪, d̪
c.	Alveolar	t, d	ʈ/*t*, ɖ/*d*
		s, z	s
d.	Palato-alveolar	tʃ, dʒ	c, ɟ
		ʃ, ʒ	ʂ
c.	Velar	k, g	k, g

Similar correspondences have been observed in the integration of lexical borrowings in Hindi (Hock 1991, Winford 2003). Hock (1991) cites the Hindi correspondences as examples of what he calls system-based substitution, an insight which will be elaborated upon in the next section. In Malayalee English, the obstruents exhibit some of the allophonic alternations which are also observed in Malayalam in similar contexts. Details of the alternations need not concern us here; interested readers should consult Mohanan and Mohanan (1984, 2003).

From the data in (2), Mohanan and Mohanan (2003) make the following observations about the source of the obstruents in Malayalee English, expressed in OT-style constraints. First, if the segment is present in both Malayalam and English, it is present in Malayalee English (OVERLAP, e.g., labials (2a)) . Second, if the segment is present in English but not in Malayalam, it may be used to substitute for a different, but phonetically similar segment in Malayalam (ADAPTATION, e.g., dentals (2b));[3] or it may be lost from Malayalee English (LOSS, e.g., voiced fricatives (2a,c,d)), or be introduced into the vernacular (RETENTION, the voiceless labial fricative (2a)). Third, if the segment is present in Malayalam but not in English, it may still be present in Malayalee English (PERSISTENCE, e.g., the alveolar-retroflex contrast). These phenomena of phonological integration, especially OVERLAP, ADAPTATION and LOSS, are familiar to the current contact linguistics literature. PERSISTENCE deserves close scrutiny. Let's take a closer look at the facts. While *t/d* and *ʈ/ɖ* are observed in Malayalee English, they occur in complementary environments. Relevant facts follow:

(3)							
	a.	take	[ʈ-]	tip	[ʈ-]	train	[ʈɽ-]
	b.	autumn	[-ʈ-]	cut	[-ʈ]	wrote	[-ʈ]
	c.	cult	[-ɭʈ]	heart	[-ɽʈ]		
	d.	atom	[-t-]	bet	[-t]	write	[-t]
	e.	built	[-lʈ]	dreamt	[-mt]	soft	[-ft]

(4)							
	a.	debt	[ɖ-]	direct	[ɖ-]	dream	[ɖɽ-]
	b.	seldom	[-ɖ-]	feed	[-ɖ]	ride	[-ɖ]
	c.	weld	[-lɖ]	cold	[-ɭɖ]	picked	[-kɖ]
	d.	fend	[-nd]	grind	[-nd]	bandage	[-nd-]

The data reveal that the English alveolar stops are realized as the Malayalam retroflex stops except when preceded, in the case of *t*, by a non-back vowel or consonant (3d,e), and in the case of *d*, by *n* (4d). Following Mohanan and Mohanan (2003), we state the alveolar-retroflex correspondence as follows:[4]

(5) a. t → t / [-back] __
  → ʈ / all other environments

b. t → d / n __
  → ɖ / all other environments

Note that in Mohanan and Mohanan's (1984, 2003) analysis the voiced alveolar stop *d* is not a segment in the underlying or lexical inventories of Malayalam. In our terms, it is not a phoneme in Malayalee English, and can at best be analyzed as an allophone of ɖ. So the persistence of the Malayalam alveolar-retroflex contrast in Malayalee English operates at distinct levels of representation. It is driven by the two principles stated below ((45) of Mohanan and Mohanan (2003)):

[3] On ADAPTATION, Mohanan and Mohanan (2003:13) explain (where NE refers to Native English): 'NE [θ, ð, ʃ] are reanalyzed as Malayalam [t, d, ʂ], illustrating the adaptation of the superstrate contrasts to the nearest substrate structures.'

[4] The [back] harmony expressed in (5) is also observed in other coronals, e.g., the lateral *l*: *cult* [-ɭ-] vs. *built* [-l-] (see (3c,e)), and the alveolar nasal: *fend* [-nd] vs. *fond* [-ɳɖ]; see Mohanan and Mohanan (2003).

(6) a. The offspring retains the structure of the substratum.
b. The output of the offspring system must match the output of the superstratum.

These principles are faithfulness constraints along the lines of Optimality Theory. Note that in Malayalam the alveolar and retroflex stops are contrastive at both the underlying and lexical levels, but the contrast is lost at the phonetic level. Principle (6a) compels the alveolar-retroflex contrast to emerge at the lexical level in Malayalee English, even though it is not contrastive at the underlying level. The process is schematized below, adapted from (50), Mohanan and Mohanan (2003):

(7) *English* *Malayalam* *Malayalee English*

English	*Malayalam*	*Malayalee English*
alveolar	→ alveolar	→ alveolar
	→ retroflex	→ retroflex

All stages are at the level of lexical representation, consistent with the three-level lexical phonology of Malayalam (cf. footnote 1). Under this analysis, the puzzling fact is that other Malayalam underlying or lexical contrasts, notably aspiration and palatalization, do not transfer to Malayalee English, contrary to PERSISTENCE.

4.3 The Filter, and the Patterns of Persistence

At the risk of simplifying matters a bit, we will interpret Mohanan and Mohanan's (2003) lexical and phonetic representations as a single surface level in opposition to the underlying representation. An examination of the underlying Malayalam contrasts that persist in Malayalee English, and those that do not, helps shed light on the roles of Malayalam and English in the emergence of the sound system of Malayalee English, the contact vernacular. From the segment inventories in (1) and (2), we can make the following observations. First, the purely lexical contrasts in Malayalam do not persist, e.g., the palatalized segments in (1c,f). These are surface segments in our two-level analysis. Second, the underlying Malayalam contrasts that are attested in English persist in Malayalee English, i.e. the places of articulation and voice contrast among stops, as shown in (2). However, the segments that realize those persistent contrasts need not have the same articulatory properties. This is the case in the Malayalee dental stops substituting for the English dental fricatives (2b), and in the voiceless retroflex fricative substituting for the English palato-alveolar fricatives (2d). This sort of substitution is common across all contact languages and among lexical borrowings. Third, the Malayalam underlying contrasts that are not attested in English do not persist in Malayalee English, a fate that befalls aspiration among stops and the alveolar-retroflex contrast, even though the latter exhibits lexical or surface complementarity.

Fourth, the underlying English contrasts that are not attested in Malayalam do not persist in Malayalee English, e.g., the voicing contrast among fricatives. Among the four types, only the first type deals with surface, or realizational, phenomena, and the rest deal with underlying phonological contrasts in the contributing languages of Malayalam and English. Focusing on underlying contrasts, we can re-cast the last three types in (8).[5]

(8)	*Malayalam*	*English*	*Malayalee English*	*Example*
a.	yes	yes	yes	voicing in stops
b.	yes	no	no	aspiration in stops
c.	no	yes	no	voicing in fricatives

Clearly, the Malayalee English obstruent system is not an exact replica of the Malayalee system, nor is it a replica of the English system. To explain the persistence patterns summarized in (8), I propose a two-step analysis. The first step calls for the entire Malayalam underlying obstruent system to transfer to Malayalee English, and the transferred system is subsequently 'sieved' through the phonology of English, filtering out those contrasts in the Malayalam system that are not part of the English system. This step is governed by the two constraints stated below:

(9) a. Substratum transfer involves an entire grammatical subsystem.
b. Morphosyntactic exponence of the transferred system conforms to the structural requirements of the lexical-source language.

In Bao (2005) and Bao and Lye (2005), these constraints are motivated to account for the aspectual system and topic prominence of Singapore English, a non-native variety with an active Chinese substratum. Constraint (9b) filters out the components of the transferred system that lack well-formed exponents in the superstratum language.

In the second step, the 'surviving' underlying contrasts are instantiated, or realized, by drawing from the available phonetic stock of Malayalam. Unlike the exponencing of morphosyntactic constructions, such as the aspectual system, which relies on morphosyntactic materials exclusively from the superstratum language, the exponencing of phonological contrasts needs to fall back on the substratum language for phonetic materials to substantiate the transferred contrasts that satisfy (9b). In the current contact linguistics literature, this step is often the only step that deals with the substitution of superstratum sounds with those of the same or similar quality from the substratum language. The Malayalee English data show that we need to look at the underlying contrasts as well.

[5]We ignore the possibility of a Malayalee English underlying contrast emerging independently of the contributing languages. Such possibilities exist in contact languages, often as a result of the internal development of the contact variety in question.

Under the two-step analysis, the persistence patterns summarized in (8) are not at all surprising. Among stops, English allows in voicing, but not aspiration (8a,b), precisely because English contrasts the former but not the latter. Lack of the voicing contrast among fricatives in Malayalam persists in Malayalee English, suggesting that English acts merely as a filter, and does not reintroduce into Malayalee English its own underlying contrasts. Similarly, the Malayalam 6-way contrast in place of articulation (excluding the palatal) is reduced to 5, the number allowed in English (see (1) and (2)). It is inconsequential which of the alveolar-retroflex contrast, alveolar or retroflex, survives in Malayalee English. We will list the retroflex ʈ/ɖ as phonemes of Malayalee English, and treat *t* as an allophone of ʈ due to back harmony (see (5)), and *d* as an allophone of ɖ due to assimilation (see (25) of Mohanan and Mohanan 2003). Need does not play a role in the process. Obviously there is no need for the surplus Malayalam contrasts in the phonological specification of English lexical items, but there is an urgent need for the voicing contrast among fricatives for the maintenance of English lexical distinctness (e.g., *few* vs. *view*, *Sue* vs. *zoo*). Nevertheless, all fricatives are voiceless in Malayalee English, causing the English minimal pairs to be homophones .

The two-step process produces the phonemic inventory of Malayalee English as shown in (10):

(10)

	Stops		Fricatives
	Voiceless	Voiced	Voiceless
Labial	p	b	f
Dental	t̪	d̪	
Alveolar/Retroflex	ʈ	ɖ	s
Palato-alveolar	c	ɟ	ʂ
Velar	k	g	

The appearance of *f* does not affect the overall system of contrasts; instead, it fills a gap in the system.

4.4 Conclusion

In the current contact linguistics literature, works on substratum phonological or phonetic influence tend to focus on surface correspondence between the substratum speech sounds and their targets; see summary accounts in Mühlhäusler (1986), Romaine (1988), Thomason and Kaufman (1988), and Winford (2003). Unlike pidgins and creoles, the so-called New English varieties typically emerge in contact ecologies in which the contributing languages, especially English and the substratum language, remain active. The contributing languages participate not only in the initial stage of the contact vernacular, but also in the subsequent stages of development. Our analysis of the Malayalee English data reveals the precise roles of the linguistic substratum and superstratum in shaping the emerging contact variety—the obstruent system of Malayalee English is essentially the Malayalam system filtered through the English system. The two competing systems do not mix randomly, as is the ca se with the aspectual system of Singapore English (Bao 2005). Furthermore, Malayalam provides the phonetic stock for the realization of the Malayalam system that has been sieved through the English system. This analysis predicts that the sound system of a new variety of English, such as Malayalam English and Singapore English, will not be radically different from the sound system of English, even when the substratum language has a far richer system of underlying contrasts.

Acknowledgments

As mentioned above, the idea reported here emerged from my discussion with Mohanan, for which I am grateful. I have also benefited from the detailed comments of two anonymous referees. All errors that remain are my own.

References

Bao, Zhiming. 2005. The aspectual system of Singapore English and the systemic substratist explanation. *Journal of Linguistics* 41:237–267.

Bao, Zhiming and Hui M. Lye. 2005. Systemic transfer, topic prominence, and the bare conditional in Singapore English. *Journal of Pidgin and Creole Languages* 20:269–291.

Bodman, Nicholas C. 1955. *Spoken Amoy Hokkien*. Kuala Lumpur: Charles Grenier.

Haugen, Einar. 1950. The analysis of linguistic borrowing. *Language* 26:210–231.

Hock, Hans. 1991. *Principles of Historical Linguistics*. Berlin: Mouton de Gruyter.

Hung, Tony T. N. 2000. Towards a phonology of Hong Kong English. *World Englishes* 19:337–356.

Mohanan, K. P. 1982. *Lexical Phonology*. Ph.D. thesis, MIT.

Mohanan, K. P. 1986. *The Theory of Lexical Phonology*. Boston, MA: D. Reidel.

Mohanan, K. P. and Tara Mohanan. 1984. Lexical phonology of the consonant system in Malayalam. *Linguistic Inquiry* 15:575–602.

Mohanan, Tara and K. P. Mohanan. 2003. Towards a theory of constraints in OT: Emergence of the not-so-unmarked in Malayalee English. Rutgers Optimality Archive ROA-416-09100.

Mühlhäusler, Peter. 1986. *Pidgin and Creole Linguistics*. Oxford: Basil Blackwell.

Romaine, Suzanne. 1988. *Pidgin and Creole Languages*. London: Longman.

Thomason, Sarah G. and Terrence Kaufman. 1988. *Language Contact, Creolization, and Genetic Linguistics*. Berkeley, CA: University of California Press.

Weinreich, Uriel. 1964. *Languages in Contact: Findings and Problems*. The Hague: Mouton.

Winford, Donald. 2003. *An Introduction to Contact Linguistics*. Malden, MA: Blackwell.

5

Repetition in Linguistic Change: Tone in Kwa Languages of Côte d'Ivoire

WILLIAM R. LEBEN AND FIRMIN AHOUA

5.1 Survey of Regular Tonal Correspondences Between Anyi and Nzema

This paper traces tonal differences in Anyi, Baule and Nzema, three languages of the Bia branch of Central Tano, a Kwa group. These languages provide evidence for a diachronic rightward shift in tone that resembles what has been found in numerous other languages, most notably neighboring Akan (Stewart 1983) but also in a wide variety of groups from sub-Saharan Africa. General resemblances aside, our real interest here is in the particulars, which differ in some ways from what is familiar from other languages and which pose some problems for description and comparison.

The Bia languages of Ghana and Côte d'Ivoire are a sister group to the better known Akan group (Stewart 1989). Gordon (2005) lists eight Bia languages, including the three dealt with here. From Northern Bia we discuss Anyi and Baule (both spoken in Côte d'Ivoire), and from Southern Bia we discuss Nzema (spoken both in Ghana and in Côte d'Ivoire).

First we compare the tones of Anyi (Northern Bia) with those of Nzema (Southern Bia). The tonal correspondences we find go a long way toward explaining the changes *within* the Baule dialects of Northern Bia.

In (1) to (5) below, tonal differences between Anyi and Nzema are grouped by tonal pattern, abstracting away from any segmental differences. In the left-most column, L and H designate one or more syllables with that tone. The tilde beneath the vowels symbolizes nasalization. Two-vowel sequences beginning with a high vowel, such as *ue*, *ʊa*, *ia*, are treated as phonologically

Reality Exploration and Discovery: Pattern Interaction in Language and Life.
Linda Uyechi and Lian-Hee Wee (eds.).

disyllabic (see Ahoua and Leben 1998, and Leben 1998). An underlined tone symbolizes a floating tone. The floating tones surface frequently, as we will show shortly.

			Anyi (Ndénié)	Nzema (Assinie)	
(1)	LHL > LHL̲	a.	èfâ	èvá `	'clay'
		b.	ɟòmâ	ɟòmá̰ `	'pestle'
		c.	bʊ̀lálɛ̀	bʊ̀làlɛ́ `	'iron'
		d.	kòkòtílè	kòkòtìlé `	'thumb'
		e.	kòlònvíà	kòlònvíá `	'egg'
		f.	bǎnà̰	bàná̰ `	'plaintain'
		g.	kǒkò	èkòkó `	'cocoyam'
		h.	èɟùḛ́ḭ́	èɟʊ̀ɛ̀nḭ́ `	'fish'
		i.	èlúè	èlùé `	'yam'
		j.	àɟê	àɣɛ̀lɛ́ `	'palm nut'
(2)	LH > LH̲	a.	cʊ̀á	cʊ̀à ´	'dog'
		b.	sùá	sùà ´	'house'
		c.	àsɥ̀é	àzùlè ´	'river'
		d.	sùmḭ́	èsùmḭ̀ ´	'pillow'
		e.	bàkǎ	bàkà ´	'tree'
		f.	nzùé	nzùlè ´	'water'
		g.	àɲɥìá̰	àŋwùmà̰ ´	'air'
		h.	sàrǎɲ	sànḭ̀ ´	'moon'
		i.	kɔ̀kɔ̀lɛ́	kɔ̀kɔ̀lɛ̀ ´	'red'
		j.	nǎɲ	nànḭ̀ ´	'meat'
		k.	ɛ̀kɛ̀lɛ̌ɲ	kɛ̀lɛ̀nɛ̰̀ ´	'toad'
(3)	HL > LHL	a.	dúà	dùálɛ̀	'tail'
		b.	nʊ̰́à̰	nnwá̰lɛ̀	'mouth'
(4)	HL > LHL̲	a.	bílê	bìlé `	'dark-colored'
		b.	ɟɛ́tɛ̀	ɟʊ̀ɛ̀tɛ́ `	'silver'
(5)	H > LH	a.	ákɔ́	àkɔ́lɛ́	'chicken'
		b.	ɛ́nɛ́	ɛ̀nɛ́	'today'
		c.	kóŋgó	kòŋgó	'business'

In (1), the Anyi sequence LHL corresponds to LHL̲ in Nzema. In (2), the Anyi sequence LH corresponds in Nzema to LH̲.

In (3), we see that Anyi HL corresponds to Nzema LHL. (4) shows cases where Anyi HL corresponds to Nzema LHL̲. In (5), the Anyi forms have an all-High melody, while the corresponding Nzema forms have a Low on the first syllable.

A sign that Nzema has lost a tonal contrast retained in Anyi is the difference between the examples in (4) and those in (1). While the Nzema has the same tone patterns for (1) and (4), the Anyi patterns differ. A second indication comes in (2d, e). Here, too, the Nzema forms share the same tonal pattern, while in Anyi there is a difference: (2d) *sùmḭ́* has Low and High on the first and second syllables respectively, while in (2e) *bàkǎ*, the same melody is realized with a Low-High sequence on the final syllable.[1]

5.2 Analysis of the Tonal Correspondences Between Anyi and Nzema

Lacking direct information about the tones of Proto-Bia, the accepted common ancestor of Anyi and Nzema (Gordon 2005), we have only present-day surface correspondences like those above to go by to determine how the tone patterns of the two languages diverged from the ancestral ones. As noted in the preceding paragraph, Nzema lacks a contrast that survives in Anyi, and so we assume that the tones of Anyi more closely correspond to those of Proto-Bia. Simplifying further, we will consider Anyi's patterns to match those of Proto-Bia, and so in this section we attempt to show how the Nzema patterns arose from those seen in Anyi.

A reasonable first hypothesis is the classic tone spreading scenario of Hyman and Schuh (1974), sketched here:

(6)
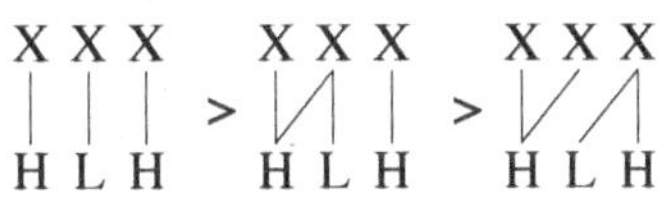

Here a tonal link on the leftmost syllable spreads one syllable to the right, creating a contour that is in turn simplified by rightward spreading from the second syllable to the third.

Applying this to Nzema, all we would need to add is an account of (i) the Low tone that appears on the first syllable in (3), (4), and (5), and (ii) the final floating tones in (1), (2) and (4). The second of these is addressed in (8) below.

For the tonal change on the initial syllable, two varieties of account are possible. Conceivably this Low tone could have been inserted historically, and its appearance could be seen as what triggered the tone spreading in the rest of the word. Or tone spreading could have occurred first as sketched in (6), with a subsequent change from initial HH to LH. Or spreading of H could have resulted in delinking of the original H, creating a toneless initial syllable which subsequently acquired a Low tone by default. The three accounts are represented schematically in (7):

[1] A conceivable alternative, one we are not in a position to evaluate, is that Anyi historically developed a new tonal contrast.

(7) a. Low tone insertion:

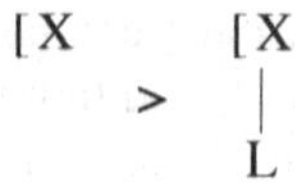

b. Level High > Rise:

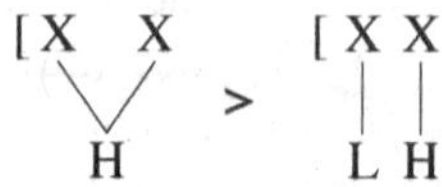

c. Tone spreading followed by delinking and default Low insertion:

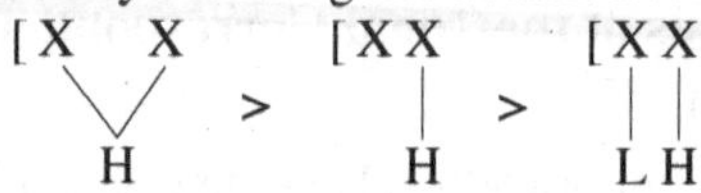

Which of these is more historically correct is an empirical matter, and without evidence the answer is just as hard to know as what K.P. Mohanan will wear for Halloween this year.[2] From a theoretical standpoint, all three analyses make good sense. The hypothesized word-initial Low tone in (7a) is supported by comparative evidence from Tano, the group containing the Bia languages Anyi and Nzema. In all six Tano languages discussed by Kouadio (1983) (Anyi, Baule, Nzema, Aboure, Eotile, Abron – also known as Brong or Bono), the noun has a Low-toned prefix. As the name pair Abron/Brong reflects, the prefix is lost historically from some of these languages under various conditions. The historical word-initial Low tone one might hypothesize for Proto-Tano would have created the conditions for the rightward spread of the remaining tones, as (7a) shows.

A second possibility is that the hypothesized level High sequence on the first two syllables of a word, shown in (7b), would have come to be realized phonetically as a rise (as attested in some other languages: see Leben 2004).

The third possibility would parallel the Kikuyu analysis of Clements and Ford (1979), involving what is commonly termed shifting instead of spreading, with insertion of a Low tone on the syllable from which the tone initially shifted. Spreading and shifting are well attested tonal processes. For example, Cassimjee and Kisseberth (2001) analyze closely related Southern Bantu languages differentiated by whether tone spreads or shifts. Without the historical facts of Bia, all three hypothetical scenarios have plausibility.

We turn now to the final floating tones in Nzema, whose correspondence with Anyi is described by (8), which delinks the final Anyi tone in the parallel Nzema forms. For convenience we break the change down into two parts.

[2]Mohanan's Halloween habits are as fabled as they are scary. One year in Stanford's Linguistics Department we were given a start when the Xerox guy unexpectedly showed up on Halloween wearing a suit and carrying the aluminum attaché that was then the vogue in the business world. The guy turned out to be Mohanan, who was unrecognizable because of the unusual garb and because he had shaved his moustache and disguised his gray hairs as black for the occasion.

(8) Tone Delinking (Nzema)

a. HL > H<u>L</u> / __]
èfâ > èvá `

b. LH > L<u>H</u> / __]
cʊ̀á > cʊ̀à ´

(8a) shows the delinking of the final Low in a word when a High precedes, and (8b) shows the delinking of a final High in a word when a Low precedes.

Note the difference in how the melody HL is realized in the two Anyi source words shown above in (4) and repeated here as (4') for convenience. Note that the fall happens on the final Anyi syllable in (4'a) but is spread over the entire Anyi word in (4'b), so that both the first and the second syllable are level in tone.

(4') HL > LH <u>L</u>

a.	bílê	bìlé `	'dark-colored'
b.	ɟétɛ̀	ɟʊ̀ɛ̀tɛ́ `	'silver'

Despite this difference, the corresponding Nzema forms on the right have the same pattern: L on the first syllable (with a simple nucleus in (4'a) and a complex one in (4'b)) and H on the second, followed by floating L.

The collapsing of the two Anyi realizations into a single one in Nzema is exactly what our account would predict.[3]

In principle, the tones historically set afloat in Nzema by the Tone Delinking in (8) could have been lost entirely. Indeed when the words transcribed here with a floating L suffix are pronounced in isolation, the L is deleted. But the tone's presence can be ascertained in several cases. The floating Low tone shows up synchronically on the Nzema suffix *-lɛ* in the examples of (3), as we see in (9):

(9) Nzema

dùálɛ̀ 'tail'
duá ` + lɛ > dùá + lɛ̀

Further evidence for Nzema's word-final floating tones surfaces when a toneless element follows. (10) and (11) illustrate two such cases.

Phrase-finally, the nouns *kúsù* 'cat' and *kɛ̀lɛ̀nɛ̰̀* ´ 'toad' are pronounced with a final Low tone: the floating H at the end of *kɛ̀lɛ̀nɛ̰̀* ´ is lost. But compare the two cases in (10), where our two nouns appear before the toneless numeral *kɔ̰* 'one'. After *kúsù*, *kɔ̰̀* has a Low tone, evidently because the preceding

[3]There is another segmental difference, whereby Anyi ɟ corresponds to Nzema ɟʊ, a labialized affricate whose labialization is often interpreted phonologically as a vowel. See Ahoua and Leben (1998) and Leben (1998) on secondary articulations and vowels vs. glides in Bia. If indeed this is a vowel, it is a Low-toned vowel – as we would predict on the basis of applying Default Low Insertion to this vowel.

syllable is L. Yet after *kɛ̀lɛ̀nɛ̰̀ ´*, *kɔ̰́* is High, a concrete manifestation of the floating H preceding it.

(10) a. kúsù kɔ̰̀ 'one cat'
b. kɛ̀lɛ̀nɛ̰̀ kɔ̰́ 'one toad'

The behavior is similar for noun-noun compounds, as in (11). In compounds, the first syllable of non-initial elements loses its underlying tone. Thus *kṵdṵ*, whose underlying tone pattern is L L, loses the L from its first syllable. The fact that the first syllable changes to H in (11b) but not in (11a) is explained by the floating H at the end of *kɛ̀lɛ̀nɛ̰̀ ´*.[4]

(11) a. kúsù kṵ̀dṵ̀ 'cat cloth'
b. kɛ̀lɛ̀nɛ̰̀ kṵ́dṵ̀ 'toad cloth'

The tonal correspondences in (1) to (4) are surprisingly close to ones that Stewart (1983) finds between two Akan languages, Fante and Asante. The correspondences within Akan and Bia must be independent of one another, since (as present-day Nzema and Asante show) they can't be posited for the parent group, Tano, of Akan and Bia.[5]

Stewart analyzes the Akan correspondences as shifting a Fante sequence of two unlike tones (HL or LH) rightward in Asante. He offers a general formula for the shift, but it is more useful for our purposes to break it down into cases:

(12)

	Fante	Asante
a.	HL	$\text{HH}\underline{\text{L}}$
b.	LH	$\text{LL}\underline{\text{H}}$
c.	$\underline{\text{H}}\text{L}$	$\text{H}\underline{\text{L}}$
d.	$\underline{\text{L}}\text{H}$	$\text{L}\underline{\text{H}}$

These schemas reveal two main similarities to the tone shift evidenced between Anyi and Nzema. First, the shift is rightward. Second, it affects both LH and HL patterns. If we probe further, a third similarity emerges as well. While the table in (12) makes it look as though the Akan shift always results in a floating tone in Asante, Stewart's examples show that this floating tone often winds up on a syllable – as it does in Nzema. Here is one of Stewart's examples, with the format modified slightly to conform to our own:

(13) Asante
ɔ̀ nhwɛ̀´ nò ⇒ ɔ̀ nhwɛ̀ nó 'he does not look at him'

Stewart proposes a historical Low tone for the object pronoun *nò*, and this tone assimilates to the preceding (floating) High tone. For him the resulting

[4]The changes described here also provide motivation for a synchronic rule of spreading in Nzema.

[5]In fact, Stewart argues that within Akan this change applied only to Asante and so did not occur at the stage of proto-Akan.

identity between the derived H on the object pronoun and the floating H in turn causes the floating tone to be deleted.

The most significant difference between the Akan case and the Anyi-Nzema correspondences is that Akan has no apparent counterpart to the change in (5), adding a Low tone in Nzema to the left of a sequence that in Anyi is all High, just as happens in Nzema to forms that in Anyi have a HL.

5.3 Tonal Correspondences Between Central Baule and Kode Baule

This section deals with two main dialects of Baule that differ markedly in their surface tones. We will refer to the dialects as Central Baule (CB) and Kode Baule (KB). Surprisingly, the tonal differences between them are similar to the ones between Anyi and Nzema sketched above. The directions given by > and < for the correspondences are the main topic of this section.

			Central Baule	Kode Baule	
(14)	LH > LH̲	a.	srǎ	srà ´	'month'
		b.	klɛ̌	klɛ̀ ´	'toad'
		c.	bɛ̌	bɛ̀ ´	'mat'
		d.	bǎ	bà ´	'child'
(15)	HL > HL̲	a.	sɛ̂	sɛ́ `	'clay pot'
		b.	blâ	blá `	'well'
		c.	búɛ̀	búɛ́ `	'liver'
(16)	HÊ< LH̲	a.	sá	sà´	'hand'
		b.	klṵ́	klṵ̀´	'stomach'
		c.	kpló	kplò´	'skin'
(17)	HL > LHL̲	a.	tá̰nḭ̀	tà̰nḭ́ `	'cloth'
		b.	lúkù	lùkú `	'Loukou'

The KB floating High surfaces synchronically when the numeral *kɔ̰* 'one' follows, as in (18a). Compare that with (18b).

(18)	a.	srà ´	srà kɔ̰́	'one month'
	b.	sɛ́ `	sɛ́ kɔ̰̀	'one clay pot'

The Low on *kɔ̰̀* in (18b) could arise from any of a number of factors: an underlying Low tone, a default Low tone, or the floating Low posited in (15), (17). Fortunately, the behavior of (18a) is more revealing. As long as the contrast between (18a) and (18b) is due to a phonological distinction, (18a) clearly documents a synchronic floating High.[6]

[6]Our recordings include citation forms in which some speakers actually pronounce the floating tones at the end of examples like those of (14), (15), (16), and (17). We have not yet deter-

Unlike Anyi and Nzema, which allowed the simplifying assumption that the tones of Anyi matched the historical tones of proto-Bia, neither the CB tones nor the KB ones can be regarded as universally reflecting the proto-Baule ones. Clearly the KB pattern L<u>H</u> in (16) matches the Proto-Baule one, as we see by comparing the words for 'hand' – CB *sá* and KB *sà´* against cognates in other Bia languages, e.g. Anyi *à-sá* 'hand.' Taking the KB pattern to reflect Proto-Baule is the only possibility consistent with the generalization that the Proto-Bia nominal prefix vowel was Low-toned. Still, the fact is that cross-linguistically, and elsewhere in Central Tano in particular, tones tend to shift to the right. This disposes us to accept the other tones of CB – the ones illustrated in (14), (15), and (17) – as retentions from Proto-Baule.

The developments between CB and KB include tone delinking on the right edge and, on the left edge, insertion of a Low tone and Tone Shift, the same combination seen in the correspondences between Anyi and Nzema. This is shown by the first two examples in (17), *tá̰nı̰̀* which becomes *tà̰nḭ́* in KB, and *lúkù* which becomes *lùkú* in KB. (Our data do not show clearly whether the predicted floating Low on the right survives synchronically in these words, and so we have not transcribed it.)

As similar as the changes within CB appear to those between Anyi and Nzema, they must have been independent. Otherwise, there is no explanation for why they would have not also have applied to the KB dialect. But this coincidence seems much less alarming when we recall Stewart's account of Akan, which also involves a highly similar but independent rightward diachronic shift that must have been independent of both of the cases discussed here, since Akan is a totally separate group from Bia.[7]

Up to this point, all of the tonal changes mentioned preserve the core melody and simply modify a link at the right end and add a default tone at the left. Are there any cases of more drastic shifts, such as tonal flip-flops, where Low changes to High and High changes to Low? Indeed some correspondences between CB and KB appear at least on the surface to be of this kind. They are given in (19), with the caveat that some of the forms in the Kode Baule column will be revisited and retranscribed in (22) and (23).

---

mined the conditions under which these variants are used.

[7]Hyman (1993) explicitly argues that two distinct rules of rightward spreading apply in a single language, Dagbani, a Gur language of northern Ghana. If that is correct, it is not surprising that spreading can enter a language group, or a single language, at several separate stages in its history.

(19)		Central Baule	Code Baule	
	a.	nànḭ́	nánḭ̀	'cow'
	b.	kòná̰	kónà̰	'Konan'
	c.	kòfi	kófi	'Koffi'
	d.	àgbá	ágbà	'cassava'
	e.	àwìé	áwìè	'rice'
	f.	ɟàmǎ	ɟámâ	'toe'
	g.	tràlɛ̌	trálɛ̂	'clothes'
	h.	ɲàmìɛ̰́	ɲámìɛ̰̀	'God'
	i.	wùmìɛ̰́	wúmíɛ̰̀	'ghost'

Conceivably, the changes that led to the forms in (19) were totally different from the ones we have been discussing. Yet there is at least one interpretation by which even these apparent tone reversals would preserve the core tonal melody.

Note that the change in (19) applies in environments largely complementary to the environments for the changes in (14). (14) applies to Low-High monosyllables (14c,d) and to words treated as monosyllabic in the standard orthography with the additional peculiarity of an orthographic CC cluster (14a,b).[8] On the other hand, the cases in (19) involve two complete syllables. Thus, it is possible – maybe even probable – that the cases in (19) first underwent the same change as in (14) – namely, Tone Delinking, as seen in the first step in (20). The rest of the change could have resulted from a KB innovation, which we could term High Tone Insertion and formulate as in (21). We sketch this scenario for the first example above, (19a):

(20)	CB nànḭ́	>	KB nà̰nḭ̀ ´	Tone Delinking
		>	KB ná̰nḭ̀ ´	High Tone Insertion

(21) Kode Baule High Tone Insertion

[L > [HL

In fact, another set of CB/KB correspondences provides independent evidence for High Tone Insertion. As seen in (22), CB Low tone corresponds to KB falling tone. Of course, the Low component of the KB fall is floating, as predicted by Tone Delinking (8).

(22)		Central Baule	Kode Baule	
	a.	ɟà	ɟá `	'foot'
	b.	bò	bó `	'bottom'
	c.	nṵ̀à̰	nʊ̰́á̰ `	'mouth'

[8] As is commonly observed, an extra-short vowel breaks up the CC cluster. See Ahoua and Leben (1998) and Leben (1998) for arguments that this is a true phonological vowel.

This alternative to flip-flop predicts that the surface forms listed for KB in the second column of (19) in fact should have (or should have had at some intermediate stage) a floating High to the right. That this is correct is shown in (23): *nánḭ̀* which in KB exhibits this floating High on the following numeral kɔ̰, the same test used above in (18). (23b) is included for completeness.

(23)	Kode Baule		
a.	nánḭ̀ ´	nánḭ̀ kɔ̰́	'one cow'
b.	bó `	bó kɔ̰̀	'one bottom'

A few additional facets of this case remain unresolved. The most problematic is illustrated in (24), which shows, inexplicably on our account, two distinct sets of correspondences in Kode Baule for Central Baule LH in words of comparable phonological structure. For (24b), the phonetic Mid tone in the Kode Baule column arises from phonological LH (Ahoua 1996).

(24) Central Baule LH = Kode Baule LH̲ or M

	Central Baule	Kode Baule	
a. LH vs. LH̲	srǎ	srà ´	'moon'
	klɛ̌	klɛ̀ ´	'toad'
	bɛ̌	bɛ̀ ´	'mat'
	bǎ	bà ´	'child'
b. LH vs. M	klɔ̌	klɔ̄	'village'
	bìá̰	biā̰	'man'

We have no solution to offer for this problem. Still, the data discussed here help to illustrate some tonal changes that can be reduced to rightward spreading plus the appearance of a Low on the left. This is consistent with a very impoverished theory of tonal operations like the autosegmental one, with ordinary rules that only add or delete tones or add or delete links. In turn, the fact that the theory is quite restricted helps to make it understandable why tone changes should appear to repeat themselves in separate developments in different languages.

Acknowledgments

This is part of an ongoing study of the comparative phonology of Kwa languages of Côte d'Ivoire. We are grateful to our students and colleagues at University of Cocody for their participation and to two anonymous reviewers for extremely helpful comments, suggestions, and corrections. The original work for this paper was supported by a grant from the National Science Foundation, SBR-9514718. The second author has also benefited from a grant from the Alexander von Humboldt Foundation while preparing an earlier version of the paper.

References

Ahoua, Firmin. 1996. *Prosodic Aspects of Baule: With Special Reference to the German of Baule Speakers*. Cologne: Koeppe.

Ahoua, Firmin and William R. Leben. 1998. The syllable template in Tano languages. Paper presented to West African Language Society Conference, Bingerville, Côte d'Ivoire.

Cassimjee, Farida and Charles W. Kisseberth. 2001. Zulu tonology and its relation to other Nguni languages. In S. Kaji, ed., *Proceedings of the Symposium, Cross-Linguistic Studies of Tonal Phenomena, Tonogenesis, Japanese Accentology, and Other Topics*, pages 327–359. Tokyo: Tokyo University of Foreign Studies.

Clements, George N. and Kevin C. Ford. 1979. Kikuyu tone shift and its synchronic consequences. *Linguistic Inquiry* 10(2):179–210.

Gordon Jr., Raymond G. 2005. *Ethnologue: Languages of the World*. Dallas, TX: SIL International, 15th edn.

Hyman, Larry M. 1993. Structure preservation and postlexical tonology in Dagbani. In S. Hargus and E. Kaisse, eds., *Phonetics and Phonology 4, Studies in Lexical Phonology*, pages 235–254. Orlando, FL: Academic Press.

Hyman, Larry M. and Russell G. Schuh. 1974. Universals of tone rules: Evidence from West Africa. *Linguistic Inquiry* 5:81–115.

Kouadio, Jérémie N. 1983. La morphologie du nom dans les langues kwa de côte d'ivoire. *Atlas des Langues Kwa de Côte d'Ivoire* 2:287–302.

Leben, William R. 1998. Weak vowels and vowel sequences in Kwa: Sounds that phonology can't handle. In O. Fujimura, B. D. Joseph, and B. Palek, eds., *Proceedings of LP '98*, pages 717–732. Prague: Karolinum Press.

Leben, William R. 2004. Rethinking autosegmental phonology. In J. M. et al, ed., *Selected Proceedings of the 35th Annual Conference on African Linguistics*, pages 1–9. Somerville, MA: Cascadilla Proceedings Project.

Stewart, John M. 1983. Asante tone shift. In I. R. Dihoff, ed., *Current Approaches to African Linguistics 1*, pages 216–245. Dordrecht: Foris.

Stewart, John M. 1989. Kwa. In J. T. Bendor-Samuel, ed., *The Niger-Congo Languages*, pages 216–245. Lanham, MD: University Press of America.

6

Syllables, Vowel Length and the Spread of Suprasegmentals

MARK DONOHUE

6.1 Introduction

The syllable has had a checkered history in linguistics, emerging from exile only relatively recently (see, for instance, Clements and Keyser 1983, Mohanan 1985, Blevins 1995). In Palu'e, an Austronesian language of southern Indonesia, we find conflicting evidence concerning the status of phonetically long vowels.[1] On the one hand we wish to consider the length to be purely due a moraicity constraint on foot size; long vowels are long (and monosyllabic) because the word needs lengths. On the other hand evidence from the interaction of a word-boundary effect that induces breathiness on the left edge (see Hajek (in press) for an areal overview), and nasal spreading from the right within the word implies that long vowels should treated as two separate segmental units, and thus two syllables. In this note I shall explore the phonetics of nasality and breathiness in Palu'e, concluding that phonetically long vowels are ambiguous, sometimes showing the behaviour of monosyllables, and sometimes that of disyllables.[2]

---

[1]Palu'e is described, briefly, only in Donohue (2005a, 2005b); this is the first work to deal with aspects of the phonology of the language. The language has the following segmental phonemes (aspiration is contrastive only initially; voiced stops are generally restricted to medial position): pʰ t̪ʰ tʃʰ kʰ; p t̪ k ʔ; b d (dʒ) g; ˀɓ mb nd ŋg; m n ŋ; v s; r l; i e a o u.

[2]Shortly after moving to Singapore and meeting Mohanan, I considered learning (some) Malayalam. I could already speak (some) Malay and (some less) Mandarin, two languages useful in Singapore (after Singlish), and it seemed only fair to learn something Dravidian as well, to be more respectful to the Indian community. Malayalam certainly is one of the great sounding languages of the world, so why not? Balanced against the presence of Tara and Mohanan, two

Reality Exploration and Discovery: Pattern Interaction in Language and Life.
Linda Uyechi and Lian-Hee Wee (eds.).

6.2 Lexical Roots in Palu'e and the Monosyllabicity of V:

The lexical root in Palu'e is bimoraic, with representative examples shown in (1); bimoraicity can be achieved by having either two short vowels, or else one long vowel, in the root. We can note that long vowels are found only in roots of the form /CV/ (or /V/), where they are obligatory, and so should not be considered to be phonemic. The forms in (2) all violate bimoraicity, by containing more than just two short vowels in one root. In (3) we see that a root that contains only one vowel cannot be realised with that vowel short: it must be long. (Many other phonotactically impossible words are of course conceivable, such as any consonant-final root; the only codas permitted are found in words with a clitic, as in (4), (6) and (7). These nasals are not moraic.) In (4) we can see that a root that shows a long vowel in isolation shows only a normal-length vowel when the 1SG nominative clitic *ak-* is added; when another mora is present, the vowel is not lengthened.

(1) a. [ˈta.ba] 'head' b. [ˈtaː] 'small bamboo'
[ˈtu.ba] 'blunt' [ˈtuː] 'knee'

(2) */CVː.CV/, */CV.CVː/, */CVː.CVː/

(3) *[CV]

(4) a. *thu* 'push' b. *ak-thu* 'I push'
[ˈtʰuː], *[ˈtʰu] [ĕ.tʰu], *[ĕ.tʰuː]

The C position in the syllable is optional: VCV, CVV and VV are also valid words, with the proviso that V_1 cannot be the same as V_2. There is a general ban on heterosyllabic long vowels, as can be seen in the behaviour of the emphatic clitic on the words in (5). While it can be added to any word, the combination of a word ending with /e/ and the emphatic clitic is a single, non-long, vowel. (Sequences of two vowels, including those seen in (5), are invariably syllabified as separate syllables; thus /teitei/ 'wait' is four syllables long, [ˌte.iˈte.i], not two, *[ˈtei.tei].)[3]

teachers available whose skills are nothing short of superlative, was the fact that Tamil is the more widespread language in Singapore, (and so more useful), and that there is no agreement system in Malayalam (which Tamil, sensibly, does display; I have my linguistic prejudices). And then there are all those pesky VOT and manner contrasts in Malayalam (pʰ p b b̤ʱ), something which Tamil does without. So Malayalam was put on the back burner, though a language in which one can say [mɪnɪˈmaɭi] for 'minimally' must be worth studying. I never got started on Tamil either; instead, by chance, I made friends with some people living on the nearest Indonesian island, and started hanging out and learning their language instead. These people are from a live volcano in the shape of a tropical island with nice food, killer chili sambal, and a wonderful language. To my surprise, I have enjoyed the experience of learning a language that has no agreement, and a number of VOT contrasts (pʰ p b ˀɓ, as well as mb). I have as yet no idea how to say 'minimally' in Palu'e, but I'm sure it will be good.

[3]Examples such as those in (1b) should not be considered to be disyllabic (that is, *[tu.u] for 'knee') since stress does not treat the two vowels as separate nuclei, and they do not show

(5) ['ti.lu] 'ear' ['ti.lu-e]
['to.bo] 'ceremonial sword' ['to.bo-e]
['ta.ba] 'head' ['ta.ba-e]
['ke.be] 'cloudy' ['ke.be], *['ke.be-e], * ['ke.beː]
['tu.bi] 'necklace' ['tu.bi-e]

We can suppose that the structures in (6a) and (6b) represent the syllables seen in (1a) and (1b), respectively; because of the ban on the occurrence of identical adjacent vowels, and the fact that long vowels are not underlyingly specified, as well as the reasons presented in the remainder of this paper, (6c) cannot be taken to represent the syllable type seen in (1b) (specifically, *ta* 'small bamboo').[4]

(6)

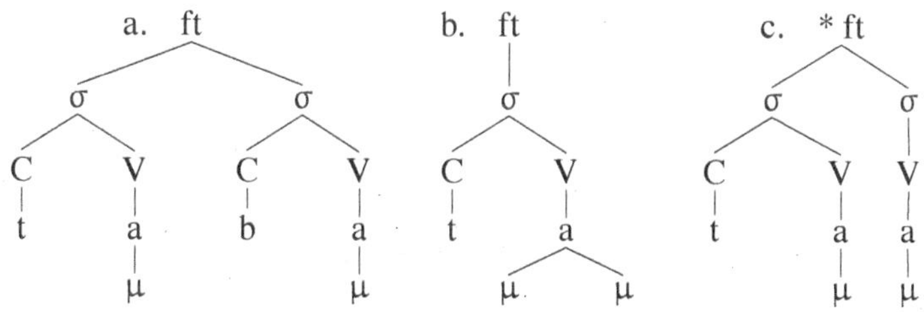

Nasality spreads leftward from a nasal consonant. This is true both of root-internal nasals, as in (7), and of nasals that are part of genitive clitics, as in (8).

(7) ['tã.na] 'land'
*['ta.nã], *['tã.nã], *['ta.na]

(8) ['ta.ba-gu] 'my/our (exclusive) head(s)'
['ta.ba-de] 'our (inclusive) head(s)'
['ta.bã-mo] 'your head(s)' ~ ['ta.bẽ̆-m] 'your head(s)'
['ta.bã-ne] 'her/his head(s)' ~ ['ta.bẽ̆-n] 'her/his head(s)'
*['tã.bã-mo], *['tã.bã-ne], etc.

---

short-vowel allophones when followed by a monoconsonantal nasal clitic (see (8); knee-3GEN is not realised as *['tu.ʊ̃̆-n] or *['tʊ.ʊ̃̆-n]; compare with (10) to see the behaviour of a true sequence of vowels in this environment). Finally, when monosyllabic verbs take the 1SG agreement prefix *ak-*, length is lost; thus ['tʰeː] 'hear', but ['akte] 'I hear.'

[4]For the purposes of this short note I shall ignore the phonology of epenthetic vowels, which are found when a root has the shape CCV. There are many reasons to believe that we should treat these CCV roots as not being completely "normal": the penultimate syllable is never stressed, in contrast to the more modal roots in (1), and this syllable always has a reduced vowel: Cɔ̆'CV, [tʰɔ̆'bu] 'grow'. Further evidence of differentiation of these roots from normal roots can be found in co-occurrence restrictions between C_1 and C_2, which are different in CCV roots than in CVCV roots.

Nasality can spread beyond a single syllable, provided there is no intervening supralaryngeal consonant. (8) additionally shows that nasality cannot spread through a supralaryngeal consonant, while (9) shows that a glottal stop is transparent for the purposes of nasal spreading.

(9) ['tẽ̆ʔ.ĩ̆-n] 'her/his faeces'
*['tĕʔ.ĩn], *['tẽ̆ʔ.ɪ̆-n], *['tĕʔ.ɪn]

(10) demonstrates that, in the absence of any intervening consonant, nasality can continue to spread leftward beyond the syllable on which it is specified.

(10) ['tũ.ẽ̆-n] 'her/his palm wine'
*['tu.ẽ̆-n] , *['tũ.ĕ-n] , *['tu.ĕ-n] (*['tʊ̃.ẽ̆-n] , etc.)

When a word does not have an initial consonant, the initial vowel is realised with breathy voice, as in (11a). In the event of a root of the form VV, (11b), the breathiness is only realised on the first vowel. In the event of a root of the form V, (11c), the vowel being necessarily long due to the bimoraicity requirement (see (6)), the entire bimoraic vowel displays breathiness.

(11) a. ['a̤.ta] 'person' *['a̤.ta̤], *['a.ta̤], *['a.ta]
b. ['ṳ.a] 'rattan; tuber' *['ṳ.a̤], *['u.a̤], *['u.a]
c. ['ṳː] 'wake' (=['ṳṳ]) *['uṳ], *['uu]

The fact that breathiness is found all through the vowel of 'wake (of a boat)' in (11c), but not all the way through the sequence of two vowels in (11b), is another argument for the treatment of (C)Vː roots such as those seen in (1b) as a single vowel that has been lengthened by a moraicity constraint, and not as a sequence of two vowels in separate syllables.[5] As seen in (11a), breathiness does not spread through the medial consonant in a VCV root.[6]

The question that confronts us can be formulated as follows. There are two processes (other than stress assignment) which apply at units greater than the segment: (i) nasalisation spreads leftward in a word; (ii) breathiness applies to a word-initial vowel. How do these two phonological factors interact? What is the realisation of a syllable that is on the one hand expected to be nasal (because of a following nasal consonant), and breathy (because of its initial position)? Answering this question is not simple, and is discussed in the following sections.

[5]An alternative analysis would block breathiness spreading in all circumstances *except* when two vowels in an uninterrupted sequence had identical qualities. It is hard to imagine the phonetic motivations of such a constraint.

[6]Medial glottal stops following an initial onsetless syllable suppress breathiness in roots such as /iʔo/ 'tail'. This is a principled exception to initial breathiness, involving the syllabification of the glottal stop (see (9)), but is not discussed here.

6.3 Competition Between Breathiness and Nasality

As a first approximation, there are four possible answers to the question posed about competition between breathiness and nasality. The obvious possibilities are:

1. the syllable is realised with nasality, and is not breathy;
2. the syllable is realised with breathy voice, and is not nasalised;
3. the syllable is realised with modal voicing and no nasalisation;
4. the syllable is simultaneously nasalised and breathy. (can an initial vowel bear both breathiness and nasality (for example, [ṳ̃])?)

Given the form in (12), the first answer appears to be correct. The lexical item is /une/, and the initial syllable is realised with nasalisation, and not with breathiness.

(12) [ˈũ.ne] 'strait; inside' *[ˈṳ.ne], *[ˈu.ne], *[ˈṳ̃.ne]

We might explain this by noting that nasalisation reflects features that are lexically specified for the word in question, while breathiness is a boundary phenomenon. The ultimate answer becomes more complicated when we consider data such as that in (13). Here the lexical root is /u/ 'wake', seen earlier in (11), shown here with the third person genitive enclitic *-ne*, seen earlier in (8).

(13) [ˈṳː-ne] 'her/his wake' (= [ˈṳṳ-ne])
*[ˈũː-ne], *[ˈu-ne], *[ˈṳ̃-ne]

Clearly the description of vowel nasalisation must refer to more than just segmental adjacency (in the model presented in Mohanan (1986), we would refer to nasalisation spreading in both strata 1 and strata 4). Based just on (13), and ignoring (12) for the moment, we see that breathiness 'wins' over nasalisation: the /u/ is both followed by a nasal consonant, and is initial, but only breathiness is realised. Note, however, that (13) is a morphologically complex word, employing a genitive clitic from the set seen earlier in (8). Any nasalisation in the root would be due to the presence of the genitive clitic, and not part of the lexical root itself, so that the explanation given following (12) would not hold. There is supporting evidence for the exceptionality of clitics: clitics are not part of the prosodic domain that determines stress (see (5) and (8)), nor do they count for moraicity requirements, as can be seen in (14). Here we see that 'my knee', formed with the lexical root seen in (1) and the morphology encountered in (8), preserves the long vowel seen in the uninflected word.[7]

[7]This fact results in surface contrasts in vowel length, such as those found when we compare /romo/ 'cloth (at the beginning of the weaving process)' versus the bimorphemic /ro-mo/ 'veranda piles+2GEN', which contrast as [rõ.mo] and [rõː.mo], respectively.

(14) [ˈtuː.-gu] 'my/our (exclusive) knee(s)'
*[ˈtu.-gu]

Additional evidence for the phonological exceptionalness of clitics can be found in the fact that there are C-only variants of clitics, as seen in (8), and that the most common vowel in the language, /a/, does not appear in any clitics (see (8) again, as well as (5)).

(13) illustrated the effect of encliticisation (with a nasal element) on a /V/ root with an NV clitic; in (15) we can see that a /VV/ root with clitic behaves somewhat differently, accommodating both the breathiness on the initial syllable, and the nasalisation on the second syllable. Breathiness applies to the first syllable, as predicted, while nasality spreads left from its segmental origin into the root, respecting the breathiness. Again, the nasality is not part of the lexical root: it has to cross a morpheme boundary, and so can be considered to be weaker than the nasalisation seen in (12). Comparing (15) with (10) we can see that nasalisation did not spread as far as might have been expected; there is clearly competition between the regressive nasalisation and the progressive breathiness, and breathiness wins.[8] (16) approximates the constraints on the realisation of quality in an initial vowel, based on (12), (13) and (15); the constraints are spelled out in (17) – (19).[9]

(15) [ˈṳ.ã-ne] 'her/his rattan'
*[ˈũ.ã-ne], *[ˈu.a-ne], *[ˈṳ̃.ã-ne], *[ˈṳ̃.ã̤-ne]

(16) $\text{Nasality}_{\text{LEXICAL}} \gg \text{InitialBreathyBoundary} \gg \text{Nasality}_{\text{NONLEXICAL}}$

(17) $\text{Nasality}_{\text{LEXICAL}}$
Realise and spread nasality that is part of the specification of a segment in the lexical root.

(18) InitialBreathyBoundary
The left edge of words should be bounded either by a segmental onset, or else by breathiness that distinguishes the first vowel.

(19) $\text{Nasality}_{\text{NONLEXICAL}}$
Realise and spread nasality that is not part of the specification of a segment in the lexical root, but appears through inflection.

The application of these constraints, along with an inviolable constraint against any syllable simultaneously showing both breathiness and nasality, is

[8] See Peng (this volume) for a similar case of two processes spreading and coming into competition; in Kikuyu place spreads regressively, and voicing spreads regressively. Peng shows that the progressive spread of voicing is blocked in highly specific circumstances; in Palu'e, as we shall see in section 1.4, it is the regressive process that is (partially) blocked.

[9] There are no known roots of the form VVNV or VVNCV. If any existed, they would be compound words spread over two feet.

shown in (20), dealing with the forms seen in (15).[10]

(20)

/ua/ + /-ne/ 'rattan-3GEN'	*Breathy Nasal	Nas_{LEX}	Initial Breath	$\text{Nas}_{\text{NON-LEX}}$
['ũ.ã-ne]			*!	
['ṳ.a̤-ne]				**!
['u.a-ne]			*!	**
☞ ['ṳ.ã-ne]				*
['ṳ̃.ã-ne]	*!			

The monomorphemic root seen in (12) is shown in (21); we presume that the initial vowel cannot be spread over two syllables to allow the same solution as was seen in (15) and (20) because of a general constraint against the proliferation of non-lexical structure ($*\text{STRUC}_{\sigma}$) (in order to allow the vowel lengthening seen in (1), we must rank this constraint below the constraint requiring bimoraicity). In (21) we can see that the fact that the nasality feature is part of the lexical item means that its preservation is more highly ranked than non-lexical nasality, such as appears in the genitive clitic, and so initial breathy voicing is not heard.

(21)

/une/ 'strait'	*Breathy Nasal	Nas_{LEX}	Initial Breath	$\text{Nas}_{\text{NON-LEX}}$
☞ ['ũ.ne]			*	
['ṳ.ne]		*!		
['u.ne]		*!	*	
['ṳ̃.ne]	*!			

For the sake of comparison, the segmentally identical, but morphologically distinct word seen in (13) is shown in (22). Because the only nasality specifications in this example are part of the genitive clitic, their preservation is less highly ranked, and the initial breathy boundary surfaces, despite the presence of the adjacent nasal segment. Note that the vowel is long, in keeping with the monosyllabic nature of the root /u/ (see (14) for discussion).

[10]This constraint might seem stipulative, but the fact that both breathiness and nasality require (significantly) greater airflow means that it is unlikely that nasalised, breathy-quality vowels can easily be produced, and certainly not that they would survive in a language in which no phonemic status is associated with either of breathiness or nasalisation.

(22)

/u/ + /ne/ 'wake-3GEN'	*Breathy Nasal	NasLEX	Initial Breath	NasNON-LEX
[ˈũː-ne]			*!	
☞ [ˈṳː-ne]				*
[ˈuː-ne]			*!	*
[ˈṳ̃ː-ne]	*!			

I shall not consider consonant-initial roots in detail, since the initial breathiness does not apply to them, and so nasalisation spreads without any competition.

6.4 Codas, A Discursion Concerning Short Vowels, and the Argument for *Disyllabic* Long Vowels

Another syllable type is relevant to this discussion, and merits a short aside for the purposes of clarity. We have seen, in (7) and (9), that when the monoconsonantal (and, consequently, nonsyllabic) variant of the third person genitive clitic *-n* is added to a root the final vowel is realised as a short, lax version of the lexical vowel; additional forms supporting this conclusion are shown in (23) and (24), where it is clear that [ʊ̆] (~ [ʉ̆]) alternates with [u], and [ɪ̆] with [i], in closed syllables. (Similar alternations between [ɛ̆] and [e], [ɔ̆] and [o], and also [ɐ̆] and [a], are also found.)

(23) a. [ˈtu.tu] 'k.o. basket'
b. [ˈtu.tʊ̃̆-n] 'her/his basket'
c. [ˈtu.tũ-ne] 'her/his basket'

(24) a. [ˈtu.bi] 'necklace'
b. [ˈtu.bɪ̃̆-n] 'her/his necklace'
c. [ˈtu.bĩ-ne] 'her/his necklace'

This clearly allows the possibility of a following nasal consonant to be in coda position in the same syllable, rather than appearing in a following syllable. The same short, lax vowels are also found monomorphemically, for instance preceding prenasalised stops, as can be seen in (25).

(25) a. [ˈtʊ̃̆m.ba] 'spear' b. [ˈtɪ̃̆m.ba] 'weigh'

Parenthetically, but to complete the phonetic picture, we can note that vowel-initial words with a medial prenasalised stop are vanishingly rare, but at least one is attested; here we can see that the short vowel does not allow enough time for the breathiness to be realised; this is a simple articulatory constraint, since breathy voice takes a longer time to activate than does modal voicing (eg., Gerfen 1999). It provides us, however, with evidence that the constraints shown in (16) do not represent the whole picture.

(26) [ˈʊ̃̌m.bu], 'door'
*[ˈʊ̤̌m.bu], *[ˈʊ̤̃̌m.bu], *[ˈʊ̌m.bu]

The other source of final nasals on vowel-initial words is the nonsyllabic genitive clitics, which we have already seen in (6) and more recently (16) and (17). Before examining their use on vowel-initial words, we need to note that when these clitics occur with a long vowel (necessarily found in a /CV/ root), the entire long vowel is nasalised, and that the open syllable allophone of the vowel is heard even when the genitive clitic is monoconsonantal.

(27) [ˈtũː-ne] 'her/his knee' (= [ˈtũũ.-ne])
[ˈtũː-n] 'her/his knee' (= [ˈtũũ-n]) *[ˈtʊ̃ːn]

Now we can examine vowel-initial roots with a nasal coda added in the form of a genitive clitic. In (28) we can see a /VV/ root with the third person clitic *-n* added. The first syllable is realised with breathy voice, and the second syllable with nasalisation. This repeats the results seen when the *-ne* clitic was added in (15): the appearance of the nasal in the coda of the second syllable does not result in patterns any different to the appearance of a nasal in a syllable following the second syllable, other than resulting in a short, lax allophone of the /a/ vowel.

(28) [ˈṳ.ɛ̃̌n] 'her/his rattan'
*[ˈũ.ɛ̃̌n], *[ˈṳ.ɛ̤̌n], *[ˈu.ɛ̌n], etc.

When we examine the addition of a *-n* clitic to monovocalic roots (/V/, thus realised as [Vː] due to the bimoraicity constraint), we find intriguing differences with the forms that have the *-ne* clitic seen earlier in (12). In (29) we see /u/ 'wake, ripple' with *-n* added. The long vowel begins with breathy voicing, and then is realised as nasalised (and modal) at the end of its length.[11] This contrasts with the forms obtained when *-ne* was added, in (12), in which breathiness is found through the entire length of the vowel.

(29) [ˈṳũn] 'her/his wake' (*[ˈũũn], *[ˈṳṳn], *[ˈuun], *[ˈṳ̃ṳ̃n])

The forms found in (29) are analogous to those seen in (28), but (28) is a /VV/ root, and (29) represents a /V/ root. Are we now to treat [uː] as being underlyingly a sequence of two identical vowels, /uu/? If so, this presents a dilemma: the new data contradict much of the evidence that we have seen earlier that supports the idea that the long vowel monosyllables are not lexical,

[11]The data shown here for *u* are identical for all monovocalic roots. Given that there are only five vowels in Palu'e, there are not many such roots: in addition to *u* 'wake' we also find *i* 'flesh' and *a* 'one' (the absence of mid vowels in monovocalic roots is not accidental, and reflects the continued operation of a low-ranked constraint against non-peripheral vowels, such as is commonly attested in Austronesian languages that have more than three vowels). Note also that these data are not simply low-level, automatic phonetic assimilations: speakers, when asked to speak very slowly, will clearly produce first a breathy mora, and then a nasalised mora.

but simply phonetic responses to foot binarity requirements. A summary of the different arguments is shown in (30).

(30)

TEST	[V :] = /V.V/	[V :] = /V/
Phonotactically restricted?		√
Instability under procliticisation		√
$[V_\alpha V_\beta]$, but $*[V_\alpha V_\alpha]$		√
Nasal spreading	(√	√)
Breathiness spreading		√
Breathiness/nasality interaction	√	

In short, the data in (11) and elsewhere overwhelmingly differentiate $[V_\alpha V_\beta]$ and [V:] roots, yet in (28) and (29) we see that these two root templates behave identically.

6.5 In Lieu of a Conclusion

There is no simple and obvious solution to the question of syllabicity for the [(C)V:] roots in Palu'e, but I hope that this brief sketch of the issues has brought home one of the points that has made Mohanan's work not only so engaging, but also so enduring: the attention to detail, and the refusal to accept a hypothesis, no matter how well argued and how well it accounts for the facts, until we can be sure that the facts really represent *all* of the available facts (see also Wee [this volume] and Peng [this volume] for examples of cases where a close attention to detail shows that the initially attractive, and simple, explanation is not adequate to the facts). If we were to have reached our final conclusions about syllable and root structure in Palu'e excluding the final two examples, we would have arrived at a weaker understanding of the complexities involved in this issue, and a poorer understanding of the challenge of linguistics. Challenge has been a by-word of Mohanan to his students and colleagues for decades, and can, I hope, continue to be the by-word of those same people as they confront their students and their research. The reason I hesitate to draw a firm conclusion is that I believe (and hope) that, as my knowledge of Palu'e deepens, I will find that the account presented here fails to cover some as-yet unearthed specific cases. The linguist never really finishes, and the analysis is never really complete.

References

Blevins, Juliette. 1995. The syllable in phonological theory. In J. Goldsmith, ed., *The Handbook of Phonological Theory*, pages 206–244. Oxford: Basil Blackwell.

Clements, George N. and Samuel J. Keyser. 1983. *CV Phonology: A Generative Theory of the Syllable*. Cambridge, MA: MIT Press.

Donohue, Mark. 2005a. The Palu'e passive: From pragmatic construction to grammatical device. In I. W. Arka and M. Ross, eds., *The Many Faces of Austronesian Voice Systems: Some New Empirical Studies*, pages 59–85. Canberra: Pacific Linguistics.

Donohue, Mark. 2005b. Syntactic and lexical factors conditioning the diffusion of sound change. *Oceanic Linguistics* 44(2):427–442.

Gerfen, Chip. 1999. *Phonology and Phonetics in Coatzospan Mixtec*. Dordrecht: Kluwer Academic Publishers.

Hajek, John. In press. Breathy voice as an areal feature of Nusa Tenggara and East Timor. In H. Steinhauer, ed., *NUSA: Linguistic Studies of Indonesian and Other Languages of Indonesia*. Badan Penyelenggara Seri NUSA.

Mohanan, K. P. 1985. Syllable structure and lexical strata in English. *Phonology Yearbook* 2:137–154.

Mohanan, K. P. 1986. *The Theory of Lexical Phonology*. Studies in Natural Language and Linguistic Theory. Dordrecht: Reidel Publishing Company.

7

Kikuyu Consonant Mutation

LONG PENG

7.1 Introduction

This article analyzes consonant mutation in Kikuyu, a Bantu language in Kenya. Like other Bantu languages, Kikuyu has stem-initial mutation caused by prefixing a placeless nasal /N-/. This prefixation yields five patterns in c-stems, consonant-initial stems. In v-stems, vowel-initial stems, it triggers the *y*-epenthesis and causes it to mutate. We show that the patterns of mutation reveal seemingly different but functionally related strategies or 'conspiracy' à la Kisseberth (1970). For instance, Kikuyu responds to *NC̥ (Pater 1996) via voicing or deletion. In addition, our analysis reveals three strategies in response to two other constraints. Unlike the languages in Pater (1996, 1999 and 2001), where the distinct strategies are distributed in different languages or in different domains/strata and can therefore be handled by constraint re-rankings or Stratal OT (Kiparsky, this volume), they appear in the same domain. In analyzing Kikuyu, the challenge lies not just in providing a description of mutation, but also in explaining how these patterns interact and how the conspiracies of seemingly distinct strategies result from one hierarchy.

7.2 The Patterns of Mutation

Kikuyu has four series of surface consonants. The voiceless series includes two stops [t, k], one palatal affricate [c] and two fricatives [θ, h]. The approximant series consists of two glides [w, y] and three sonorant continuants [β, r, ɣ]. The nasal series includes four nasal stops[m, n, ɲ, ŋ] while the NC series comprise the four homo-organic nasal-oral clusters [mb, nd, ɲj, ŋg] (with [j] representing a voiced palatal affricate).

Reality Exploration and Discovery: Pattern Interaction in Language and Life.
Linda Uyechi and Lian-Hee Wee (eds.).

There are four morphologically distinct prefixes that are made up phonologically of a placeless nasal /N-/ in Kikuyu. /N-/ indicates plurality on nouns, marks the 1st first person singular subject and object on verb stems and is an adjective marker when prefixed to abstract noun stems. When /N-/ comes in contact with the voiceless, approximant and nasal series of consonants in stem-initial position, five patterns of mutation emerge: a) the NC pattern, b) the nasal deletion pattern, c) the anti-gemination pattern, d) the fusion pattern, and e) the anti-fusion patterns. We describe the five patterns here on the basis of the data taken mostly from Armstrong (1967), Barlow (1960), Mugane (1997) and my own field work.

The NC pattern involves two types of stems: /t, c, k/-initial and /β, w, r, y, ɣ/-initial stems. /t, c, k/ undergo postnasal voicing (1a), while /β, w, r, y, ɣ/ harden into stops or affricate [b, d, j, g] (1b). In (1), the data with the /N-/ prefix appear in the second column. "-" signals the morpheme boundary.

(1)	a.	ko-a-tuur-a	koo-n-duur-a	'to ache him/me'
		ro-cuθe	ɲ-juθe	'backbone/backbones'
		a-ker-eet-ɛ	ŋ-ger-eet-ɛ	'he/I have crossed (street)'
	b.	o-βuθu	m-buθu	'rottenness/rotten'
		ro-wɔra	m-bɔra	'sting/stings of bees'
		a-re-et-ɛ	n-de-et-ɛ	'he/I have eaten'
		ko-mo-yur-i-a	koo-ɲ-jur-i-a	'to let him/me fill'
		ro-oa	ɲj-oa	'skin/skins, hide/hides'
		a-ɣor-eet-ɛ	ŋ-gor-eet-ɛ	'he/I has bought'

In (1b), the approximants must appear before an oral consonant in order for the NC cluster to surface. This is true of c-initial and v-initial stems: cf. *koo-ɲ-jur-i-a* (c-initial) vs. *ɲj-oa* (v-initial). The only difference is that *y* is inserted in v-initial stems, with epenthesis driven by alignment (Peng 2004 and 2007). When a nasal or NC cluster follows, the approximants emerge with fusion from (1b): see (4). We follow Herbert (1977, 1986) and Downing (2005) in assuming that [mb, nd, ɲj, ŋg] are clusters. This view suggests that postnasal voicing and hardening should not be analyzed via co-occurrence restrictions such as *[+nasal, -voiced].

Two types of stems trigger the deletion of /N-/. One involves a stem-initial dental fricative /θ/ and the other /h/-initial stems.

(2)	a-θɛk-ɛɛt-ɛ	θɛk-ɛɛt-ɛ	'he/I have laughed'
	o-θɛru	θɛru	'brightness/bright'
	a-hɛ-ɛt-ɛ	hɛ-ɛt-ɛ	'he/I has/have given'
	ro-hio	hio	'knife/knives'

We analyze the deletion in θ-/h-initial stems in an identical fashion for two reasons. First, they pattern alike in triggering the /N-/ deletion. Second, they pattern like t/c/k-initial-stems in blocking fusion in (5). Under our analysis, θ/h-initial stems behave alike because they are [-voiced] and [+continuant].

The anti-gemination pattern, which involves nasal-initial stems, is similar to (2) in that /N-/ appears to be deleted. But the motivation is different, conditioned by a prohibition against geminate consonants.

(3)	a-mɛɲ-ɛɛt-ɛ	mɛɲ-ɛɛt-ɛ	'he/I have known'
	o-nɔru	nɔru	'fatness/fat'
	o-ɲiiɲi	ɲiiɲi	'smallness/small'
	ko-mo-ŋorek-ia	koo-ŋorek-ia	'to annoy him/me'

To see this, consider the following. As /N-/ assimilates in place, we would find geminate nasals such as [mm, nn] if /N-/ were to surface. This is what we find in LuGanda, a Bantu language that allows geminates: e.g. /N-muli/ ⇒ [mmuli] 'reed' and /N-naku/ ⇒ [nnaku] 'days' (Cole 1967: 37-41).

The fusion pattern involves the stems with initial approximants. What distinguishes (4) from (1b) is that they appear before a nasal or NC. The outcome here is a single nasal. This pattern applies to c-initial and v-initial stems: i.e. *ɲ-embɔ* (a v-initial stem). Mentioned earlier, v-initial stems involve the epenthesis of *y*, which fuses with /N-/. This pattern is referred to in the Bantu literature as Meinhof's Law, Meinhof's Rule or Ganda Law.

(4)	mo-βain-a	main-a	'fine him/me'
	ro-reme	neme	'tongue/tongues'
	ro-embɔ	ɲ-embɔ	'song/songs'
	ro-ɣɛɛndɔ	ŋɛɛndɔ	'journey/journeys'

We view (4) as the result of fusing /N-/'s nasality with the place of stem-initial consonants. Fusion emerges from three requirements: a) Meinhof's Law (oral segments flanked by nasals agree in nasality), which triggers /N-β/⇒[Nm], b) place assimilation, which triggers /Nm/⇒[mm] and c) anti-gemination, which triggers /mm/⇒[m]. As neither [Nm] nor [mm] is legitimate, a single nasal appears.

The anti-fusion pattern involves /t, c, k/- (5a) and /θ, h/-initial stems (5b). The outputs are identical to (1a) and (2). What distinguishes (5) from (1a) and (2) is that a nasal or NC follows stem-initial consonants like (4). Unlike (4), neither surfaces with a fused nasal. These stems block fusion.

(5)	a.	o-tɔɔŋga	n-dɔɔŋgu	'wealth/wealthy'
		a-cin-eet-ɛ	ɲ-jin-eet-ɛ	'he/I have burned'
		o-kɛnu	ŋ-gɛnu	'happiness/happy'
	b.	a-θɔɔm-ɛɛt-ɛ	θɔɔm-ɛɛt-ɛ	'he/I have read'
		ro-hɛni	hɛni	'flash/flashes of lightning'

Why are (5a) and (5b) considered separately if they do not differ from (1a) and (2)? Meinhof's Law demands that segments surrounded by nasals agree in nasality. The stem-initial oral consonants in (5) are surrounded by nasals with the /N-/ prefix. /N-/ should fuse with stem-initial consonants. The fact that they do not calls for an explanation.

7.3 Analysis

The Two NC Patterns. The mapping from the inputs to the two NC patterns in (1) involves five feature changes. Place assimilation /N/⇒[m, n, ɲ, ŋ] involves the acquisition of the following consonant's place by /N-/. Postnasal voicing /t, c, k/⇒[d, j, g] involves a change in [voice]. The mappings from /β, w, r, y, ɣ/ to [b, d, j, g] involve postnasal hardening and de-sonorization, that is, changes in [continuant] and [sonorant]. Lastly, the mappings from /N-w/ and /N-y/ to [mb] and [ɲj] involve consonantization, that is, a change in [consonantal]. In (6), we lay out the ten constraints responsible for these feature changes:

(6) a. AG (pl) Adjacent consonants must agree in place
b. ID (pl) Input and output segments are identical in [place]
c. *NC̥ A nasal-voiceless obstruent sequence is prohibited
d. ID (vc) Input and output segments are identical in [voice]
e. *NF A nasal must not be followed by a [+cont] consonant
f. ID (ct) Input and output segments are identical in [continuant]
g. *C/S If [-continuant], then not [+sonorant]
h. ID (sn) Input and output segments are identical in [sonorant]
i. *C/C If [-continuant], then not [-consonantal]
j. ID (cs) Input and output segments are identical in [consonantal]

We analyze nasal place assimilation as involving the interaction of AG(pl) and ID(pl). AG(pl) dominates ID(pl), forcing adjacent consonants to agree in place. Stem-initial consonants could in principle assimilate to the preceding nasal. This option is not available because /N-/ is placeless.[1] Thus, short of deletion or fusion, /N-/ must assimilate to satisfy AG(pl).

Postnasal voicing stems from the domination of *NC̥ over ID (vc). *NC̥ is a markedness constraint that bans NC̥ sequences. It was proposed by Pater (1996) and argued for in a number of subsequent works including Hayes and Stivers (2000) and Pater (1999, 2001). One advantage for *NC̥, according to Pater (1996) and Hayes & Stivers (2000), is that it captures the fact that postnasal voicing is crosslinguistically common, but prenasal voicing is not. *NC̥ penalizes NC̥ clusters, not C̥N clusters. A further advantage is that *NC̥ explains why [b, d, j, g] are restricted to the postnasal setting in Kikuyu.

[1] It is not crucial to assume that /N-/ is placeless. This assumption is made because we see no evidence favoring any one of /m, n, ɲ, ŋ/ as underlying. The analysis would differ somewhat if /N-/ were assumed to have a place specification.

Postnasal hardening results from the ranking of *NF over ID (ct). *NF prefers nasal-stop to nasal-fricative (NF) sequences. In an extensive study of NC sequences, Herbert (1986) concludes that NF clusters are rare and fricatives often harden to stops or affricates in postnasal position. Ohala and Ohala (1993) provide phonetic reasons why hardening is desirable. These studies led Steriade (1993) and Padgett (1994) to propose representations that eliminate NF sequences. Like *NC̥, *NF captures the fact that postnasal hardening is common, but prenasal hardening is not. Moreover, it allows us to explain why [b, d, j, g] appear only in postnasal setting. The responses to *NF may vary just like the responses to *NC̥. Besides hardening, languages may opt for consonant epenthesis (English), nasal deletion (Kikuyu) and fusion (Kikuyu, Setswana). *NF unifies the seemingly unrelated outcomes. It is hard for the representational solution to capture the conspiracy effect.

The mapping from /β, w, r, y, ɣ/ to [b, d, j, g] transforms sonorants and glides into obstruents. We analyze these changes via feature co-occurrence restrictions. Following Archangeli and Pulleyblank (1994), we express these restrictions via implicational statements. Desonorization stems from the requirement that if a segment is [-continuant], then it is not [+sonorant]. The only exceptions are [m, n, ɲ, ŋ], whose sonorancy is protected by an undominated ‘If [+nasal], then not [-sonorant]’. Consonantisation emerges from the pressure for [-continuant] segments to be [+consonantal] via *C/C. As glides and vowels are [-consonantal] and [+continuant], *C/C is never violated. Under our analysis, desonorization and consonantisation result from the change from [+continuant] to [-continuant]. As this change is driven by *NF, desonorization and consonantisation are localized to postnasal /β, w, r, y, ɣ/. /β, w, r, y, ɣ/ in other positions are not affected as nothing pressures them to change their input [+continuant] specification.

In Kikuyu, voicing is not contrastive, as [b, d, j, g] appear only in postnasal position. This fact follows from the ranking of *VO (which states that voiced obstruents are not allowed) over ID (vc). In order for voiced obstruents to emerge in a postnasal setting, *NC̥ must outrank *VO. This suggests that *VO is sandwiched between *NC̥ and ID (vc).

(7) AG (pl), *NC̥, *NF, *C/C, *C/S ≫ *VO ≫ ID (pl), ID (vc), ID (ct), ID (cs), ID (sn)

To understand this ranking, consider the two tableaux in (8) and (9), which illustrate how voiceless obstruents and approximants become voiced and obstruent stops

(8) Tableau for /N-tɛ-ɛt-ɛ/ ⇒ [ndɛɛtɛ] 'I have thrown away'

/N-tɛ-ɛt-ɛ/	AG (pl)	*NC̥	*VO	ID (pl)	ID (vc)
a. mtɛɛtɛ	*!	*		*	
b. ntɛɛtɛ		*!		*	
☞ c. ndɛɛtɛ			*	*	*

(9) Tableau for /N-yur-i-a/ ⇒ [ɲjuria] 'to let me fill'

/N-yur-i-a/	*NF	*C/C	*C/S	*VO	ID (pl)	ID (ct)	ID (cs)	ID (sn)
a. ɲyuria	*!				*			
b. ɲy̱uria		*!			*	*		
c. ɲj̱uria			*!		*	*	*	
☞ d. ɲjuria				*	*	*	*	*

The option for approximants to preserve their feature specifications is illustrated in (9a). This option is ruled out by ranking *NF over *VO. To comply with *NF, /y/ must change its [continuant] specification. The candidates in (b), (c) and (d) contain a palatal whose [+continuant] specification is altered to [-continuant]. [y̱] in (9b) represents a palatal that is [-continuant], [-consonantal] and [+sonorant], a candidate eliminated by *C/C. The underlined [j̱] in (9c) denotes a [-continuant] and [+consonantal] and [+sonorant] palatal. This candidate is knocked out by *C/S. These tableaux demonstrate that *NC̥, *NF, *C/C and *C/S must outrank *VO.[2]

The Nasal Deletion Pattern. In Kikuyu, nasal deletion is attested in θ/h-initial stems. We attribute this to the claim that [θ] and [h] are [-voiced] and [+continuant]. This analysis is inspired by Bantu languages with similar mutation. As a phenomenon, nasal deletion is widely seen in stems with voiceless fricatives in Bantu languages, such as Venda and Yaka (Steriade 1993). Take Venda for instance. According to Steriade (1993: 415), when /N-/ abuts a voiced fricative such as [z], they emerge as a prenasalized affricate: e.g. /N-ziamedzo/⇒[**ndz**iamedzo] 'place onto'. But if the segment is a voiceless fricative such as [s], /N-/ is elided, leaving an affricate in its wake: e.g. /N-sengo/⇒[**ts**engo] 'court hearing'. In Kikuyu, the evidence that these two segments pattern alike comes from two sources. First, both trigger the elision of /N-/. Second, they behave like [t, c, k] in blocking fusion. These facts provide support for classifying [θ] and [h] as [-voiced] and [+continuant] and for linking nasal deletion to their classification as [-voiced] and [+continuant].

Consider the constraints responsible for nasal deletion. First, MAX-IO is clearly involved. Moreover, MAX-IO must outrank *VO, as shown in (10).

[2]One candidate not considered in (9) is [ɲuria]. This candidate will be evaluated and eliminated once the fusion pattern is analyzed, as illustrated in the tableau in (17).

(10) Tableau for /N-tɛ-ɛt-ɛ/ ⇒ [ndɛɛtɛ] 'I have thrown away'

/N-tɛ-ɛt-ɛ/	MAX-IO	*VO	ID (vc)
a. tɛɛtɛ	*!		
☞ b. ndɛɛtɛ		*	*

As nasal deletion is attested, MAX-IO must be violated and ranked below constraints such as *NC̥ and *NF. As (11) shows, ranking MAX-IO below *NC̥ and *NF is not sufficient because it incorrectly predicts that deletion is not optimal.

(11) Tableau for /N-θɛk-ɛɛt-ɛ/⇒[θɛ.kɛɛ.tɛ] 'I have laughed'

/N-θɛk-ɛɛt-ɛ/	*NC̥	*NF	MAX-IO	*VO	ID(vc)	ID(ct)
a. n̪t̪ɛkɛɛtɛ	*!					*
b. n̪ðɛkɛɛtɛ		*!			*	
☹ c. n̪d̪ɛkɛɛtɛ				*	*	*
☞ d. θɛkɛɛtɛ			*!			

The problem comes from (11c) in which /θ/ undergoes both voicing and hardening and becomes a voiced dental stop [d̪]. The question is: Why is [n̪d̪] not desirable? Re-ranking MAX-IO and *VO is not an option, as (10) shows. The solution lies in the recognition that a voiceless fricative must undergo both voicing and hardening to become a voiced stop while a voiceless stop or a voiced fricative needs to undergo voicing or hardening, but not both. Under this analysis, a cluster such as [nd] that originates from /N-t/ or /N-r/ violates ID(vc) or ID(ct). But if /N-θ/ is to become [n̪d̪], it must violate both ID(vc) and ID(ct). What distinguishes [n̪d̪] from [nd] is the extent to which these outputs may deviate from their inputs. In Kikuyu, an output may deviate from its input in either [voice] or [continuant], but not both.

With this understanding, we see why local conjunction of constraints is necessary. Local conjunction (Smolensky 1995, 1997), allows two constraints – C_1 and C_2 – to be joined to form a new constraint, C_1&C_2. C_1&C_2 does not replace C_1 or C_2. It is a separate constraint, ranked separately and violated only if both C_1 and C_2 are violated. It is shown to be necessary to a host of phenomena including the chain shift (Kirchner 1996), dissimilation (Alderete 1995) and phenomena that require counter-feeding ordering in derivational accounts (Itô and Mester 1998, 2001). We see here that it can explain nasal deletion here and anti-fusion later.

To block [n̪d̪] requires ID(vc)&ID(ct). As long as it dominates MAX-IO, [n̪d̪] is eliminated in favor of nasal deletion.

(12) Tableau for /N-θɛk-ɛɛt-ɛ/⇒[θɛ.kɛɛ.tɛ] ‘I have laughed’

/N-θɛk-ɛɛt-ɛ/	ID(vc) &ID(ct)	MAX-IO	*VO	ID(vc)	ID(ct)
a. ndɛkɛɛtɛ	*!		*	*	*
☞ b. θɛkɛɛtɛ		*			

ID(vc)&ID(ct), like ID(vc) or ID(ct), limits the degree to which an output can deviate from the input. Unlike them, local conjunction of faithfulness constraints can describe phenomena in which only some degree of departure from the input is tolerated (Kirchner 1996).

The Anti-gemination Pattern. The anti-gemination pattern is attested in nasal-initial stems. Following Itô and Mester (1998), we formulate NO-GEM(INATE) as a ban against double-linking one root node to two syllabic slots. As the root node dominates segmental features such as [nasal], NOGEM penalizes **only** complete geminates. Partial geminates such as [mb, nd, ɲj, ŋg], which share the place, do not violate NOGEM because they have two independent root nodes with distinct [nasal] specifications (see Wee [this volume] for a different characterization of gemination and antigemination via *MULT ASSOC and INTER-TIER FAITH. Complete geminates emerge from two requirements: AG (pl) and the Obligatory Contour Principle (OCP).

(13)

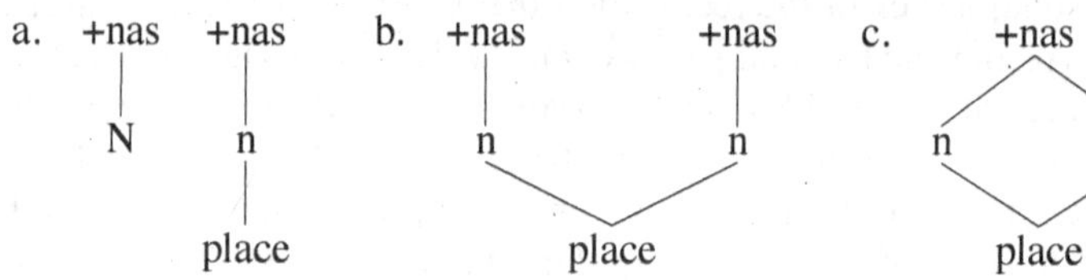

Consider the representation in (13a). This form cannot surface because of AG(pl). To satisfy AG(pl), /N-/ must assimilate as in (13b). This representation is problematic for the OCP. The geminate structure in (13c) emerges in response to the OCP.

(14) Tableau for /N-nɔru/ ⇒ [nɔru] ‘fat’

/N-nɔru/	AG (pl)	OCP	NO-GEM	MAX-IO	*VO
a. Nnɔru	*!				
b. $n_i n_j$ɔru		*!			
c. $n_i n_i$ɔru			*!		
☞ d. nɔru				*	

[$n_i n_j$ɔru] in (14b) and [$n_i n_i$ɔru] in (14c) correspond to (13b) and (13c), respectively. As long as AG (pl), OCP and NOGEM rank above MAX-IO, the anti-gemination outcome is optimal.

The Fusion Pattern. The fusion pattern is found in stems where the initial approximants appear before a nasal or NC cluster. Though fusion results in segment loss, it is distinct from deletion. In a deletion, the output retains the specification of only one of the input segments, while a fused segment serves as a correspondent for both input segments. Thus fusion, unlike deletion, does not violate MAX-IO. Fusion violates UNIF(ORMITY)-IO, which McCarthy and Prince (1995) states as "No element of the output has multiple correspondents in the input."

We claim that the pressures for fusion come from four constraints: AG (pl), MEINHOF'S LAW (ML henceforth), OCP and NOGEM. AG(pl) demands that /N-/ shares the place of the stem-initial approximant, preferring [n-r] to [N-r]. ML, formulated in (15), forces /r/ to be nasalised, preferring [n-n] to [n-r]. The OCP requires that adjacent identical consonants such [n-n] have the geminate structure in (13c). Finally, NOGEM pressures [n-n] to degeminate, favoring [n] over [n-n]. These constraints are jointly responsible for forcing /N-/ and stem-initial segments to fuse.

(15) MEINHOF'S LAW (ML):

$$* \ \underset{[+n]}{C}\ \{\ \underset{[-n]}{C}\ \ V(V)\ \underset{[+n]}{C}$$

Following Herbert (1986), we consider the trigger to ML as the [+nasal] specification of /N-/ and the stem-medial [+nasal]. These [+nasal] specifications form what he calls the 'hyper-nasal' environment, causing the stem-initial [-nasal] consonant to change. We state ML as a negative constraint. The left curly bracket ({) marks the left stem boundary. ML is activated only when a [+nasal] consonant, that is, /N-/, appears to the left of the stem. The parenthesis surrounding the vowel is intended to suggest that the [-nasal] consonant and [+nasal] consonant can be separated by up to two vowels. ML prohibits an oral consonant surrounded by nasals. It does not dictate a specific outcome, unlike Herbert's rule (1986: 82). The selection of a particular strategy results from constraint interactions. Apart from nasalization, denasalization or nasal deletion can both remove the hyper-nasal environment in compliance with ML.

Consider why fusion, but not denasalization or nasal deletion, is optimal. To prevent denasalization, we adopt Pater's (1996) ID I⇒O (nasal), which states that any correspondent of an input segment specified as [+nasal] must be [+nasal]. We reject MAX (nasal) because it forbids nasal deletion as well as denasalization. As nasal deletion is allowed, a high-ranking MAX (nasal) incorrectly predicts that nasal deletion is not possible.

We illustrate the analysis of fusion in (16). In (16a) *drame* represents a denasalization output. This output, though satisfying ML, violates ID (ns). The reasons for the elimination of (16b) through (16e) are straightforward;

they each violate *NF, AG (pl), OCP, and NOGEM.

(16) Tableau for /N-rame/ ⇒ [name] 'tongue'

/N-rame/	ID (ns)	*NF	AG (pl)	OCP	NO-GEM	MAX -IO	ML	UNIF -IO
a. drame	*!							
b. nrame		*!					*	
c. mrame			*!				*	
d. $n_in_j$ame				*!				
e. $n_in_i$ame					*!			
f. rame						*!		
g. ndame							*!	
☞ h. name								*

The comparison between [ndame] and [name] shows why ML must outrank UNIF-IO. This ranking accounts for why fusion is preferred. Why is nasal deletion not optimal? This follows from ranking MAX-IO over UNIF-IO: cf. (16f) and (16h). The high ranking of MAX-IO explains why deletion is not desirable and used as a last resort, when fusion is not allowed. The evidence for ranking MAX-IO over ML will come later from the anti-fusion data.

Recall that postnasal hardening is attested in stems where the approximants appear before stem-medial oral consonants such as /N-yur-i-a/ ⇒ [ɲjuria] 'to let me fill'. Why is postnasal hardening preferred to fusion in such stems? This follows from ranking UNIF-IO above *VO.

(17) Tableau for /N-yur-i-a/ ⇒ [ɲjuria] 'to let me fill'

/N-yur-i-a/	UNIF-IO	*VO	ID (pl)	ID (ct)
a. ɲuria	*!		*	*
☞ b. ɲjuria		*	*	*

Ranking UNIF-IO above *VO accounts for the fact that fusion is used when forced by ML. In cases where ML is not violated, the preferred strategy is postnasal hardening.

The Two Anti-fusion Patterns. One type of anti-fusion outputs emerges with NC clusters as in (5a). This pattern originates from the contact of /N-/ to [t, k, c]: e.g. /N-tɔɔŋgu/ ⇒ [n-dɔɔŋgu] 'wealthy'. The other pattern, seen in θ-/h-initial stems in (5b), shows up with the deletion of /N-/: e.g. /N-θɔɔm-ɛɛt-ɛ/ ⇒ [θɔɔm-ɛɛt-ɛ] 'I have read'. In analyzing t/c/k-initial stems, we must consider why neither fusion nor deletion is used, because both can satisfy ML. In analyzing θ/h-initial stems, we must explain why deletion is preferred to fusion and hardening, an option allowed in t/c/k-initial stems. The constraint hierarchy proposed so far wrongly predicts that fusion is optimal for t/c/k-initial stems.

(18) Tableau for /N-kɛnu/ ⇒ [ŋ-gɛnu] 'happy'

/N-kɛnu/	MAX-IO	ML	UNIF-IO	*VO
a. kɛnu	*!			
b. ŋ-gɛnu		*!		*
☹ c. ŋɛnu			*	

MAX-IO knocks out the deletion candidate in (18a), while ML eliminates the correct candidate in (18b), predicting that fusion is optimal.

As ML must dominate UNIF-IO to account for fusion, reversing the ranking is not possible. The solution must lie in some other constraint, one that the fusion candidate violates but that the correct outcome in (18b) does not. This constraint must outrank ML and cannot block fusion. To understand the issue, consider the three fusion configurations in (19).

(19)
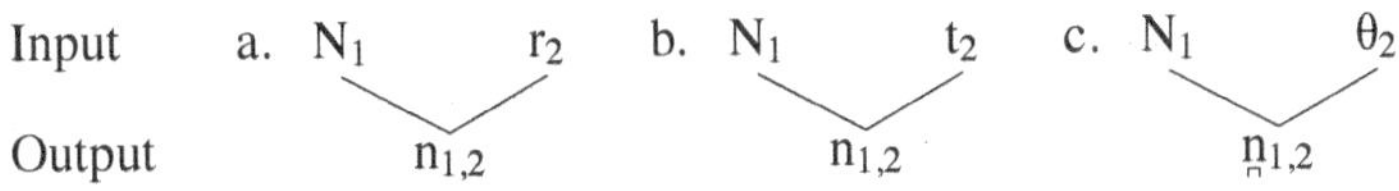

(19a), (19b) and (19c) represent β/w/r/y/ɣ-initial, t/c/k-initial and θ/h-initial stems, respectively. What we need to explain is why fusion is permitted in (19a), not in (19b) and (19c). Under fusion, the output nasal serves as a correspondent to /N-/ in each configuration. Thus the difference is not in the correspondence between /N-/ to the fused nasal. The solution lies in the relation between /r, t, θ/ to the output nasal. These three input-output relations all involve the change from [-nasal] to [+nasal], which cannot distinguish /r/⇒[n] from /t/⇒[n] or /θ/⇒[n̪]. Moreover, the change in [continuant] does not help to explain why t/c/k- and θ/h-initial stems resist fusion, as this change is relevant only to /θ/⇒[n̪]. The difference between fusion and anti-fusion patterns resides in [voice] and [sonorant], both of which are involved in /t/⇒[n] and /θ/⇒[n̪], but not in /r/⇒[n]. The question becomes: Can imposing a high ranking ID(vc) or ID(sn) prevent fusion? The answer is no. In Kikuyu, voiceless segments can undergo voicing while sonorants can become obstruents. Thus, changes in [voice] or [sonorant] are permitted.

The key lies in the recognition that the mappings from /t, θ/ to [n, n̪] involve changes in both features, while postnasal voicing and hardening trigger a change in one feature. To prevent /t, c, k, θ, h/ from undergoing fusion, we can appeal to ID(vc)&ID(sn), the conjunction of ID(vc) and ID(sn). This constraint, if ranked above ML, eliminates the fusion candidate.

(20) Tableau for /N-kɛnu/ ⇒ [ŋ-gɛnu] 'happy'

/N-kɛnu/	MAX-IO	ID(vc)&ID(sn)	ML	UNIF-IO	*VO
a. kɛnu	*!				
b. ŋɛnu		*!		*	
☞ c. ŋ-gɛnu			*		*

This tableau also provides crucial evidence for ranking MAX-IO over ML.

In analyzing θ/h-initial stems, we must explain why deletion is preferred to fusion and hardening attested in t-/c-/k-initial stems.

(21) Tableau for /N-θɔɔm-ɛɛt-ɛ/ ⇒ [θɔɔm-ɛɛt-ɛ] 'I have read'

/N-θɔɔm-ɛɛt-ɛ/	ID(vc)& ID(sn)	ID(vc)& ID(ct)	MAX-IO	ML	UNIF-IO
a. n̪ɔɔmɛɛtɛ	*!	*			*
b. n̪d̪ɔɔmɛɛtɛ		*!		*	
☞ c. θɔɔmɛɛtɛ			*		

The preference for deletion results from ID(vc)&ID(sn) and ID(vc)&ID(ct). They rule out fusion while ID(vc)&ID(ct) eliminates hardening. This analysis of the anti-fusion pattern again shows the need for ID(vc)&ID(ct).

To summarize, this analysis of consonant mutation reveal nineteen constraints arranged into six layers in (22).

(22) AG (pl), *NC̥, *NF, *C/C, *C/S, NOGEM, ID(vc)&ID(ct), ID(vc)& ID(sn), ID (ns), OCP ≫ MAX-IO ≫ ML ≫ UNIF-IO ≫ *VO ≫ ID (pl), ID (vc), ID(ct), ID(sn), ID(cs).

Mutation pressures stem mainly from *NC̥, *NF, NOGEM, and ML, which trigger changes in stem-initial segments, producing five distinct patterns.

7.4 Conclusion

Kikuyu mutation provides a dramatic illustration of pattern interactions and the claim that distinct surface outcomes may be motivated by one constraint. We see this in the responses to *NC̥, *NF and ML. With respect to *NC̥, Kikuyu employs voicing and nasal deletion. In the case of *NF, we witness hardening, fusion, and nasal deletion. Kikuyu responds to ML in three ways. Fusion and deletion result in compliance with ML. The third outcome, seen in the anti-fusion data, violates ML. Unlike the *NC̥ languages in Pater, these strategies are concentrated within one domain. While the languages analyzed by Pater lend to constraint re-rankings or Stratal OT (Kiparsky, this volume), Kikuyu mutation does not. We show that one hierarchy can handle the conspiracies of seemingly unrelated strategies and uncover their functional unity.

This hierarchy brings to light the relations of different strategies. With respect to *NC̥, voicing is preferred; nasal deletion is deployed as a last resort. With regard to *NF, hardening is preferred, followed by fusion with deletion least preferred. Moreover, the responses to ML illustrate elegantly the OT claim that constraints are violable. Even while ML exerts pressure for /N-/ to delete or fuse, its demand can be outweighed, resulting in optimal outputs that violate ML.

This analysis provides an account of the asymmetry in the distribution of [b, d, j, g], which, though attested, are restricted to the post-nasal position. Because voiced obstruents emerge from mutation, any analysis of this mutation should explain this asymmetry. Under this analysis, this asymmetry follows partially from *VO≫ID (vc). This ranking wipes out the voicing contrast by penalizing voiced obstruents. As voiced obstruents are not permitted by *VO ≫ ID (vc), we must address how [b, d, j, g] emerge and b) why they are restricted to the postnasal setting. Our answer is that *VO is outranked by *NC̥ and *NF, yielding *NC̥, *NF ≫ *VO ≫ ID (vc). *NC̥ and *NF are responsible for the emergence of [b, d, j, g] in postnasal position, as they impact only postnasal consonants.

This analysis draws its data from one Bantu language. It remains to be seen whether the re-rankings of these constraints can handle similar mutations in other Bantu languages. While we recognize the limitations imposed by any analysis of one language, we hope that the readers can see the benefits not only for offering an understanding of Kikuyu mutation, but also for stimulating interest in this Bantu-wide phenomenon.

Acknowledgements

One of K.P. Mohanan's central contributions to linguistics is his insistence and ability to unpack linguistic theories, as exemplified in many of his works (see, e.g.,Mohanan (1991)). In deconstructing linguistic theories and unearthing their claims and assumptions he shows that linguistic theories are not packages which can only be examined in whole, but a set of claims and assumptions whose validity can and should be tested individually. In so doing, he helps us all to obtain a better understanding of not only linguistic theories but also the phenomena they seek to explain. This study of Kikuyu consonant mutation is conducted in this spirit.

References

Alderete, John. 1995. Dissimilation as local conjunction. In K. Kusumoto, ed., *Proceedings of the North East Linguistic Society 27*, pages 17–31. NELS, Amherst, MA: GLSA.

Archangeli, Diana and Douglas Pulleyblank. 1994. *Grounded Phonology*. Cambridge, MA: MIT Press.

Armstrong, Lilias E. 1967. *The Phonetic and Tonal Structure of Kikuyu*. London: Dawsons of Pall Mall.

Barlow, Ruffell A. 1960. *Studies in Kikuyu Grammar and Idiom*. Edinburgh: William Blackwood & Sons Ltd.

Cole, Desmond T. 1967. *Some Features of Ganda Linguistic Structure*. Johannesburg: Witwatersrand University Press.

Downing, Laura J. 2005. On the ambiguous status of nasals in homorganic NC sequences. In M. van Oostendorp and J. M. van de Weijer, eds., *The Internal Organization of Phonological Segments*, pages 183–216. Berlin: Mouton de Gruyter.

Hayes, Bruce and Tanya Stivers. 2000. Postnasal voicing. Ms., University of California, Los Angeles.

Herbert, Robert K. 1977. Phonetic analysis in phonological description: Prenasalized consonants and Meinhof's Rule. *Lingua* 43:339–373.

Herbert, Robert K. 1986. *Language Universals, Markedness Theory and Natural Phonetic Processes*. Berlin: Mouton de Gruyter.

Itô, Junko and Armin Mester. 1998. Markedness and Word Structures: OCP Effects in Japanese. Ms., University of California, Santa Cruz. [Rutgers Optimality Archive (http://roa.rutgers.edu), #255-0498].

Itô, Junko and Armin Mester. 2001. Structural preservation and stratal opacity in german. In L. Lombardi, ed., *Segmental Phonology in Optimality Theory*, pages 261–295. Cambridge, UK: Cambridge University Press.

Kirchner, Robert. 1996. Synchronic chain shifts in optimality theory. *Linguistic Inquiry* 27(2):291–306.

Kisseberth, Charles W. 1970. On the functional unity of phonological rules. *Linguistic Inquiry* 1:291–306.

McCarthy, John and Alan Prince. 1995. Faithfulness and reduplicative identity. *University of Massachusetts Occasional Papers in Linguistics: Papers in Optimality Theory* 18:249–384.

Mohanan, K. P. 1991. On the bases of radical underspecification. *Natural Language and Linguistic Theory* 9:285–325.

Mugane, John. 1997. *A Paradigmatic Grammar of Gĩkũyũ*. Stanford, CA: CSLI Publications.

Ohala, John J. and Manjari Ohala. 1993. The phonetics of nasal phonology. In M. K. Huffman and R. A. Krakow, eds., *Phonetics and Phonology 5: Nasals, Nasalization, and the Velum*, pages 225–249. San Diego, CA: Academic Press.

Padgett, Jaye. 1994. Stricture and nasal place assimilation. *Natural Language and Linguistic Theory* 12:465–513.

Pater, Joe. 1996. *NC̥. In K. Kusumoto, ed., *Proceedings of the North East Linguistic Society 26*, pages 227–239. NELS, Amherst, MA: GLSA.

Pater, Joe. 1999. Austronesian nasal substitution and other NC̥ effects. In R. Kager, H. van der Hulst, and W. Zonneveld, eds., *The Prosody-Morphology Interface*, pages 310–343. Cambridge, UK: Cambridge University Press.

Pater, Joe. 2001. Austronesian nasal substitution revisited: What's wrong with *NC̥ (and what's not). In L. Lombardi, ed., *Segmental Phonology in Optimality Theory*, pages 159–182. Cambridge, UK: Cambridge University Press.

Peng, Long. 2004. The prosodic basis of Bantu glide epenthesis. In *WECOL 2003: Proceedings of the Thirty-Second Western Conference on Linguistics*, pages 15:221–233. University of Arizona, Tucson.

Peng, Long. 2007. LuGanda glide epenthesis and prosodic misalignment. *South African Journal of African Languages* 25(4):273–282.

Smolensky, Paul. 1995. On the structure of the constraint component Con of UG. Handout to talk presented at University of California. Los Angeles, [Rutgers Optimality Archive (http://roa.rutgers.edu), #86-0000].

Smolensky, Paul. 1997. Handout of talk given at John Hopkins Optimality Theory Workshop. University of Maryland Mayfest.

Steriade, Donca. 1993. Closure, release, and nasal contours. In M. K. Huffman and R. A. Krakow, eds., *Phonetics and Phonology 5: Nasals, Nasalization, and the Velum*, pages 401–470. San Diego, CA: Academic Press.

8

Vowel Harmony in Kimaragang as a Lexical Rule

PAUL R. KROEGER

8.1 Introduction

This paper discuss the vowel harmony system of Kimaragang Dusun, an endangered language spoken in northeastern Borneo, from the perspective of Lexical Phonology (Kiparsky 1982, Mohanan 1986, Mohanan and Mohanan 1984, Kaisse and Shaw 1985). The paper is primarily a typological sketch, rather than a formal analysis. I offer it here because the data are interesting, and K.P. Mohanan has always loved interesting data; and because Mohanan himself helped me to look at the corresponding Timugon Murut data in a new way, a very long time ago.

Vowel Harmony (VH) in Kimaragang has the classic properties of a lexical rule: it is obligatory, categorical, and structure preserving (Kiparsky 1985). It does not apply across clitic boundaries, and appears to be sensitive to different levels, or strata, of affixation, applying to some prefixes but not to others. Moreover, there appear to be a small number of lexical exceptions, roots which idiosyncratically fail to undergo VH. I begin in section 2 by outlining the basic pattern of Vowel Harmony, contrasting it with a second (and competing) process which I call Vowel Neutralization. Section 3 lays out the evidence referred to above which supports the identification of VH as a lexical rule. Section 4 provides a brief comparison of the Kimaragang facts with a similar pattern of vowel alternations found in a related language, Timugon Murut.

Reality Exploration and Discovery: Pattern Interaction in Language and Life.
Linda Uyechi and Lian-Hee Wee (eds.).

8.2 Vowel Harmony and Vowel Neutralization

Kimaragang is a member of the Dusunic family, a cluster of closely-related languages belonging to the Northeast Borneo subgroup of Western Malayo-Polynesian (Wurm 1993). Dusunic languages generally exhibit a basic 4-vowel system: /i,a,o,u/. The back mid vowel, which is traditionally represented as /o/, is normally unrounded or only slightly rounded in most Dusunic languages. It has a fairly wide range of phonetic variants, but its most basic realization is generally as a central or back unrounded vowel, [ʌ] or [ɤ] (Miller 1993). Kimaragang uses slightly more rounding for this vowel, with the pronunciation ranging from [ɔ] in stressed or long syllables to [ə] in short, pre-stress syllables. Kimaragang has also developed a 5th contrastive vowel, /e/, but this development is not of major significance to the present study and will be largely ignored in what follows.[1]

Vowel Harmony, which affects only the non-high vowels, changes /o/ to /a/ when the next vowel to the right is /a/. In other words, the low vowel /a/ spreads from right-to-left, replacing adjacent non-high vowels (/o/), one syllable at a time. The following examples illustrate this pattern:

(1) **Kimaragang Vowel Harmony** (roots are italicized)[2]

Underlying		**Surface**	**gloss**
ondom-an	⇒	andaman	'remember'
noko-*dagaŋ*	⇒	nakadagaŋ	'sold'
po-*ogom*-an	⇒	paagaman	'place where you set something'
po-*rolop*-an	⇒	paralapan	'cause to be gobbled up'
m-*ponoN*-sawo	⇒	manansawo	'to marry'
poN-*omot*-an	⇒	paŋamatan	'harvest time'
poN-*loboŋ*-an	⇒	paŋalabaŋan	'time/place of burial'
poN-*tanom*-an	⇒	pananaman	'time/place of planting'
<in>poN-*olos*-an	⇒	pinaŋalasan	'the person you borrowed from'
<in>poN-*asok*-an	⇒	pinaŋasakan	'the place where dry rice is planted'

High vowels /i,u/ are opaque; they neither trigger nor undergo vowel harmony, and the process cannot apply when a high vowel intervenes between the /a/ and a preceding /o/, as illustrated in (2a). Semivowels /y,w/, however, do not block vowel harmony, as shown by the examples in (2b):

[1] The /e/ developed through the coalescence of the sequences *o(h/ʔ)i and *a(h/ʔ)i. Thus even though /e/ is a non-high vowel, it is not affected by VH because the /i/ in the historical form was opaque to VH. Synchronically, this coalescence is still productive in the post-lexical rule of Vowel Merger discussed in sec. 3 below. See Kroeger (1993) for further discussion.

[2] The phonemic contrast between implosive /ɓ,ɗ/ and normal /b,d/ is not consistently written in the materials available to me, and so is suppressed in this paper. This contrast has no effect on the vowel alternations under discussion here. For a description of nasal assimilation patterns see Kroeger (2005).

(2) a.

a.	*sogit*-an	⇒ sogitan	'feel cold'
	oliŋ-an	⇒ oliŋan	'forget'
	noko-*pilat*	⇒ nokopilat	'accidentally wounded'
	sobu-an	⇒ sobuwan	'be urinated on'
	m-poN-*duat*	⇒ moŋoduat	'to ask'
b.	o-*sodoy*-an	⇒ asadayan	'all day long'
	o-*lobow*-an	⇒ alabawan	'receive muddy water'
	o-DUP-*lowoŋ*-an	⇒ alalawaŋan	'consider someone stupid'
	o-*roloy*-an	⇒ aralayan	'to be overgrown (e.g. with vines)'

Examples like those in (3) demonstrate two additional facts about the harmony process. First, it is unidirectional: /a/ does not spread from left-to-right, but only from right-to-left. Second, although both non-high vowels are involved in the process, only one of them (/a/) can trigger it; /o/ does not spread to the left when preceded by /a/.

(3)

dagaŋ-on	⇒ dagaŋon	'to buy'
surat-on	⇒ suraton	'to write'
rapaʔ-on	⇒ rapaʔon	'to boil'
lapak-on	⇒ lapakon	'to split'

However, there is another context in which the change from /a/ to /o/ can be triggered. This process, which I refer to as Vowel Neutralization, is illustrated in (4). The generalization here is that any pre-penultimate /a/ which is not immediately followed by another /a/ gets changed to /o/.

(4) **Vowel Neutralization**

a.	*talib*-an	⇒ toliban	'to pass by'
b.	*lasu*-an	⇒ losuan	'to feel hot'
c.	*anu*-on	⇒ onuwon	'to take'
d.	*sawo*-on	⇒ sowoʔon	'to marry'
e.	*tanom*-on	⇒ tonomon	'to plant'
f.	*rayow*-on	⇒ royoʔon	'to praise'

Each of the examples in (4) involves a disyllabic root whose first vowel is /a/ and whose second vowel is something else. When a suffix is added, the /a/ becomes pre-penultimate and so changes to /o/. If the suffix vowel is /a/, as in (4a) and (4b), which could trigger vowel harmony, this change is observed only when the second root vowel is high. If the suffix vowel is /o/, which cannot trigger vowel harmony, the change is observed no matter what the second root vowel is.[3]

[3] In Kimaragang, unlike Timugon, there are no suffixes whose nucleus is a high vowel.

I believe that this neutralization is related to stress placement. A number of Sabah languages outside of the Dusunic family have similar processes which neutralize non-high vowels in pre-stress syllables, and most if not all of these languages have regular penultimate stress. Labuk Kadazan (Hurlbut 1981) is a Dusunic language very closely related to Kimaragang, with a similar pattern of vowel harmony. It also has regular penultimate stress, and exhibits the same pattern of neutralization illustrated in (4): any /a/ in the penultimate syllable of a root is reduced to /o/ when a suffix is added, because of the shift in stress placement which is triggered by suffixation.

The pattern of stress placement in Kimaragang is slightly more complex. As in Penampang Kadazan (Miller 1993), stress in Kimaragang seems to be neither contrastive nor fully predictable. Stress may fall on either the penultimate or the final syllable, and in some words appears to be equally distributed over the final two syllables. Nevertheless, it is safe to say that stress always falls within the final disyllabic foot of the word, and that any /a/ occurring before the final foot is a target for neutralization.[4]

Notice that Vowel Harmony wins out over Neutralization in environments where both rules could apply, as illustrated by the occurrences of pre-penultimate /a/ in (1) above. In terms of rule ordering, this means that VH must follow Neutralization;[5] in terms of constraints, VH must outrank Neutralization.

Another interesting aspect of the VH alternation in Kimaragang is that it is (somewhat unexpectedly) constrained by Geminate Inalterability (Hayes 1986): "true" (i.e. morpheme-internal) geminate vowels systematically fail to undergo Vowel Harmony, as seen in (5a), while "fake geminates" (sequences of identical vowels across a morpheme boundary) do undergo vowel harmony, as seen in (5b). Due to limitations of space I will not discuss this issue further here; but see Wee (this volume) for a discussion of tautomorphemic vs. heteromorphemic geminates.

(5)	a.	n-o-*loot*-an	⇒	nolootan	'was covered with sand/dirt'
		o-*toor*-an	⇒	otooran	'long-lasting'
		*toboo*ŋ-an	⇒	tobooŋan	'to muzzle; tie the mouth (of a dog)'
		-in-*sood*-an	⇒	⟨in⟩soodan	'helped to pound rice'
		po-*tood*-ay	⇒	potooday	'cause to go slowly' (imper.)
		n-o-*sook*-an	⇒	nosookan	'was dished up for' (ben.)
		tiŋgoob-ay	⇒	tiŋgoobay	'cover' (imper.)
		n-*oob*-an	⇒	nooban	'brooded' (hen on eggs)

[4]Recall that Kimaragang /o/ is pronounced as schwa in pre-stress positions, so VN can be seen as neutralization of an unstressed vowel to schwa.

[5]This is a "counter-feeding" ordering, since if the order were reversed the forms created by VH would be neutralized by VN.

poN-*woog*-an	⇒ pomoogan	'washing place'
poN-in-*loow*-an	⇒ poŋinloowan	'term of address'

b.	po-*ogom*-an	⇒ paagaman	'place where you set something'
	ko-*omot*-an	⇒ kaamatan	'harvest'
	n-o-*ondom*-an	⇒ naandaman	'was remembered'
	noko-*abur*	⇒ nakaabur	'spilled, wasted' (IV)

8.3 VH as a Lexical Rule

As mentioned in the introduction, Vowel Harmony in Kimaragang has the properties predicted for a lexical rule within the theory of Lexical Phonology. In environments where it can apply, it is obligatory. It is categorical, meaning that it changes /o/ to /a/ without producing varying degrees of lowness or roundness. It is structure preserving in the sense that it does not create segments (or combinations of features) not found in underlying representations (Kiparsky 1985). Moreover, there seem to be a small number of lexical exceptions, roots which idiosyncratically fail to undergo VH. Most of these are loan words, such as: *podar* 'soap powder', *kodak* 'film', *biola* 'violin', *kokola* 'coca-cola', *sojar* 'soldier'. A rare example of a native root that resists VH is the root *konan* 'negotiate bride price'. However, some speakers pronounce and write this word as *koonan*, with the geminate vowel resisting VH as mentioned above; and this seems likely to be the historical form of the word. Another example of a lexical exception is the third person plural pronoun which some speakers pronounce as *yoʔalo* (others pronounce it as *yaalo*).[6]

We may contrast these features of VH with a process I will call Vowel Merger, which changes the sequences /o+u/ and /o+i/ to [oo] and [ee] respectively, as illustrated in (6).

(6) **Vowel Merger**

ko-*uli*	⇒ kooli	'able to return'
i-po-*udung*	⇒ ipoodung	'cause to put in fire'
n-o-*ugut*	⇒ noogut	'has been gathered'
o-*uni*	⇒ ooni	'used to produce sound'
po-*inum*-on	⇒ peenumon	'cause to drink'
ko-*ilo*	⇒ keelo	'to know'
noko-*igit*	⇒ nokeegit	'has gotten engaged'

Impressionistically, the long vowel [oo] which is created by this process is more tense and more rounded than other /oo/ clusters, whether within a single morpheme or across morpheme boundaries (example: *ko-uli* [kooli] 'able to return' vs. *ko-ogom* [kɔɔgɔm] 'able to sit'). Lip rounding is not contrastive

[6]This form is historically bimorphemic, derived from the root **alo*.

for non-high vowels; thus Vowel Merger is not structure preserving, since it creates a tense rounded vowel [o] which is not part of the underlying phoneme inventory of Kimaragang.

Another interesting difference between the two processes is that Vowel Merger frequently applies across clitic (or particle) boundaries, whereas Vowel Harmony does not. Some examples of /o+i/ merger across clitic boundaries are presented in (7). (When the long [ee] in these examples is unstressed, it often shortens to [e].)

(7) *no* 'compl' +*ilo?* 'that (DIST)' ⇒ *ne(e)lo?*
po 'incompl' +*ilo?* 'that (DIST)' ⇒ *pe(e)lo?*
no 'compl' + *ino* 'that (MED)' ⇒ *ne(e)no*
no 'compl' + *iri* 'that (SALIENT)' ⇒ *ne(e)ri*
po 'incompl' + *iri* 'that (SALIENT)' ⇒ *pe(e)ri*
irad ko? 'like' +*ilo?* 'that (DIST)' ⇒ *irad keelo?*
aso 'not exist' + =*i?* 'emphatic' ⇒ *asee?*

Some examples showing the failure of VH to apply across similar boundaries are presented in (8). Examples (8f) and (8g) involve clusters of second position particles, as shown by their pre-verbal position following the initial NEG.

(8) a. *po* 'incompl' + *ka* 'hearsay' ⇒ *poka*
b. *po* 'incompl' + *ma* 'prtcl' ⇒ *poma*
c. Waroo no kaka irih ... (*na kaka)
exist FOC HEARSAY SALIENT
'Once upon a time ...'
d. Ba-banar no ka. (*na ka)
DUP-true FOC HEARSAY
'It is true, so they say.'
e. ...ong alaku ko amu ... (*ka amu)
if sellable or NEG
'... if it will sell or not.'
f. Amu no yalo gumoos ... (*na yalo)
NEG COMPL 3sg.NOM tolerate
'He can no longer tolerate ...'
g. Amu po yalo nopongo ... (*pa yalo)
NEG INCOMPL 3sg.NOM finished
'He is not yet finished ...'

When a disyllabic root is reduplicated, a process that is only productive for vowel-initial roots, Vowel Merger can apply across the reduplicative boundary as illustrated in (9a). Vowel Harmony cannot apply across these boundaries, as illustrated in (9b).[7]

(9)	a. *iso-iso*	⇒	ise(e)so	'just one; all alone'
	m-pi-*iyo-iyo*	⇒	miyeeyo	'look like each other'
	ko-*ilo-ilo*	⇒	keeleelo	'source of knowledge'
	b. *yalo-yalo*	⇒	yalo-yalo (*yala-yalo)	'he himself'
	o-*angod-angod*	⇒	aangod-angod (*aangad-angod)	'somewhat fragrant'
	ko-*abos-abos*	⇒	kaabos-abos (*kaabas-abos)	'occasion for loss'
	m-pi-*ambot-ambot*	⇒	miambot-ambot (*miambat-ambat)	'speak/sing at the same time'
	m-pi-*aŋgol-aŋgol*	⇒	miaŋgol-aŋgol (*miaŋgal-aŋgol)	'a good match for each other'

Vowel Harmony appears to be sensitive to different levels, or strata, of affixation. We have already seen many examples of prefixes which undergo VH in the expected way; but there are a number of other prefixes in which /o/ fails to alternate. Some examples are provided in (10). This kind of morphological selectivity is a characteristic feature of lexical rules, and one that is not normally found in post-lexical rules.[8]

(10)	soro-DUP-*walu*	⇒	sorowawalu	'eight apiece'
	soro-DUP-*opod*-an	⇒	soroapapadan	'having 10 each'
	soŋ-DUP-*akan*	⇒	soŋakanakan	'each one eating'
	soŋ-DUP-*ago*	⇒	soŋagaago	'all hurrying around'
	ponoko-DUP-*lamin*	⇒	ponokolalamin	'use as a room'
	ponoko-DUP-*talib*	⇒	ponokotatalib	'keep passing by'
	oŋo-*gayo*	⇒	oŋogayo	'big (pl.)'
	oŋo-DUP-*maal*	⇒	oŋomamaal	'expensive (pl.)'
	oŋo-DUP-*lambat*	⇒	oŋolalambat	'widely spaced (pl.)'
	n-oŋo-*babak*	⇒	noŋobabak	'all got broken'
	n-oŋo-*kalabus*	⇒	nongokalabus	'all escaped'
	soŋ-ko-DUP-*gamit*	⇒	soŋkogagamit	'grab wildly'
	soŋ-ko-DUP-*sako*	⇒	soŋkosasako	'accept rides carelessly' (e.g. with unknown driver)

[7] Note that Vowel Harmony does apply in CV reduplication; some examples are seen in (10).

[8] I assume that the change of /o+a/ to [aa] in the fourth form in (10), *soŋ*-DUP-*ago* ⇒ *soŋagaago*, is due to Vowel Merger rather than Vowel Harmony.

soŋ-ko-po-*loboŋ* -ay ⇒ soŋkopalabangay 'buried carelessly' (i.e. in a bad place)
soŋ-ko-po-*boros*-ay ⇒ soŋkopabarasay 'passed message carelessly (i.e. to wrong person)

My tentative hypothesis is that the prefixes which fail to alternate belong to a separate level from those to which VH can apply. The non-alternating prefixes are phonologically unusual in other respects as well, such as failure to undergo nasal assimilation in forms such as */soŋ-balanga/ [soŋbalaŋa]* 'one clay pot full'; */soŋ-tulud/ [soŋtulud]* 'all flying around'. However, more work is needed to develop and test the details of this hypothesis.

In the preceding section we showed that a "fake" (i.e., heteromorphemic) geminate /o+o/ can undergo vowel harmony (5b). However, this is not true for the geminate [oo] created by Vowel Merger, as seen in examples like *n-o-ubat-an [noobatan]* 'treated with medicine'; *i-po-ugas [ipoogas]* 'cause to erase'; *ko-ubas-an [koobasan]* 'custom; habit'. This is immediately explained if VH is a lexical rule while VM is post-lexical, under the assumption that all lexical rules apply before any post-lexical rule. (VH will not apply to the underlying /o/ in the prefixes, because of the opacity of the high vowel /u/.) So these forms are not instances of geminate inalterability but simply a result of the relationship between lexical and post-lexical rules, which in this case produces a counter-feeding order.

8.4 Timugon Murut

The Dusunic and Murutic families, two of the main branches within the Northeast Borneo subgroup, are closely related to each other. The closeness of the relationship is seen not only in shared vocabulary items (roughly 50% shared cognates; Smith 1984), but also in extensive phonological and grammatical similarities. The distribution of non-high vowels in Timugon Murut is at first glance very similar to the Kimaragang patterns discussed in section 1.2; but on closer inspection some interesting differences emerge. The change of /o/ to /a/ in (11a), triggered by a suffix containing /a/, looks superficially very similar to the Kimaragang VH pattern illustrated in (1) above. But in Timugon, as (11b) demonstrates, the same change can be triggered by a suffix whose vowel is /i/.

(11) Timugon Murut[9]

a. *orop*-an ⇒ arapan 'perch' (LocF)
oŋoy-an ⇒ aŋayan 'go' (LocF)
sakoy-an ⇒ sakayan 'mount, ride' (LocF)
in-*abot*-an ⇒ inabatan 'belt' (RF, past tense)
paG-*sigo*-an ⇒ pansigaan 'spying place' (LocF)

b.	*tanom*-in	⇒	tanamin	'plant' (RF)
	abot-in	⇒	abatin	'belt' (RF)
	atod-in	⇒	atarin	'escort' (RF)
	rukop-in	⇒	rakapin	'catch (with noose)' (RF)
	oŋoy-in	⇒	aŋayin	'go' (RF)
	sigo-in	⇒	sigain	'spy on' (RF)
	orop-in	⇒	arapin	'perch' (RF)
	pa-*korojo*-in	⇒	pakarajain	'cause to work on' (RF)
	sakoy-iʔ	⇒	sakayiʔ	'mount, ride' (RF imper.)

Similarly, the change of /a/ to /o/ in (12a) looks superficially very similar to the Kimaragang Neutralization pattern illustrated in (4). But in Timugon, as (12b) demonstrates, pre-penultimate /a/ cannot change to /o/ when followed by a high vowel. Moreover, pre-penultimate /a/ does not change to /o/ unless the suffix vowel is /o/, as shown by comparing the first four examples of (11b) with (12a).

(12) Timugon Murut

a.	*tanom*-on	⇒	tonomon	'plant' (OF)
	patoy-on	⇒	potoyon	'kill' (OF)
	abot-on	⇒	oboton	'belt' (OF)
	rakop-on	⇒	rokopon	'catch (w/ noose)' (OF)
	pa-*sakoy*-on	⇒	posokoyon	'cause to mount' (OF)
	paN-*takod*-on	⇒	ponokoron	'live-with' (OF)
	paG-*latok*-on	⇒	porotokon	'cause to mix' (OF)
b.	*tampio*-on	⇒	tampioon	'drought-stricken'
	anduʔ-on	⇒	anduon	'marry' (OF)
	pali-on	⇒	palion	'abstain from' (OF)
	sapuk-on	⇒	sapukon	'shoot with blow-gun' (OF)
	taŋiʔ-in	⇒	taŋiin	'weep for' (RF)
	paG-*alig*-in	⇒	pagaligin	'exchange' (RF)
	paG-*saruy*-an	⇒	pansaruyan	'swim' (LocF)

It turns out that in Timugon, the vowel that spreads to the left is /o/, not /a/; and Neutralization changes /o/ to /a/. So VH and Neutralization in Timugon are almost the mirror images of the corresponding processes in Kimaragang. Prentice (1971:22, Sec. 2.3.4.1.1) summarizes the distribution of non-high vowels in Timugon with the following two descriptive generalizations:

[9] Much of the data for Timugon Murut is taken from Prentice (1971); the rest was provided by Richard Brewis and Silipa bte. Majius (p.c.), supplemented by examples from K. Brewis (1988) and Brewis & Brewis (1988). The labels for voice categories are those adopted by Prentice, following the terminological norm for Philippine languages in the 1960s and 70s: AF 'actor focus', OF 'object focus', RF 'referent focus', LocF 'locative focus'.

(i) /o/ may occur in non-final syllables of morphemes and words only if /o/ also occurs in all following syllables.

(ii) if /o/ occurs in the last two syllables of a word, /a/ may not occur in preceding syllables of the word unless another vowel intervenes.

Generalization (i) is responsible for the change from /o/ to /a/ when a suffix is added whose vowel is not /o/. This pattern of alternation was seen in (11). Generalization (ii) is responsible for the pattern of alternation seen in (12a): when a suffix containing the vowel /o/ is added to a root whose last two syllables contain the vowels /a/ and /o/ in that order, the antepenultimate /a/ together with any /a/ further to the left change to /o/. This leftward spreading of /o/ is blocked by the intervention of a high vowel, as seen in (12b).

Let me note in passing that Generalization (i) has an interesting parallel in Selayarese, where [-ATR] mid vowels may occur only (a) in final open syllables, or (b) in a syllable immediately preceding a [-ATR] mid vowel (Basri and Chen 1999).

K.P. Mohanan (p.c.) has pointed out to me[10] that Prentice's two generalizations can be understood in autosegmental terms by making the following assumptions:

(13) a. The melodic features [o] may not appear in non-final position on the V-melody tier.
b. Any [o] which violates this constraint is delinked and subsequently deleted (through stray erasure).
c. /a/ is the neutral vowel in Timugon; unspecified vowels are realized as /a/ by default spell-out rules.
d. An [o] which is linked to more than one V slot spreads to a non-high (or unspecified) vowel on its left (that is, doubly linked /o/ replaces /a/ from right-to-left).

Since Timugon has regular penultimate stress, the effect of assumption (13d) could also be achieved by specifying that "An [o] which is linked to the stressed syllable spreads...", since (13a) and (13b) ensure that a penultimate /o/ must be followed by /o/. The somewhat surprising fact that a single /o/ does not spread is illustrated in (14).

(14) *akan*-on ⇒ akanon 'eat' (OF)
baal-on ⇒ baalon 'make' (OF)
lunsay-on ⇒ lunsayon 'demolish' (OF)
ukab-on ⇒ ukabon 'open' (OF)
ansak-on ⇒ ansakon 'cook' (OF)
rasaŋ-on ⇒ rasaŋon 'sweat' (OF)

[10]This would have been sometime in the early 1990s, during Mohanan's first few years in Singapore.

Taken together, the assumptions in (13) result in two kinds of alternations. First, a non-final /o/ which is not immediately followed by /o/ is delinked and surfaces as /a/; I refer to this pattern as Timugon Neutralization. Second, a non-final /o/ which is immediately followed by /o/ spreads to the left if there is an /a/ in the preceding syllable; I refer to this pattern as Timugon Vowel Harmony. The vowel /o/ is independently licensed only in the final syllable.

Notice that if we change /a/ to /o/, and vice versa in the preceding paragraph, we have a system very similar to that of Kimaragang. The other two changes that would need to be made to achieve a perfect fit are (a) refer to "pre-penultimate" position rather than "non-final" position; and (b) remove the requirement for VH triggers to be doubly linked (or stressed). The resulting description would read: "First, a pre-penultimate /a/ which is not immediately followed by /a/ is delinked and surfaces as /o/; I refer to this pattern as Kimaragang Neutralization. Second, any /a/ spreads to the left if there is an /o/ in the preceding syllable; I refer to this pattern as Kimaragang Vowel Harmony. The vowel /a/ is independently licensed only in the final disyllabic foot."

On this view, both languages have a rule of Vowel Harmony which spreads a "marked" vowel from right to left replacing the default vowel; and a second rule of Neutralization that replaces a "marked" vowel in a non-licensed position with the default vowel. This approach requires us to assume that /a/ is the default vowel in Timugon while /o/ is the default vowel in Kimaragang.

An alternative approach would be to restate these generalizations in terms of features, rather than phonemes. It seems quite plausible that the active feature in Timugon, i.e. the feature that spreads via Vowel Harmony, could be different from the active feature in Kimaragang. One relevant fact is that the phonetic features of /o/ are different in the two languages. As noted above, /o/ is normally unrounded or only slightly rounded in most Dusunic languages, something like [ʌ] or [ɤ]. In Timugon, however, /o/ is actually pronounced as a round vowel. Let us tentatively adopt the following classification of Timugon vowels, and assume that the harmonic feature is [+ round]:

(15) **Timugon Vowels**

	i	**u**	**a**	**o**
High	+	+	–	–
Round	–	+	–	+

In principle we could use these same two features to distinguish the four basic Dusunic vowels, but there are at least two obvious problems with this analysis. First, it does not seem to reflect the actual pronunciation of /o/ in Dusunic languages. Tongue position, rather than rounding, seems to be the primary feature which distinguishes /o/ from /a/ in these languages. Second, a two-feature system leaves no room for the emergence of the fifth vowel /e/ in Kimaragang.

Most descriptions of Dusunic languages assume that the feature which minimally distinguishes /a/ from /o/ is [low] (see, for example, Hurlbut 1993, Pekkanen 1993). However, "lowness" harmony (spreading of [+low] in this traditional sense) seems to be quite rare. One could plausibly suggest that the harmonic feature is actually [ATR], at least for those dialects where /o/ is pronounced as a tense back unrounded vowel [ɤ].[11] I would like to propose a third option, namely that the active feature, i.e. the feature that distinguishes /a/ from /o/, is [RTR], as suggested by Basri and Chen (1999) for Selayarese. I propose the classification shown in (16) for the Kimaragang vowels.

(16) **Kimaragang Vowels**

	i	u	a	o	(e)
High	+	+	–	–	–
Back	–	+	+	+	–
RTR	(–)	(–)	+	–	–

Under these assumptions, we can say that both languages have a rule of Vowel Harmony which spreads the active feature from right to left, and a second rule of Neutralization that deletes the active feature when it occurs in a non-licensed position. For Timugon, we would need to stipulate that high vowels are opaque; for Kimaragang, this follows from the feature analysis in (16). The main differences between the two languages reduce to (a) the identity of the active feature, and (b) the position in which it is independently licensed (final syllable vs. final foot).

8.5 Conclusion

Kimaragang VH is typologically interesting in several respects. First, it appears to be an example of a unidirectional dominant-recessive harmony system, in that the dominant vowel (/a/) always spreads from right to left, whether from suffix to root or from root to prefix. Bakovic (2000) states that such systems are "unattested". Second, it seems to be unusual for vowel harmony to exhibit Geminate Inalterability effects. Maltese and Tigre have a process of rounding harmony that does not affect long vowels (McCarthy 1979, Schein & Steriade 1986), but this is the only comparable case that I am aware of.

This paper has argued that Kimaragang VH has properties typically associated with lexical phonological processes, notably the existence of lexical

[11] The [ATR] analysis seems counter to the phonetic facts of Kimaragang, in which /o/ is generally pronounced as a lax ([ÐATR]) vowel, like /a/. However, it is not uncommon for lexical rules to preserve morpho-phonemic alternations long after the phonetic motivation for those alternations has been lost due to historical change.

exceptions and sensitivity to specific classes of affixation. VH has been shown to "outrank" (i.e., stand in a counter-feeding relationship to) Neutralization, a competing pattern of vowel alternations. I have also argued that the vowel alternations of Timugon Murut are essentially the same as those of Kimaragang except for the identity of the active feature (alternatively, the default vowel) and the domain within which that feature (or segment) is licensed.

References

Bakovic, Eric. 2000. *Harmony, Dominance and Control*. Ph.D. thesis, Rutgers University, New Brunswick, NJ. [Rutgers Optimality Archive (http://roa.rutgers.edu/) #360-1199].

Basri, Hasan and Yiya Chen. 1999. When harmony meets reduplication in Selayarese. In C. Smallwood and C. Kitto, eds., *Proceedings of AFLA VI*, pages 37–49.

Brewis, Kielo and Richard Brewis. 1988. *A Trilingual Phrase Book: Timugon Murut, Bahasa Malaysia, English*. Kota Kinabalu: Sabah Museum and State Archives.

Brewis, Kielo A. 1988. *Learn to Speak Timugon Murut: A Series of 25 Language Lessons*. Sabah Museum and State Archives.

Hayes, Bruce. 1986. Inalterability in CV phonology. *Language* 62:321–352.

Hurlbut, Hope. 1981. Morphophonemics of Labuk Kadazan. In A. Gonzalez and D. Thomas, eds., *Linguistics Across Continents: Studies in Honor of Richard S. Pittman*, pages 46–53. Manila: Summer Institute of Linguistics and Linguistic Society of the Philippines.

Hurlbut, Hope. 1993. Labuk-Kinabatangan Kadazan phonemics. In M. Boutin and I. Pekkanen, eds., *Phonological descriptions of Sabah languages*, pages 47–58. Kota Kinabalu: Sabah State Museum.

Kaisse, Ellen and Patricia Shaw. 1985. On the theory of Lexical Phonology. *Phonology Yearbook* 2:1–30.

Kiparsky, Paul. 1982. Lexical phonology and morphology. In I.-S. Yang, ed., *Linguistics in the Morning Calm*, pages 3–91. Seoul: Hanshin.

Kiparsky, Paul. 1985. Some consequences of lexical phonology. *Phonology Yearbook* 2:83–138.

Kroeger, Paul. 1993. Kimaragang phonemics. In M. Boutin and I. Pekkanen, eds., *Phonological descriptions of Sabah languages*, pages 31–45. Kota Kinabalu: Sabah State Museum.

Kroeger, Paul. 2005. Kimaragang. In S. Adelaar and N. Himmelmann, eds., *The Austronesian Languages of Asia and Madagascar*, pages 397–428. London and New York, NY: Routledge.

McCarthy, John. 1979. *Formal Problems in Semitic Phonology and Morphology*. Ph.D. thesis, MIT, Cambridge, MA.

Miller, Carolyn P. 1993. Kadazan/Dusun phonology revisited. In M. Boutin and I. Pekkanen, eds., *Phonological descriptions of Sabah languages*, pages 1–14. Kota Kinabalu: Sabah State Museum.

Mohanan, K. P. 1986. *The Theory of Lexical Phonology*. Dordrecht: Reidel.

Mohanan, K. P. and Tara Mohanan. 1984. Lexical Phonology of the consonant system in Malayalam. *Linguistic Inquiry* 15:575–602.

Pekkanen, Inka. 1993. Tatana' phonemics. In M. Boutin and I. Pekkanen, eds., *Phonological descriptions of Sabah languages*, pages 15–30. Kota Kinabalu: Sabah State Museum.

Prentice, D. J. 1971. *The Murut Langauges of Sabah*. Pacific Linguistics C-18.

Schein, Barry and Donca Steriade. 1986. On geminates. *Linguistic Inquiry* 17:691–744.

Smith, Kenneth D. 1984. The languages of Sabah: A tentative lexicostatistical classification. In J. K. King and J. W. King, eds., *Languages of Sabah: A Survey Report*, pages 1–57. Pacific Linguistics, C-78.

Wurm, Stephen A. 1983. Language atlas of Borneo. In S. Wurm and S. Hattori, eds., *Language Atlas of the Pacific Area*. Canberra: Pacific Linguistics.

9

Exploring the Dilemma of the Split-L Geminate Pattern in Hong Kong English

LIAN-HEE WEE

9.1 Basic Patterns

In Hong Kong English (HKE, see Hung 2000 for phonological inventory), and also other Englishes, such as Australian English (Borrowsky and Hovarth 1997, Borrowsky 2001), Estuary English (Alterndorf 2003) and Singapore English, the lateral /l/ vocalizes to [w] when it is in the coda, as may be seen in (1).

(1) L-vocalization (data from Hong Kong English, HKE)

a.	i.	[smaiw]	'smile'	ii.	[smailiŋ]	'smiling'
b.	i.	[peiw]	'pale'	ii.	[peilisʃ]	'palish'
c.	i.	[meiw]	'mail'	ii.	[meiliŋ]	'mailing'
d.	i.	[kɔː]	'call'	ii.	[kɔːliŋ]	'calling'
e.	i.	[puː]	'pull'	ii.	[puːliŋ]	'pulling'

Given the [w]~[l] alternation in (1), it is clear that the stems must contain an underlying /l/ that surfaces as [w] (i.e. vocalized) when that /l/ is syllabified into the coda.[1] If the preceding vowel is [+labial], /l/ deletes, and the vowel undergoes compensatory lengthening.

[1] In studying non-native varieties of English, one should not make fallacious assumptions that underlying representations are identical to the Received Pronunciation. Underlying representations are after all hypothetical and must be supported by evidence. As shown in Mohanan (1992), Mohanan and Mohanan (2003) and also Bao (this volume), unprejudiced and rigorous approaches to non-native varieties of English and other contact languages can often lead to very intriguing discoveries.

Reality Exploration and Discovery: Pattern Interaction in Language and Life.
Linda Uyechi and Lian-Hee Wee (eds.).

(2) a. /l/ ⇒ [w] / ($_{\text{rime}}$ [-labial]__)
/smail/ ⇒ [smaiw]
/peil/ ⇒ [peiw]
/meil/ ⇒ [meiw]

b. /l/ ⇒ ø / ($_{\text{rime}}$ [+labial]__)
/kɔl/ ⇒ [kɔː]
/pul/ ⇒ [puː]

The facts in (1d) and (1e) need not necessarily be analyzed as the deletion presented in (2b). It is also possible to treat this as the lengthening of V due to the vocalization of L (henceforth L-voc)[2]. This matter is immaterial here because both options require /l/ to vocalize. Armed with (2), consider now the data in (3).[3]

(3) L-vocalization or preservation (HKE)

a.	i.	[piw]	'peel'	ii.	[piwliŋ]	'peeling'
b.	i.	[hɛw]	'hell'	ii.	[hɛwliʃ]	'hellish'
c.	i.	[kiw]	'kill'	ii.	[kiwliŋ]	'killing'

(cf. /piː/ ⇒ [pi.iŋ] / *pi.liŋ 'peeing')

At first blush, the data in (3) behave like those in (1d) and (1e) and therefore should be analyzed in a way consistent with (2b), where the [w] would be assumed as part of the underlying representations. That way, /l/ would be deleted unless followed by a vowel initial suffix. However, since /l/ must be underlying (without this, there will be no way of predicting the occurrence of the [l] in (3ii) without making erroneous predictions to cases like 'pee' ~ 'peeing'), the [w] in (3i) is predictable given the L-voc rule in (2a). It is important to note the predictability of pre-L [w], because by this property, [w] should not be part of the underlying representations in (3). One has ended in a dilemma.

THE L-VOC DILEMMA

I. If one assumes that there is no underlying /w/ in the stems in (3), the [w] in (3i) must have come from the vocalization of /l/. In which case, how can there be a [-wl-] sequence in (3ii)? Either the /l/ has become a [w] or not, but in this case, it seems to do both, which is paradoxical (akin to the particle-wave duality of light).

---

[2] Mark Donohue, Bruce Hayes and James Myers have on separate occasions suggested that L-voc implies labiality in the UR, as in /l^{w}/ (following Sproat and Fujimura 1993), which loses the labiality in the onset position; otherwise it would be difficult to explain why L-voc does not take the form of [-labial] vowels. But this issue is tangential to the focus of this paper.

[3] Syllabic /l/ is vocalized as [əw] in HKE, but since it is irrelevant for the purposes here, it shall not be discussed further.

II. If one assumes that the /w/ is underlying in the stems in (3), one would miss the fact that [w] is predictable when there is a final /l/, as in (2).

Although assuming no underlying [w] leads to a paradoxical situation, this paper argues that it is in fact the correct choice. The paradox can be resolved if one assumes that (i) phonological information percolates across the various tiers of the structural representations and (ii) the correspondence of percolated phonological information is not necessarily perfect. This approach allows for an analysis of a wider range of facts, a set of which is presented in the following section.

9.2 Relating to Patterns of Gemination

The first clue to resolving the L-voc Dilemma is to be found in the robust pattern of root-final consonants. They geminate when followed by a vowel initial suffix.[4]

(4) Root-final Consonant Geminates (HKE data)[5]

a.	i.	[stɔp]	'stop'	ii.	[stɔppiŋ]	'stopping'
b.	i.	[pin]	'pin'	ii.	[pinniŋ]	'pinning'
c.	i.	[put]	'put'	ii.	[puttiŋ]	'putting'

The process shown in (4) is also widely attested across varieties of English as well as other languages. In HKE, such gemination does not extend to cases where the rime has 3 segments, as in (5).

(5) Final Consonant Non-Geminates (HKE data)

a.	i.	[weit]	'wait'	ii.	[weitiŋ]	'waiting'
b.	i.	[paip]	'pipe'	ii.	[paipiŋ]	'piping'
c.	i.	[lain]	'line'	ii.	[lainiŋ]	'lining'

The reason behind this is that HKE, by virtue of its origins as a contact language between Cantonese and English, has an inclination for syllables that conform to the Cantonese syllable structure where the rime maximally contains two segments. The patterns in (4) and (5) can be captured in Optimality Theory with the ranking of two fairly straightforward constraints, as in (6) and (7).

---

[4]But see also Silverman (1992:323) for morpheme-internal geminates in HKE where gemination happens only when the preceding nucleus is simplex. The data is slightly different from suffix-triggered gemination, but the motivation for both kinds of gemination lies in the bimoraicity of the Cantonese syllable.

[5]These are not true geminates in that the CC is heterosyllabic. Evidence for the geminates comes from the clear presence of both pre- and post-pausal Cs when informants are asked to insert pauses into multi-syllabic words. Thus, 'stopping' is [stɔp^{v}piŋ], where ^{v}=pause with two clear [p]s. In (5), there is no geminate because there is no pre-pausal C, 'waiting' is [wei^{v}tiŋ]).

(6) BI-RIME[6] The rime contains exactly 2 segments
MAX Do not delete input segments
DEP Do not insert segments
ONSET All syllables have onsets.

MAX ≫ BI-RIME; ONSET ≫ Dep

(7) a. No Gemination without Suffixation

/CVVC/	MAX	BI-RIME
i. CVVC		*
ii. CVC	*!	

b. Suffixation Triggering Gemination (cf. (4))

/CVC/ + iŋ	BI-RIME	ONSET	DEP
i. CV.Ciŋ	*!		
ii. CVC.Ciŋ			*
iii. CVC.iŋ		*!	

c. Suffixation Not Triggering Gemination (cf. (5))

/CVVC/ + iŋ	BI-RIME	ONSET	DEP
i. CVV.Ciŋ			
ii. CVVC.Ciŋ	*!		*
iii. CV.Ciŋ	*!		

Thus, in (5), prior to suffixation, the final consonant is kept. Also, the final consonant does not geminate after suffixation since that would give the initial syllable a rime with three segments. Instead it is better to simply syllabify the morpheme-final consonant as the onset of the suffix syllable. In (4), where the root morpheme has only two segments in the rime, consonant gemination preserves the unmarked rime structure while providing an onset for the suffix syllable.

There is a clear connection between final consonant gemination and the L-voc dilemma. Notice that the root morphemes in (1) all have trisegmental rimes. So, where there is no suffix, the /l/ vocalizes rather than deletes. The cases in (3) are analogous to (5): the [-wl-] sequence is really a case of consonant gemination that has split into two distinct phones.

[6] BI-RIME is most likely the effect of two constraints involving (i) the bimoracity of the Cantonese syllable which is the minimal phonological word and (ii) the biuniqueness correspondence of the mora and the segment (a markedness constraint that forbids multiple linking).

(8) Comparing the Morpheme-final L with Morpheme-final C

a. /stɔp+iŋ/ ⇒ stɔp+iŋ
/pil+iŋ/ ⇒ pil+liŋ ⇒ piw.liŋ
gemination *L-voc*

b. /weit+iŋ/ ⇒ wei.tiŋ
/smail+iŋ/ ⇒ smai+liŋ ⇒ smai.liŋ
gemination n/a *L-voc n/a*

There are now two compelling reasons for us to take the apparently paradoxical position that [w] is not underlying in (3). Firstly, the presence of [w] is predictable from the underlying /l/ (see (2) and (8)). If there is /l/, then suffixation with a vowel-initial morpheme will yield [-wl-] only when the nucleus preceding /l/ is simple; without suffixation, /l/ will be syllabified into the coda as [w]. Secondly, the distribution of [-wl-] and [-l-] is identical to that of other consonants such as [-pp-] and [-p-]. They all depend on the complexity of the preceding nucleus. Although the alternative solution that requires underlying [w] would also yield the same surface forms, it would be at the cost of generality.[7]

An account such as (8) where there is no underlying [w] will require /l/ to send its proxy to be the onset of the suffix syllable while it stays in the rime to become vocalized, very much akin to the king sending his viceroy on unpleasant missions while he becomes fat in the comfort of his palace. This split-gemination that is the L's Viceroy Effect is opaque in derivational terms and not easily dealt with in classical OT.[8]

[7]L-voc in Adelaide English (AdE, Simpson 1980, Steriade p.c.) is like HKE but without geminates for cases like 'stopping', etc. This may cast doubts on whether greater generality is attained in analyzing HKE L-voc by reference to gemination. Like all attempts at theorizing, it is sometimes a matter of what set of facts a theory hopes to capture. Here, one is faced with the choice of relating a set of facts in one language, or with relating a phenomenon across languages. There is no a priori reason for the choices, though this paper represents an attempt at the former which could appeal to available mechanisms of faithfulness or to certain UR specificities for blocking gemination in AdE. Thus, one would have an account of all the relevant facts after all: HKE and AdE would be typological variations of the same set of universal principles (see section 9.4). However, taking the position of not relating HKE L-voc with gemination would require two sets of accounts for HKE: one for L-voc which it shares with AdE and one for gemination. I therefore submit, a posteriori, that the choice to analyze L-voc by reference to gemination is the superior approach. Further, Hammond (1997), citing Halle and Mohanan (1985), presents a variety of American English where gemination appears to be sensitive to the weight of the preceding syllable, similar (though not identical) to HKE.

[8]Classical OT has always had problems with opacity, and in this case one has a combination of transparent and opaque effects in (8). Later models such as Sympathy Theory (McCarthy 2003), Stratal OT (Kiparsky 2003, this volume) and Candidate Chains (McCarthy 2006) address opacity within OT but due to space constraints, the reader is invited to review Wee (2004) for an exploration of some of these enhanced OT models. It is also noteworthy that the opacity in (8a) is attributed to the opaque intermediate form **pilliŋ*. Although Voc and Gem do not appear to trigger or block each other, the ordering of processes is crucial for producing the right results.

9.3 A Pattern with a Paradox

Recall the L-voc Dilemma where taking the position that [w] is not underlying, though desirable, appears to be paradoxical because one would have the sequence [-wl-] corresponding to the one underlying element /l/. At first blush, section 9.2 seems to have the answer. It is not that /l/ has become [w] and stayed [l] at the same time, rather, it is that there are two /l/s so that one stays in the rime to be vocalized while the proxy is syllabified as the onset of the suffix syllable.

However, the gemination under consideration here is triggered by ONSET and would have to be accounted for in terms of progressive spreading, shown in (9).

(9) ONSET-triggered Consonant Spreading

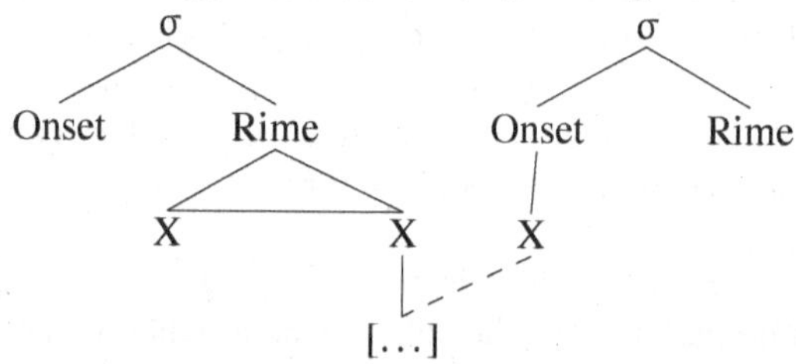

The main idea in (9) is the multiple association of the melodic content which accounts for a wide variety of facts including compensatory lengthening (Hayes 1989), vowel harmony (Kroeger, this volume), homorganic NC clusters (Peng, this volume) and glide formation (Mohanan 1986:75-77, where such spreading not only occurs across the syllable boundary but also across word boundaries in Malayalam).

Such spreading blurs syllable boundaries and may lead to complications where phonological processes target one part of the association (essentially Selkirk's 1990 two-root approach, cited in Broselow 1995, and Doug Pulleyblank p.c.). In Donohue (this volume), Palu'e shows precisely such characteristics where spreading nasality across syllable boundaries competes with vowel phonation, resulting in apparently paradoxical situations. Here too, a spreading account of L-voc returns us to the paradox of having one /l/ corresponding to two segments [-wl-]. Looking at (9), if the two skeletal slots are associated to [l], then there would be an L-geminate. If there is vocalization, then there would be a W-geminate. Either way, one does not arrive at a [-wl-] split-geminate sequence.

A simplistic solution at this point is to return to SPE type rules and account for the data by ordering two rules as in (10).

(10) An Undesirable Rule-Ordering Approach

Step 1:	Ø	$\Rightarrow$ C / $[_{\text{rime}}$VC$]$ +__V
Step 2:	/l/	$\Rightarrow$ w / $[_{\text{coda}}$__$]$

Step 1 ensures gemination when the environment is right while Step 2 ensures that /l/ syllabified into the coda becomes vocalized. Such an account is clearly undesirable because it offers us no insight into why the phonological system is the way it is. Further, it predicts that languages would vary typologically by the re-ordering of the rules, producing such languages that would yield **[pi-wwiŋ]* for 'peeling' and *[stɔppiŋ]* for 'stopping' if Step 2 is ordered before Step 1. To the best of my knowledge, this is unattested. Thus, a satisfactory theory of any explanatory power must retain the autosegmental representation of gemination as well as the parallel between root-final consonant gemination and the L's Viceroy Effect.[9]

9.4 Correspondence of Information Across Tiers

If the autosegmental representation of gemination is to be preserved, then the parallel L's Viceroy Effect with consonant gemination would require a theory that encodes the derivational complexity of splitting the L geminate within an enriched representation. This can only be done within the framework of Inter-tier Correspondence Theory (ICT, Wee 2004), where derivational histories are recoverable from hierarchical structures via correspondence of information across tiers. In such a conception, derivations are no longer necessary since the effect of derivation can be derived from the primacy of terminal nodes coupled with the non-faithful correspondence of information at higher nodes.

(11) Inter-tier Correspondence Theory (ICT)

i. Carriage of information
   All nodes (terminal or non-terminal) are information-bearing.[10]

ii. Correspondence of information
   There is a correspondence of the information content between nodes that stand in immediate domination.

iii. Violability of correspondence
   Correspondence of information between nodes is not necessarily perfect:

[9]Analyzing /l/ as a dorsal lateral complex along the lines of Sproat and Fujimura (1993) may offer fission as an explanation to the split-gemination paradox. However, this would falsely predict that [-wl-] should appear when CV prefixes to L-initial stems. In short, though /l/ may have a [dorsal] feature, it must be treated like all other consonants in terms of where [-wl-] occurs, making the fission account unviable.

[10]This idea is not new and is in fact found in endocentric models of syntactic representation. ICT also shares this assumption with Orgun's (1996) treatment for cyclic phenomenon in morphology-phonology interleaving. (See Wee 2004 for the similarities and differences.)

Given the setup in (11), ICT stands phonological representations on their heads in that terminal nodes are now exactly identical to underlying (input) strings. What is traditionally construed as the phonetic output is now the entire representation with the root node looking identical to the traditional notion of surface strings. To illustrate, consider a hypothetical language where /A+A/ ⇒ [BA]. In ICT, this would be represented as follows:

(12)

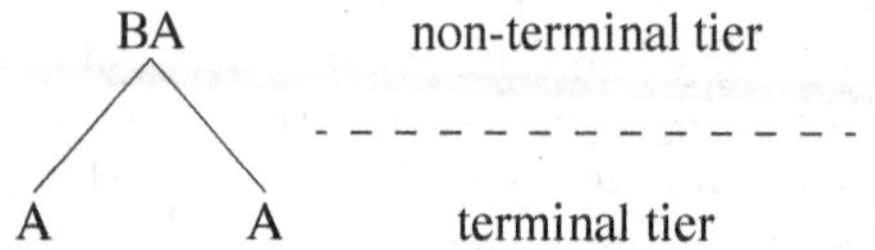

As can be seen in (12), it is the constituency of two adjacent A-s that triggers the unfaithful correspondence at the root node. To get the effect in (12), one would of course need a constraint that favors preservation of information from the right branch. This can be easily done with positional faithfulness constraints and general faithfulness constraints. To illustrate the power of ICT, consider now the effect of (12) to ternary strings. With the help of an additional rule CB ⇒ CD, the examples in (13) should suffice:

(13) ICT with reference to Rule-ordering Effects[11]

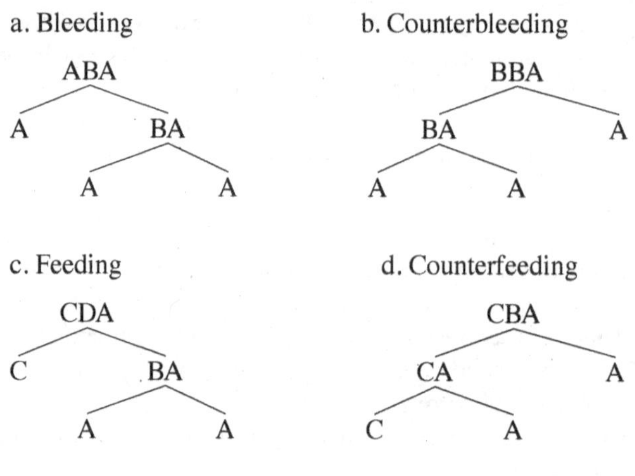

It should be clear from (13) that ICT captures directly the insight that opacity (and for that matter effects of derivation) is often structurally moti-

Goldrick's (2000) Turbidity presents a closely related idea of accounting for opacity where a covert element X may be realized by its sister Y through the dominating node. The parallel between Turbidity and ICT is somewhat oblique, but both point to structural representations for capturing opacity within a output driven framework.

[11]The same effects can be achieved with a progressive rule AA ⇒ AB coupled with the mirror-images of these structures.

vated, something that was built into the levels of Lexical Phonology or the mechanisms of bracket erasures (Mohanan 1986 and Kiparsky, this volume).

There are a few advantages with ICT. Firstly, it predicts that opacity is only as deep as there are hierarchical structures, since the number of unfaithful percolations is directly proportionate to the number of tiers. In other words, the depth of opacity is not arbitrary. Secondly, it predicts that adjacency does not trigger phonological alternation, rather alternation happens only in marked constituencies. Both predictions are generally supported by patterns across languages. The third advantage is that ICT provides a natural account for opacity within a non-derivational framework such as Optimality Theory (OT). ICT no longer requires derivations because the history of derivation would be a consequence of gradual mismatched inter-tier correspondences from the terminals to the root of the candidate tree.[12]

The only price one has to pay in accepting ICT is that output forms are no longer strings but structures. This is not a tall price to pay at all since one also has structural outputs in various other domains such as morphology, syntax and prosody. In fact, ICT lends greater coherence to phonological theorizing in general since we can now treat segmental phonology the same way we treat prosody (i.e. in having structural outputs rather than linear ones).[13]

9.5 ICT and L's Viceroy

Having gotten this far, the solution to L's Viceroy is now apparent. The optimal candidate for a given input /CVL+VX/ is as follows:

(14) Optimal Candidate for L's Viceroy Effect

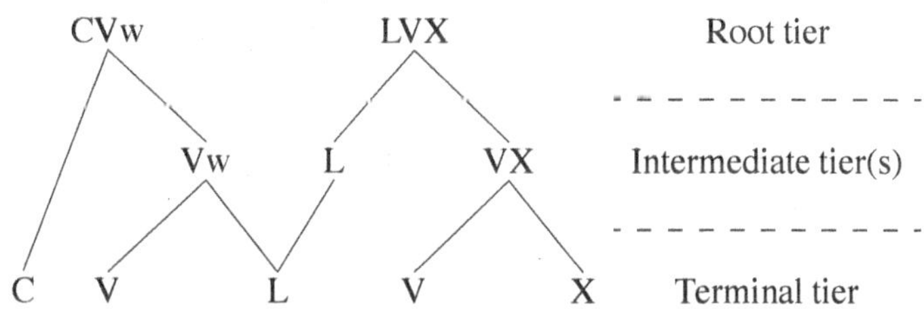

As may be seen in (14), the terminal tier is identical to the input string /CVL+VX/. This string is then parsed into a structure equivalent to two syllables such that the input 'L' is doubly associated, similar to the auto-segmental

[12]There is a fourth advantage in that ICT marries the insights of both the containment model (Prince and Smolensky 1993/2004; McCarthy and Prince 1993/2001) and the correspondence model (McCarthy and Prince 1995) of OT. In ICT, the input is contained as the terminal nodes and Correspondence is captured across tiers. See Wee (2004) for discussion.

[13]Implicit in treatments for prosody, such as parsing of elements into Onsets, Syllables or Feet, etc, is the hierarchical, hence structural organization of material. As such, these outputs are not strings per se.

representation in (9). Information from the terminal tier corresponds to that in the higher tiers (akin to percolation, though not necessarily construed derivationally). With one exception, all inter-tier correspondences have been faithful. The one exception is where L has not percolated faithfully in its first association: it has [w] as a correspondent. This unfaithful correspondence is triggered by a constraint that prohibits [l] in the coda of a syllable, which would yield the effect of split gemination.

To see how ICT works with the examples in HKE, consider first a set of possible candidates when given an input such as /pil+iŋ/ 'peeling' and /meil+iŋ/ 'mailing'.

(15) Candidates for /pil+iŋ/ 'peeling'

a. Faithful

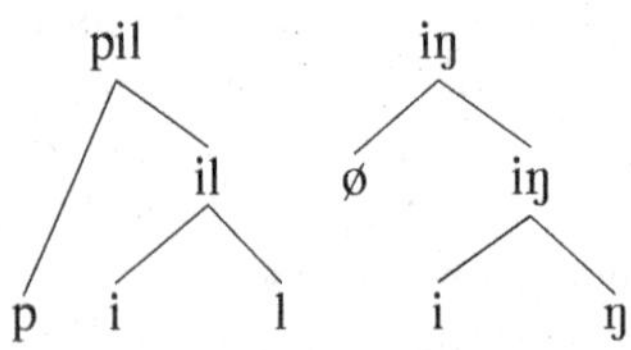

b. Vocalize

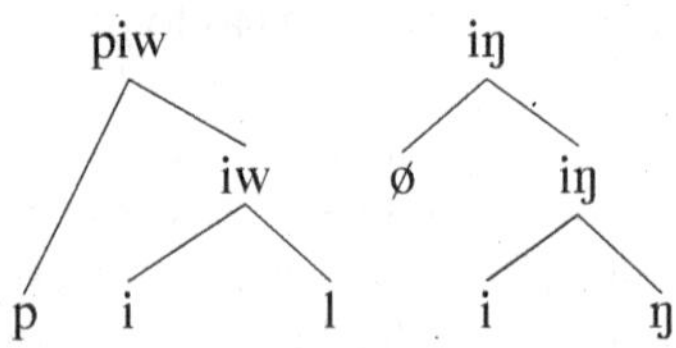

c. Geminate

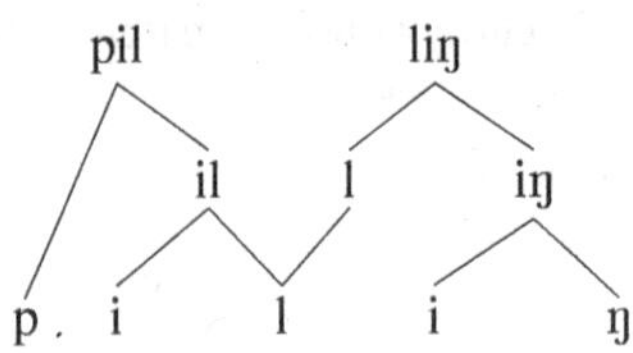

d. Geminate and Vocalize

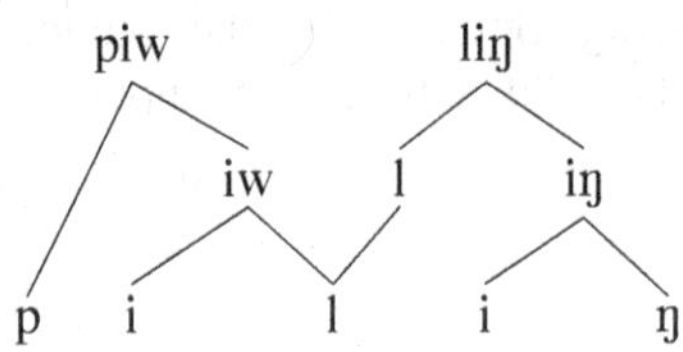

e. Vocalized Geminates

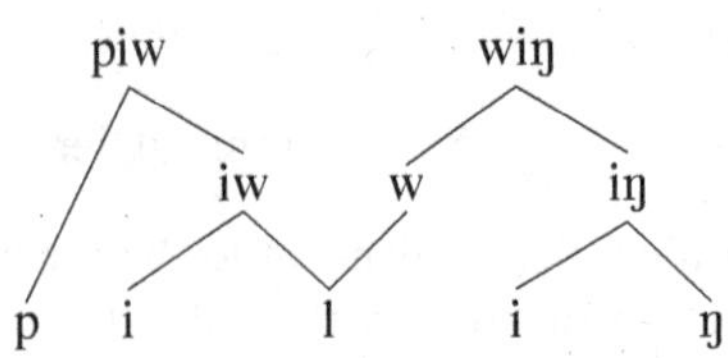

(16) Candidates for /meil+iŋ/ 'mailing'

a. Faithful

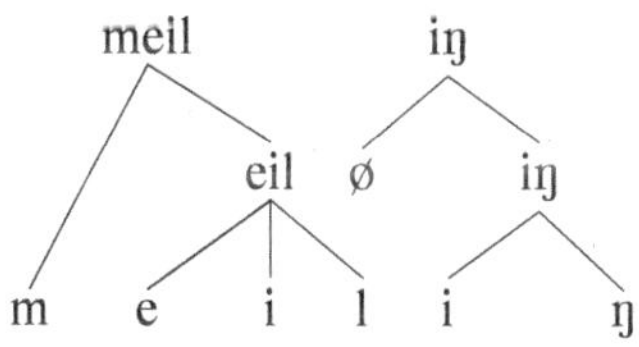

b. Vocalize

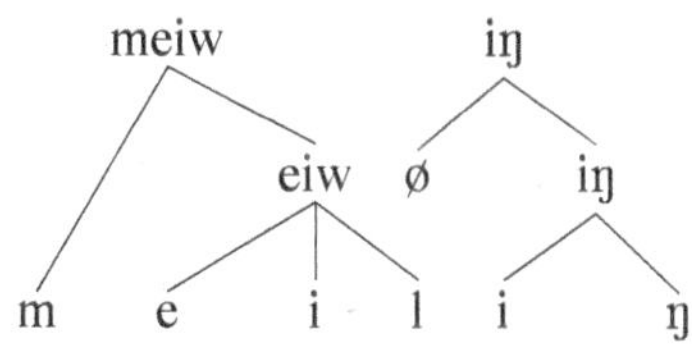

c. Resyllabified

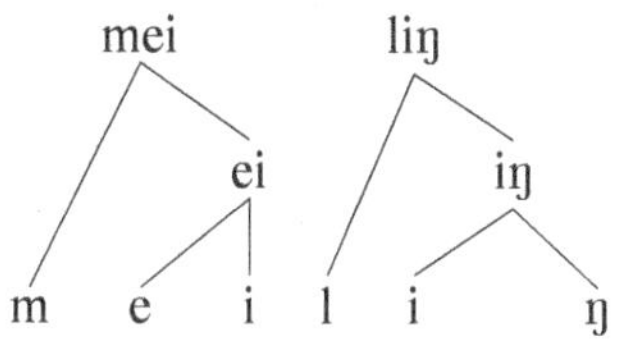

d. Geminate and Vocalize

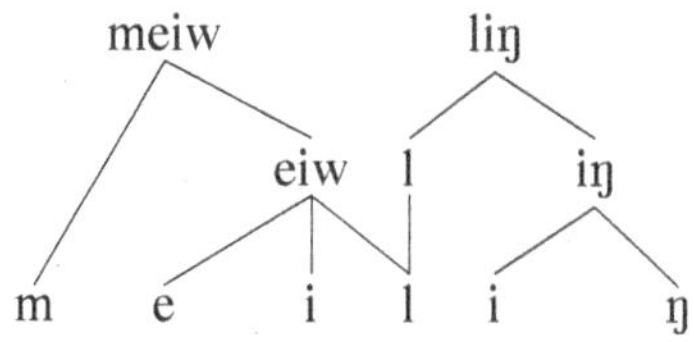

e. Vocalized Geminate

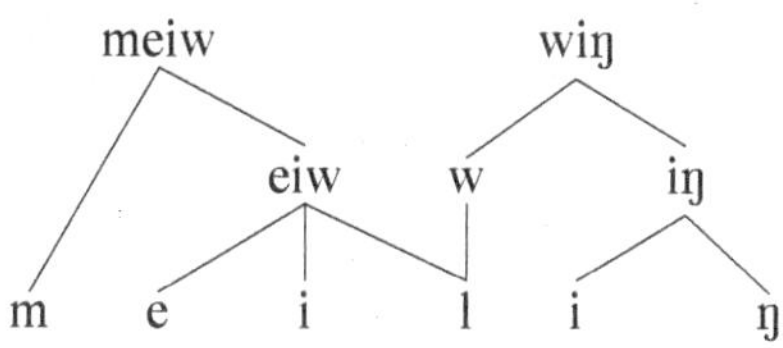

The above candidates are only a subset of all possible candidates, but this representative set should suffice to illustrate how ICT would correctly predict the presence of the L's Viceroy when the rime has two elements and the absence of that effect when the rime has three elements (parallel to the presence or absence of root-final consonant gemination). The above candidates vary along various parameters: (i) where the final L is syllabified; (ii) if that L is geminate; and (iii) if percolation of the L is faithful.

Armed now with the set of candidates, one can evaluate each candidate with respect to the constraints in an OT tableau.[14]

[14]Doug Pulleyblank (p.c.) suggests a classical OT solution where the input $/l_i/$ has two correspondences $[w_i]$ and $[l_i]$. There are two problems: (i) this predicts languages that allow long distance split correspondence $/X_j/$ corresponds to $[Y_j \ldots Z_j]$ by virtue of GEN's capacity, which as far as I know are unattested. ICT restricts such split correspondence to adjacency because cross-branching structures are impossible to GEN; and (ii) multiple correspondences require different IDENT to apply to each correspondent. These IDENT constraints would have to be positional in nature, which is the insight of ICT. So, while the split correspondence approach could in principle generate the L-voc effects of HKE, it overgenerates.

(17) ICT account of L's Viceroy

*MULT ASSOC

A node cannot be dominated by more than one node.

INTER-TIER FAITH[15]

Dominating nodes must have identical information with subordinate nodes.

*L-CODA[16]

[l] is not allowed in the coda.

/pil+iŋ/	*L-CODA	ONSET	*MULT ASSOC	INTER-TIER FAITH
a. Faithful	*!	*		
b. Vocalize		*!		*
c. Geminate	*!		*	
☞ d. Gem & Voc			*	*
e. Voc'd gem			*	**!

/meil+iŋ/	*L-CODA	ONSET	BI-RIME	*MULT ASSOC	INTER-TIER FAITH
a. Faithful	*!	*	*		
b. Vocalize		*!			*
☞ c. Resyllabified					
d. Gem & Voc			*!	*	*
e. Voc'd gem				*!	**

Violation counts in the above tableaux are obtained by evaluating each representation candidate at every tier against the constraints. For example, in the faithful candidates (a), /l/ is kept as it is in the corresponding higher tier which constitutes a violation of *L-CODA at that level. It is important to bear in mind that in ICT representations, adjacency and constituency are clearly different. When the /l/ is at the terminal tier, there is no indication of it being in the coda. That information is only available in the dominating tier when /l/ and the preceding vowel form a constituent.

As may be seen in (17), vocalization is only triggered when /l/ is syllabified into the coda, which happens only at the behest of BI-RIME.[17] The same is

[15]This is really a collection of constraints parallel to Faithfulness in classical OT frameworks. For current purposes, this simplification suffices.

[16]Whether or not this is universal is immaterial here, but across languages [l] is often vocalized when in the rime.

[17]Donca Steriade (p.c.) pointed out that in attributing the geminate and vocalization combination in HKE to resyllabification, there must be either (i) no morpheme-internal geminates in words like *silly*, *vanilla* or *dilly-dally* or (ii) these geminates, which do not stem from resyllabifi-

true for gemination, which is the result of two forces combined: BI-RIME and ONSET. This explains why /meil+iŋ/ and /pil+iŋ/ is so different. In /pil+iŋ/, gemination and vocalization are both necessary if the constraints of BI-RIME and *L-CODA are to be fulfilled. Of crucial importance here is the possibility of 'unfaithful' inter-tier correspondence because it is this that allows for the same /l/ to surface differently according to its context (i.e. onset or coda positions).

9.6 Concluding Remarks

This paper began with a simple-looking and common puzzle where [l] alternates with [w] and not others. A straightforward but simplistic solution would have been to assume underlying /w/ in some cases and not others. However, when that pattern is studied with additional patterns of consonant gemination (or lack thereof) during suffixation, a clear parallel with the L-voc facts can be seen. The puzzle deepens: it involves the making of a proxy and the alternation of the original, characterized in this paper as the L's Viceroy Effect (or Split L-geminate).

The L's Viceroy Effect leads to the apparently paradoxical situation where /l/ must at once be [l] and [w]. The paradox arose out of our understanding of gemination as two skeletal positions associated to one melody, so perhaps one should consider the simplistic option of discarding autosegmental representations for ordered SPE type rules. The SPE rules, though capable of generating the set of facts, provide little conceptual understanding to why the facts should be the way they are. Further, one would expect typological differences to stem from the differences in the ordering of the rules. I know of no languages that would attest to this. In other words, one needs a deeper characterization to generate the patterns of L-voc.

In exploring this apparently paradoxical pattern, a discovery is made when one arrives at an ICT account which resolves the paradox by appealing to the structures for correspondence of information. This exploration thus extends beyond arguing that ICT is the right framework for understanding phonological patterns as evidenced by its usefulness in tackling the puzzling L's Viceroy facts. The real purpose is perhaps to demonstrate the spirit of scientific inquiry that sometimes leads one to face apparent dilemmas and paradoxes, and to find resolution in newer conceptions of old ideas (albeit sometimes requiring us to stand our earlier beliefs on their heads such as what the ICT does to phonological representations).

---

cation, function differently. It turns out that in HKE, *silly* is [siːliː], *vanilla* [wan.lei.laː] and dilly dally [diː.liː.dɛː.liː]. Without being Anglo-centric, positing that HKE has geminate UR is unmotivated for these cases, so (i) is most likely true, even with proviso to fn.4. *Vanilla* [wan.lei.laː] presents a complication with the heterosyllabic [-n.l-], which if a geminate, is certainly unlike the kind studied here and would still be consistent with (ii).

Acknowledgments

In 1994, Mohanan presented the Teacher's Dilemma in class saying that, "The teacher's job is to make himself useless to the students as soon as possible", and always taught us in that spirit (see Ann, this volume for more similar stories). At the LFG 2005 conference in Bergen, I caught Mohanan at an obscure corner, quietly supporting the timid Karene (who was in that class in 1994) as she presented her poster, slowly shedding off her reliance on Tara and Mohanan. I wonder if such teachers ever become useless to their students. Perhaps, that is how this dilemma is resolved.

This project is supported by FRG/05-06/I-51 (Hong Kong Baptist University). The author is grateful to Donca Steriade, Doug Pulleyblank, Long Peng, Tony Hung and Mark Donohue for inspiring discussions; and to Fung Kwok Bong, Daffodil Yeung, Liu Hoi Pui, Kwan Nga Tang and Kam Hiu Ying for their services as informants or/and research assistants.

References

Altendorf, Ulrike. 2003. *Estuary English: Leveling at the Interface of RP and South-Eastern British English*. Tübingen: Gunter Narr Velag.

Borowsky, Tony. 2001. The vocalisation of dark-l in Australian English. In D. Blair and P. Collins, eds., *English in Australia*, pages 69–87. Amsterdam/Philadelphia: John Benjamins Publishing Company.

Borowsky, Tony and Barbara Horvath. 1997. L-vocalization in Australian English. In F. H. et al, ed., *Variation, Change, and Phonological Theory*, pages 101–123. Amsterdam: John Benjamins Publishing Company.

Broselow, Ellen. 1995. Skeletal positions and moras. In J. Goldsmith, ed., *The Handbook of Phonological Theory*, pages 175–205. Oxford: Basil Blackwell.

Goldrick, Matthew A. 2000. Turbid output representations and the unity of opacity. In *Proceedings of NELS 30*. GSLA, Amherst, MA. [Rutgers Optimality Archive (http://roa.rutgers.edu) #368-1299].

Halle, Morris and K.P. Mohanan. 1985. Segmental phonology in Modern English. *Linguistic Inquiry* 16:57–116.

Hammond, Michael. 1997. Vowel quantity and syllabification in English. *Language 73* 73(1):1–18.

Hayes, Bruce. 1989. Compensatory lengthening in moraic phonology. *Linguistic Inquiry* 20(2):253–306.

Hung, Toni T. 2000. Towards a phonology of Hong Kong English. *World Englishes* 19(3):337–356.

Kiparsky, Paul. 2003. Syllables and moras in Arabic. In C. Fery and R. van de Vijver, eds., *The Optimal Syllable*, pages 147–182. Cambridge: Cambridge Univ. Press.

McCarthy, John. 2003. Sympathy, cumulativity, and the Duke-of-York gambit. In C. Fery and R. van de Vijver, eds., *The Optimal Syllable*, pages 23–76. Cambridge: Cambridge Univ. Press

McCarthy, John. 2006. Slouching towards optimality: Coda reduction in OT-CC. Ms., Univ. of Mass., Amherst. [Rutgers Optimality Archive (http://roa.rutgers.edu) #878-1006].

McCarthy, John and Alan Prince. 1993/2001. Prosodic phonology 1: Constraint interaction and satisfaction. Tech. Rep. 3, Rutgers Univ. Center for Cognitive Sciences. [Rutgers Optimality Archive (http://roa.rutgers.edu) #482-1201.

McCarthy, John and Alan Prince. 1995. Faithfulness and reduplicative identity. In L. W. D. Jill Beckman and S. Urbanczyk, eds., *Univ. of Mass. Occasional Papers in Linguistics 18: Papers in optimality theory*, pages 249–384. Amherst, MA: University of Massachusetts. Also in René Kager, Harry van der Hulst and Wim Zonneveld eds. *The Prosody Morphology Interface*. [Rutgers Optimality Archive (http://roa.rutgers.edu) #60-0000].

Mohanan, K.P. 1992. Describing the phonology of non-native varieties of a language. *World Englishes* 11:111–128.

Mohanan, K. P. 1986. *The Theory of Lexical Phonology*. Dordrecht: Reidel Publishing Company.

Mohanan, Tara and K.P. Mohanan. 2003. Towards a theory of constraints in OT: Emergence of the not-so-unmarked in Malayalee English. MS., National Univ. of Singapore. [Rutgers Optimality Archive (http://roa.rutgers.edu) #601-0503].

Orgun, Cemil O. 1996. *Sign-based morphology and phonology with special attention to optimality theory*. Ph.D. thesis, Univ. of California, Berkeley. [Rutgers Optimality Archive (http://roa.rutgers.edu) #171-0197].

Prince, Alan and Paul Smolensky. 1993/2004. *Optimality Theory: Constraint Interaction in Generative Grammar*. Blackwell.

Selkirk, Elisabeth. 1990. A two-root theory of length. MS., University of Massachusetts, Amherst, MA.

Silverman, Dan. 1992. Multiple scansions in loanword phonology: Evidence from Cantonese. *Phonology* 9:289–328.

Simpson, Jane. 1980. Cyclic syllabification and the first cycle rule of vowel-rounding in some dialects of Australian English. Ms., MIT.

Sproat, Richard and Osamu Fujimura. 1993. Allophonic variation in English /l/ and its implications for phonetic implemenation. *Journal of Phonetics* 21:291–311.

Wee, Lian Hee. 2004. *Inter-tier Correspondence Theory*. Ph.D. thesis, Rutgers Univ. [Rutgers Optimality Archive (http://roa.rutgers.edu) #654-0404].

10

Optimality Theory as a Probabilistic Model

JOHN C. PAOLILLO

10.1 On Seeing Things as They Really Are

Like many others represented in this volume, I met Mohanan at Stanford University when I was a graduate student in linguistics and he was a lecturer. More than anything else, what characterized Mohanan's influence on our cohort was his total engagement with our intellectual development as linguists. Whether we wrote about phonology, syntax, South Asian languages, or the philosophy of linguistics, Mohanan was there in his office patiently explaining just where the thread of coherence in our writing came unraveled. Often he would startle me – I suspect others had this experience, too – with a revelation about my own beliefs, much as if he had just extracted a rabbit I was unaware was hiding in my own hat (for an alternative perspective on these encounters, see Ann this volume).

It is one of those encounters that comes persistently to mind when I think about how I arrived at my current understanding of grammar. We were discussing the notion of subject in South Asian Languages, particularly Sinhala, about which I held a committedly agnostic view, seeing subject as an indeterminate category around which certain pragmatic, semantic and other factors tend to converge (see, e.g., the considerations expressed in Butt, et al. this volume). Seemingly out of nowhere, Mohanan suggested that I wasn't agnostic at all about subjects; rather, if I believed what I had just said, I was claiming that subjecthood needed to be decided by a weighted sum of the relevant semantic, pragmatic and syntactic contextual influences. Moreover, this wasn't Mohanan's view, but it was contained in the argument I had just made, so it

Reality Exploration and Discovery: Pattern Interaction in Language and Life.
Linda Uyechi and Lian-Hee Wee (eds.).

could only be my own view of grammar. Being familiar only with generative grammar, I found this idea utterly alien and bizarre. For years, I couldn't grasp how such an idea was compatible with my views, or how it could work in a coherent notion of grammar. All I really wanted at the time was for the notion of subject to leave me alone, so that I could try to do syntax without it.

I have come to understand that Mohanan was right about my preferred mode of grammatical analysis. Today I see most things in grammars as having weights attached to them, and recognize some form of weighting in a number of linguists' formal devices. I now understand that weighting permits a division of labor between the rational/deductive approaches to the substantive aspects of a theory and its empirical, data-driven evaluation. This aspect of the quantitative paradigm is well developed in the empirical social sciences, but less so in linguistics. I am nonetheless amazed today that twenty years ago Mohanan was better able to recognize my true meta-theoretical disposition than I was.

My aim in this contribution is to try to show how others might similarly believe, without realizing it, that grammars have weights. Moreover, I aim to illustrate the benefits of separating substantive and empirical considerations in the formal model for linguistic theory-building, observing that a well-structured model for the weights allows us to clearly identify the independent statements made in an analysis, and thereby say something about its complexity. I do this by examining the version of Optimality Theory (OT) in Anttila (1997), and comparing it with the Variable Rule (VR) model.

OT (Prince and Smolensky 2004 [1993], 1997) is widely accepted in generative phonology, and has a strong following in syntax, especially in Lexical Functional Grammar (see e.g. Bresnan 2001, Bresnan and Nikitina this volume). OT promises more elegant analyses of natural language by appealing to a system of strictly-ranked competing constraints, whose relative ranking winnows down a large (potentially infinite) set of candidate forms to a single optimal candidate. Analysis is conducted by deductively identifying constraints and their rankings to account for the observations. VR, in contrast, emphasizes rigorous empirical methods for studying linguistic variation. Analysis proceeds by sampling and classifying linguistic phenomena, and estimating and testing a statistical model to fit the data (Labov 1969, Paolillo 2002, Sankoff 1988). Such methods are desirable in an empirically accountable approach to grammar. While OT and VR approaches are sometimes used together (e.g. Borowsky and Horvath 1997, Nagy and Reynolds 1997), the analyses produced are fundamentally disjoint, concerning different questions. Hence, the methodological aspects of VR remain unavailable for guiding analysis in OT. The comparison here shows that this need not be the case.

The remainder of this chapter is organized as follows. Section 2 outlines a schema for relating rules in VR to constraint systems in OT. Section 3 introduces the concept of weighting and explains how it relates to implicational scales, ranking in OT and frequency predictions in VR. Section 4 completes the probabilistic model for OT by specifying its functional form. Section 5 illustrates the application of the probabilistic model for OT using Anttila's (1997) analysis of the Finnish genitive plural alternation. Finally, Section 6 presents some general concluding remarks.

10.2 OT and String-Rewriting Rules

The first step in translating between OT and VR is understanding the formal relationship of constraint-based and rule-based analyses. VR uses the string-rewriting rule formalism of Chomsky and Halle (1968), in which one string, the *input*, is transformed into another, the *output*. For example, suppose we have a language with a number of forms characterized as strings of the form CaD, where capital letters C and D represent natural classes of segments. Now suppose that instead of the expected form CaD, what is observed turns out to be CbD. In this case the SPE-style analysis posits a rule relating the two sets of forms, written CaD → CbD. This is conventionally re-arranged to highlight the roles of the different elements in the rule, the environment and the process, separated by a slash and written as in (1).

(1) a → b / C __ D

In OT, the same observations lead to a different treatment. First, the observed alternation between a and b tells us that there should be candidates CaD, and CbD,[1] By observing the shape of the alternating forms, we may come to a conclusion that there is a constraint against the string CaD, and another against CbD, which we write as *CaD, and *CbD, respectively. Furthermore, since CaD is not observed, we can also assume that *CaD is higher-ranked than *CbD, because *CaD is never violated, but *CbD is. This is represented in the constraint evaluation tableau in (2). Note that the SPE form of the rule in (1), CaD → CbD, corresponds closely to the tableau in (2). Specifically, the string description to the left of the arrow corresponds to the higher-ranking of the two constraints, as well as to the non-optimal candidate form. The two analyses are formally equivalent; all that is different is the division of labor among the different formal elements.

[1]Normally, the candidate set is said to be potentially infinite, but given that there are no other output forms to consider, we can assume that some high-ranked constraints determined by the rest of the grammar have whittled the candidate set down to the two alternants.

(2) Constraint evaluation tableau matching the rule in (1)

/CaD/	*CaD	*CbD
CaD	*!	
+ CbD		*

The above example somewhat over-simplifies what phonologists do in undertaking an analysis, where many decisions are made about the correct description of the alternant strings, and a large set of facts about a language are taken into account. Rule-based analyses acknowledge interactions of many different rules in a phonological system, and OT analyses recognize interactions among a large set of constraints. Nonetheless, the comparison indicates that OT constraint rankings can be read as collections of rules when the candidate set is known. We adopt this assumption below.

10.3 Rankings and Weights

Suppose now that there is variation in the output, and that CaD and CbD are both observed. SPE regarded such situations as requiring that a rule be optional, i.e., that its application not be required in all circumstances. This type of rule provided the basis for the variable rule developed in VR. The primary difference between the variable rule and the optional rule is that the application of the variable rule is governed by a set of weights attached to different parts of the rule's environment. These weights are obtained by estimating them within the constraints of a statistical model, usually a logistic regression model.

To elaborate the example used in section 2, suppose it were the case that /CaD/ was realized 30% of the time as CaD, and 70% of the time also as CbD. Suppose further, that /CaE/ is realized with different proportions of *a* and *b*, 60% CaE and 40% CbE. To express this distribution, we can attach probability weights to the rule elements D and E, as in (3). Here, the angle brackets indicate a disjunction in the rule environment between D and E. The numbers after the environment elements D and E represent the observed probability of *a* being realized as *b* in that context. This is the basic form of a variable rule.

(3) $\mathrm{a} \rightarrow \mathrm{b} \,/\, \mathrm{C}\_\_ \left\langle \begin{array}{c} \mathrm{D}: 0.7 \\ \mathrm{E}: 0.4 \end{array} \right\rangle$

For empirical analyses of linguistic variation, in which many such environment disjunctions are possible, there are two issues. Cosmetically, it can be cumbersome to write all of the probabilities into the rule itself; consequently, the probability weights are usually written in a separate table, where statistical tests and other information may also be given. Practically, one has to know how to combine different environment weights to derive a predicted probability, i.e. the *functional form* of the model. Suppose we determine that a preceding environment F, as distinct from C, also observes the same alternation, but at a different rate – how then do we combine the preceding environment weights, C or F, with the following environment weights, D or E, to predict the frequencies of *a* and *b* in all four environments, C __ D, C __ E, F __ D, and F __ E?

VR uses a functional form known as the *logit-additive* or *logistic regression* model; this model has certain desirable properties that avoid some of the problems of simpler models (Paolillo 2002). In the logit-additive model, probability weights, which range from 0 to 1, are first transformed using the logit function (4a), into numbers that range from negative to positive infinity.[2] These logit weights can then be added to give a combined value, which is then transformed back into the range from 0 to 1, using the logistic function (4b, the inverse of the logit), to give the predicted frequency of the variant. The reasons for this transformation are somewhat technical, but can be found in Paolillo (2002). Probability weights required for this model are easily estimated using logistic regression software such as the VARBRUL 2 program typically used in VR (Sankoff 1988).[3]

(4) (a) $\text{logit}(p) = \ln(p/(1-p))$

(b) $\text{logistic}(x) = e^x/(1+e^x)$

The logit and logistic functions are both S-curves, but their orientation with respect to the x and y axes differs. For the logit function, probability weights (falling between zero and one) are represented on the x-axis, and logit weights (falling between negative and positive infinity) are represented on the y-axis. The logistic function is exactly like the logit function but flipped around the line $y = x$. In both curves, probability weights of one and zero correspond to logit weights of infinity and negative infinity, respectively. The curves are non-linear in these two regions, so that a small change in probability means a large change in the corresponding logit. A probability of 0.5 corresponds to a logit of zero; at this value the rule has an equal probability of applying and not applying. Finally, the curves are symmetrical about the 0.5 probability weight. Equal distances from this value represent equally favoring and disfavoring effects.

Probability weights of zero and one are important because they represent categoricity, and the non-linearity of the logit and logistic functions in these regions allows us to account for ranking effects as well. The corresponding logit weights are infinite, so any smaller (i.e. finite) quantity added to them

---

[2] The symbol p throughout this chapter refers to a probability; $\ln(x)$ is the natural logarithm of x, the logarithm whose base is the irrational number $e (\approx 2.718282)$. Exponentiation of the base $e(e^x)$ is the inverse of $\ln(x)$: $e^{ln(x)} \equiv x$, or equivalently, $\ln(e^x) \equiv x$.

[3] Other widely-used statistical packages for logistic regression include R, SPSS, SAS, and Stata. These programs report estimated weights as logits rather than as probabilities.

effectively disappears. These properties allow the logit-additive model to express both variable and categorical linguistic alternations.

While the standard OT model results in predictions that are always categorical, these predictions are derived from an implicational hierarchy of competing constraints. Implicational hierarchies, sometimes called implicational scales, are common in linguistic analysis. In sociolinguistics, they are encountered in descriptions of creole continua (Bickerton 1971, DeCamp 1971) and language shift (Gal 1979), as well as language variation (Bailey 1973). Rousseau and Sankoff (1978) demonstrate that implicational scales represent an instance of the VR model where weights take extreme values, and hence express categoricity in the logit-additive model. This treatment extends unmodified to standard OT constraint rankings.

To develop our previous example, suppose we have a rule $a \rightarrow b$, influenced by the preceding environments D, E, F, and G, and following environments P, Q, and R. The rule outputs form an implicational scale if they can be tabulated as in Table 1. In practice, the table can be of any size or extent, depending on the number of environments to be considered, the only requirement is that some ordering of rows and columns yields a strictly diagonal pattern of *a* and *b* outputs. The VR approach to implicational scales exploits the notion of a mathematical limit, under which extreme, even infinite probability weights can differ significantly in size. All of the probability weights assigned to factors in an implicational scale can be effectively one or zero, but their transformed weights (the logits of the probability weights) vary in size appropriately, achieving the effect of ranking.

TABLE 1 Example of an implicational scale.

	D	E	F	G	*Rank*
P	b	a	a	a	K^6
Q	b	b	a	a	K^4
R	b	b	b	a	K^2
Rank	K^7	K^5	K^3	K	

To see this, consider again the scale in Table 1. Note that column D overwhelmingly favors the rule. Consequently let us assume that columns categorically favor *b*, and rows favor *a*.[4] Note, however, that column G does not actually show any favoring of *b*. Even though it categorically favors *b*, the other environments it combines with (all of the rows in the table) override it. In OT terms, G is a low-ranked yet categorical constraint.

[4]Nothing actually hinges on this assumption. Other assumptions lead to equivalent models with different values for the weights, but which predict the same empirical outcomes.

Suppose we pick a weight to assign to column G; since it categorically favors b, its p should be close to one. Let us pick such a weight whose logit is $\ln(K)$, where K is a "ranking constant", which we can choose to be an arbitrarily large positive number.[5] Now consider environment R, which categorically favors a, the rule input. The p for R must also be extreme, but in the opposite direction (near zero). As with G, all of the environments (columns) that combine with R override it, except for column G (the corresponding cell has a, not b). Since G's logit is $\ln(K)$, R's logit must be larger and negative, because if they were equal in size they would sum to zero: $\text{logit}(p) = \text{logit(R)}+\text{logit(G)} = -\ln(K)+\ln(K) = 0$. The p corresponding to a logit of zero is 0.5, indicating an equal probability of a and b – pure chance variation, not categoricity, as needed. If we set R's logit at $-\ln(K^2)$, then R will outrank G by a factor of K, because $\text{logit}(p) = \text{logit(R)}+\text{logit(G)} = \ln(K^2)+\ln(K) = -\ln(K)$. Hence, the intersection of R and G shows a categorically, rather than b.

This process of assigning weights continues through the remaining environments in the same way. Environment R is out-ranked in turn by F, since the cell at their intersection is b, and not a, so F should be larger yet in magnitude, e.g., $\ln(K^3)$, and so on, until all of the environmental factors have been assigned weights from an ascending exponential scale of weights based on K. The ranks of all nine environmental factors in this scheme are indicated in the row and column labeled "Rank" in Table 1. The resulting variable rule always predicts categorical variation in all its combinations of environmental factors, while nonetheless recognizing a ranking relationship among them. Of course, the VR model is foremost a model of variation, and relaxing assumptions about the strict ranking of weights permits values of p between 0 and 1. When this is done, all such variable cells fall on the diagonal of the table, with larger probabilities always being closer to cells containing 1 and smaller ones closer to cells containing zero. Any implicational scale may be analyzed in a manner similar to this example.[6]

OT Tableaux are merely different arrangements of the same information. For Table 1, the corresponding OT constraint order is *Da > *bP > *Ea > *bQ > *Fa > *bR > *Ga, and this is mirrored in the magnitude of the assigned weights. In many analyses, multi-way tables are needed to unravel all of the constraint-candidate interactions, but the fundamental concept of OT, constraint ranking, is expressible by the weighting scheme given above. Consequently, the VR model subsumes implicational scales, which include OT constraint hierarchies.

---

[5] K actually represents the odds of the probability weight p, and $p = K/[1+K]$.

[6] Statistically, this is also a model of independence. Hence, implicational scales are consistent with the independence assumptions of many statistical models.

10.4 A Functional Form for Weighting in OT

OT analyses that account for linguistic variation typically have some way of generating multiple rankings for some set of constraints. These rankings, when considered with an appropriate candidate set, result in multiple tableaux with different optimal outcomes. The proportion of each variant realized is the proportion of tableaux for which each variant is optimal. There are various methods for generating the alternative rankings, but any of them can be translated into VR in much the same way. The most straightforward of these employs *crucial unranking* (Anttila 1997), in which a set of constraints has no specified rank with respect to one another.[7]

In Anttila's formulation, the tableaux that need to be counted correspond directly to constraints. All constraints in a given rank have an equal weight, but violation of each constraint in that rank adds an increment of weight to the model. For the corresponding OT model, this means that in a constraint set weighted $\ln(K)$, two constraints violated would be counted as weighing $\ln(2K)$, three as $\ln(3K)$, etc. As long as there are fewer than K violations of the constraint, the weight of additional violations will not exceed the value of the next-ranked constraint, which is $\ln(K^2)$ $(=\ln(KK))$. Since we can take the limit of this system as K goes to infinity, violation of any number of lower-ranked constraints never outweighs a single violation of a higher-ranked constraint. One probability model with these properties has the form given in (5), where each rank r has a ranking constant K_r, a multiplier m_r which is $+1$ (favoring) or -1 (disfavoring), and a number of constraints n_r matching a particular cell.

(5) $\text{logit}(p_{cell}) = \sum_r m_r[\ln(n_r K_r)]$

For this model, constraints favoring and disfavoring a particular variant must be split into separate ranks. For example, suppose we again have an alternation between a and b, with the constraints *Cb, *Db, and *Ea together in a crucially unranked set. Again we have $a \rightarrow b$, with environments C__ and D__ favoring, and E__ disfavoring. If all three constraints apply simultaneously to the same form (see Section 5 for an example), two out of three of the resulting tableaux favor b, giving a probability of 0.67 of finding *b* rather than *a*. In the translated model, the two constraints *Cb, *Db are counted together in a rank of weight $\ln(K)$ whose multiplier m is positive, while the remaining constraint *Ea is counted in a rank of the same weight with a negative multiplier m. Thus, following (5) we have $\text{logit}(p) = m_{r1}\ln(n_{r1}K_{r1}) +$

[7]Another version uses "floating constraints", in which the alternative rankings are obtained by a specific constraint or constraints "floating" to various positions in the hierarchy (Nagy and Reynolds 1997). Such models of ranking may be addressed by introducing variance and/or interaction parameters into the functional form in (5).

$m_{r2}\ln(n_{r2}K_{r2}) = +1\ln(2K) - 1\ln(1K) = \ln(2)$, and transforming back into probability weights, logistic(logit(p)) = logistic(ln(2)) = 0.67. By counting favoring and disfavoring constraints in separate ranks, we ensure the same result as in Anttila's model, using a functional form general enough for OT analyses without crucially unranked constraints. The model in (5) compares closely to the logit-additive model of VR, given in (6). Both models combine a number of terms to produce a transformed weight for the cell, logit(p_{cell}), which is then transformed back into a probability weight with the logistic function.

(6) $\text{logit}(p_{cell}) = \sum_i [\text{logit}(p_i)]$

The model in (5) involves several different modes of combining variables, rather than the single mode of combination used in the logit-additive model of VR in (6). Constraints in each rank have to be counted before the terms of the model can be combined.[8] For this reason, (5) may be criticized as more complex than (6). It also fails to make the usual statistical distinction between main effects and interaction effects, under which main effects represent simple environmental conditions and interaction effects represent a conjunction of two or more environmental conditions. Since interaction effects are generally taken to be more complex, it is harder to evaluate the complexity of (5).

For a specific analysis, it is possible to reorganize the model parameters to conform with the model in (6) while distinguishing main and interaction effects and keeping a close correspondence between constraints and model parameters (see Paolillo 2000). The reorganized model predicts, using a form like (6), the same logit(p_{cell}) as the model derived from (5), and hence is empirically indistinguishable from it. Here, we will not be further concerned with complexity in the functional form of the probabilistic model, but will focus our attention on the number of parameters required to express an analysis. These parameters are the real-number valued quantities of the form ln(K), etc. and are matched to corresponding environments or constraints, as developed in Section 5. Hence they represent the independent statements of an analysis, and can be used to evaluate its complexity.

10.5 Example: The Finnish Genitive Plural

In this section, we illustrate the translation of OT into the probability model of (5) for the Finnish genitive plural as analyzed by Anttila (1997). The

[8] Anttila's analysis of one and two-syllable words requires counting multiple violations of the same constraint differently from violations of two constraints at the same rank. This form of counting requires a further complication of (5). It is unclear whether all multiple violations are counted consistently in Anttila (1997); hence, they will not be considered further here.

strong/weak alternation of the Finnish genitive plural exhibits a complex but predictable pattern of both categorical and non-categorical variation. The strong variant has a diphthongized and stressed stem-final vowel, and the stem is suffixed with [-iden]. In the weak variant the stem-final vowel is an unstressed monophthong and the suffix is [-ien]. Weakening is conditioned by stem-final vowel quality and metrical factors depending on word length. This process is expressed as a variable rule in Figure 1, where the strong form is taken as the rule input.[9] Examples of strong and weak forms for nouns with *i*-, *o*-, and *a*-stems appear in Table 2.

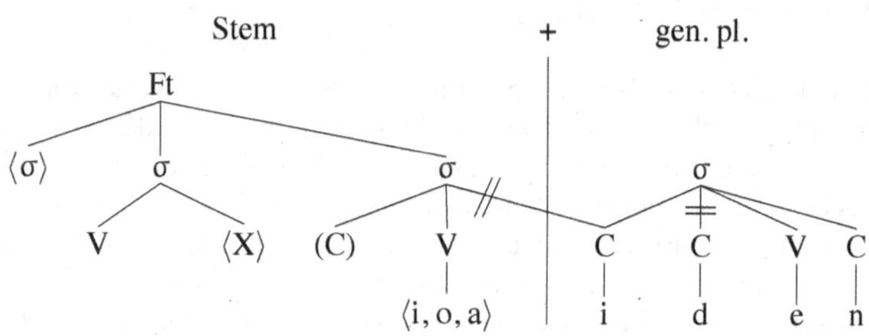

FIGURE 1 Finnish genitive plural weakening

Strong and weak variation is accounted for in Anttila's analysis by assuming that some sets of constraints are crucially unranked. The analysis furthermore gives an apparently reasonable fit to an observed corpus of Finnish data (see Paolillo 2002 for criticism on this point). In this section, we follow Anttila's analysis closely, to arrive at a probabilistic model that is directly comparable to his original analysis.

TABLE 2 Finnish genitive plural variants (Anttila 1997:40)

V	*Penult*	*Form*	*Gloss*	*Strong Form*	*Weak Form*
i	heavy	/poliisi/	'police'	pó.lii.sèi.den	pó.lii.si.en
	light	/naapuri/	'neighbour'	náa.pu.réi.den	náa.pu.ri.en
o	heavy	/korjaamo/	'repair shop'	kór.jaa.mòi.den	kór.jaa.mo.jen
	light	/hetero/	'hetero'	hé.te.ròi.den	hé.te.ro.jen
a	heavy	/maailma/	'world'	máa.il.mòi.den	máa.il.mo.jen
	light	/kollega/	'colleague'	kól.le.gòi.den	kól.le.go.jen

[9] Anttila (1997) presents the genitive plural as a morphological alternation, without delving deeply into its phonological character.

Anttila's analysis posits twelve constraints ranked in four sets, as given in Table 3. Constraints within each rank are crucially unranked. The "no stress clash" constraint of Set 1, as the highest-ranked constraint, prohibits any word-stress patterns in which adjacent syllables bear stress. The two constraints in Set 2 ensure that Finnish words tend to have stressed heavy syllables and light unstressed syllables. These three constraints condition categorical alternation in genitive plurals with one and two syllable stems or with a stressed antepenult, ruling out the strong variant, except in one-syllable words, where the weak variant is prohibited.

TABLE 3 Constraint rankings for Finnish genitive plurals

Rank	Syllable	Weight & Stress	Vowel	Weight & Stress
Set 1	*X́ . X́	No stress clash		
Set 2	*Ĺ	No stressed light		
	*H̆	No unstressed heavy		
Set 3	*L . L	No weight lapse	*H/I	No heavy [i]
			*Í	No stressed [i]
Set 4	*H . H	No weight clash	*H/O	No heavy [o]
	*H́	No stressed heavy	*Ó	No stressed [o]
	*X̆ . X̆	No stress lapse	*L/A	No light [a]

In words with other metrical patterns, Set 2 constraints do not directly select strong or weak genitive plural forms, but merely ensure that stem-final weight and stress coincide in all realized variants. Together with the other four syllable weight and stress constraints, these constraints collectively enforce a stress pattern of foot-initial stress that allows two possible foot structures: two syllables, [σσ] and three syllables, when the last syllable is light [σσ L]. Furthermore, three-syllable feet are dispreferred, and occur when required by another constraint, such as *H/I in Set 3, which disfavors [i] as the nucleus of a heavy syllable. The alignment of primary stress with word-initial syllables is not covered in the analysis.

The constraints conditioning the genitive plural alternation are translated into rule environments in Table 4, using the examples *italiaano* 'Italian', *naapuri* 'neighbor', *maailma* 'world', *hetero* 'hetero', and *korjaamo* 'repair shop'. Environments are generated by eliding the part of the constraint that is specific to the rule, i.e. the strong/weak form of the genitive plural. In all cases Table 4 shows candidates that would violate the constraints, including some candidates that are unobserved. The column headed "Active Site" indicates the syllable(s) in the candidate where the corresponding constraint acts. The particular variant filtered out by the constraint appears in the next column.

The last column represents the corresponding environment, i.e. the constraint minus whatever bit of structure the selected variant provides. As can be seen in Table 4, the environments represented reduce to preceding stress (X́__ and X̆__) preceding syllable weight (L__ and H__), and the stem-final vowel (a__, o__ or i__). These are written in the rule of Figure 1 inside angle brackets ⟨ ⟩, to indicate that they are weighted factors in a variable rule. Note that the first syllable of a foot always bears stress, so the optionality of the leftmost syllable in the rule is equivalent to stating preceding syllable stress.

TABLE 4 Translation of categorical constraints into rule environments

Set	*Constraint*	*Active Site (bold)*	*Variant*	*Environment*
1	*X́ . X́	í.ta.li.**áa.nói**.den	*strong	X́ __
	*H/I	náa.pu.**rèi**.den	*strong	i __
3	*Í	náa.pu.**rèi**.den	*strong	i __
	*L . L	náa.**pu.ri**.en	*weak	L __
	*H́	máa.il.**mòi**.den	*strong	(all)
	*X̆ . X̆	hé.**te.ro**.jen	*weak	X̆ __
4	*H . H	máa.**il.mòi**.den	*strong	H __
	*L/A	máa.il.**mo**.jen	*weak	a __
	*H/O	kór.jaa.**mòi**.den	*strong	o __
	*Ó	kór.jaa.**mòi**.den	*strong	o __

The three different types of environmental factors, preceding stress, preceding weight, and stem-final vowel, combine to produce a total of twelve environments (2 × 2 × 3) in which predictions about the distribution of strong and weak variants are made. Anttila (1997) illustrates these with examples of stems from three to five syllables in length, in 27 partially redundant environments. Table 5 presents Anttila's predictions for the twelve environments as proportions of weakened variants, where the three-way arrangement is structured as a three-dimensional implicational scale. Only the diagonal elements among unstressed preceding syllables are variable (light *i*-stems and heavy *o*- and *a*-stems).

The translated probabilistic model is presented in Table 6. The rows of the table represent the twelve different stem environments from Table 4. The columns, as in OT tableaux, indicate the constraint ranks and their weights from Table 3; constraints are indicated in the row labeled *Con*, and corresponding rule environments in the row labeled *Env*. Constraint Sets 3 and 4 (from Table 4) are split into two ranks as required by the functional form in (5) to separate constraints favoring and disfavoring weakening. Constraint Set 4 is the lowest ranked set, so its ranking constant is $\ln(K)$; Set 3 has $\ln(K^2)$;

TABLE 5 Genitive plural weakening by stem vowel, preceding stress and weight

Stress	*Weight*	*i*	*o*	*a*
X́	H	1.00	1.00	1.00
X́	L	1.00	1.00	1.00
X̆	H	1.00	0.80	0.50
X̆	L	0.67	0.00	0.00

etc., as indicated in the row labeled *Rank*.[10] Constraint violations are indicated by asterisks (in ranks favoring weakening, with positive weights, it is the strong variant that incurs the violations; in ranks disfavoring weakening, with negative weights, it is the weak variant). The final two columns of each table give the total weight for each candidate set (simplified according to the rules of adding logarithms), and the predicted proportion of weak variants (p). Table 6 is a complete translation of Anttila's analysis into a probabilistic model that preserves its essential properties using a functional form similar to the logit-additive model of VR. Categoricity and variability are predicted as desired, the same as in the original OT analysis.

TABLE 6 OT model for Finnish genitive plural.

Rank	$\ln(K^2)$	$\ln(K^2)$		$-\ln(K^2)$	$\ln(K)$				$-\ln(K)$		*Total*	*p*
	*X́				*H́				*X̆.X̆			
Con	.X́	*H/I	*Í	*L.L		*H.H	*H/O	*Ó		*L/A		
Env	X́	i	i	L	all	H	o	o	X̆	a		
H́ . i	*	*	*		*	*					$\ln(4K^7)$	1.00
H́ . o	*				*	*	*	*			$\ln(4K^5)$	1.00
H́ . a	*				*	*				*	$\ln(2K^4)$	1.00
Ĺ . i	*	*	*	*	*						$\ln(2K^5)$	1.00
Ĺ . o	*			*	*		*	*			$\ln(3K^3)$	1.00
Ĺ . a	*			*	*					*	$\ln(K^2)$	1.00
H̆ . i		*	*		*	*			*		$\ln(4K^2)$	1.00
H̆ . o					*	*	*	*	*		$\ln(4)$	0.80
H̆ . a					*	*			*	*	0	0.50
L̆ . i		*	*	*	*				*		$\ln(2)$	0.67
L̆ . o				*	*		*	*	*		$-\ln(K^2/3)$	0.00
L̆ . a				*	*				*	*	$-\ln(2K^2)$	0.00

At this point one could compare the OT analysis of Finnish genitive plurals to VR analyses of the same data. For instance, one could apply measures

[10] Set 2 is assigned a ranking constant K^3 to preserve Anttila's analysis of footing, stress and one- and two-syllable words. It is not shown here for reasons of space.

of model fit used for logit-additive models, such as the log-likelihood ratio or Pearson chi-squared statistic, to assess the fit of the OT model as compared with alternative VR models (Paolillo 2002). Here, we undertake a simpler evaluation, by comparing the above model, with ten parameters, one for each active constraint, against an alternative VR model of the same data. This comparison helps illuminate the nature of the OT model more directly.

To identify an appropriate VR alternative, we need to predict the same p values as in the OT model. For this model, which uses the functional form in (6), weights are not confined to values of the form $m_r[\ln(n_r K_r)]$;any suitable values may be used. We proceed by first attending to the location of the categorical cells in Table 5. Preceding stress is clearly a strongly-weighted factor favoring weakening, since it occurs categorically in all six cells. An appropriate value for this parameter should exceed all other parameter values in the model; as before we use $\ln(K^4)$. Among stems with unstressed penults, since light syllables disfavor weakening with respect to heavy ones, let us assign $-\ln(K^2)$ to that factor, following the OT analysis again. Then, for the p_{cell} for light i-stems to work out to 0.67, its logit must be ln(2); therefore the parameter value assigned to i-stems must be $\ln(2K^2)$. For o-stems, whose p is 0.80, the parameter value must be $\ln(4)$. For a-stems, no value need be specified: when no environmental factors apply, all of the terms of the model sum to zero ($\text{logit}(p_{cell}) = 0$), which means that $p_{cell} = 0.50$. No further parameters need to be specified for this model, which is given in full in Table 7.

TABLE 7 A VR analysis for the Finnish genitive plural

Env	*logit(p)*	*p*
X́ _	$\ln(K_4)$	1.00
i _	$\ln(2K_2)$	1.00
L _	$-\ln K_2)$	0.00
o _	$\ln(4)$	0.80

That the predictions of this model are identical to those of the translated model can be seen in Table 8, which presents a display parallel to that of Table 6, using the environments and their corresponding weights from Table 7. The values in the cells of the last column (p) are identical to those in Table 6, indicating that the translated OT model and the VR model make identical predictions.

We are now in a position to compare the complexity of the two forms of analysis, in terms of the statements they are required to make in the analysis of Finnish genitive plurals. The model in Table 8 has only four parameters (one

TABLE 8 VR model for Finnish genitive plural

Rank	ln(K⁴)	ln(2K²)	–ln(K²)	ln(4)	*Total*	*p*
Env	X́	i	L	o		
H́ . i	*	*			ln(2K⁶)	1.00
H́ . o	*			*	ln(4K⁴)	1.00
H́ . a	*				ln(K⁴)	1.00
Ĺ . i	*	*	*		ln(2K⁴)	1.00
Ĺ . o	*		*	*	ln(4K²)	1.00
Ĺ . a	*		*		ln(K²)	1.00
H̆ . i		*			ln(2K²)	1.00
H̆ . o				*	ln(4)	0.80
H̆ . a					0	0.50
L̆ . i		*	*		ln(2)	0.67
L̆ . o			*	*	–ln(K²/4)	0.00
L̆ . a			*		–ln(K²)	0.00

per column), where the model in Table 6 has ten (one per constraint). Hence, for the same empirical predictions, the OT model requires six more statements. The redundant constraints or parameters are mandated by the strict ranking assumption of the OT analysis and the functional form it requires. Since (5) has no place for weights that are not some multiple of K, the only way it can achieve probability outcomes between zero and one is through the variable n_r i.e. through increasing the number of constraints at a given rank. This problem does not afflict the VR analysis, where parameter values are not restricted to powers of K. For the redundancy to be justified, it should serve some other purpose than that of the specific analysis. Such justification could come, for example, from language change or acquisition: if we were to observe discrete, step-wise changes in the frequency of a variant in a particular environment, this could correspond to discrete changes in the number of parameters at specific ranks, and the functional form needed for OT could gain support. Historical variation studies do not point to this conclusion (see, e.g. Kroch 1989). In the absence of such evidence, we are compelled to accept the simplest model that accounts for the data. Given that the OT and VR models are empirically indistinguishable, it is difficult to recommend the more complex OT model.

Potential objections to this conclusion have been addressed throughout this section by keeping a close correspondence between the OT analysis of Anttila (1997) and its probabilistic manifestation. No entities have been introduced that do not correspond to entities in the original analysis, namely the constraints, their rankings, and the assumptions for counting violations. Both OT and VR models require real-valued parameter weights of the form $\ln(K)$, etc., so they are equivalent in this respect. The functional form of the OT model, with its different modes of violation counting, is revealed to be more complex than that required for VR. Moreover, the same functional form requires more statements to make identical empirical predictions.

10.6 The Red Pill or the Blue One?

In the foregoing, we have seen that both formally and quantitatively, OT analyses can be translated into probabilistic models that correspond closely to VR models. Formally, a set of ranked constraints can be read as an SPE-type rule, by recognizing the distinct contributions of the environment and the alternating variants in each constraint. Quantitatively, the logit-additive statistical model permits a unified treatment of categorical and non-categorical variation. A special case of this model describes implicational scales (Rousseau and Sankoff 1978) or standard OT constraint hierarchies (Kager 1999, Prince and Smolensky 2004 [1993]). The relationship between the OT and VR probabilistic models is thus one where VR subsumes standard OT as a special and restricted case. The logit-additive model can be further generalized to reflect the structure of alternative OT versions, and competing OT and VR analyses of the same phenomena can thus be compared.

The analysis above focuses on a particular variant of OT in which crucially unranked constraints are used to account for non-categorical variation (Anttila 1997, Anttila and Cho 1998, Anttila and Fong this volume). Other versions of OT, in which constraints have continuously varying values, rather than ordinal ranks (Boersma 1998, Boersma and Hayes 1999, Bresnan 2001, Bresnan and Nikitina this volume, Zubritskaya 1997) resemble the VR model even more closely. In fact, the VR model of Finnish genitive plural weakening could be interpreted as specifying constraint rankings for continuous OT.[11] Yet other versions of OT that address variation with tableau-counting (Kiparsky 1993, Nagy and Reynolds 1997, Reynolds 1994) may be treated similarly by specifying appropriate parameter restrictions or functional forms. For this reason, OT and VR approaches to linguistic analysis need not be viewed as fundamentally distinct. To the extent that they differ, it is in terms of the functional form of the probabilistic model implied, and the relative economy of the analyses supported.

I mentioned at the beginning of this chapter that Mohanan was the first to reveal to me that I believed grammars should have weights. For reasons like those above, I now recognize this as true, and that probabilistic models

[11]The mathematical details of the Boersma (1998) and Boersma and Hayes (1999) continuous OT differ from those of the logit-additive model of VR, but both models fall into the class of Generalized Linear Models (McCullagh and Nelder 1989, Paolillo 2002).

have additional benefits, such as the ability to frame competing analyses in a common, theoretically neutral meta-language where empirical adequacy and descriptive complexity can be assessed.

Beyond this, the properties of probabilistic models themselves – expressed through concepts like independence, sampling, estimation, significance testing, main and interaction effects, and the like – may be used to guide the development of substantive theories in other ways (Paolillo 2002). In fact, the deductive mode of argument in this chapter is atypical of research using probabilistic models. Notwithstanding the importance of a well-reasoned substantive theory, emphasis is placed on empirical aspects of the analysis, which is now my preferred mode of inquiry. For this reason, whenever I next need to address the syntax of subjects in South Asian languages, it will be with weights for all of the relevant environmental factors, just as Mohanan recognized I would need in our discussion twenty years ago.

Acknowledgement

An earlier version of this work was presented at NWAVE 28, Toronto 1999 and appeared as Paolillo (2000). I am indebted to Arto Anttila, Julie Auger, other NWAVE participants, two reviewers and the editors of this volume for comments and suggestions.

References

Anttila, Arto. 1997. Deriving variation from grammar. In F. Hinskens, R. van Hout, and W. L. Wetzels, eds., *Variation, Change and Phonological Theory*, pages 35–68. Amsterdam: Benjamins.

Anttila, Arto and Y.-M. Cho. 1998. Variation and change in Optimality Theory. *Lingua* 104:31–56.

Bailey, Charles-James. 1973. *Variation and Linguistic Theory*. Arlington, VA: Center for Applied Linguistics.

Bickerton, Derek. 1971. Inherent variability and variable rules. *Foundations of Language* 7:457–492.

Boersma, Paul. 1998. *Functional Phonology*. Amsterdam: Netherlands Graduate School of Linguistics.

Boersma, Paul and Bruce Hayes. 1999. Empirical tests of the gradual learning algorithm. Rutgers Optimality Archive ROA-348-10991.

Borowsky, Toni and Barbara Horvath. 1997. L-vocalization and Australian English. In F. R. v. H. Hinskens and W. L. Wetzels, eds., *Variation, Change and Phonological Theory*, pages 101–123. Amsterdam: Benjamins.

Bresnan, Joan. 2001. Explaining morphosyntactic competition. In M. Baltin and C. Collins, eds., *Handbook of Contemporary Syntactic Theory*, pages 11–44. Oxford: Blackwell. Rutgers Optimality Archive ROA-299-0299.

Chomsky, Noam and Morris Halle. 1968. *The Sound Pattern of English*. New York, NY: Harper and Row.

DeCamp, David. 1971. Toward a generative analysis of a post-creole speech continuum. In D. Hymes, ed., *Pidginization and Creolization of Languages*, pages 349–370. Cambridge: Cambridge University Press.

Gal, Susan. 1979. *Language Shift: Social Determination of Linguistic Change in Bilingual Austria*. New York, NY: Academic Press.

Hinskens, Frans, Roland van Hout, and W. Leo. Wetzels. 1997. *Variation, Change and Phonological Theory*. Amsterdam: Benjamins.

Kager, René. 1999. *Optimality Theory*. Cambridge: Cambridge University Press.

Kiparsky, Paul. 1993. Variable Rules. Handout distributed at the Rutgers Optimality Workshop (ROW1).

Kroch, Anthony. 1989. Reflexes of grammar in patterns of language change. *Language Variation and Change* 1:199–244.

Labov, William. 1969. Contraction, deletion and inherent variability of the English copula. *Language* 45:715–762.

McCullagh, Peter and John A. Nelder. 1989. *Generalized Linear Models*. London: Chapman and Hall/CRC, 2nd edn.

Nagy, Naomi and William Reynolds. 1997. Optimality theory and variable word-final deletion in Faetar. *Language Variation and Change* 9(1):37–55.

Paolillo, John C. 2000. A probabilistic model for Optimality Theory. In Auger and A. Word-Allbritton, eds., *The CVC of Sociolinguistics: Contact Variation and Culture, Indiana University Working Papers in Linguistics*, pages 89–107. Bloomington, IN: Indiana University Linguistics Club.

Paolillo, John C. 2002. *Analyzing Linguistic Variation: Statistical Models and Methods*. Stanford, CA: CSLI Publications.

Prince, Alan and Paul Smolensky. 1997. Optimality: From neural networks to Universal Grammar. *Science* 275:1604–1610.

Prince, Alan and Paul Smolensky. 2004 [1993]. *Optimality Theory: Constraint Interaction in Generative Grammar*. Oxford: Blackwell.

Reynolds, William T. 1994. *Variation and Phonological Theory*. Ph.D. thesis, University of Pennsylvania, Pennsylvania.

Rousseau, Pascale and David Sankoff. 1978. Singularities in the analysis of binomial data. *Biometrika* 65(3):603–608.

Sankoff, David. 1988. Variable rules. In U. Ammon, N. Dittmer, and K. Mattheier, eds., *Sociolinguistics: An International Handbook of the Science of Language and Society*, vol. 2, pages 984–997. Berlin: Walter de Gruyter.

Zubritskaya, Katya. 1997. Mechanism of sound change in Optimality Theory. *Language Variation and Change* 9(1):121–148.

11

Reduplication in Stratal OT

PAUL KIPARSKY

11.1 Stratal OT

In Stratal OT, morphology and phonology are stratified and interleaved, as in traditional Lexical Phonology (Mohanan 1986), but the strata (Stem, Word, Postlexical) are characterized by systems of parallel constraints.[1] The output of each morphological operation is submitted to the phonological constraints on its stratum: stems must satisfy the stem phonology, words must satisfy the word phonology, and phrase must satisfy the phrasal phonology.[2] For example, an affix which is added to stems to form words would enter into the derivation in the following fashion:

(1)

$[\,A\,]_{\text{STEM}}$	
$\downarrow$	Phonological constraints on stems are enforced
$[\,A'\,]_{\text{STEM}}$	
$\downarrow$	B affixed to A′; selectional requirements of B are checked
$[\,A' + B\,]_{\text{WORD}}$	
$\downarrow$	Phonological constraints on words are enforced
$[\,A'' + B'\,]_{\text{WORD}}$	
$\downarrow$	
$\vdots$	
output	

[1]Thanks to Stephen Anderson, John Frampton, Donca Steriade, and the editors for comments on a draft of this paper.

[2]As in Lexical Phonology, roots are not themselves directly subject to phonological constraints, though they are indirectly constrained via the stems and words they enter into. This idea has been taken over in OT, except that under parallelism it has to be the entire phonology that constrains underlying representations, not just the stem level phonology, with very different empirical consequences.

Reality Exploration and Discovery: Pattern Interaction in Language and Life.
Linda Uyechi and Lian-Hee Wee (eds.).

On the phonological side, Stratal OT accounts for opacity and paradigmatic transfer phenomena (Kiparsky 2000, Bermúdez-Otero 1997, 2007; see also the related approach in Wee, this volume). Although constraint interaction is locally parallel and transparent, the interleaving of phonology and morphology and the intrinsic seriality of strata gives rise to "derivational" effects. On the morphological side, the assumption that the selectional restrictions of an affix are checked at the point of affixation has two important consequences. First, if an affix (such as B in (1)) selects a base with some phonological property, this requirement must crucially be satisfied at an intermediate representation (A′ in (1)); it need *not* be satisfied in the underlying form A (which does not show the derived phonology of the base) nor in the output form (which shows an overlay of phonological effects, triggered by B and by any later layers of derivation). Secondly, checking selectional restrictions at the point of affixation correctly predicts a range of morphological locality effects, among them notably the generalization of Carstairs (1987) that morphological selection is not "outwardly sensitive", i.e. that in the configuration (2), A and B cannot be morphologically dependent on (selected by) the presence of the morpheme C, or by the particular shape of C.

(2) [[A + B] C]

One of the things that makes prosodic morphology interesting is the rich additional phonology/morphology interactions that it gives rise to. With respect to selection, reduplication is more revealing than other kinds of morphology, for the copying operation mirrors the phonological shape of the base, thereby providing some of the clearest evidence that when a base undergoes affixation, it has already undergone the lexical phonology applicable at that point, but not yet any phonology triggered by later morphology or by postlexical processes.

Furthermore, prosodic morphology is a massive source of opacity, for two reasons. First, prosodic morphology can involve operations that mask phonological conditioning. For example, a phonological process may seem to "overapply" in a reduplicant or truncatum when a superimposed prosodic template wipes out its trigger. (Although the traditional term "overapplication" is a misnomer from our point of view, it will serve as a descriptive term for the effect that such constraint masking creates.) Importantly, our view of the morphology/phonology interface says not just that phonological processes *can* "overapply" under these conditions, it says that they *must*. Here Stratal OT makes a stronger claim about overapplication than theories which treat it an exceptional situation that requires special stipulations or special mechanisms of some kind.

The second predicted new type of opacity associated with prosodic morphology is just the opposite: phonology masks morphology. This arises specifically with reduplication. Because Stratal OT requires the output of prosodic morphology to satisfy the phonological constraint systems at any subsequent layer of derivation, the application of phonological processes may disturb the prosodic template or obscure the melodic parallelism between base and reduplicant.

11.2 Parallel OT

For these reasons, the complex phonology/morphology interactions in reduplication provide an ideal testing ground for assessing the relative merits of Stratal and parallel OT. The parallel OT approach to reduplication relies on special correspondence relations between a reduplicant and two representations of the base, its *output* form, and its *input* form (McCarthy and Prince 1995). These correspondence relations are independent of those which hold between the input and output representations of the base itself, but they are formally parallel to it. For every MAX-I/O, DEP-I/O, and IDENT-I/O constraint this theory posits a corresponding Base/Reduplication (B/R) constraint, and a corresponding Input/Reduplication (I/R) constraint. Thus, a reduplicated output participates simultaneously in four faithfulness relations (not counting Sympathy and whatever other faithfulness relations are invoked for opacity):

(3)

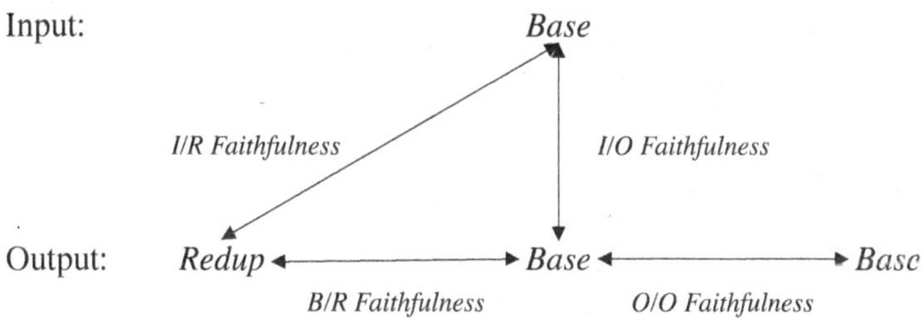

Parallel OT treats reduplication as a separate type of phenomenon governed by B/R and I/R correspondence constraints, and allocates truncation with paradigmatic effects to Output/Output (O/O) correspondence constraints.

In Stratal OT, there are no reduplication-specific correspondence constraints, i.e. no B/R or I/R constraints, and no O/O constraints either. The shape of a reduplicated or truncated element — the REDUPLICANT or TRUNCATUM — is determined by the interaction of normal Input/Output (I/O) faithfulness constraints with markedness constraints in a morphologically selected constraint ranking (a co-phonology, along the lines of Inkelas & Zoll 2005). Overapplication phenomena and other apparent anomalies associated with prosodic morphology are no different in principle from any other so-called cyclic effects. They are just more spectacular. The reduplicant+base combination obeys the general phonology of the category to which it belongs (allowing for lexical exceptions and morpheme-specific idiosyncratic behavior, as with any morphology). There is nothing morphologically special about prosodic morphology; phonologically its outputs behave like ordinary affixed forms and compounds. Truncation and reduplication do not differ in the constraint families they are subject to, but in the form of the template (represented by a ranking of prosodic markedness constraints) and in whether it is imposed on the base itself, or on a copy of the base.

I shall argue that the phonology/morphology interface phenomena, far from motivating B/R and I/R constraints, tell decisively *against* them, and support Stratal OT. They predict unattested base/reduplication phonological interactions of at least two types, BACK-COPYING and RECOPYING. Furthermore, some reduplication systems are intractable in parallel OT; this is shown for Sanskrit below. In each case, Stratal OT not only accommodates the correct phonology/morphology interaction, but predicts it. In short, the parallelist theory of reduplication is too weak in some respects and too strong in others, and both failings are traceable to the parallelist architecture. The Stratal OT approach provides a superior treatment of the actually occurring cases and generates a reasonable typology.

11.3 Back-copying and Recopying: The Excess Richness of Parallel OT

Back-copying is the putative phenomenon of overapplication in the reduplicant of a process triggered by the reduplicant in the base. McCarthy and Prince (1995) support their claim that back-copying exists with an example from Malay which they cite from Kenstowicz (1981), who has it from Farid Onn (1980), apparently the original source of the datum. In Malay, nasality spreads postlexically rightwards over vowels, glides, and laryngeal consonants, and is blocked by obstruents and liquids. This spreading process crosses a reduplication boundary, and — this is the back-copying — nasality which spreads from the first member of a reduplicated compound onto the second is then said to be copied from the second member back onto the first. In consequence, the nasalization appears in a context where it is not phonologically licensed.

(4) [w̃ãŋĩ-w̃ãŋĩ] 'very fragrant' (from [waŋĩ] 'fragrant')

In the model proposed here, such cases would actually be impossible to deal with.

In Farid Onn's examples, the extra nasalization abuts a nasal consonant, as in the first syllable of (4). So it is important to rule out the possibility that the putative back-copying nasalization is just a coarticulation effect, reinforced by the fact that the *entire rest of the word* is nasal. The crucial evidence will have to come from longer examples, which allow a bit more separation between the nasal and oral spans. During a delightful visit to the Mohanans in Singapore, I tried to verify the back-copy phenomenon with such data. I interviewed four (non-linguist) native speakers of the dialect of Malay described by Farid Onn, using examples like (5).[3]

(5) a. *(warna bajunya) ke-hitam-hitam-an*
'(the color of the dress) is blackish'

b. *(taman bunganya terasa) ke-harum-harum-an*
'(the garden terrace) is full of fragrance'

In (5), back-copying would predict *three* nasal spans interleaved with three oral spans. The crucial prediction is the first, boldfaced little island of nasality:

(6) a. *[kə-**h̃ĩ**tam-h̃ĩtamãn]

b. *[kə-**h̃ã**rum-h̃ãrumãn]

However I heard no nasality in this part of the words in the speech of any of the informants. Therefore, until solid phonetic evidence is produced for longer words like (6), to exclude the interpretation of the apparent overapplication effect as phonetic coarticulation, the report of back-copying in Malay remains in limbo.

Inkelas and Zoll (2005) examine a number of other putative back-copy examples and conclude that none of them stand up to scrutiny. So at this point it is reasonable to doubt whether the whole phenomenon even exists.

The second kind of global base-reduplication interaction predicted by B/R constraints is RECOPYING, the overapplication in the base of a process in the reduplicant (whether the application in the reduplicant is itself conditioned by the base or not). Not even an apparent example of this pattern has ever been exhibited as far as I know, but here is what it would look like. In Sanskrit, the intensive is formed with a reduplicating prefix of the form CVC-. The coda of the reduplicating prefix is subject to regular process of Sanskrit phonology, including coda neutralization and place assimilation. For example, a medial *-mn-* created by reduplication shows up as *-nn-*, as in the intensive 3.Sg. *nan-namīti* 'bends' (from *nam-*, *namati*). Base-Reduplicant identity would cause the assimilated *-n* of the reduplicant to be recopied into the root, giving **nan-nanīti*. This is not merely the wrong Sanskrit form, it represents a typologically undocumented phenomenon. It is not derivable in Stratal OT, since this theory has no mechanism for enforcing stem-reduplicant identity other than copying itself, which, as explained above, accesses the melody of the base at

[3]Here I would like to express my thanks to Lian Hee and his colleagues Dahliyah Kasmani, Pakcik Sahari, Rumna, Fatima Ahmad, and Ismail Talib at the National University of Singapore, who helped me construct the examples and graciously answered my questions.

the point of affixation. OT with B/R constraints, on the other hand, straightforwardly predicts that recopying should emerge simply when the relevant B/R constraint is ranked high enough:[4]

(7)

Sanskrit	AGREE	IDENT-B/R(Lab)	IDENT-I/O(Lab)	IDENT-I/R(Lab)
Input: /R-namīti/, Base: *-namīti*				
a. nan-namīti		*		*
b. nam-namīti	*			
☞ c. nan-nanīti			*	*

Since Stratal OT has neither I/R constraints nor B/R constraints, nor of course sympathy constraints or O/O constraints, these overgeneration problems simply do not arise.

I now turn to a case of the opposite type, where even this rich machinery is descriptively insufficient, while Stratal OT still gives the right results.

11.4 Where Parallel OT is Too Weak

In this section I turn to the phonology of reduplication in classical Sanskrit. The forms in (8) are perfect stems of classical Sanskrit, marked by a well-defined type of reduplication unique to this particular morphological category. (8a,c) have simple roots, and (8b,d) have prefixed roots. We are interested in the initial consonant of the root and its reduplicant.

(8) a. /sic/ *si-ṣec-* 'pour'
b. /ni-sic/ *ni-ṣi-ṣec-* 'pour down'
c. /sañj/ *sa-sañj-* 'stick to'
d. /pari-ṣañj/ *pari-ṣa-ṣañj-* 'be attached to'
e. /ḍhauk/ *ḍu-ḍhauk-* 'approach'

In (8a,b,c), *s* is retroflexed to *ṣ* by a phonological process that applies after *r*, a nonlow vowel, or a velar,[5] a process known mnemonically after its context as *ruki*. (The retroflex *ḍh* in (8e) is underlying, and contrastive.) So the *s* ∼ *ṣ* alternation is phonologically transparent. But the phonological parallelism between reduplicant and stem is not: in (8a), the reduplicant's *i* triggers retroflexion of the root-initial *s*, whereas the reduplicant itself has plain *s*. In

[4]Theoretically, I/O, B/R, and I/R faithfulness constraints should be able to rank anywhere with respect to each other and with respect to markedness constraints, to yield a complete factorial typology. But McCarthy and Prince show that allowing I/R constraints to outrank I/O constraints would badly compromise the typology of reduplication, and propose that I/R constraints are universally ranked below I/O constraints because of a "metaconstraint" that ranks root faithfulness over affix faithfulness. The tableau in (7) respects this stricture.

[5] Palatals cannot precede [s] for other reasons. It should also be said that, in what seems to be an OCP effect, *ruki* is normally blocked by an immediately following *r* (e.g. *su-sruv-úḥ* 'they flowed', *si-srev-iṣa-ti* 'wants to fail')

other words, there is no recopying, just as Stratal OT predicts. How can these data be dealt with in parallel OT?

First let us introduce the phonological constraints required in any OT analysis, stratal or parallel. Retroflexion is driven by a context-sensitive constraint — call it **Is* — which prohibits *s* in the *ruki* context, symbolized here by *I*. **Is* dominates a context-free markedness constraint *[+R] that bars retroflex consonants, including *ṣ* (where [R] is just a placeholder for the feature or features that define retroflexion).[6] *[+R] is also dominated by IDENT-I/O(R), since /ṣ/ and the retroflex stops are distinct phonemes of Sanskrit.

(9) a. **Is* [s] cannot occur after a nonlow vowel, after /r/, or after velars.
b. *[+R] No retroflex [ṣ] (i.e., elsewhere).

Uncontroversially, the specific CV-template of perfect reduplication is defined by a set of prosodic constraints (such as NOCODA). The neutralization of certain features such as aspiration is general for prefixes in Sanskrit, and is accounted for by ranking the relevant markedness constraints (such as *ASPIRATED) highly for that class of morphemes. Setting these things aside, let us focus on how retroflexion works in reduplicated forms.

On the parallel theory, reduplication-specific faithfulness constraints require identity between the reduplicant and the base. One such constraint is IDENT-B/R(R): "corresponding segments in the base and the reduplicant have the same value with respect to retroflexion". IDENT-B/R(R) is not surface-true in *si-ṣec-*, for the retroflexion triggered by the reduplicant in the root is not "back-copied" into the reduplicant itself. Some higher-ranking constraint or constraints must dominate IDENT-B/R(R) to compel its violation in such forms. It must be either a markedness constraint, namely (9b) *[+R], or a faithfulness constraints, namely ID-I/O(R).[7] The first alternative can be immediately rejected on the basis of *ḍu-ḍhauk-*, which shows that retroflexion *is* retained in reduplicants. So the data cannot be accounted for by a markedness constraint, as shown by the tableau in (10) (where the solid hand marks the wrong output that is derived, and a checkmark the desired output that is not derived).

[6] I set aside the question what the context *I* and the affected feature or feature bundle [R] are phonologically; [+High] is very likely one feature that they share..

[7] Actually it could also be a Sympathy constraint ❀ IDENT-B/R(R) (with ★ ID-I/O(R) as the selector). I will ignore this possibility because of the by now familiar general objections to sympathy theory, and because of the specific objection that, in early stages of Sanskrit, /ṣ/:/s/ is not contrastive in roots. Sympathy to noncontrastive features should be precluded, for otherwise sympathetic reduplication could indeed result in the impossible *[ṣa-svaj-], or for that matter in *[s̃a-svaj-] or what have you.

(10)

Sanskrit	ID -B/R(Lab)	*Is	ID -I/O(R)	*[+R]	ID -B/R(R)
a. Input: /sic-sic/					
i. si-sic-		*			
☞ ii. si-ṣic-			*	*	*
iii. ṣi-ṣic-			*	**	
iv. ba-sic-	*				
b. Input: /sañj-sañj/					
☞ i. sa-sañj-					
ii. ṣa-sañj-				*	*
iii. ṣa-ṣañj-			*	**	
iv. sa-ṣañj-			*	*	*
v. ba-sañj-	*				
c. Input: /ḍhauk-ḍhauk/					
i. du-dhauk-			*		
ii. ḍu-dhauk-			*	*	*
✓ iii. ḍu-ḍhauk-				**	
☛ iv. du-ḍhauk-				*	*
v. ba-ḍhauk-	*			*	*

The dominant template-defining constraints, and the candidates that violate them, are omitted in the tableau. Other IDENT-B/R constraints than ID-B/R(R) must dominate the corresponding markedness constraints in order to block candidates with unmarked reduplicants from ousting the more marked but faithful candidates. In (10), *ba-* represents all these party-crashers, and IDENT-B/R(Labial) represents the IDENT-B/R constraints needed to keep them out.

The other way to defeat ID-B/R(R) would be through domination by the faithfulness constraint IDENT-I/R(R) (see (3)), which would have to be crucially ranked between **Is* and *[+R].[8] Tableau (11) shows that it yields the right results for the data considered so far.

[8]Thanks to Stephen Anderson for pointing this out. The tableau respects the stipulation that IDENT-I/O constraints universally outrank IDENT-I/R constraints (McCarthy and Prince 1995.)

(11)

Sanskrit	ID -B/R(Lab)	*Is	ID -I/O(R)	ID -I/R(R)	*[+R]	ID -B/R(R)
a. Input: /R-sic/, Base: *sic-*						
i. si-sic-		*				
☞ ii. si-ṣic-			*		*	*
iii. ṣi-ṣic-			*	*	**	
iv. ba-sic-	*			*		
b. Input: /sañj-sañj/						
☞ i. sa-sañj-						
ii. ṣa-sañj-				*	*	*
iii. ṣa-ṣañj-			*	**	**	
iv. sa-ṣañj-			*	*	*	*
v. ba-sañj-	*					*
c. Input: /R-ḍhauk/, Base: *ḍhauk-*						
i. du-dhauk-			*	*		
ii. ḍu-dhauk-			*		*	*
☞ iii. ḍu-ḍhauk-					**	
iv. du-ḍhauk-				*	*	*
v. ba-ḍhauk-	*		*		*	*

But this analysis also fails, albeit in a less obvious way. What it claims is that retroflex consonants appear in reduplicants only under two conditions: (i) in an overt *ruki* environment (i.e. after a high vowel, *r*, or *ṣ*), where retroflexion is forced by **Is*, and (ii) if they correspond to an *underlying* retroflex consonant, in which case ID-I/O(R) takes effect regardless of the overt environment. A clear prediction for Sanskrit follows: *retroflexion overapplies in reduplicants if and only if it is specified in the underlying form of the base.*

This prediction is false, as shown by (8d) *pari-ṣa-ṣañj-* (which represents the regular classical Sanskrit outcome in such cases).[9] Here *derived* retroflex *ṣ* appears in an environment where it is *not* overtly licensed by a surface *ruki* context. ID-B/R(R) would select the desired (4c) *pari-ṣa-ṣañj-*, but because it must be ranked below ID-I/R(R) (see (11)), it is effectively invisible.

[9]There is a set of Prefix+Root combinations that show transparent retroflexion (e.g. *pari-ṣasvaj-e* 'embraced' (Wackernagel 1957:235). These are remnants of the older Vedic system where *ruki* was restricted to the word-level. Secondly, there are Prefix+Root combinations that are compound-like and do not undergo *ruki* at all, *a fortiori* whether the root is plain, reduplicated, or augmented (Wackernagel 1957:234).

(12)

Sanskrit	ID -B/R(Lab)	*Is	ID -I/O(R)	ID -I/R(R)	*[+R]	ID -B/R(R)
Input: /pari-sañj/						
i. pari-sa-sañj-						
☞ ii. pari-ṣa-sañj-				*	*	*
✓ iii. pari-ṣa-ṣañj-			*	**	**	
iv. pari-sa-ṣañj-			*	*	*	*
v. pari-ba-sañj-	*					*

We have arrived at a ranking paradox: no single ranking of the available constraints can derive all the forms in (11) and (12).

Stratal OT's phonology/morphology interleaving does predict the correct outputs, provided we make one crucial assumption about the morphological derivation: that the verb combines lexically with its prefix prior to suffixation. The theory then dictates that the prefix triggers retroflexion of the root-initial *s*- prior to reduplication.

The assumption that the verb combines lexically with its prefix prior to inflectional affixation is plausible because the prefix+verb combination often has an unpredictable meaning and unpredictable grammatical properties (such as active vs. middle voice). Prefixation is thus derivational: it forms new lexemes, which are then inflected. More compellingly, the priority of derivational prefixation over inflection is required by the selectional restrictions on affixes, which distinguish between bare and prefixed roots. The strongest selectional evidence that the prefix+root combination is the constituent to which inflectional affixes are added comes from suffix allomorphy. Several suffixes vary in form depending on whether the root is prefixed or not. The gerund (absolutive) suffix, which makes temporal adverbials with the meaning 'having V-ed', 'after V-ing', has two basic allomorphs: *-tvā*, which occurs after simple roots, and *-ya*, which occurs after prefixed roots. The latter allomorph gets a *t* added before it if the root is light, in order to make the one-mora root syllable into a minimal foot. The allomorphy is illustrated by the simple form and a compounded form of the root */bhr̥/* 'carry' in (13).

(13) a. *bhr̥-tvā́* 'having brought' (*-tvā* after a simple root)
b. *saṃ-bhŕ̥-tya* 'having brought together' (*-t-ya* after a light prefixed root)

In *bhr̥-tvā́*, the root, being simple, selects the allomorph *-tvā́*. In (13b) *saṃ-bhŕ̥-tya*, the prefixed root selects the gerund allomorph *-(t)ya*. This shows that the gerund is formed off the prefixed root.[10]

[10]More precisely, it shows this provided we agree that the right allomorph is selected at the point at which the morphological operation introducing the affix takes place, and in particular

Additional evidence is the special behavior of the negative prefix *a-*. Unlike verbal prefixes, such as *sam-* in (13b), *a-* has no effect on the choice of gerund allomorph. For example, *á-bhṛ-tvā* 'not having carried' has the gerund allomorph that is otherwise selected by simple roots. Why does *a-* differ from the verbal prefixes in this way? The solution to this puzzle is that *a-* is prefixed not to roots but to gerunds, and gerunds are formed from simple roots, hence with the allomorph *-tvā*. The evidence that *a-* not prefixed to roots but to gerunds is that *a-* selects nominal and adverbial stems, and it is only in virtue of the gerund suffix *-tvā* that the verbs become adverbs eligible for *a-*prefixation. Conversely, verbal prefixes select verbal stems, and hence must be added to roots before they become adverbs. The allomorphy reflects this derivational history.

(14) a. saṃ-bhṛ → $(\text{saṃ})_{\text{Stem}}(\text{bhṛ́-tya})_{\text{Stem}}$ (suffixation to a prefixed root)
b. bhṛ-tvā́ → $(\text{á})_{\text{Stem}}(\text{bhṛ-tvā})_{\text{Stem}}$ (prefixation to a suffixed stem)

The prosodic structure of the words is the same, as far as we can tell, as indicated in (14). Specifically, phonology shows that there is a compound boundary between the prefix and the root in both words. Examples like this show that level ordering cannot be simply reduced to the domains defined by prosodic structure. Rather, the morphophonology reveals that the order of prefixation and suffixation is determined by the different selectional requirements of the prefixes and suffixes, even for what surfaces as the same prosodic structure.

Therefore the derivation of *pari-ṣa-ṣañj-* proceeds from the prefixed root, after retroflexion has been triggered by the prefix-final vowel *i-*.

(15)
sañj-	Root
pari-ṣañj-	Prefixation, *ruki*-retroflexion
pari-ṣa-ṣañj-	Reduplication

This derives the correct output.

A second class of opaque retroflexion contexts that follows from this morphology/phonology interleaving involves the augment *a-* which is prefixed to the root to mark past tense. In roots whose initial *s-* is retroflexed to *ṣ-* by a prefix, the *ṣ-* appears also when the *a-* is prefixed to the root, even though it interrupts the conditioning *ruki* context.

(16)
abhy-a-ṣiñc-a-n	'poured on'	(from *abhi* + *siñc-* → *abhi-ṣiñc-*)
adhy-a-ṣṭhā-m	'stood on'	(from *adhi* + *sthā-* → *adhi-ṣṭhā-*[11])

that there are no "allomorphy processes" that could, for example, replace *-tvā́* by *-tya* after the prefix has been added.

[11]Glide formation takes effect at the word level. Coronal assimilation applies there also, as described below: *adhi-a-ṣthā-m* → *adhyaṣṭhām*.

In sum: when verbs receive inflectional suffixes or the augment *a*-, their prefix (if they have one) with any phonological effects that it may trigger on the root, are already in place. In the case of augmentation with *a*-, the effect is to make the *ruki* context opaque.

This morphological derivation also explains the phonology of reduplication under discussion. The Stratal OT account works as follows.

Morphologically, the input is a full copy of the stem. The stem-level constraint system includes the template-defining constraints (again omitted here, with the candidates that violate them), and the general phonological constraints in their normal Sanskrit ranking:

(17)

		Sanskrit	IDENT -I/O(Lab)	**Is*	IDENT -I/O(R)	*[+R]
a. Input: /sic-sic/						
	i.	si-sic-		*		
☞	ii.	si-ṣic-			*	*
	iii.	ṣi-ṣic-			**	*
	iv.	ba-sic-	*		*	
b. Input: /sañj-sañj/						
☞	i.	sa-sañj-				
	ii.	sa-ṣañj-			*	*
	iii.	ba-sañj-	*			
c. Input: /pari-sañj/						
	i.	pari-sañj-		*		
☞	ii.	pari-ṣañj-			*	*
d. Input: /pari-ṣañj-ṣañj/ (by reduplication from (c))						
	i.	pari-sa-sañj-		*	*	
	ii.	pari-ṣa-sañj-			*	*
☞	iii.	pari-ṣa-ṣañj-				**
	iv.	pari-sa-ṣañj-		*	*	*
	v.	pari-ba-ṣañj-	*		*	*
d. Input: /ḍhauk-ḍhauk/						
	i.	du-dhauk-			*	
	ii.	ḍu-dhauk-			*	*
☞	iii.	ḍu-ḍhauk-				**
	iv.	du-ḍhauk-			*	*
	v.	ba-ḍhauk-	*		*	*

Perfect reduplication doubles the root after prefixation and, therefore, with the stem-level phonology triggered by the prefix in place. Where consistent with the dominant templatic constraints (such as *ASPIRATED), IDENT-I/O(R), its ranking independently motivated by the rest of the phonology, keeps the output faithful to the copy. In this setup IDENT-I/O(R) does the job of the parallel theory's IDENT-B/R(R), with the important benefit that back-copying and recopying becomes impossible.

Augment forms like those in (16) are unproblematically derived by insertion of past-marking *a-*, followed by glide formation. The retroflex *ṣ* persists in spite of the intervening augment *-a-*.

(18)
siñc-	Root
abhi-ṣiñc-	Prefixation, *ruki*
abhi-a-ṣiñc-	Augmentation
abhy-a-ṣiñc-	Glide formation (Word level)

The observational generalization is that reduplication and the augment are "transparent" to *ruki*. The descriptive generalization behind it seems to be that they are added to prefixed roots after it undergoes *ruki*.[12] Stratal OT is a theoretical framework that accommodates that descriptive generalization.

A final point of interest is that stops which are adjacent to *ṣ* (whether derived or underlying) assimilate to it in retroflexion. In contrast to *ruki* retroflexion, this process is automatic and applies obligatorily across word boundaries. Interestingly, the retroflex stops derived by this process reduplicate as plain stops, never as retroflexes. This can be seen in initial *s*+stop clusters, which reduplicate with the stop (and not with the *s*).

(19) *vi-ta-ṣṭh-e* (not **vi-ṭa-ṣṭh-e*) 'stood apart'

We now have a good explanation for the behavior of these clusters: *ruki* enforces *ṣ* at the stem level, and this process consequently is rendered opaque by subsequent inflection and phonology. Assimilation of retroflexion in coronal clusters (such as *ṣt* → *ṣṭ*) applies at the word level, and consequently is not visible to, and therefore not made opaque by, stem-level inflection and phonology.

The behavior of *derived* retroflex stops contrasts with that of *underlying* retroflex stops, which do enter into reduplication as predicted, e.g. *ḍu-ḍhauk-*. A particularly interesting case is root-initial *ṣṭh-* in *ṣṭhīv-* 'spew'. In Classical

[12]A similar account is needed for other inflections, such as the nasal infix in case forms like /havis/ → *haviṣ* → *havīṃṣ-i* 'oblations' (Neuter Nom.-Acc. Plural).

Sanskrit, as prescribed by Pāṇini's grammar, it has the perfect *ṭi-ṣṭhev-a*.[13]

This intricate web of connections should not be surprising from the traditional perspective on reduplication, for since Marantz (1982) and Clements (1985) it has been known that contrastive features tend to be transferred from the base to the reduplicant. This insight is captured in Stratal OT. What it means for a feature F to be contrastive is to be protected by a sufficiently high-ranked IDENT-I/O(F) faithfulness constraint, and precisely this ranking guarantees also faithfulness to the copy of F in the reduplicant. For the global B/R correspondence approach, distinctiveness should be irrelevant to transfer. Distinctiveness is a matter of whether I/O faithfulness constraints dominate markedness constraints, and transfer is a matter of whether B/R constraints and I/R faithfulness constraints dominate markedness constraints. Parallel OT provides no principled reason why these rankings should be correlated at all. For Stratal OT, a corollary of the generalization that distinctive features are transferred from base to reduplicant in virtue of high-ranked IDENT-I/O(F) faithfulness is that the rise of a contrast in a language might entail changes in its reduplication patterns. This is exactly what we have seen.[14]

11.5 A Derivational Alternative

The putative existence of global phonology/morphology interactions in reduplication has prompted several novel proposals. Raimy (2000) incorporates an arrow symbol "→" into phonological representations to denote the precedence relation between segments. In order to represent reduplication, the arrow is allowed to loop back, so that a segment can in effect precede itself (Raimy 2000:12). For example, *sañj-* and its reduplicated form For example, *sañj-* and its reduplicated form *sa-sañj-* look like this:

(20) a. # → s → a → ñ → j → %

b. # → s → a → ñ → j → %

[13]In contrast, Vedic has *ti-ṣṭhev-a* (ŚB. 1.2.3.1). This can be explained directly from our assumptions. Unlike Classical Sanskrit, Vedic has no distinctive retroflex stops in verb roots. The root's lexical representation at that stage is therefore /ṣthīv/. Since the assimilatory retroflexion of stops next to *ṣ* is not registered in reduplicants – because it is not present at the stem level – the Vedic data follow. In Classical Sanskrit, retroflex stops become admissible in the lexical representations of verb roots (e.g. *ḍhauk* 'approach', *ghaṭ* 'strive', *aṭ* 'wander', *raṭ* 'howl'). At this point, *ṣṭhīv-* is restructured from /ṣthīv/ to /ṣṭhīv/ (lexicon optimization), and *ṭ* starts being copied in reduplicants.

[14]Donca Steriade *in litt. el. binis* points out that the cyclic effects seen in Sanskrit can be dealt with by Base/Output constraints, provided we give up the usual requirement that Bases be free forms (i.e. Output/Output constraints will not work). This takes us back to the more general point that under Stratal OT, plain vanilla I/O constraints do the work for which parallelism must posit numerous additional types of constraint, including Base/Output constraints, Output/Output constraints, Base/Reduplication constraints, Input/Reduplication constraints, not to speak of Sympathy constraints and company.

Raimy proposes that looped representations such as (20b) provide insight into the phonology of reduplication. He introduces a UNIFORMITY PARAMETER with two settings, which "determines whether a rule requires all environments that a segment appears in to satisfy the structural description of the rule or if only a single environment is sufficient to trigger the rule" (Raimy 2000:20). To illustrate, let us consider the reduplication of *siñc* to *si-ṣiñc*. A Raimy-style phonological representation of the reduplicated form looks like this:

(21) # → s → i → ñ → c → %

How does *ruki* apply to this structure? It depends on the setting of the Uniformity Parameter. When it is *off*, the fact that *s* appears is a *ruki* environment (namely *i* → *s*) suffices to trigger the *ruki*. This corresponds to overapplication: *siñc* → **ṣi-ṣiñc*. When it is *on*, the rule is blocked, because *s* also appears in a non-*ruki* environment (namely # → s). This corresponds to a type of underapplication: *sic* → **si-siñc*.

The correct output is neither **ṣiṣiñc* nor **sisiñc*; it is *siṣiñc*. The forms **ṣiṣiñc* and **sisiñc* are not only wrong, their derivation instantiates nonexistent types of global phonology/morphology interactions – back-copying, and a type of globality that even parallel OT does not allow, where a process fails to apply in the base just in case its reduplicated copy is not subject to it.[15] These forms could not be generated in Sanskrit under Stratal OT assumptions. Stratal OT has no mechanism for blocking *ruki* through a requirement of phonological parallelism between reduplication and base. Of course, if (contrary to what is the case in Sanskrit) the *ruki* rule were inapplicable across prefix boundaries, or at least between reduplication prefixes and their bases, and the grammar were otherwise the same, then **sisiñc* would not only be derivable, it would be the only possible output. In other words, if Sanskrit had **ti-stha-ti* 'stands', rather than *ti-ṣṭha-ti* (from *sthā*), and so on across the board, then Stratal OT would predict **si-siñc*; as it is, the actual form *ti-ṣṭha-ti* entails the actual form *si-ṣiñc-*.

Could the actual forms *ti-ṣṭha-ti, si-ṣiñc-* be derived in the looping theory? Raimy posits that phonological representations are linearized at some point in the derivation, so that loops between segments are translated into multiple copies of those segments in the phonetics. Raimy suggests that this linearization process takes place *before* the phonetics-phonology interface, between the cyclic and postcyclic rules (Raimy 2000:50). From that point on, phonological rules take effect on each copy independently of the others. So, to derive *si-ṣiñc-*, the *ruki* rule would have to be postcyclic. But *ruki* in clas-

[15]The early literature on reduplication sometimes analyzed Luiseño as having a process that fails to apply in the base just in case its reduplicated copy is not subject to it, but as noted by Marantz (1982) the 'underapplication' can also be located in the reduplication.

sical Sanskrit is clearly cyclic, for it interacts cyclically with morphology in cases such as (16).

The upshot is that Raimy's theory predicts two impossible patterns of *ruki* application in Sanskrit reduplication (depending on how the Uniformity Parameter is set), and fails to provide a coherent descriptive account of the actual observed pattern.[16]

11.6 Conclusion

In sum: the parallel approach both overgenerates and undergenerates. Stratal OT, where the only phonological correspondence relation is I/O correspondence, gives better results.

References

Bermúdez-Otero, Ricardo. 1999. *Constraint Interaction in Language Change: Quantity in English and Germanic*. Ph.D. thesis, University of Manchester.

Bermúdez-Otero, Ricardo. 2007. Dichronic phonology. In P. de Lacy, ed., *The Cambridge Handbook of Phonology*. CUP.

Carstairs, Andrew. 1987. *Allomorphy in Inflexion*. Beckenham: Croom Helm.

Clements, George N. 1985. The problem of transfer in nonlinear morphology. *Cornell Working Papers in Linguistics* 7.

Frampton, John. 2004. Distributed reduplication. MS, MIT.

Inkelas, Sharon and Cheryl Zoll. 2005. *Reduplication*. Cambridge: CUP.

Kenstowicz, Michael. 1981. Functional explanations in generative phonology. In D. L. Goyvaerts, ed., *Phonology in the 1980's*. Ghent: E. Story-Scientia.

Kiparsky, Paul. 2000. Opacity and cyclicity. *The Linguistic Review* 17:351–567.

Marantz, Alec. 1982. Re reduplication. *Linguistic Inquiry* 11:497–509.

McCarthy, John and Alan Prince. 1995a. Faithfulness and reduplicative identity. In L. W. D. Jill N. Beckman and S. Urbanczyk, eds., *Papers in Optimality Theory*, vol. 18, pages 249–384. University of Massachusetts Amherst, GLSA.

Mohanan, K.P. 1986. *The Theory of Lexical Phonology*. Dordrecht: Reidel.

Onn, Farid M. 1980. *Aspects of Malay Phonology and Morphology: A Generative Approach*. Ph.D. thesis, Universiti kebangsaan Malaysia, Kuala Lumpur.

---

[16]Frampton (2004) develops another descriptively rich derivational theory of reduplication which makes provision for some of the unwanted types of morphology/phonology interactions discussed here. The space at my disposal here does not allow me to do the justice to it that it deserves.

Raimy, Eric. 2000. *The Phonology and Morphology of Reduplication*. Berlin: Mouton de Gruyter.

Wackernagel, Jakob. 1957. *Altindische Grammmatik I*. Göttingen: Vandenhoeck & Ruprecht.

12

The Emergence of Optimality Theory

K.P. MOHANAN, D. ARCHANGELI, D. PULLEYBLANK

12.1 Introduction

Generative phonology has been dominant for roughly fifty years[1] (Chomsky & Halle 1968, etc.) with Optimality Theory (OT) being the prevailing framework in phonology for over a decade (Prince & Smolensky 2004, etc.). Both theories share the assumption that Universal Grammar (UG) provides an inventory of universal distinctive features; OT also assumes that UG provides an inventory of universal constraints. The feature inventory defines the set of potential input segments in human languages that serve as phonemic, i.e., contrastive segments across languages, while the combination of feature inventory and constraints define the set of cross-linguistically possible sets of (i) phonetic segments,[2] (ii) sequences of phonetic segments, and (iii) pairings of phonemic-phonetic segments/segment sequences. The features and constraints provided in UG are available to all individual grammars, hence it follows that all individual grammars contain the same set of distinctive features and constraints. Individual grammars vary in their interactions between con-

[1]This is roughly the same length of time that KPM has been around. Note that the authors' names appear in order of shortest to longest, of course (or was that older to younger? senior to junior? wiser to less wise?...). We should add that Mohanan, though an author of the paper, can only partially be held responsible for anything in it. He thought the paper was for another volume, and as we cut, chopped, edited and formatted for this volume, we kept him significantly out of the loop. So if you like anything in the paper, the credit should go to Mohanan (and also Tara Mohanan, Lian-Hee Wee and Joe Pater, all of whom gave us comments before or after an earlier draft); if your reaction is less positive to anything, blame Diana and Doug...

[2]Here and throughout, we use 'phonetic' to refer to the output of the phonology. Following Keating (1990), Pulleyblank (1986), and others, we assume that the output of the phonology is interpreted by a language-specific phonetic component.

Reality Exploration and Discovery: Pattern Interaction in Language and Life.
Linda Uyechi and Lian-Hee Wee (eds.).

straints, formally expressed as ranking. Structural differences between individual grammars are due solely to differences in ranking. Constraints hold on phonetic representations (output constraints, i.e. markedness constraints), as well as on the pairing between phonemic and phonetic representations (input-output constraints, i.e. faithfulness constraints). There are no constraints on input (phonemic) representations (Richness of the Base). Thus, all individual grammars have the same potential set of contrastive units (phonemic inventory) and there are no limits on input sequences. However, languages vary in the set of permissible phonetic segments and in the permissible sequencing of those segments. The assumption that UG provides universal inventories of features and constraints allows us to explain phonological patterns that appear recurrently across genetically unrelated languages while the assumption that individual grammars vary in the ranking of universal constraints allows us to explain the typological variations between such recurrent patterns.

While the advantages of shifting the focus of attention from language-specific rules to the resolution of conflict between universal constraints are widely acknowledged, there has been growing evidence during recent years that the 'natural' patterns of contrast, distribution and alternation in human languages, i.e., those that appear repeatedly in human languages, are strongly influenced by the human articulatory and perceptual systems (Archangeli & Pulleyblank 1994, Flemming 1995, Boersma 1998, Hume & Johnson 2001, Hayes, Kirchner & Steriade 2004, Blevins 2004, Barnes 2006, Boersma & Hamann 2007, etc.). In other words, natural phonological patterns are grounded in, or emerge from, the interaction of sub-phonological forces in the 'phonetic space'.

We might capture this grounding by restructuring UG such that it does not include an inventory of universal features and constraints, replaced by some other structure. Possibilities include: (i) supplement the phonological component of UG with a theory of the generation of features, constraints, and rankings[3] to derive the universal inventories of each; (ii) allow each grammar to generate features and constraints, simply abandoning any universal set of features and any universal set of constraints.

This paper explores aspects of the second option, specifically:

(1) a. While UG may provide basic units of linguistic representation, UG does not provide an inventory of specific distinctive features.

b. From (a) above, it follows that UG does not provide an inventory of universal feature-constraints either.

c. Inventories of features, contrastive segments and feature-constraints emerge in an individual grammar in the course of language devel-

[3]The harmonic ranking of constraint sets posited in standard OT suffers because the constraints that are harmonically ranked are themselves stipulated, i.e. simply listed in UG.

opment through exposure to data, shaped by the forces of articulation and perception and constrained by the units of representation provided by UG.

d. Thus, individual grammars vary in their inventories of features and constraints (as well as in standard OT constraint interaction).

We refer to a theory that subscribes to (1a-d) as Emergent Optimality Theory (EOT).[4]

This chapter lays out a research paradigm to explore the implications of EOT, with particular attention paid to the notions of inventories (featural and segmental), feature behavior typology, and the role of the interaction of phonetic forces. Given the scope of this short paper, our goal is not to provide detailed motivation for the points made or a detailed model of emergentist OT (see, e.g., Boersma 1998, Boersma & Hamann 2007); instead, our goal is to sketch an alternative to the heavily nativist assumptions of standard phonological theory, outlining a few of the ways that an emergentist view causes a shift in the way we regard phonological problems.

12.2 Problems in OT

While 'standard OT' provides new insight into the workings of language, we discuss two areas here that call for reconceptualization.

First, standard OT posits that UG simply includes a list of the universal constraints that account for the cross-linguistically recurrent patterns of distribution and alternation. This view posits no synchronic connection between the physical medium through which language is manifested and the substantive aspects of the phonological system: similarities are accidental or due to effects of human genetics that took place in the distant past. EOT explores the hypothesis that recurrent phonological patterns are derivable through a functionally grounded theory of constraint generation that supplements the OT theory of constraint interaction (Hayes 1999, Boersma 1998, etc.).

Second, the so-called 'factorial typology' in OT seeks to provide an explanation not only for legitimate typological differences between languages (i.e., properties of patterns that are repeatedly found in genetically unrelated languages) but also for accidental differences (i.e., idiosyncratic properties that happen to exist only in one language or a group of genetically related languages). For example, while both nasals and plosives undergo place assimilation in English, only nasals undergo place assimilation in Malayalam (Mohanan 1993). Since there are many languages that behave like English

[4]Note that the core of this proposal is (1a), that features are emergent, or the Emergent Features Hypothesis. The remaining points follow if one adopts both this hypothesis and the Optimality Theory hypothesis. The Emergent Features hypothesis is not inherently bound to Optimality Theory.

and many that behave like Malayalam, this is a typological difference. In contrast, that an onset in Malayalam does not allow the palatalized [r^j] after [k] or a velarized [$r^ɣ$] after [g] (though each is allowed as an onset by itself) does not seem to have a parallel in any other language, and is therefore not of typological significance. If OT is understood to account for these patterns using universal constraints, it obscures the distinction between systematic differences and accidental differences, and makes both the theory and individual analyses unnecessarily complicated. If OT is understood to allow language-specific constraints whenever the universal ones fail, then the theory is severely weakened. A third option is that such patterns are simply not accounted for by the grammar, raising the question of why a grammar should account for any patterns at all.

The research program proposed here explores how assumptions (1a-d) of EOT can provide a solution to such problems.

12.3 Defining the Problem

Let us assume that an adult phonological system consists of a reasonably standard OT grammar, but let us assume that features and constraints emerge from experience. Under this view, mechanisms are needed to ensure the development both of appropriate features and of appropriate constraints. In both instances, there are two general types of solutions that can be proposed. At one extreme, we could imagine that the emergent systems are tightly controlled by UG. That is, even though UG might not include actual feature sets and actual constraints, it might include heavy predispositions towards particular types. At the other extreme, UG might contain only very general predispositions; the extreme version of this possibility would be to postulate no language-specific mechanisms at all, with 'UG' subsumed by applying general-purpose learning mechanisms to language.

We would expect the modality of speech perception and production to at least partially determine the nature of the units appropriate for a particular grammar. Spoken language must be auditorily perceived and vocally produced, just as signed language must be visually perceived and manually produced. As noted in work such as Halle (1982), distinctive features are defined by both auditory properties (as they must be perceived) and articulatory properties (as they must be produced).

Consider a macro-view of how a grammar might develop. During the first year of life (Werker & Tees 1984, etc.), infants form perceptually motivated categories, categories that correspond to output segments of the language that they are exposed to. This stage of language acquisition clearly involves categories whose primary characteristics are perceptually defined. As acquisition moves into the production phase, these perceptually motivated categories must be mapped onto articulation – and the mapping of categories onto both perception and articulation is crucial to any adult use of language. Two important points can be made.

First, one challenge facing the language learner who has identified a finite set of segmental categories is how to map those categories to feature combinations. The challenge is somewhat simplified because the average phonological system has a relatively small number of segments (Maddieson 1984). However, it is easy to demonstrate that the mapping is in many (perhaps most) cases underdetermined by the evidence (Archangeli & Pulleyblank 1994, Pulleyblank 2006) since particular segments are realized phonetically and physically in different ways in different languages, and phonological patterns referring to features vary across languages.

Second, this problem is present whether UG includes pre-specified features or not. Consider first the situation if UG contains an inventory of features. In this case, the phonetic segments observed in a language must be mapped onto the hard-wired features (abstracting away from details of phonetic realization in different languages), and segments must be examined to determine which of the pre-existing features are appropriate. The universal set of features is large enough to handle every segment found in any language, even though the learner needs only to figure out mappings for the segments of the target language. Thus, the learner is trying to map a relatively small set of feature combinations into the thousands of possible combinations given the full set of universal features.

The problem may actually be simpler in an emergent approach. The small finite set of segments identified during the first year of life must be classified according to (a) perception, (b) articulation, and (c) phonological patterning. These classifications give rise to the number of features necessary to characterize exactly the segments found in the target language. Thus, the number of such features is highly limited in the emergent approach, determined precisely by those segments identified in the first year of acquisition, cross-classified by whatever patterns are explicitly motivated in observed data.[5]

12.4 Identifying Patterns

Fundamental to the EOT program is the hypothesis that cross-linguistically recurrent phonological patterns result from phonetic or cognitive properties while patterns to specific languages or related groups of languages may have their source in idiosyncratic, unprincipled happenstance. Central to EOT, therefore, is the notion that children acquiring language look for patterns. We

[5]Note the incoherence of the position that the learner's job is to extract the *universal* feature set from the available data, in a model where UG does not contain a list of features, but all features are derived by every learner, since not all languages make use of every feature.

illustrate this with an example where speakers of English establish grammatical regularities in a case without significant perceptual effect, hence without an output that is observable to other speakers.

Mielke et al. (2009) examine the articulation of American English /ɹ/ adjacent to /i,a,o/ and voiceless consonants. These studies show that the class of speakers who use different articulatory gestures for /ɹ/ are quite systematic in which articulation is used in a given context. These contexts are systematic within each speaker but vary across speakers. The across-speaker variation in articulation reflects in part the variability speakers have in their articulation of adjacent sounds, with such contextual factors raising issues of articulatory ease. Compare, for instance, the distribution below: these two speakers are very similar in some contexts, but exactly the opposite from each other in other contexts. Responses are 100% unless marked.

(2)

	kri, θri	krV, θrV	ʃrV	Cri
Subject R08	bunch	retroflex	bunch	bunch
Subject R17	bunch	bunch	retroflex (70%)	bunch

A further striking property of the way individuals articulate /ɹ/ is the remarkable complexity of the patterns. Two of the simpler prevocalic patterns are illustrated in (3), where the distribution of bunched or retroflexed articulation depends on both the quality of the preceding consonant (or lack thereof) and the quality of the following vowel.

(3)

	Subject R19	Subject R01
always bunch	ʃri, tri, θri	all other #rV and #CrV
often bunch	θro	#ro, fro, fra
50-50	—	#ra
often retroflex	ʃro, tro	—
always retroflex	#rV, all other #CrV	—

As Mielke et al. conclude, these data reveal the willingness of the human mind to embrace and use patterns, even when there is no strong acoustic evidence for doing so (cf. Twist et al 2007). Finally, the variety shown here appears to be strongly influenced by the articulation of the sounds near /ɹ/, bolstering support for the view that sound patterns are driven, in part at least, by articulatory considerations.

The data also provide evidence for a further point, namely that the more similar two segments are to each other, the more likely they will be to interact with each other. As demonstrated in Baker et al. (2006), Mielke et al. (2009), in word-initial /stɹ/ clusters the retraction of /s/ to something rather ʃ-like is more common among speakers whose articulations for /s/ and for /ɹ/ are already quite similar to each other. Crosscutting the similarity tendency, however, there is a subset of speakers who retract anyway, despite having very different articulations for /s/ and /ɹ/. In these cases, it appears that the articulatory pressure is not present, yet there is perceptual evidence for learning the allophonic pattern. There are also speakers who do not retract the /s/ in this environment and who have very different articulations for /s/ and /ɹ/: these speakers do not succumb to the perceptual pressure to form an allophonic pattern. These cases present opposite ends of the spectrum under consideration, and can be summarized as follows: Where articulatory pressure is high and perceptual pressure is low, the result is individual systematic patterns for different articulations of /ɹ/ despite imperceptible and/or conflicting cues. Where articulatory pressure is low and perceptual pressure is high, individuals who are strong 'retractors' retract /s/ despite an absence of coarticulatory pressure to do so, while individuals who are nonretractors do not retract /s/ in spite of the perceptual pressure to do so.

It is well-known that perceptual and articulatory pressures may conflict: the ways that such conflicts are resolved lead to the emergence of different patterns of contrast, distribution and alternation in different languages. Fundamental to the emergentist option for phonological grammar is the position that cross-linguistically recurrent phonological patterns of contrast, distribution and alternation are to be explained in terms of phonetics or cognitive properties, not stipulations of phonological substance in UG. It follows that:

> **Typological differences** (i.e. cross-linguistically recurrent patterns of contrast, distribution and alternation) not attributable to shared origins or language contact must be explained in terms of articulatory, perceptual or general cognitive factors.

Idiosyncratic differences between languages in their patterns of contrast, distribution and alternation should be attributed to the accidents of historical changes rather than the forces of articulation and perception.

12.5 The Model

The model of emergence in phonology that is consistent with the proposal in (1a-d) is shown in (4). This is to be taken as a model of the growth of an internal grammar in the mind of a learner. Markedness constraints on phonetic representations define (part of) the patterns of distribution at the phonetic level (see, e.g., Boersma & Hamann 2007). These patterns are governed by the forces of articulation and perception, the typological differences between languages stemming from the differences in their interaction. These forces also govern the emergence of segmental contrasts as well as the classification of these contrasts in terms of phonological features at the lexical level.

The model in (4) lends itself to constraints holding on any one of these levels (markedness) or on the correspondence between two levels (enriched faithfulness). Input-output correspondence constraints define the relation between the phonetic-lexical levels and lexical-underlying levels of representation, while markedness constraints define properties of each level of representation; these issues merit further investigation (see, e.g. Kiparsky, this volume).

(4) Abstract — Underlying representations

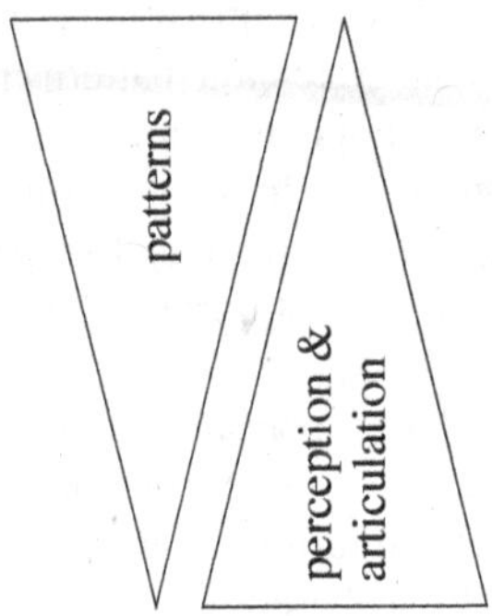

↑

Lexical representations

↑

Phonetic representations

↑

Concrete — Speech signal (data)

While SPE phonology takes alternation as primary and distribution as derivative, standard OT takes distribution as primary and alternation as derivative. One consequence is that OT restricts input-output constraints to faithfulness constraints that express only the relation of identity. Rather than taking either alternation or distribution as primary, EOT views the relative responsibilities of distribution (level-internal constraints) and alternation (inter-level constraints) open to empirical investigation on a case-by-case basis. That is, in the absence of an architecture built into UG, we expect the grammar selected by a learner to be the one that provides the simplest set of correspondence (input-output) constraints and markedness constraints consistent with observed patterns. This may entail allowing input-output constraints that state correspondences beyond the identity relation.

In the next sections, we answer questions that arise from positing (1a), that UG does not provide an inventory of specific distinctive features.

12.6 Typology

Without inherent features, must we abandon all feature-based cross-linguistic comparison, sacrificing the insights about typology of features, segments, and (feature-based) phonological patterning resulting from the permutation of constraint rankings? For example, the statement that the constraint *[+nasal, –consonantal] holds in English but not French has a meaningful interpretation only if the features referred to in the constraint, [+nasal] and [–consonantal], have valid cross-linguistic meanings spanning both English and French. How is this possible if UG does not contain a universal list of pre-defined features?

What is needed is a cross-linguistically valid currency of distinctive features: such a currency can obtain without reference to a set of features stipulated in UG. To take an analogy, comparison between different species often need to appeal to a cross-species vocabulary such as 'eye', 'hand', and 'leg'. Even though such entities are not identical across species, they share a set of family resemblances that make them homologous in biology, allowing for cross-species comparison. For the legitimization of such cross-species homologies, however, it is not necessary for biological theory to stipulate an inventory of entities with invariant definitions across species. All that is necessary is a theory of evolution and morphogenesis in biology to include the emergence of homologous entities.

Likewise, what is needed in phonology for typological comparison is a theory of feature emergence that expresses the family resemblances of features, connecting the concrete aspects of the articulation and perception of speech to a cross-linguistically shared set of features. If the concepts of [+high] and [–consonantal] in phonology are analogous to the concepts of [+masculine] and 'noun' in syntax and to the concepts of 'eye', 'hand' and 'leg' in biology, then we may say that [+high], [–consonantal], [+masculine] and 'noun' are homologous entities in language structure. Neither [+masculine] nor 'noun' can be universally defined, though these categories do have non-trivial associations with certain meaning clusters. Similarly, even though we may not be able to provide universal definitions for [+high] and [–consonantal] in terms of necessary and sufficient conditions, we expect a theory of features to outline their prototypical associations with articulatory and perceptual properties, as well as the limits of the cross-linguistic variability in their phonetic manifestations.

12.7 Segment Inventories

Without inherent features, why do individual segment inventories exhibit relatively symmetric organization? As Clements (2003) notes, at the gestural level, if languages have voiced and voiceless coronal stops, then if one is dental so will the other be; if one is alveolar, then so will the other be (Clements 2003: 325). With no universal set of features, shouldn't we expect segment inventories to include random sets of segments, rather than relatively symmetric sets?

Clements (2003) argues that economy principles hold of phonetic gestures as well as of distinctive and redundant phonological feature specifications, going on to speculate that '[a]s an abstract cognitively based principle, economy ... may not be unique to spoken language, and a worthwhile programme of research might be to examine its applications in non-spoken language forms and other types of communication systems' (Clements 2003: 331-2). In addition, though Clements treats phonological feature economy as separate from phonetic gestural economy, he notes that the two are complementary: 'feature economy can be seen, in some instances, as a grammaticalisation of gesture-economy effects operating at the more abstract feature level' (Clements 2003: 326).

We hypothesize that the crucial point here is the cognitive requirement for maximizing the use of established categories. That is, we take gestural-economy as prior not only in a historical sense but also in the process of language acquisition. We hypothesize that learners identify phonological categories (see comments in Section 1.3 concerning acquisition in the first year of life) and categorize them according to their phonetic properties. Economy, in this view, drives the establishment of distinctive features, but does so in a way that requires no UG stipulation about those features.

At the phonological level, economy dictates that features active in a particular language tend to be used maximally, subject to constraints on perceptibility and articulation. A voicing contrast on fricatives, for example, is more likely if there is a voicing contrast on stops; laryngealization on sonorants is more likely if there is a distinction between plain stops and ejectives.

A final point to note is that category economy is an expected result within Optimality Theory. If faithfulness to some feature F outranks a prohibition on F (Faith[F] $\gg$ *F), then F will be active in a language's phonology, while the opposite ranking will result in a feature playing no role. Unless constrained by specific feature cooccurrence constraints, if F is active, it will be generally active. For example, if faithfulness to nasality outranks a prohibition on nasal vowels, then the predicted result is that the language will have both oral vowels and a full set of nasalized vowels.

12.8 Inventories of Segment Contrasts

The segment inventory issues do not stop with the systematicity of a single language's inventory. Cross-linguistic generalizations can be drawn about the great similarity among inventories of unrelated languages. Doesn't the absence of a universal set of features lead to much greater cross-linguistic diversity? After all, if features emerge through categorization based on language-specific data, then the set of features are unlimited.

Our response has two parts. First, according to Maddieson (1984), a typical language has about 5 vowels and 20 consonants. Interestingly, even though this is the modal size, it is not the case that systems with 20 consonants systematically exhibit the 20 most common consonants. For example, Maddieson notes that of the 29 languages with 21 consonants in his database, no member of this set of languages contains all 20 of the most frequent consonants. He notes that 'at the modal inventory size for consonants there is no greater tendency for more frequent segments to occur than in the UPSID data file as a whole' (Maddieson 1984:13).

Thus, while there are generalizations that can be drawn, there are also significant differences in the details as specific different inventories are examined. And while inventories of even modal size do not contain a deterministic set of sounds, they tend towards feature economy (Clements 2003), with the necessary features playing a significant classificatory role.

The second point has to do with these features. With some features, it is extremely likely that *all* languages employ some variant of them. For example, a segment produced with an open vocal tract and modal voicing will probably be found in all languages; 'consonantal' interruptions of such a vocal tract configuration will also be universal, typically produced without voicing since closing the vocal tract inhibits vibration of the vocal folds; and so on. Given such segments, classification involving opening/closure, voicing/voicelessness, and so on will be quasi-universal. As inventories become elaborated, however, noncore features will tend to be more variable.

12.9 Variability of Features

The final question that we address is whether there is evidence from linguistic behavior supporting the view that learners create and define features rather than simply aligning their language data with an inherent set of such features. In this section we present four different types of such evidence.

First, as the behavior of features in different languages is examined, it becomes apparent that different languages rely on different sets of features, different active values of the 'same' features, even different features involving the same basic articulator movements. For example, Yoruba and Wolof use tongue root retraction actively where Akan and Fula use tongue root advancement (Archangeli & Pulleyblank 1994); Lango (Archangeli & Pulleyblank 1994) and Turkana (Noske 1996) use both tongue root advancement and tongue root retraction actively; most languages (Maddieson 1984) do not use any independent tongue root type feature at all, making no relevant differentiation of 'high', 'mid' and 'low' (Spanish, Japanese, etc.).

Second, economy may push certain segment classes to be analyzed in one way in one language and in a second way in a second language. In such a case, a feature may develop atypical properties. For example, Dholuo has a stop inventory that contrasts a voiced oral series with a voiceless oral series, and a prenasalized series with a nasal sonorant series:

(5) Dholuo stops

Oral stops	p	t	c	k
	b	d	ɟ	g
Nasal stops	mb	nd	ɲɟ	ŋg
	m	n	ɲ	ŋ

Two types of featural analyses may be contemplated for such segments. On the one hand, we might see the distinction in the oral stops as involving a feature [voiced], while the distinction in the nasal stops is some other feature (there is less agreement about how prenasalized stops should be represented, so we will not commit to what this 'other' feature should be). Considerations of economy, on the other hand, would lead us to a different possibility, one where voiceless oral stops and prenasalized stops share one value of a feature whose opposite value is shared by voiced oral stops and plain nasal stops. The latter solution has been argued for on other grounds in Pulleyblank (2006), with segments like [p, mb] analyzed as fortis and segments like [b, m] analysed as lenis.

In this short sketch of such cases, three points are important. First, principles like economy may lead to different analyses of inventories than would a theory of universal constraints. Second, allowing featural categories to vary from language to language may result in the simplification of individual grammars. Third, since language learning involves mapping of perception onto production, learned/emergent classes are expected by and large to be preferred to the extent that the mappings are transparent (Wilson 2003, 2006; Boersma & Hamann 2007); a UG-based account of features makes no such prediction since innately specified features could or could not have transparent mappings to the articulations found in any given language. On the other hand, an emergent feature approach predicts that the existence of robust phonological patterns in a language could override phonetic transparency, with more 'exotic' features resulting.

An additional type of variability in features is predicted by the emergent approach. Based on an extensive cross-linguistic review of the motivation for natural classes, Mielke (2004, 2005) argues that variability in phonological class behavior mirrors phonetic ambivalence in how a class is defined. For example, plosives are phonetically 'stops' both in terms of their articulation (complete oral closure) and in terms of air-flow (no air-flow); glides, in contrast, are 'continuants' both articulatorily and in terms of air-flow. Unlike such nonambivalent cases, nasals are definitionally intermediate. If the class of stops is defined in terms of oral articulation, then nasals are stops; if stops are defined in terms of air-flow, then nasals are continuants. As shown by Mielke, phonetically ambivalent segment classes such as nasals exhibit variability cross-linguistically in precisely the sort of fashion predicted by a theory envisioning emergent features, hence features that will vary in their definition from language to language.

As a last point, we note that under the Emergent version of OT, featural markedness is (as traditionally understood) defined by tendencies rather than absolutes. For example, a UG theory of featural markedness within OT is usually taken to mean that a single scale of markedness is universal, for example, a scale stipulating that labials are more marked than coronals that are more marked than laryngeals (e.g. Lombardi 2002). Under this view, a default segment could be coronal only if some specific constraint ruled out laryngeals, and a default segment could be labial only if specific constraints ruled out both coronals and laryngeals. Such specific constraints would need to be motivated by some consideration other than general markedness. As shown by Hume & Tserdanelis (2002), however, Sri Lankan Portuguese Creole constitutes a case where labial consonants are the least marked. Such a markedness reversal is predicted to exist in an emergentist framework, though it should be rare for precisely the substantive reasons that motivate the markedness scale in the first place.

12.10 Conclusion

The research proposal sketched here lays out a strategy to account for the fact that phonological principles (such as distinctive features and their behavior) mimic preferences of the human vocal tract and human auditory capabilities. The approach addresses problems inherent to classic Optimality Theory. For example, the OT stipulation that constraints are universal fails to account for the similarities between these constraints and purely phonetic behavior, and the OT effort to account for all differences across languages as typological, rather than to understand some differences as legitimately typological and others as accidental.

The model in (4) above is an attempt to address these issues. The direction of the arrows from the speech signal to the underlying representation is meant to capture the first point: that the constraints and the representations are derived from the data rather than by matching the data to a set of universal elements and constraints. Additionally, because the grammar is built from the speech signal data, patterns without articulatory or perceptual motivation are understood to be idiosyncratic and not requiring a universal explanation. Finally, markedness constraints may be permitted at each of these levels; this may allow for markedness constraints to hold of the input, thereby allowing a notion of lexical contrast that is impossible under a version of OT including Richness of the Base.

Central to this research program is the need to deepen our understanding of how the speech signal is interpreted to result in a phonological system. We have presented two different strategies in approaching this problem. One is phonetic research, delving into the perceptual and articulatory properties of speech sounds, determining mismatches, and understanding what speakers do with those mismatches. The second builds on that phonetic analysis, to develop an abstract hierarchizing of phonetic (articulatory or perceptual) preferences, which can be rewritten as constraints, in order to characterize the patterns observed in a given language.

References

Archangeli, Diana and Douglas Pulleyblank. 1994. *Grounded Phonology*. Cambridge, MA: MIT.

Baker, Adam, Jeff Mielke, and Diana Archangeli. 2006. Top-down and bottom-up influences in English s-retraction. Presented at NWAV 35.

Barnes, Jonathan. 2006. *Strength and Weakness at the Interface*. Berlin: Mouton de Gruyter.

Blevins, Juliette. 2004. *Evolutionary Phonology: The Emergence of Sound Patterns*. Cambridge, MA: Cambridge University Press.

Boersma, Paul. 1998. *Functional Phonology: Formalizing the interactions between articulatory and perceptual drives*. Ph.D. thesis, University of Amsterdam, The Hague. Holland Academic Graphics.

Boersma, Paul and Silke Hamann. 2007. The evolution of auditory contrast. Ms., Universiteit van Amsterdam & Utrecht University.

Chomsky, Noam and Morris Halle. 1968. *The Sound Pattern of English*. New York, NY: Harper & Row.

Clements, George N. 2003. Feature economy in sound systems. *Phonology* 20:287–333.

Flemming, Edward. 1995. *Perceptual Features in Phonology*. Ph.D. thesis, UCLA, Los Angeles, CA.

Halle, Morris. 1982. On distinctive features and their articulatory implementation. *Natural Language & Linguistic Theory* 1:91–105.

Hayes, Bruce. 1999. Phonetically-driven phonology: the role of Optimality Theory and inductive grounding. In M. Darnell, E. Moravcsik, M. Noonan, F. Newmeyer, and K. Wheatly, eds., *Functionalism and Formalism in Linguistics*, pages 243–285. Amsterdam: John Benjamins.

Hayes, Bruce, Robert Kirchner, and Donca Steriade. 2004. *Phonetically Based Phonology*. Cambridge: Cambridge University Press.

Hume, Elizabeth and Keith Johnson. 2001. *The Role of Speech Perception in Phonology*. San Diego: Academic Press.

Hume, Elizabeth and Georgios Tserdanelis. 2002. Labial unmarkedness in Sri Lankan Portuguese Creole. *Phonology* 19:441–458.

Keating, Patricia A. 1990. The window model of coarticulation: Articulatory evidence. In J. Kingston and M. E. Beckman, eds., *Papers in Laboratory Phonology I: Between the Grammar and Physics of Speech*, pages 451–470. Cambridge: Cambridge University Press.

Lombardi, Linda. 2002. Coronal epenthesis and markedness. *Phonology* 19:219–251.

Maddieson, Ian. 1984. *Patterns of Sounds*. Cambridge: Cambridge University Press.

Mielke, Jeff. 2004. *The Emergence of Distinctive Features*. Ph.D. thesis, Ohio State University, Ohio.

Mielke, Jeff. 2005. Ambivalence and ambiguity in laterals and nasals. *Phonology* 22(2):169–203.

Mielke, Jeff, Adam Baker, and Diana Archangeli. 2009. Variability and homogeneity in American English /ɹ/ allophony and /s/ retraction. In C. Fougeron, ed., *Laboratory Phonology 10: Variation, Detail, and Representation*. Berlin/New York: Mouton de Gruyter.

Mohanan, K. P. 1993. Fields of attraction in phonology. In J. Goldsmith, ed., *The Last Phonological Rule: Reflections on Constraints and Derivations*, pages 61–116. Chicago, IL: University of Chicago Press.

Noske, Manuela. 1996. [ATR] harmony in Turkana. *Studies in African Linguistics* 25:61–99.

Prince, Alan and Paul Smolensky. 2004. *Optimality Theory: Constraint Interaction in Generative Grammar*. Malden, MA: Blackwell.

Pulleyblank, Douglas. 1986. *Tone in Lexical Phonology*. Dordrecht: Reidel.

Pulleyblank, Douglas. 2006. Minimizing UG: Constraints upon Constraints. In D. M. D. Baumer and M. Scanlon, eds., *Proceedings of the 25th West Coast Conference on Formal Linguistics*, pages 15–39. Somerville, MA: Cascadilla Proceedings Project. www.lingref.com, document #1430.

Twist, Alina, Adam Baker, Jeff Mielke, and Diana Archangeli. 2007. Are covert /ɹ/ allophones really indistinguishable? In T. Cook and K. Evanini, eds., *Penn Working Papers in Linguistics 13(2)*, pages 207–216. Papers from NWAV 35.

Werker, Janet F. and Richard C. Tees. 1984. Cross-language speech perception: evidence for perceptual reorganization during the first year of life. *Infant Behavior and Development* 7:49–63.

Wilson, Colin. 2003. Experimental investigation of phonological naturalness. In G. Garding and M. Tsujimura, eds., *WCCFL 22 Proceedings*, pages 533–546. Somerville, MA: Cascadilla Press.

Wilson, Colin. 2006. Learning phonology with substantive bias: an experimental and computational study of velar palatalization. *Cognitive Science* 30:945–982.

Part III

Exploration of Interaction in Structural Patterns

13

The Gradience of the Dative Alternation

JOAN BRESNAN AND TATIANA NIKITINA

Natural uses of dative constructions in English reveal that the boundaries between categoricity and gradience are fluid in both lexicon and grammar.[1] In the lexicon, the mapping between semantic classes of dative verbs and alternative syntactic constructions rests on probabilistic biases rather than strict categories. In the grammar of argument type positioning, even the strongest of constraints on ditransitive complements shows variability, while a very weak statistical pattern corresponds to near categorical regularities elsewhere. Both the lexical and the grammatical gradience can be modeled within Stochastic Optimality Theory, and combining them has surprising empirical consequences.

13.1 Lexical Gradience

Many English ditransitive verbs appear in alternative dative PP and dative NP constructions:

(1) "You don't know how difficult it is to find something which will please everybody—especially the men."
"Why not just **give them cheques**?' I asked.
"You can't **give cheques to people**. It would be insulting."[2]

(2) "You **carrying a doughnut to your aunt** again this morning?" J.C. sneered. Shelton nodded and turned his attention to a tiny TV where

[1] We thank our collaborator Anna Cueni, and for many stimulating discussions when we were first formulating the ideas of the present study, K.P. and Tara Mohanan. This work is based in part on research supported by the National Science Foundation under Grant No. BCS-9818077.

[2] Davidse (1996a: 291), from Graham Green (1980) *Doctor Fischer of Geneva or the Bomb Party*. London: The Bodley Head.

Reality Exploration and Discovery: Pattern Interaction in Language and Life.
Linda Uyechi and Lian-Hee Wee (eds.).

"Hawaii Five-O" flickered out into the darkness of the little booth. "Looks like you **carry her some breakfast** every morning."[3]

Examples (1) and (2) involve denial and repetition, which presuppose that *give* and *carry* have the same meaning in both constructions. Here the alternative syntactic constructions are apparently used primarily for a shift of emphasis. Elsewhere, however, different constructions are clearly associated with different semantics. For example, spatial goals normally do not alternate in English, as the contrasting examples in (3) show (Bresnan 1978, cited by Gropen et al. 1989):

(3) I sent a package to the boarder ~ I sent the boarder a package.
I sent a package to the border. ~ *I sent the border a package.

Human recipients usually resist the spatial interpretation—

(4) I sent a book to the library ~ I sent a book there.
I sent a book to you ≁ I sent a book there.

—but PPs can be vague or ambiguous between spatial and dative uses, as in the following attested example from the Switchboard corpus (Godfrey et al. 1992) discussed by Cueni (2004), which could be either a spatial goal or a recipient:

(5) They take everything to the pawn shops and just hock everything.

Semantic approaches to explaining the dative alternation have proposed that alternative dative syntax always expresses alternative meanings, whether constructional (Goldberg 1995, Kay 1996) or lexical (Green 1974, Oehrle 1976, Gropen et al. 1989, Pinker 1989, Levin 1993, Davidse 1996b, Krifka 2001).

Abstracting away from differences in choice of syntactic representation, a central idea in these approaches is that dative verbs or idioms which have possessive semantics as in (i) are uniquely associated with the dative NP syntax [V NP NP], while datives with allative semantics as in (ii) are uniquely associated with the dative PP syntax [V NP [to NP]$_{PP}$]:

(i)	'x causes y to have z'	(possessive)	⇒	NP V NP NP
(ii)	'x causes z to go to/be at y'	(allative)	⇒	NP V NP [to NP]

On these approaches, the dative NP and PP constructions are not alternative expressions of the same meaning, they are expressions of different meanings.

Semantic restrictions on the dative alternation, such as those involving motional transfer, communication, and idioms, respectively illustrated in (6), (7), and (8), have been taken to support these approaches (examples adapted from Pinker 1989:110–111, Levin 1993:46, 114, Krifka 2001).

[3] www.flagpole.com/Issues/12.23.98/shortstory.html

(6) I threw the box to John. ∼ I threw John the box.
I lowered the box to John. ≁ *I lowered John the box.

(7) Ann faxed the news to Beth. ∼ Ann faxed Beth the news.
Ann yelled the news to Beth. ≁ *Ann yelled Beth the news.

(8) The lighting here gives me a headache. ≁ *The lighting here gives a headache to me.

For example in (8), giving someone a headache is causing them to have a headache, not transferring the headache from one location to another. Hence, by virtue of its meaning, it is argued, this idiom occurs only in the possessive dative NP construction (i) and does not alternate. Likewise, in (6) the meaning of *throw* specifies the causing event in the schema (i), while the meaning of *lower* specifies both the causing event and the movement event in schema (ii), since there is a homomorphoric mapping between the two events in lowering actions (Krifka 2001; Pinker 1989). Therefore *lower* and similar verbs cannot have the syntax associated with schema (i) because it omits an essential part of their meaning. With *yell* in (7), there is "a homomorphism between speech production (e.g. the activity of yelling) and the transfer of information," according to Krifka (2001), while with *fax* there is no homomorphism between the causing event and the movement event; only the initial stage of the transfer is specified as with *throw* in (6).

When the same verb appears with both dative NP and dative PP syntax on this account, the meanings of the two constructions differ. Either the verbs *throw, fax*, and the like are lexically polysemous, or polysemy is imposed by the differing constructional contexts they appear in, depending on the specific grammatical assumptions (lexical or constructional) of the approach. For cases where the meanings of the verbs do not obviously differ, such as the examples in (1) and (2) of denial and repetition, Krifka (2001), building on Gropen et al. (1989) and Pinker (1989), proposes for *give* that "every transfer of possession entails an abstract movement event in the dimension of possession spaces."[4] This proposal makes some polysemies empirically indistinguishable from the monosemy hypothesis (Levin and Rappaport Hovav 2002), which asserts that when verbs in the broad semantic classes (i) and (ii) have recipient rather than purely spatial arguments, each can occur with both dative NP and PP syntax, giving rise to alternation. We will see that alternation in this sense occurs with far more verb classes than has been recognized.

[4]The *give a headache* idiom is not affected by this meaning postulate, according to Krifka (2001), because the theme does not just change possession but comes into existence. The latinate verbs (*donate, contribute*, etc.) remain an exception to this generalization for morphophonological reasons.

Case 1: Verbs of imparting of force

"Verbs of instantaneous imparting of force in some manner causing ballistic motion" (Pinker 1989) occur with both dative NP and PP syntax:

(9) Lafleur throws/tosses/flips/slaps/kicks/pokes/flings/blasts him the puck; he shoots, he scores!
(cf. Lafleur throws/tosses/flips/slaps/kicks/pokes/flings/blasts the puck to him; he shoots, he scores!)

In contrast, according to Pinker (1989:110–111) and Krifka (2001) among others, "verbs of continuous imparting of force in some manner causing accompanied motion" occur only in the dative PP construction:

(10) *I carried/pulled/pushed/schlepped/lifted/lowered/hauled John the box.
(cf. I carried/pulled/pushed/schlepped/lifted/lowered/hauled the box to John.)

Yet we find from an examination of documents available on the internet that verbs of continuous imparting of force are linguistically construable as depicting changes of possession, and are in current use. The following examples are a selection of our findings.

(11) VERBS OF CONTINUOUS IMPARTING OF FORCE

Karen spoke with Gretchen about the procedure for registering a complaint, and **hand-carried her a form**, but Gretchen never completed it.

As Player A **pushed him the chips**, all hell broke loose at the table.

Therefore, when he got to purgatory, Buddha **lowered him the silver thread of a spider** as his last chance for salvation.

Nothing like heart burn food. "I have the tums." Nick joked. He **pulled himself a steaming piece of the pie**. "Thanks for being here."

"Well...it started like this..." Shinbo explained while Sumomo **dragged him a can of beer** and opened it for him, "We were having dinner together and..."

Note that the context of the second example is a tournament poker game. Whoever wins the pot receives all of the chips, and the transfer can be achieved simply by pushing the chips across the table to the winner. In the last example, Sumomo is a very small servant robot, small enough to dance on a table, climb up his master's leg and perch on his shoulder. Sumomo serves the beer to the visitor Shinbo by dragging a can to him.

Case 2: Verbs of communication

Another widely repeated contrast occurs among verbs that can be used for describing types of communication (Pinker 1989, Levin 1993, Krifka 2001, among others). "Verbs of instrument of communication" have uses with both dative NP and PP syntax:

(12) Susan cabled/emailed/faxed/phoned/telegraphed/... Rachel the news. (cf. Susan cabled/emailed/faxed/phoned/telegraphed/... the news to Rachel.)

In contrast, manner-of-speaking verbs are marked as ungrammatical with dative NP syntax:

(13) *Susan whispered/yelled/mumbled/barked/muttered... Rachel the news. (cf. Susan whispered/yelled/mumbled/barked/muttered...the news to Rachel.)

Despite the reported ungrammaticality of manner-of-speaking verbs with dative NP syntax, we again find representatives of the starred types of examples in current use:

(14) MANNER-OF-SPEAKING VERBS

Shooting the Urasian a surprised look, she **muttered him a hurried apology** as well before skirting down the hall.

"Hi baby." Wade says as he stretches. You just **mumble him an answer**. You were comfy on that soft leather couch. Besides ...

The shepherd-dogs, guardians of the flocks, **barked him a welcome**, and the sheep bleated and the lambs pattered round him.

I think he was poking fun at the charges that Blackmore has been making that he chronically forgets words — he went over to Jon Lord during 'Smoke' and seemed to be getting Jon to **yell him the words**!!

I still can't forget their mockery and laughter when they heard my question. Finally a kind few (three to be exact) came forward and **whispered me the answer**.

Case 3: *give* NP NP idioms

Idioms have been long and widely cited as showing that the dative NP and dative PP constructions differ semantically. Expressions like *give me a headache* and *give him a punch* cannot be said to describe transfers of possession, either literally or figuratively. Yet these idioms are in fact used with dative PP syntax, as are all of the possibly idiomatic *give* NP NP collocations we found in the Treebank Switchboard corpus (Marcus et al. 1993). The following is a representative selection.

(15) GIVE A HEADACHE TO

From the heads, offal and the accumulation of fishy, slimy matter, a stench or smell is diffused over the ship that would **give a headache to**

the most athletic constitution.

Design? Well, unless you take pride in **giving a headache to your visitors** with a flashing background?

(16) GIVE A PUNCH TO

When the corpse was bloodless, he got up and grinned to Ethan-vampire, oh so happy. "Oh yesssss!" He **gave his old mate**. "Let's find a bar, Ethan." ...

"Well, mate, you asked for it."- And he **gave a punch to the guy** in the middle of his face, splotching ...

All three headed toward Mulan. She dropped kicked the first. Next she **gave a punch to the second man**. He blocked so she grabbed his arm and flipped him. ...

She **gave a punch to the evil reporter that had asked the dumb ass question**.

(17) GIVE A BREAK TO

PUC **gives a break to big users of energy**.

"Why can't we **give a break to the people who organise them** [the matches]?"

Give a break to the overburdened who have no place to rest.

That's been the fairest way I can think of to protect the people who do register, and still **give a break to the people who have contributed to the project**...

They wonder what citizenship means if you **give a break to people who are here illegally**.

(18) GIVE A HARD TIME TO

The silly clowns sometimes **give a hard time to the emperor**.

The Necromancer has a wide area of spells he can use to either stay out of trouble or **give a hard time to his opponents**.

Those who have come before traditionally **give a hard time to those who have just come**.

(19) GIVE GRIEF TO

Still, I took it back today and **gave some grief to the assistant** and came out with a better scanner than I had paid for on Tuesday.

He **gave grief to those taking their time near the rear**, I remember watching him from outside the bus while we stood on the yellow footprints.

For further discussion of idioms in relation to usage data, see Snyder (2001), Davidse (1998), and especially Levin and Rappaport Hovav (2002).

Case 4: Verbs of prevention of possession

Even the verbs *cost* and *deny*, which are widely described as occurring only with dative NP syntax, we found to alternate. Contrast (20) (Krifka 2001, among many others) with (21) and (22):

(20) The car cost Beth $5000. ↛ *The car cost $5000 to Beth.
Ann denied Beth the ice cream. ↛ *Ann denied the ice cream to Beth.

(21) COST ... TO

The IRS is unionized, and the union apparently has the fear that outsourcing will **cost jobs to their members**.

Any reduced rate, however, will still **cost jobs to Californians in the teleservices profession**, drive up costs, increase inefficiency, and place an undue restraint on technology.

He did so thinking it would **cost nothing to the government**.

(22) DENY ... TO

Most grievances will involve only a dispute between the griever and the employer. The employer has underpaid, or disciplined, or **denied a leave to a teacher**; resolution of the grievance does not impact directly on others.

definition of 'abnegate'. *The American Heritage Dictionary of the English Language*, 4th Edition: 1. To give up (rights or a claim, for example); renounce. 2. **To deny (something) to oneself**: The minister abnegated the luxuries of life.

After all, who could **deny something to someone** so dedicated to the causes of international friendship and collaboration?

We observe that the meanings of *give a headache, give a punch, give a break, give a hard time*, and *give grief* do not appear to vary across the dative NP and dative PP contexts. Likewise, the verbs of deprivation of possession *cost* and *deny* mean the same in the dative PP constructions. The verbs of continuous imparting of force *drag, carry, push, pull*, and *lower* still specify the same distinguishing manners of motion in the dative NP contexts cited as they do in the dative PP context. Likewise, the manner-of-speaking verbs *mutter, mumble, bark, yell, whisper* continue to specify the same characteristic emissions of sound continuously accompanying the speech acts in the dative NP contexts cited as in the dative PP contexts.

13.2 Sources of Lexical Differences

Although both dative NP and dative PP constructions can be used to express transfers of possession, as we have seen, the fact is that there is a strong skewing of the syntax of alternating dative verbs toward the dative NP construction in conversational English usage. Dative NP constructions are 78.6% of a set of all alternating dative constructions collected from the Switchboard corpus of English telephone conversations by Bresnan et al. (2007). 51% of the total dative dataset are headed by the verb *give*, which favors the dative NP construction 84.6% of the time. If we take *give* to be prototypical of the class of transfer of possession verbs, then dative NP syntax is by far the preferred syntactic expression for this class of verbs.

Transfers of possession may occur in many ways. In a sport like hockey, possession of the puck can take place by means of a number of sudden actions in play, and there is much varied discourse about it. In the world more generally, or at least in present-day American life, if a person accompanies and holds, clings to, or otherwise stays in contact with a possession, it seems to us less likely that a transfer of possession is going on, and in many cases there is probably much less talk about it than about possession of a ball or puck in sports. A transfer of possession between people under normal circumstances is surely more common in situations where walking is a major mode of transportation. The previously given web examples are from present-day English, but many examples of *carry* with dative NP can be found on the web in depictions of life in rural areas, often predating the rise of the automobile.

(23) Pre-automotive uses of ditransitive *carry*

Aurie and Pearl went to Humboldt that afternoon. I went back to Mrs. Kate's to **carry her some mustard salad**.

"This evening she was late starting dinner because her second granddaughter has a cold, and she had to **carry her some pepper sauce** for her cough."

Polly had been sick and Sara wanted to **carry her some food**.

"Go, my dear, and see how thy grandmamma does, for I hear she has been very ill; **carry her a custard and this little pot of butter**." [from *Little Red Riding Hood*]

For the same reasons, *push* is probably less likely to be discussed as a mode of transferring possession than *carry*, with *pull* perhaps less so, and *lower* and *drag* the least. These observations raise the possibility that our grammaticality judgments of the contrasting pairs of examples are being systematically biased by the probability of similar descriptions of the event types depicted by the examples.

In summary, our hypothesis is this. We can use both dative NP and dative PP syntax to express transfers of possession, but the prototypical descriptions of giving are heavily biased toward the dative NP construction. These days transfers of possession are more likely to be described in the discourse of sports where motional verbs of instantaneous imparting of force (*throw, toss, kick, flip, slap, fling, etc.*) are more heavily used than in discourse about dragging, lowering, pushing, pulling, and even carrying. Hence, we are more likely to judge verbs in the *throw* class as acceptable with dative NP syntax than verbs in the *drag* class.

We can pursue a similar line of thinking about the verbs of communication. Both means-of-communication verbs and manner-of-speaking verbs are grammatically possible with alternative dative syntax, yet dative NP syntax seems to be preferred in grammaticality judgments of the former.

Notice that activities of cabling, emailing, faxing, phoning, telegraphing, and the like almost always involve communication—that is transfers of the possession of information. The most frequent verb of communication that occurs in dative constructions is *tell*. Over 95% of all dative uses of *tell* in the Switchboard corpus occur in the dative NP construction.[5]

In contrast to the activities described by means-of-communication verbs, whispering, yelling, mumbling, barking, muttering, and the like are more often, to varying degrees, noncommunicative. When used intransitively and with certain directional phrases, the manner-of-speaking verbs "describe the physical characteristics of a sound" rather than "an intended act of communication by speech" (Zwicky 1971:225,226):

(24) He whispered/yelled/mumbled/barked/muttered (but he wasn't saying anything).
He whispered/yelled/mumbled/barked/muttered at us/in our direction.

In fact, a search of the Treebank Switchboard corpus yields 17 occurrences of the five manner-of-speaking verbs, of which 12 are noncommunicative and 3 are semi-communicative (like "yelling for help", for which an interlocutor need not be present and, hence, the message may not be successfully communicated). Only 2 have complements which denote "the products of a speech act".

Granted that the uses of manner-of-speaking verbs are probably disproportionately describing noncommunicative activities, why should their commu-

[5]This count excludes nonalternating uses such as concealed questions (*I will tell you another plant that is purply*) and occurrences of the fixed expression *I('ll) tell you what*.

nicative uses favor the dative PP over the dative NP? Zwicky (1971:226) observes that the directional *at, toward* phrases that modify manner-of-speaking verbs are in complementary distribution with the *to* PPs.

(25) He whispered/yelled/mumbled/barked/muttered at us/in our direction (*to John).

This fact suggests that these verbs have a variant of the allative type lexical semantics; here the PP denotes the orientation of the actor toward the goal rather than a path of movement. With these verbs the theme argument is usually a noncommunicative sound and less often the product of a speech act. The same PP syntax expresses both situations, with *at* selected for the former and *to* for the latter.

These observations are only suggestive, but they motivate our conjecture that *grammaticality judgments of contrasting pairs of examples may be systematically biased by the probability of similar descriptions of the event types depicted by the examples*.

We reemphasize that it is the probability of the *descriptions* of event types, not the events themselves, that we conjecture to be important in judging grammaticality. We have no idea whether yelling or muttering events are more or less probable than emailing or faxing events, but the proportions of yellings or mutterings that are described as communicative transfers of possession of information are much smaller, we suspect, than the proportions of emailings or faxings.

Thus, for communication verbs our hypothesis can be summarized in this way. We can use both dative NP and dative PP syntax to express communications, viewed as transfers of possession of information, but the prototypical dative verb of communication, *tell*, is heavily biased toward the dative NP construction. Now communication is more likely to be described in discourse about faxing, emailing, and other events involving means of communication than in discourse about whispering, yelling, mumbling, barking, and muttering. Hence, we are more likely to judge verbs in the *mutter* class as unacceptable with dative NP syntax than verbs in the *fax* class simply because there are far fewer instances of mutterings, mumblings, and yellings that are likely to be described as instances of tellings.

Empirical support for the hypothesis that frequencies of *descriptions* of events influence judgments of well-formedness comes from an experiment conducted by Bresnan (2006). Bresnan (2006) asked English speakers to rate various verbs in the dative NP construction in two conditions—either with a pronoun recipient (by far the most frequent usage in spontaneous conversations) or with the recipient headed by a lexical noun (much less frequent). The reportedly non-alternating verbs of motion and communication were rated higher with a pronominal recipient than the theoretically alternating verbs with a lexical noun recipient. Thus the relative probabilities of descriptions of event types in usage appear to influence judgements of the well-formedness of the syntactic construction.

13.3 Grammatical Gradience

As we have seen, the gradience of the dative alternation pervades the lexicon, with the flexible and overlapping mappings of verbs and idioms to syntax. We now show that gradience also characterizes the grammar of datives, in two constraints on argument type positioning.

13.3.1 The *NP PRON constraint

The *NP PRON constraint is widely cited in English linguistics. Personal pronouns, but not demonstrative or indefinite pronouns, are avoided when following lexical NPs if both are objects:

(26)	John gave it to Mary.	*Tom gave an aunt them.	*She gave John it.
	John gave Mary it.	Tom gave them to an aunt.	I gave John that.
			She gave John one.
	(Erteschik-Shir 1979:452)	(Collins 1995:39)	(Kay 1996)

In fact, however, the avoidance of NP Pronoun sequences appears to be gradient and not categorical in English. It is true that the Treebank Switchboard corpus has no examples of ditransitives with the NP Pronoun sequence, but the following examples are representative of those found in active use on the much larger corpus of web documents.

(27) VERB NP PRONOUN

Note: I don't give children peanut butter until they are 3 years old since it is recommended not to **give children it** to avoid possible allergies.

You should never give out your address or phone number online and you should never **send someone them** in the mail either.

Per[c]eptions about God's absence are due to our lack of **showing people him** through our life.

Mega Blast beam: This is kakuri's strongest ki attack only he has what it takes to know how to use it he can **teach people it** but it takes at least 2 years.

Please follow these simple rules and **teach your children them**, however most dogs are friendly.

Second graders finished their underwater scenes and are very proud of these. They could not wait to **show their parents them** and can't wait to bring them home.

Speakers also vary in that some avoid pronouns in second object position even when the primary object is also pronominal:

(28) *...gave her it (Erteschik-Shir 1979: 452)
...gave him it (Hawkins 1994: 312)

13.3.2 A soft effect of person

Bresnan, Dingare, and Manning (2001) found that there is a soft constraint in English aligning first and second persons with the subject argument and third persons with non-subject argument of dyadic verbs, whether active or agentive passives. This constraint matches a 'hard', or near-categorical constraint on the distribution of person in Salish languages like Lummi .

A similar constraint appears in the complements of English dative verbs (active voice). In the full Switchboard corpus, dative NPs of all types (pronominal and nominal) are more frequent than dative PPs of all types: 78.6% ($n = 1859$) of all the dative arguments collected are expressed as dative NPs, and only 21.4% ($n = 505$) as dative PPs. If we split up these dative arguments by person, we find that the distribution of local (first and second) persons is skewed toward dative NPs while the distribution of nonlocal (third) persons is skewed toward dative PPs (Fisher's exact test, p-value $= 1.874e - 14$).[6] See Table 1.

TABLE 1 Person of Recipient by Dative Construction in SWITCHBOARD

	NP		PP		Total	
1ST, 2ND PERSON	688	(91%)	72	(9%)	760	(100%)
3RD PERSON	1171	(73%)	429	(27%)	1600	(100%)
ALL PERSONS	1859		501		2360	

A major problem with interpreting this finding is that person is highly correlated with other properties: for example, pronouns are short, definite, and tend to be given, and local person pronouns are in addition animate and seem nearly always given in conversations. We know that there is an effect of weight (correlated with word-length) on the dative alternation (Thompson 1990, 1995; Hawkins 1994:212–213,311–313; Collins 1995; Wasow 1997,

[6]Here Fisher's exact test measures the strength of the association between person and recipient syntax—specifically, whether the ratio of local- to third-person recipients expressed as NPs differs significantly from the ratio of those expressed as PPs. This statistic is not affected by small cell counts or large imbalances in the table of data (such as the fact that there are many fewer prepositional dative constructions in the dataset than ditransitives). The extremely small p-value indicates that the association is unlikely to be accidental.

2002). Since local person pronouns are all short while nonlocal person NPs are longer on average, the weight or length effect would be in the same direction as the person effect: the shorter would tend to precede the longer. That would bias local-person recipients toward dative NP position adjacent to the verb and away from dative PP position following the often heavier or longer themes. Several regression studies have shown that weight and information status have distinct effects on ordering in alternating dative and possessive constructions in English (Arnold et al. 2000, Wasow 2002, Bresnan et al. 2007, Rosenbach 2005), but none to our knowledge have previously addressed whether the asymmetrical distribution of person observed in Table 1 can be explained by the other properties of weight, pronominality, animacy, givenness, and verbal semantics.

To answer this question we annotated the Treebank Wall Street Journal (WSJ) data from the Bresnan et al. study for person of recipient. We then fit a mixed-effect logistic regression model which added to the combined-corpus model of Bresnan et al. (2007) the factor of 'person' as a fixed effect and retained verb senses as a random effect. We found that there is indeed a small but significant effect of person, shown in Table 2.

TABLE 2 Dative Model Effects (95% Confidence Intervals)

Fixed Effects Odds Ratios for V NP PP Realization

			lower	est.	upper
(Intercept)			1.21	2.40	4.77
RECIPIENT accessibility	=	non-given	3.00	4.31	6.18
THEME accessibility	=	non-given	0.14	0.22	0.35
modality	=	WSJ	1.34	1.90	2.69
RECIPIENT pronominality	=	noun	3.99	6.21	9.67
THEME pronominality	=	noun	0.10	0.15	0.24
length difference (log scale)			0.27	0.31	0.36
RECIPIENT definiteness	=	indefinite	1.49	2.10	2.97
THEME definiteness	=	indefinite	0.20	0.28	0.39
RECIPIENT person	=	non-local	1.19	1.81	2.76
RECIPIENT animacy	=	inanimate	2.71	4.44	7.28

Table 2 shows the estimated parameters of the model and their 95% confidence limits. The fixed effects are those that hold across all of the verb senses. They show, for example, that a non-local person recipient is about 1.8 times more likely to be realized as a dative PP than a local person recipient, after adjusting for the larger effects of animacy and pronominality of the recipient. All of the fixed effects including person of recipient are significant, with the

95% confidence intervals all well-bounded away from 1.

Notice further in the table that the recipient predictor values all have magnitudes greater than 1, thus favoring the V NP PP structure, while the same values for the theme predictors all have magnitudes less than 1, favoring the V NP NP structure. In other words, nominality, non-givenness, indefiniteness, inanimacy, and non-locality of person in the recipient favor the non-Core (PP) realization, compared to the contrasting values of the recipient (pronominality, givenness, definiteness, animacy, and locality of person), which favor the core (NP) realization. (The complementary effects hold for the theme.) This is a pattern of *harmonic alignment*, softly manifested in probabilities (see Bresnan et al. 2007 for a more detailed discussion).

13.3.3 A hard effect of person

We have seen that the boundaries between categoricity and gradience are fluid. We therefore might expect to find languages in which the gradient but broadly motivated person pattern we have discovered in English dative constructions is hardened into categorical rule systems.

Why person in particular would play a large role in the grammar of argument positioning is discussed by Evans (1997:398): "… [I]s only the role important, or does the choice of cast also influence the way an event is portrayed?" As Evans observes, the dative alternation (and the behavior of applicatives) depends not only on the verbal semantics of the roles of possessor or goal, but also on the properties of the cast of referents that fill the roles: animacy, person, information status (Evans 1997). He cites cases where comitative applicative constructions depend on 'cast' properties such as animacy and person.

Several languages show categorical pronominal and person splits in the dative alternation (Haspelmath 2004), but we consider just one here. Kanuri, a Nilo-Saharan language spoken in Nigeria, Niger, and Cameroon, shows a person split across alternative dative structures (Hutchison 1981). In Kanuri with the verb *give* a non-local person recipient can be expressed only in a postpositional phrase, (29a). However, if the recipient is second or first person, it is normally expressed as a direct object prefix on the verb, as in (29b). It appears to be highly dispreferred to drop the third person recipient, (29c).[7]

(29)	(a) *shí-rò* *yíkə́nà*	(b) *nj-íkìn*	(c) ?*yíkə́nà*
	him-to give.PRF	2SG.OBJ-give.IMP	Ø-give.PRF
	'I gave (it) to him'	'I give (it) to you'	'I give (it) to him'

Note that in Kanuri only the single verb meaning *give*, according to Hutchison, shows a dative alternation. All other verbs express all recipients,

[7]All third person recipients found with the verb *give* in Hutchison (1981), Ellison (1937) and Lukas (1937) are marked by the postposition. (All of these examples are also specific.)

whether local or nonlocal persons, by means of postpositional phrases.

13.4 A Stochastic Optimality Theoretic Model

A simple Optimality Theoretic (OT) model of the dative alternation can be based on two conflicting constraint families, a faithfulness constraint family FAITH(REC) requiring that the recipient role of the verb be expressed by a morpholexical form which carries recipient meaning and a constraint family HARMONY penalizing disharmonic combinations of semantic argument type and type of syntactic expression. This model assumes the same input for each candidate set; the choice of syntax is always relative to a given meaning to be expressed. To model variability, we assume stochastic ('noisy') evaluation of constraints ranked on a continuous scale (Boersma 1998, Boersma and Hayes 2001). See Figure 1.

FIGURE 1 Constraint ranking on a continuous scale with stochastic evaluation

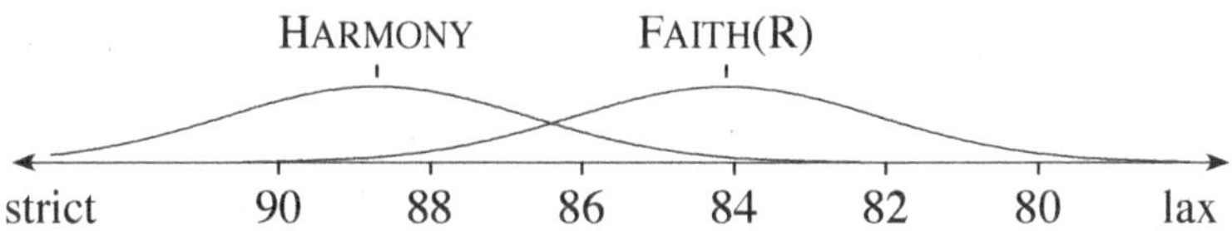

	HARMONY	FAITH(REC)
☞ give them cheques		*
give cheques to them	*!	

	FAITH(REC)	HARMONY
give them cheques	*!	
☞ give cheques to them		*

In OT with stochastic evaluation the variable rankings of HARMONY and FAITH(REC) produced by noisy evaluation will lead to constraint ranking reversals at a frequency which is a function of the distance between the constraints on the continuous ranking scale. Given variable ranking normally distributed around a mean, the closer together the constraints are, the more the ranking reversals, and the more variable the outputs. In this way an OT grammar with stochastic evaluation can generate both categorical and variable outputs. Categorical outputs arise when crucially ranked constraints are distant. As the distance between constraints increases, interactions become vanishingly rare.

Our grammatical constraints on argument type positioning can be modeled by the HARMONY constraint family. We make use of a hierarchy of constraints schematized in Figure 2 which align nominal expression types with Core and Non-Core argument positions (Prince and Smolensky 1993, Aissen 1999, 2003). Prominent argument types are preferentially aligned with core positions, and Non-prominent, with non-core. In the English verb phrase, as illustrated in (30), bare NP complements are Core arguments, while prepositional phrase complements are non-Core.

FIGURE 2 Constraint Hierarchy Schema

*CORE=non-prom,NON-CORE=prom

*CORE=prom,NON-CORE=prom *CORE=non-prom,NON-CORE=non-prom

*CORE=prom,NON-CORE=non-prom

(30) Prominent: give NP NP (Core) Non-Prominent: give NP to NP (Non-Core)

The *NP Pron constraint. Pronouns are more prominent than lexical NPs on the hierarchy of nominal expression types (Silverstein 1976, Aissen 1999, 2003). In Figure 2, therefore, by instantiating "prom" and "non-prom" with "Pron(oun)" and "Noun", respectively, we generate a hierarchy of constraints HARMONY(PRON) that can model the *NP PRON phenomena. Each constraint penalizes a disharmonic alignment of argument-types and positions, with the top of the hierarchy representing the most disharmonic combination and the bottom, the most harmonic.

The FAITH(REC) constraint ensures a faithful expression of the recipient and is violated when the recipient is not expressed in a canonical way (e.g. with a dative preposition). If FAITH(REC) dominates the entire prominence sub-hierarchy, all prominence types of the adpositional constructions will be optimal; conversely, if FAITH(REC) is dominated by the entire sub-hierarchy, no prominence types of adpositional constructions will be optimal. At intermediate points where it can be interleaved in the sub-hierarchy, FAITH(REC) splits possible constructions according to their harmony; for example, only the most disharmonic adpositional constructions are avoided when FAITH(REC) is dominated by the top constraint(s). Thus, the theory of harmonic alignment logically entails an implicational scale of construction types.[8]

(31)

	FAITH(REC)	*CORE=Pron, NON-CORE=Noun
give Mary them	*!	
☞ give them to Mary		*

For example, the bottom constraint in the hierarchy—*CORE=Pron,NON-CORE=Noun—can be ranked so much lower than FAITH(REC) that the result is effectively a categorical absence of variation for [VERB NP PRON] inputs.

The middle constraints on the hierarchy of Figure 2 are mutually unordered. The speaker differences in (28) are captured by the rankings in (32).

(32) FAITH(REC) ≫ *CORE=Pron, NON-CORE=Pron ≫ *CORE=Pron, NON-CORE=Noun
FAITH(REC) , *CORE=Pron, NON-CORE=Pron ≫ *CORE=Pron, NON-CORE=Noun

In the first set of ranked constraints, FAITH(REC) is ranked high enough to suppress noticeable alternation when the recipient is pronominal, accounting for speakers who reject **gave her it*. In the second set, FAITH(REC) and *CORE=Pron, NON-CORE=Pron are ranked closely enough together to create a threshold of alternation through noisy evaluation, which results in allowing instances of double object construction with pronominal recipients, as for those speakers who accept *gave her it*.

Person effects. As for the soft and hard person effects, note that as designators of speech act participants, local (1ST, 2ND) persons are considered more prominent than non-local (3RD persons, and person shows harmonic alignment with Core and Non-Core argument positions (Aissen 1999, 2003; Bresnan, Dingare, and Manning 2001; Dingare 2001). In Figure 2, therefore, by now instantiating "prom" and "non-prom" with "Local" and "Non-Local", respectively, we generate a hierarchy of constraints HARMONY(PERS) that can model the person effects.

The Kanuri person split is straightforwardly captured by the constraint ranking in (33).

(33) *CORE=3,NON-CORE=1,2 ≫ FAITH_{give}(REC) ≫ OTHER HARMONY

[8]Equivalently, we can model the harmonic alignment by providing an implicational semantics to the constraints rather than using a fixed hierarchical order, for example, by designing the constraint violations to have a subset relation. Both formulations must make equivalent stipulations of what constitutes the 'top' of the prominence hierarchy, either through constraint ordering relations or by constraint definition.

/give it to him/	*CORE=3,NON-CORE=1,2	FAITH(REC)	OTHER HARMONY
☞ him-to (it) give			*
(it) him-give		*!	

/give it to you/	*CORE=3,NON-CORE=1,2	FAITH(REC)	OTHER HARMONY
you-to (it) give	*!		*
☞ (it) you-give		*	

In Kanuri *CORE=3, NON-CORE=1,2 is ranked above FAITH$_{give}$(REC), and so if the input is 'I give it to you', the candidate with the recipient expressed in a postpositional phrase is excluded by highly ranked *CORE=3, NON-CORE=1,2. All other harmony constraints on person (*CORE=3, NON-CORE=1,2, *CORE=3, NON-CORE=3, *CORE=1,2, NON-CORE=3) are ranked far below the opposing constraint FAITH$_{give}$(REC). If the input is 'I give it to him' (the recipient is non-local person), the variant with postpositional expression of the Recipient (satisfying FAITH$_{give}$(REC)) wins.

Lexical variation and gradience. We can easily incorporate lexical variation into our model by distinguishing FAITH(REC) for smaller lexical and constructional semantic classes, as already shown in (33).[9] Then the greater resistance to alternation of some dative verbs will correspond to their more faithful observance of the constraint to mark a Recipient role. Thus a model of the Kanuri constraint system is shown in (34).

(34) FAITH$_{other}$(REC) $\gg$ *CORE=3,NON-CORE=1,2 $\gg$ FAITH$_{give}$(REC)) $\gg$ OTHER HARMONY

The Kanuri constraint system for the dative alternation resembles that of English, but the Kanuri constraints will be spread sufficiently far apart on the continuous scale to produce a (near-)categorical person split.

13.5 Consequences

If frequency differences among semantic classes of verbs in English are modeled in the same way as the lexical variation in Kanuri (namely, by lexical specializations of FAITH(REC)), then an interesting prediction is derived from the model: *the more highly biased a verb is toward the dative NP construction, the more driven by harmonic alignment it should be*. We illustrate this prediction with reference to the English verb *give*.

The verb *give* is often taken to be the prototypical dative verb; it is the highest-frequency dative verb in the Treebank Switchboard corpus, constituting 53% of all alternating dative verbs. Yet it does not have the same distribution of syntactic argument types as the pool of other dative verbs. Many uses of *give* are abstract, as in the attested examples *Um, but still, it gives **it** some*

[9] This idea was suggested to us by Stemberger's (2001) work.

*variety; but I'm going to give **it** thumbs down; you know, give **it** a great deal of thought; and you can add hamburger if you want to give **it** a little more body.* To test our prediction, we should confine ourselves to semantically comparable cases of concrete event descriptions of transfer of possession.

Table 3 counts the realized constructions of dative verbs describing transfers of possession with animate recipients and concrete theme arguments in the full Switchboard corpus (Godfrey et al. 1992). It shows that *give* is more biased toward the ditransitive NP NP construction than the general pool of dative verbs (binomial test $x = 164, n = 233, p = 0.59, p\text{-value} = 0.0003$).

TABLE 3 Construction Type for 'Concrete' Transfers, *give* vs. All Dative Verbs

	give		All Dative Verbs	
NP NP	164	(70%)	304	(59%)
NP PP	69	(30%)	213	(41%)
Total	233	(100%)	517	(100%)

Analyzing the proportions of human and pronominal recipients of transfer of concrete possession uses of dative verbs, we show in Table 4 that person is harmonically aligned more strongly for *give* than for the dative verbs in general, as predicted by our model, (proportion test, $\chi^2_2 = 7.1036$, p-value $=$ 0.02867). Thus *give* has a stronger preference for local-person recipients than the set of all dative verbs. This difference, though small, is still statistically significant and is in the direction implied by the model.

TABLE 4 Animate Pron. Recipients in 'Concrete' Transfers, *give* vs. All Dative Verbs

	give		All Dative Verbs	
1ST, 2ND person	92	(39%)	187	(36%)
3RD person personal pronoun	90	(39%)	187	(36%)
3RD person not personal pronoun	51	(22%)	143	(28%)
Total	233	(100%)	517	(100%)

The combined model of lexical and grammatical gradience has a further very interesting consequence: *the more highly biased a verb is toward the dative PP construction, the less driven by harmonic alignment it should be.* PP-biased dative verbs will show at most *partial* alignment effects, so that they will alternate (if at all) only with those dative NP configurations that avoid the most disharmonic PP constructions in Figure 2.

In our model, PP-biased verbs are represented by lexically specialized FAITH(REC) constraints which must dominate the constraint hierarchies of

Figure 2 to avoid alternation with the dative NP construction. But variation – modeled by noisy constraint ranking reversals – occurs at a frequency which is a function of the distance between the constraints on the continuous ranking scale. Hence reranking a dominating FAITH(REC) constraint, if it occurs, will occur most often at the top of the constraint hierarchy. For example, the first and second constraints in (35) will rerank more than the first and third.

(35) FAITH_{drag}(REC) ≫ *CORE=Noun, NON-CORE=Pron ≫ *CORE=Noun, NON-CORE=Noun

In this way the model explains contrasts like those in (36) and (37) (Bresnan et al. 2007, Bresnan 2006).

(36) He dragged him a can of beer. *vs*. ??He dragged a guest a can of beer.

(37) Karen hand-carried him a form. *vs*. ??Karen hand-carried a man a form.

This hitherto unexplained phenomenon is well illustrated by the verbs sampled from usage in Sections 1 and 2.

In conclusion, by incorporating both lexical and grammatical variation into the same stochastic model, we have shown how it is possible to model the fluid boundaries between categoricity and gradience in dative constructions and to derive new quantitative predictions of the relation of verb bias to argument harmony.[10]

An Anecdote

Mohanan is very fierce in argument, but for him it is a form of play. We have argued so often with Mohanan that in the end we gave up all pretense of argument and simply played. We drank beer with lime. We went jogging in the park before the sun rose in Singapore. We drove around strange places at night looking for strange cloth with our eyes rolling in our head and our head rolling on our neck. 'We' excludes the second author, who wishes she had been there, we think.

References

Aissen, Judith. 1999. Markedness and subject choice in optimality theory. *Natural Language & Linguistic Theory* 17:673Ũ–711.

Aissen, Judith. 2003. Differential object marking: Iconicity vs. economy. *Natural Language & Linguistic Theory* 21:435–483.

[10]We note that the stochastic OT model used in the present study belongs to a family of new probabilistic approaches that permit unifying explanations of categorial and gradient effects in syntax. Other promising models include partially ordered constraint ranking (Anttila and Fong 2004, Fong and Anttila, this volume), the wide range of probabilistic models discussed in Bod, Hay, and Jannedy (eds) (2003), Manning (2003), and the pioneering cumulative stochastic model of OT of Mohanan and Mohanan (2003).

Anttila, Arto and Vivienne Fong. 2004. Variation, ambiguity, and noun classes in English. *Lingua* 9–10:1253Ű–1290.

Arnold, Jennifer, Thomas Wasow, Anthony Losongco, and Ryan Ginstrom. 2000. Heaviness vs. newness: The effects of complexity and information structure on constituent ordering. *Language* 76:28–55.

Bod, Rens, Jennifer Hay, and Stefanie Jannedy. 2003. *Probabilistic Linguistics*. Cambridge, MA: MIT.

Boersma, Paul. 1998. *Functional Phonology: Formalizing the Interactions Between Articulatory and Perceptual Drives*. Ph.D. thesis, University of Amsterdam, Amsterdam. http://www.fon.hum.uva.nl/paul/.

Boersma, Paul and Bruce Hayes. 2001. Empirical tests of the gradual learning algorithm. *Linguistic Inquiry* 32:45–86.

Bresnan, Joan. 1978. A realistic transformational grammar. In M. Halle, J. Bresnan, and G. A. Miller, eds., *Linguistic Theory and Psychological Reality*, pages 1–59. Cambridge, MA: MIT.

Bresnan, Joan. 2007. Is syntactic knowledge probabilistic? Experiments with the English dative alternation. In S. Featherston and W. Sternefeld, eds., *Roots: Linguistics in Search of its Evidential Base (Studies in Generative Grammar)*. Berlin: Mouton de Gruyter.

Bresnan, Joan, Anna Cueni, Tatiana Nikitina, and Harald Baayen. 2007. Predicting the dative alternation. In G. Boume, I. Kraemer, and J. Zwarts, eds., *Cognitive Foundations of Interpretation*, pages 69–94. Amsterdam: Royal Netherlands Academy of Science.

Bresnan, Joan, Shipra Dingare, and Christopher D. Manning. 2001. Soft constraints mirror hard constraints: Voice and person in English and Lummi. In *Proceedings of the LFG '01 Conference*. CSLI Publications. on-line.

Collins, Peter. 1995. The indirect object construction in English: An informational approach. *Linguistics* 33:35–49.

Cueni, Anna. 2004. Coding notes. Ms., Stanford University.

Davidse, Kristina. 1996a. Ditransitivity and possession. In R. Hasan, C. Aoran, and D. Butt, eds., *Functional Description: Theory in Practice*, pages 85Ű–144. Amsterdam: John Benjamins.

Davidse, Kristina. 1996b. Functional dimensions of the dative in English. In W. V. Belle and W. V. Langendonck, eds., *The Dative, Volume 1: Descriptive Studies*, pages 289Ű–338. Amsterdam: John Benjamins.

Davidse, Kristina. 1998. Agnates, verb classes, and the meaning of construals. The case of ditransitivity in English. *Leuvense Bijdragen. Leuven Contributions in Linguistics and Philology* 87:281–313.

Dingare, Shipra. 2001. *The Effect of Feature Hierarchies on Frequencies of Passivization in English.* Master's thesis, Stanford University, Stanford. Rutgers Optimality Archive: http://roa.rutgers.edu.

Ellison, Randall E. 1937. *An English-Kanuri Sentence Book.* London: Oxford University Press.

Erteschik-Shir, Nomi. 1979. Discourse constraints on dative movement. In T. Givt'on, ed., *Discourse and Syntax. Syntax and Semantics*, pages 441Ű–467. New York: Academic.

Evans, Nick. 1997. Role or cast? Noun incorporation and complex predicates in Mayali. In A. Alsina, J. Bresnan, and P. Sells, eds., *Complex Predicates*, pages 397Ű–430. Stanford: CSLI Publications.

Godfrey, John J., Edward C. Holliman, and Jane McDaniel. 1992. SWITCHBOARD: Telephone speech corpus for research and development. In *Proceedings of the International Conference on Acoustics, Speech, and Signal Processing (ICASSP)'92*, pages 517Ű–520. San Francisco, CA.

Goldberg, Adele. 1995. *Constructions: A Construction Grammar Approach to Argument Structure*. Chicago, IL: University of Chicago Press.

Green, Georgia. 1974. *Semantics and Syntactic Regularity*. Bloomington, IN: Indiana University Press.

Gropen, Jess, Steven Pinker, Michelle Hollander, Richard Goldberg, and Ronald Wilson. 1989. The learnability and acquisition of the dative alternation. *Language* 65:203Ű–257.

Haspelmath, Martin. 2004. Explaining the ditransitive person-role constraint: A usage-based approach. *Constructions* 2.

Hawkins, Jack. 1994. *A Performance Theory of Order and Constituency*. Cambridge: Cambridge University Press.

Hutchison, John P. 1981. *A Reference Grammar of the Kanuri Language*. Madison, WI: African Studies Program.

Kay, Paul. 2002. An informal sketch of a formal architecture for construction grammar. *Grammars* 5(1):1–19.

Krifka, Manfred. 2001. Lexical representations and the nature of the dative alternation. Handout. University of Amsterdam, November 9, 2001.

Levin, Beth. 1993. *English Verb Classes and Alternations. A Preliminary Investigation*. Cambridge, MA: MIT.

Levin, Beth and Malka Rappaport Hovav. 2002. What alternates in the dative alternation? In *The 2002 Conference on Role and Reference Grammar: New Topics in Functional Linguistics: The Cognitive and Discoursive Dimension of Morphology, Syntax and Semantics*. Universidad de La Rioja, Logrono, Spain. Available on Levin's webpage.

Lukas, Johannes. 1937. *A Study of the Kanuri Language*. London: Oxford University Press.

Manning, Christopher D. 2003. Probabilistic syntax. In R. Bod, J. Hay, and S. Jannedy, eds., *Probabilistic Linguistics*, pages 289Ű–341. Cambridge, MA: MIT.

Marcus, Mitchell, Beatrice Santorini, and May Ann Marcinkiewicz. 1993. Building a large annotated corpus of English: The Penn Treebank. *Computational Linguistics* 19:313–330.

Mohanan, K. P. and Tara Mohanan. 2003. The logical structure of OT constraints. Stanford University Department of Linguistics Colloquium.

Oehrle, Richard T. 1976. *The Grammar of the English Dative Alternation*. Ph.D. thesis, MIT Department of Linguistics, Cambridge, MA.

Pinker, Steven. 1989. *Learnability and Cognition. The Acquisition of Argument Structure*. Cambridge, MA: MIT.

Prince, Alan and Paul Smolensky. 1993. Optimality theory: Constraint interaction in generative grammar. RuCCS Technical Report 2, Rutgers University Center for Cognitive Science, Piscataway, NJ.

Rosenbach, Anette. 2005. Animacy versus weight as determinants of grammatical variation in English. *Language* 81:613–644.

Silverstein, Michael. 1976. Hierarchy of features and ergativity. In R. M. W. Dixon, ed., *Grammatical Categories in Australian Languages*, pages 112–171. Canberra: Australian Institute of Aboriginal Studies. NJ: Humanities Press.

Snyder, Kieran. 2001. What can the pragmatics of the double object construction tell us about their syntax? In *37th Annual Meeting of the Chicago Liguistic Society (CLS)*, pages 565–580.

Stemberger, Joseph. 2001. Overtensing within optimality theory. Rutgers Optimality Archive: http://roa.rutgers.edu.

Thompson, Sandra. 1990. Information flow and dative shift in English discourse. In J. A. Edmondson, F. Crawford, and P. Mühlhäusler, eds., *Development and Diversity, Language Variation Across Space and Time*, pages 239–253. Dallas, TX: Summer Institute of Linguistics.

Thompson, Sandra. 1995. The iconicity of 'dative shift' in English: Considerations from information flow in discourse. In M. E. Landsberg, ed., *Syntactic Iconicity and Linguistic Freezes*, pages 155–175. Berlin: Mouton de Gruyter.

Wasow, Tom. 1997. Remarks on grammatical weight. *Language Variation and Change* 9:81–105.

Wasow, Thomas. 2002. *Postverbal Behavior*. Stanford: CSLI Publications.

Zwicky, Arnold. 1971. In a manner of speaking. *Linguistic Inquiry* 2:223–233.

14

A Comparison of the English and Korean Double Object

EUNJEONG OH AND MARIA LUISA ZUBIZARRETA

14.1 Introduction

This paper examines the so-called Double Object (DO) constructions in English and Korean. Two kinds of DO constructions are under investigation: goal and benefactive DOs. Following the usual convention, a DO whose prepositional dative (henceforth PP) counterpart is headed by *to* is termed a goal DO and a DO whose PP counterpart is headed by *for* is termed a benefactive DO. The two types of DOs are exemplified below.

(1) a. John gave a book to Mary. (Goal PP)
b. John gave Mary a book. (Goal DO)

(2) a. Mary baked a cake for John. (Benefactive PP)
b. Mary baked John a cake. (Benefactive DO)

In this paper we examine two issues. First, we examine the syntactic and semantic properties of English and Korean DO constructions. Through this crosslinguistic comparison, we show that they share certain structural and semantic similarities, but that they also differ in some important respects. Secondly, we provide a more in-depth study of the DO constructions in Korean, which have been less extensively studied than their English counterparts.

A close examination of the DO constructions in the two languages reveals that goal DOs in English and Korean are structurally comparable: Both are 'low applicatives' (in the sense of Pylkkänen (2002)). On the other hand, benefactive DOs in the two languages are structurally distinct. While English benefactive DOs are low applicatives, Korean benefactive DOs are high ap-

Reality Exploration and Discovery: Pattern Interaction in Language and Life.
Linda Uyechi and Lian-Hee Wee (eds.).

plicatives. This syntactic distinction has a semantic correlate. While goal DOs in both languages and benefactive DOs in English encode a (prospective) possession relation, which is claimed to be a property of low applicatives in general, Korean benefactive DOs encode a wider benefactive meaning and are not restricted to the prospective possession relation that characterizes the English benefactive DO. Turning to Korean DO constructions, we first show, on the basis of the low adverb placement and scrambling tests, that the goal argument and benefactive argument occupy different structural positions. Specifically, the beneficiary in the benefactive DOs is structurally higher than the goal argument. The beneficiary is located above *v*P, while the goal argument is located below *v*P. We then take the question of whether the beneficiary is base-generated higher than *v*P, or it is moved into a *v*P external position. We provide evidence in favor of the first position.

14.2 The Syntax and Semantics of Goal and Benefactive DOs in English

As is well-known, English DOs exhibit asymmetric c-command properties with respect to binding and NPI licensing, which suggests that the first DP complement is structurally higher than the second one (cf. Barss and Lasnik 1986, Larson 1998, Aoun and Li 1989, Pesetsky 1995, among others).

(3) a. I showed Mary herself.
b. *I showed herself Mary.

(4) a. I showed no one anything
b. *I showed anyone nothing.

The same c-command asymmetries between the two objects are also attested with benefactive DOs.[1]

(5) a. I got every worker$_i$ his$_i$ paycheck.
b. *I got its$_i$ owner every paycheck$_i$.

(6) a. (?) I bought no one anything.
b. *I bought anyone nothing.

Turning to the semantic properties of English DOs, the DO construction is semantically different from the PP construction in subtle ways (cf. Green 1974, Oehrle 1976, Tremblay 1991, Pesetsky 1995, den Dikken 1995, Harley 1995, 2002, among others).[2]

[1] Note that reflexives are not possible as themes in benefactive DO constructions. Thus, we cannot construct a benefactive counterpart of goal DOs in (3a).

[2] Our discussion of PP constructions here is restricted to the goal PP construction, excluding the benefactive PP construction.

In the DO construction, the first DP complement is understood as the prospective possessor of the second DP complement (i.e. the direct object), where 'possessor of x' is an abstract and very general relation (comparable to the relation entertained by the possessor and its sister NP in nominal phrases); see the implication below in (7a), (8a), and (9a). We will refer to this layer of meaning proper to the DO construction as the Poss meaning or Poss constraint.[3] The PP construction, on the other hand, is interpreted as transfer of the object denoted by the direct object to a physical location denoted by the PP, as shown by the contrast in (10). In other words, the goal argument in the PP construction is uniquely locational.

(7) a. The revolution gave the country a new government.
Cf. The country has a new government.
b. *The revolution gave a new government to the country.

(8) a. The war years gave the journalist a new perspective.
Cf. The journalist has a new perspective.
b. *The war years gave a new perspective to the journalist.

(9) a. The noise gave Mary a headache.
Cf. Mary has a headache.
b. *The noise gave a headache to Mary.

(10) a. *John sent New York a letter.[4]
b. John sent a letter to New York.

There has been much debate in the literature as to whether the relation between the DO and the PP forms is derivational (e.g. Larson 1988, den Dikken 1995) or projectional in nature (e.g. Pesetsky 1995, Pylkkänen 2002, Harley 1995, 2002). We endorse here the general view outlined in den Dikken (1995), in which the prospective possessor relation arises from an extra-layer of verbal structure headed by an abstract (low applicative) V*, generated above the prepositional structure, as shown in (11a). The lowest V (with the P incorporated) moves to V*, forming a complex predicate, and the goal argument moves to the Spec of this complex predicate, as shown in (11b). This com-

[3]Along with the semantic constraint on the DO form, there is a 'morphological' constraint. This constraint states that verbs of Germanic (or native) origin can readily appear in that construction, but not verbs of Latinate origin. Examples violating the morphological constraint are illustrated below. There is no deep grammatical reason why this morphological constraint should hold. It is a remnant of the Germanic origins of the construction (cf. Green 1974, Oehrle 1976, Stowell 1981). The discussion in this paper is restricted to the DO constructions violating the semantic constraint.

(i) Sue built us the house.
(ii) *Sue constructed us the house. (Pinker 1989: 45)

[4]The following pair shows the restriction on DOs is not due to animacy per se: *We gave the house a new roof./*We gave a new roof to the house.*

plex predicate establishes the Poss relation between the DP goal and the DP theme.

(11) a. [Bill [v [[V* [a book [give [P Mary$_i$]]]]]]]
b. [Bill [v [Mary$_i$ [V*-give-P [a book [(give-P) (Mary$_i$)]]]]]]

In the case of A-movement, it is generally the case that the lowest copy in the chain is deleted. This explains the contrasts in (7)-(9) and in (12) below (from Richards 2001).

(12) a. The Count gave Mary the creeps.
b. *The Count gave the creeps to Mary.

Yet, there is some evidence that a prepositional layer of structure does underlie the DO construction. As noted by Richards op.cit. (note 4), when the object of the Preposition is heavy, examples like (12b) become grammatical. See also Bresnan and Nikitina (this volume) for similar examples with varying degree of PP heaviness.

(13) The Count gives the creeps to anyone who talks to him for five minutes.

We analyze such cases as having a structure comparable to (11b), in which the highest copy of the A-chain has been deleted. This option is available only for "heavy" constituents, possibly due to a strong preference for placing such constituents at the end of the sentence.

As for the English benefactive DO, in the absence of evidence to the contrary, it is reasonable to assume that it has essentially the same grammar as the goal DO. Besides the asymmetric c-command relation between the first and second DP complements illustrated in (5) and (6), it also exhibits comparable semantic properties. Indeed, benefactive DOs in English also obey the Poss constraint, as illustrated by the following contrasts from Jackendoff (1990), who attributes them to Jane Grimshaw:

(14) a. Bill poured Mary some coffee.
b. *Bill poured Mary some cement.

(15) a. Bill fixed Mary a sandwich.[5]
b. *Bill fixed Mary the car.

The impossibility of stative verbs (e.g. *hold*) and verbs of consumption or removal (e.g. *steal*) to appear in the benefactive DOs in English also follows from the same constraint; cf. Pylkkänen (2002).[6] Compare these verbs with verbs of creation such as *bake* or *draw*.

[5]Note that the two verbs *fix* in (15) have different meanings, albeit the same phonetic realization. While *fix* in (15a) means *make* and thus, it is a verb of creation, *fix* in (15b) means *repair*.

[6]We have found examples like *I like **me** a clean man; I want to sit home and watch **me** some TV* (from the novel *Big Stone Gap* by A. Trigiani). Note that in all of these examples the

(16) a. *Bill held Mary the bag.
b. *Bill stole Mary the money.

(17) a. Bill baked Mary a cake.
b. Bill drew Mary a picture.

On the other hand, the benefactive PP covers a wider benefactive construal. Since the benefactive PP is not an argument of the low applicative V*, it is not subject to the Poss constraint. Thus, the benefactive PP counterparts of the DOs in (16) are well-formed: *Bill held the bag for Mary. Bill stole the money for Mary.*

Note that the benefactive *for*-PP is not an argument; it is not entailed by the meaning of the lexical verb. Therefore, the benefactive DO form cannot be derived from the benefactive PP form. In the benefactive DO, the dative DP is directly merged with low applicative V*, as shown below. As in (11b), the prospective possession relation between the first and second DPs is established via the complex predicate V*-*bake*.

(18) [Bill *v* [Mary [V*-baked [a cake (baked)]]]]

14.3 The Syntax and Semantics of Goal and Benefactive DOs in Korean

We now turn to DO constructions in Korean, in which the first DP complement is marked Dative (*-eykey*) and the second DP complement is marked Accusative (*-ul*). The Dative DP asymmetrically c-commands the Accusative DP (cf. Lee 1991, 1993, Cho 1994, Ko 2005):

(19) a. John-i Bill-kwa Mary-eykey selo-uy
John-Nom Bill-and Mary-Dat each other-Gen
chinkwu-lul sokayhay-ss-ta.
friend-Acc introduce-Past-Decl
'John introduced Bill and Mary each other's friends.'

b. *John-i selo-uy chinkwu-eykey
John-Nom each other-Gen friend-Dat
Bill-kwa Mary-lul sokayhay-ss-ta.
Bill-and Mary-Acc introduce-Past-Decl
'John introduced each other's friends Bill and Mary.'

---

benefactive argument is a pronoun coreferential with the subject and the direct object is indefinite. The question arises as to whether the pronoun originates within the DP direct object or within the VP. This dialect merits further investigation before we can draw a conclusion as to its theoretical significance.

Given the asymmetric c-command relationship between the two objects, we refer to DAT-ACC construction in Korean, both goal and benefactive, as the Korean DO construction.

Unlike English DOs, Korean DOs lack a PP counterpart. In other words, there is no DO-dative PP alternation in Korean. Therefore, Korean lacks contrasts like the English ones in (9) and (10). Nevertheless, Korean does have forms such as (9a).

(20) khu-n soum-un Mary-eykey twuthong-ul cwu-ess-ta.
big-Rel noise-Top Mary-Dat headache-Acc give-Past-Decl
'The big noise gave Mary a headache.'

Based on this similarity, we will make the reasonable assumption that goal DOs in Korean have a structure comparable to that of benefactive DOs in English; see (18) above.

We next turn to the benefactive DOs in Korean. There is an interesting difference between benefactive DOs in the two languages with respect to verbal morphology. Note that in the Korean benefactive DO construction, the presence of the dative case-marked DP (i.e. the beneficiary) is licensed by the presence of the light verb *cwu-*. This implies that *cwu-* introduces the dative-marked argument.[7] In the absence of the benefactive morpheme *cwu-*, only the PP form headed by the benefactive postposition *–ulwihay* is possible.[8]

(21) a. John-i *Mary-eykey* kheyikh-ul kwu-e*(*cwu*)-ess-ta.
John-Nom Mary-Dat cake-Acc bake-L Ben-Past-Decl
'John baked Mary a cake.'

b. John-i *Mary-lulwihay* kheyikh-ul kwu-e (*cwu*)-ess-ta.
John-Nom Mary-for cake-Acc bake-L Ben-Past-Decl
'John baked a cake for Mary.'

The benefactive DOs in Korean and the benefactive DOs in English differ in other important respects. The Korean benefactive DO and its English counterpart do not have exactly the same meaning. In Korean benefactive DOs, the Dative DP has a general benefactive meaning. Thus, there is no oddity in the benefactive DO sentence given in (22). In this sentence, *Mary* is interpreted as benefiting from the event of "John's baking the cake" (on-behalf-of interpretation), but she is not the intended recipient of the cake. On the other hand, its English DO counterpart cannot be used with the on-behalf-of interpretation. In the case of the English benefactive DO, it is clearly the case

[7] When *cwu-* is used as a lexical verb, it corresponds to the English *give*.

[8] A reviewer reminded us of the following example, which lacks *cwu-* (Maling 2001:433), *Na-nun Tom-eykey cenyuk-ul sa-ss-ta* 'I bought Tom dinner'. This is the only example of that type and it is clearly idiomatic, as shown by the fact that a change in the choice of object gives rise to an ungrammatical example.

that the subject's intention is for the entity denoted by the first object to be the intended recipient of the entity denoted by the second object. In other words, the benefactive DO construction is unambiguously associated with a prospective possessor meaning.

(22) Pappu-n Mary-lulwihay John-i Mary-eykey kheyikh-ul
be busy-Rel Mary-for John-Nom Mary-Dat cake-Acc
kwu-e*(cwu)-ess-ta.
bake-L Ben-Past-Decl
'John baked a cake for the benefit of Mary, who is busy.'

Furthermore, the Korean benefactive DO construction, unlike its English counterpart, is perfectly compatible with stative verbs as well as verbs of consumption and removal.

(23) a. John-i Mary-eykey kapang-ul tul-e *(cwu)-ess-ta.
John-Nom Mary-Dat bag-Acc hold-L Ben-Past-Decl
'John held the bag for Mary.'

b. John-i Mary-eykey ton-ul hwumchi-ess-ta.
John-Nom Mary-Dat money-Acc steal-Past-Decl
'John stole Mary the money.'

Even intransitive verbs can appear in the benefactive construction in Korean, as shown below. Recall that the benefactive construction in English denotes a prospective possession relation between the two objects and as such, it cannot appear in a structure lacking a direct object.

(24) a. John-i Mary-eykey wus-e cwu-ess-ta.
John-Nom Mary-Dat smile-L Ben-Past-Decl
'John smiled for Mary.'

b. John-i Mary-eykey mwuposwu-lo ilhay cwu-ess-ta.
John-Nom Mary-Dat no wage-with work Ben-Past-Decl
'John worked for Mary for free.'

c. John-i Mary-eykey malhay cwu-ess-ta.
John-Nom Mary-Dat speak Ben-Past-Decl
'John spoke for Mary.'

According to Pylkkänen (2002) which identifies two types of applicative heads (i.e. high and low applicatives), the semantic properties discussed above are exactly those of the high applicative construction. The high and low applicatives have distinct semantics. While the low applicatives denote a relation between two individuals entering into a possessive relation with each other, the high applicatives denote a relation between an individual and an event. More concretely, in the Korean benefactive construction illustrated above, the Dative case-marked argument is the benefactor of the event denoted by verbal complement of *cwu-*. As in Korean, the DO construction in

Venda, which is classified as a high applicative is also compatible with stative verbs, (25b), and intransitives, (25a).

(25) a. Ndi-do-shum-el-a musadzi
Ndi-FUT-work-APPL-FV lady
'I will work for the lady.'

b. Nd-o-far-el-a Mukasa khali
1sg-PAST-hold-APPL-FV Mukasa pot
'I held the pot for Mukasa.' (Pylkkänen 2002:25)

Given the resemblance between the DO constructions in Venda and Korean, we assume that the benefactive DO in Korean is a high applicative. We furthermore assume that the light verb *cwu-*, which licenses the Dative case-marked argument, is generated higher than the lexical verb, as shown in (26) (the structure corresponds to the example in (21a)). In the remainder of this section, we will provide supporting evidence for the proposed structure.

(26)

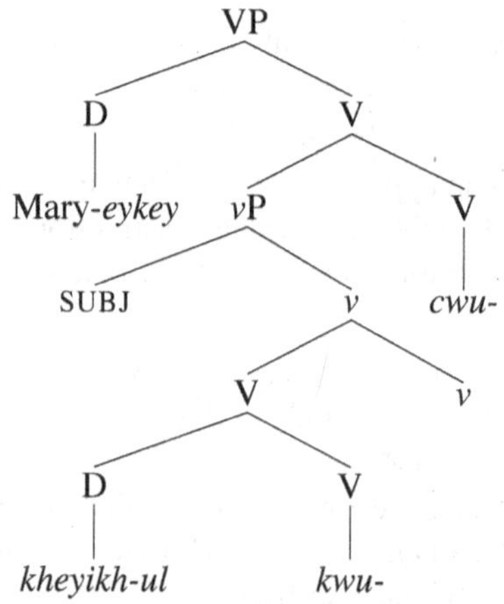

The first piece of evidence can be gleaned from the low adverb placement test. Given the assumption that low adverbs like the manner adverb *ppalli* 'quickly' and the instrumental adverb *phokhu-lo* 'fork-with' demarcates the *v*P boundary (cf. Ko 2005), the relative positioning of these low adverbs in the constructions under discussion reveals the relative structural positions of the dative arguments and, indirectly, of the V that licenses them. Neither the manner nor the instrumental adverbs can precede the *–eykey* marked argument in the benefactive DO; see (27) and (28). On the other hand, they can precede the *–eykey* marked argument in the goal DO construction; see (29) and (30). These contrasts provide evidence that the *–eykey* marked argument in the benefactive DO construction is located above *v*P, while the *–eykey* marked argument in the goal DO construction is located below *v*P. Furthermore, the low adverb placement test indirectly reveals the position of *cwu-*. The co-dependency between the Dative case-marked argument and *cwu-* implies that *cwu-* introduces (or licenses) that argument, which is projected above the *v*P. This fact suggests that *cwu-* is higher in the structure than the *v*P, which in turn suggests that *cwu-* is also higher than the abstract V*.

(27) a.??John-i *ppalli* Mary-eykey kapang-ul tul-e cwu-ess-ta.
John-Nom quickly Mary-Dat bag-Acc hold-L Ben-Past-Decl
b. John-i Mary-eykey *ppalli* kapang-ul tul-e cwu-ess-ta.
c. John-i Mary-eykey kapang-ul *ppalli* tul-e cwu-ess-ta.

(28) a.??John-i *tulaipe-lo* Mary-eykey computer-lul
John-Nom screwdriver-with Mary-Dat computer-Acc
kochi-e cwu-es-ta.
fix-L Ben-Past-Decl
b. John-i Mary-eykey *tulaipe-lo* computer-lul kochi-e cwu-ess-ta.
c. John-i Mary-eykey computer-lul *tulaipe-lo* kochi-e cwu-ess-ta.

(29) a. John-i *ppalli* Mary-eykey steak-lul cwu-ess-ta.
John-Nom quickly Mary-Dat steak-Acc give-Past-Decl
b. John-i Mary-eykey *ppalli* steak-lul cwu-ess-ta.
c. John-i Mary-eykey steak-lul *ppalli* cwu-ess-ta.

(30) a. John-i *phokhu-lo* Mary-eykey steak-lul cwu-ess-ta.
John-Nom fork-with Mary-Dat steak-Acc give-Past-Decl
b. John-i Mary-eykey *phokhu-lo* steak-lul cwu-ess-ta.
c. John-i Mary-eykey steak-lul *phokhu-lo* cwu-ess-ta.

The scrambling test lends further support for the proposed structure of the Korean benefactive DO and concomitantly for the proposal that the Dative case-marked arguments in the goal DO and in the benefactive DO are associated with distinct structural positions in Korean. The results of the scrambling test show that the Dative case-marked argument in the goal DO construction is contained within *v*P, while the Dative case-marked argument in the benefactive DO construction is outside the *v*P. As illustrated by the contrast between (31) and (32), the Accusative-marked object may scramble across the Dative-marked object in the goal DO construction, but not in the benefactive DO construction.

(31) a. John-i Mary-eykey kapang-ul tul-e cwu-ess-ta.
John-Nom Mary-Dat bag-Acc hold-L Ben-Past-Decl
'*John held Mary the bag.'
b.??John-i kapang-ul Mary-eykey tul-e cwu-ess-ta.
John-Nom bag-Acc Mary-Dat hold-L Ben-Past-Decl

(32) a. John-i Mary-eykey steak-lul cwu-ess-ta.
John-Nom Mary-Dat steak-Acc give-Past-Decl
'John gave Mary steak.'

b. John-i steak-lul Mary-eykey cwu-ess-ta.

Interestingly, the benefactive applicatives in Bantu languages, which are classified as a high applicative by Pylkkänen (2002), pattern together with the Korean benefactive DOs with respect to scrambling. This resemblance adds additional support to the high applicative status of the Korean benefactive DO construction. As in Korean, in Bantu the theme argument cannot precede (i.e. scramble over) the benefactive argument in the absence of object agreement. This is illustrated by the examples below.

(33) a. Chitsiru chi-na-gul-ir-a atsikana mphatso
fool SP-Past-buy-APPL-fv girls gift
'The fool bought a gift for the girls.' (Chicheŵa: Marantz 1993)

b. *Chitsiru chi-na-gul-ir-a mphatso atsikana
fool SP-Past-buy-APPL-fv gift girls

(34) a. N-a-i-lyi-i-a m-ka k-elya
Foc-SP-Prs-eat-APPL-fv wife food
'He is eating food for his wife.' (Chaga: Bresnan and Moshi 1993)

b. *N-a-i-lyi-i-a k-elya m-ka
Foc-SP-Prs-eat-APPL-fv food wife

To summarize, in this section we have shown that the goal and benefactives in the English DO constructions, as well as the goal in the Korean DO, are low applicatives (merged in a position located within *v*P), while the benefactive in the Korean DO construction is a high applicative (merged in a position located above *v*P).

An alternative that comes to mind for the Korean benefactive DO is the following. It could be the case that the benefactive dative in Korean (as in English) is generated within *v*P and is then moved to a *v*P external position when *cwu-* is present. We argue against this alternative in the next section.[9]

[9]Given the assumption that a numeral quantifier and its host NP form a constituent (cf. Sportiche 1988), the easiest way to decide between these two positions (i.e. base generation and movement) is to check the positions of the benefactive dative and its associated numeral quantifier in relation to the position of the low adverbs. If it is possible for the numeral quantifier associated with the benefactive dative to surface to the right of the low adverb such as the manner or instrumental adverb, then it may be assumed that the benefactive dative is base-generated below the low adverb which demarcates the *v*P boundary. However, this prediction is not testable since a Dative case-marked object in Korean (whether it be a benefactive or goal argument), cannot license a floating quantifier; see examples below. Thus, in order to establish the base position of the benefactive dative, we have to resort to some other (indirect) test. We investigate this issue through the relative position of the benefactive dative in relation to the base position of the

14.4 The Korean Benefactive Dative: Base-generated or Not?

The interesting point about the structure in (26) is that the Dative case-marked argument in the benefactive DO construction in Korean not only asymmetrically c-commands the Accusative case-marked argument (i.e. the theme), but it also asymmetrically c-commands the base position of the subject. Indeed, if the proposed structure is the correct one, we expect to see an asymmetry between the benefactive dative and the goal dative in terms of their relative structural position in relation to the subject's base position. The weak crossover facts discussed below suggest that the benefactive is merged higher than the subject's base position, while the goal is merged lower than the subject's base position.

As is well-known, when fronting a wh-phrase that is c-commanded by a DP containing a pronoun, the pronoun cannot be interpreted as bound by the wh-phrase (i.e. the so-called weak crossover effect). As shown below, the benefactive dative, but not the goal dative, gives rise to a weak crossover effect.

(35) a. Etten sacang-nim$_i$-kkeyse ku$_i$-uy cikwon-eykey wolkup-ul
which president-Hon-Nom he-Gen worker-Dat paycheck-Acc
ponay-ss-ni?
send-Past-Q?
'Did which president$_i$ send his$_i$ worker a paycheck?'

b.??Etten sacang-nim$_i$-kkeyse ku$_i$-uy cikwon-eykey kapang-ul
which president-Hon-Nom he-Gen worker-Dat bag-Acc
tul-e cwu-ess-ni?
hold-L Ben-Past-Q?
'Did which president$_i$ hold his$_i$ worker a bag?'

The goal-benefactive dative asymmetry in (35) suggests that the benefactive dative asymmetrically c-commands the subject while the goal dative does not. This in turn suggests that the benefactive dative is higher than the subject, which in turn is higher than the goal dative. This leads to the conclusion that the benefactive dative is structurally higher than the goal dative, precisely the conclusion that we have reached independently in the preceding section based on the distribution of low adverbs and the scrambling test.

---

subject and to the position of the goal dative.

(i) John-i sey-myeng-uy chinkwu-tul-eykey senmwul-ul cwu-ess-ta.
John-Nom 3-CL-Gen friend-PL-Dat present-Acc give-Past-Decl
'John gave three friends a present.'

(ii) *John-i chinkwu-tul-eykey sey-myeng senmwul-ul cwu-ess-ta.
John-Nom friend-PL-Dat 3-CL present-Acc give-Past-Decl
'John gave three friends a present.'

Further evidence for the claim that the benefactive dative is directly merged above *v*P comes from the distribution of numeral quantifiers. The benefactive dative may intervene between the subject and the numeral quantifier associated with the subject. On the other hand, when the goal dative splits the subject and its associated numeral quantifier, the resulting sentence is degraded; see the contrast between (36b) and (37b). While the latter is less than perfect, the former is worse. It should be noted that both the benefactive and the goal dative can precede the subject and its associated numeral quantifier; see (36c) and (37c).

(36) a. *Haksayng-tul-i* *sey-myeng* Mary-eykey senmwul-ul
student-PL-Nom 3-CL Mary-Dat present-Acc
cwu-ess-ta.
give-Past-Decl
'Three students gave Mary a present.'

b. ??*Haksayng-tul-i* Mary-eykey *sey-myeng* senmwul-ul
student-PL-Nom Mary-Dat 3-CL present-Acc
cwu-ess-ta.
give-Past-Decl

c. Mary-eykey *haksayng-tul-i* *sey-myeng* senmwul-ul
Mary-Dat student-PL-Nom 3-CL present-Acc
cwu-ess-ta.
give-Past-Decl

(37) a. *Haksayng-tul-i* *sey-myeng* Mary-eykey kulim-ul kuli-e
student-PL-Nom 3-CL Mary-Dat drawing-Acc draw-L
cwu-ess-ta.
Ben-Past-Decl
'Three students drew Mary a drawing.'

b. ?*Haksayng-tul-i* Mary-eykey *sey-myeng* kulim-ul kuli-e
student-PL-Nom Mary-Dat 3-CL drawing-Acc draw-L
cwu-ess-ta.
Ben-Past-Decl

c. Mary-eykey *haksayng-tul-i* *sey-myeng* kulim-ul kuli-e
Mary-Dat student-PL-Nom 3-CL drawing-Acc draw-L
cwu-ess-ta.
Ben-Past-Decl

How can we account for the above goal-benefactive dative asymmetry? The asymmetry can be attributed to the *Cyclic Linearization Principle* (CLP) put forth by Fox and Pesetsky (2005) and Ko (2005). According to the CLP, the relative ordering contained in a spell-out domain is established through a spell-out operation at each cycle (namely, *v*P and CP). The linear ordering established at the end of each spell-out domain cannot be erased and must be preserved at PF. As such, an ordering information in a lower spell-out domain should be consistent with a new one computed in a higher spell-out domain in order to avoid an ordering contradiction at PF. Consider the case of a subject and its numeral quantifier (NumQ) in Korean. These originate in Spec of v and they are linearized with respect to other elements contained within *v*P (such as the goal argument) at the *v*P cycle. Within that cycle, the subject and its NumQ is recorded as preceding the goal argument. Consequently, subsequent scrambling (at higher cycles) cannot contradict that order. This explains the ungrammaticality of (36b). On the other hand, a *v*P-external element (such as the benefactive argument) does not get linearized with the subject and its NumQ until the CP cycle. Therefore, scrambling of the subject across the benefactive argument (with NumQ stranding) at the CP cycle (prior to spell-out) can occur without giving rise to a linearization contradiction at PF. This explains the wellformedness of (37b). Thus, if we assume the CLP, we can account for the above asymmetry provided that the goal dative originates within *v*P while the benefactive dative originates above *v*P.

14.5 Conclusion

In this paper, we have examined the structural and semantic properties of English and Korean DO constructions. We have argued that the goal and benefactive argument in the English DO are contained within the same verbal projection in which the subject is generated (namely, *v*P) and that this is also the case for the goal argument in the Korean goal DO. On the other hand, we have argued that the benefactive argument in the Korean benefactive DO is generated outside the *v*P, namely in the Spec of the high applicative verb *cwu* . These results have important implications. If the arguments of the lexical verb are contained within the lowest verbal projection, the results suggest that while the goal is directly selected by the lexical verb, the benefactive is not (see Jackendoff (1990) for the same conclusion). Furthermore, the fact that the benefactive can either be generated higher than the subject (as in Korean) or lower than the subject (as in English) suggests, mutatis mutandis, that the subject is not directly selected by the verb either (as argued by Marantz (1984) and Kratzer (1999)).

Dedication

Maria Luisa dedicates this article to Mohanan in fond memory of their graduate years together and the many fruitful discussions on metrical theory and vowel harmony.

References

Aoun, Joseph and Audrey Li. 1989. Scope and constituency. *Linguistic Inquiry* 20:141–172.

Barss, Andrew and Howard Lasnik. 1986. A note on anaphora and double objects. *Linguistic Inquiry* 17:347–354.

Bresnan, Joan and Lioba Moshi. 1993. Object asymmetries in comparative Bantu syntax. In S. A. Mchombo, ed., *Theoretical Aspects of Bantu Grammar*, pages 50–93. Stanford, CA: CSLI Publications.

Cho, Jai-Hyoung. 1994. *Scrambling: Crossover, Reconstruction and Binding Theory*. Ph.D. thesis, University of Connecticut.

den Dikken, Marcel. 1995. *Particles: On the Syntax of Verb-Particle, Triadic, and Causative Constructions*. Oxford: Oxford University Press.

Fox, Danny and David Pesetsky. 2005. Cyclic linearization of syntactic structure. *Theoretical Linguistics: Object Shift* 31(1–2):1–46.

Green, Georgia M. 1974. *Semantics and Syntactic Regularity*. Bloomington: Indiana University Press.

Harley, Heidi. 1995. *Subjects, Events, and Licensing*. Ph.D. thesis, MIT.

Harley, Heidi. 2002. Possession and the double object construction. In *Linguistic Variation Yearbook 2*, pages 29–68. John Benjamins Publishing Company.

Jackendoff, Ray. 1990. *Semantic Structures*. Cambridge, MA: MIT Press.

Ko, Heejeong. 2005. *Syntactic Edges and Linearization*. Ph.D. thesis, MIT.

Kratzer, Angelika. 1999. Severing the external argument from its verb. In J. Rooryck and L. Zaring, eds., *Phrase Structure and the Lexicon*, pages 109–137. Dordrecht: Kluwer.

Larson, Richard K. 1988. On the double object construction. *Linguistic Inquiry* 19(3):335–391.

Lee, Young-Shik. 1991. Scrambling and pronoun binding. In S. K. et al., ed., *Harvard Studies in Korean Linguistics IV*, pages 329–338. Cambridge, MA: Harvard University.

Lee, Young-Sook. 1993. *Scrambling as Case-Driven Obligatory Movement*. Ph.D. thesis, University of Pennsylvania.

Maling, Joan. 2001. Dative: The heterogeneity of the mapping among morphological case, grammatical functions, and thematic roles. *Lingua* 111:419–464.

Marantz, Alec. 1984. *On the Nature of Grammatical Relations*. Cambridge, MA: MIT Press.

Marantz, Alec. 1993. Implications of asymmetries in double object construction. In S. Mchombo, ed., *Theoretical Aspect of Bantu Grammar*, pages 113–150. Stanford, CA: CSLI Publications

Oehrle, Richard T. 1976. *The Grammatical Status of the English Dative Alternation*. Ph.D. thesis, MIT.

Pesetsky, David. 1995. *Zero Syntax: Experiencers and Cascades*. Cambridge, MA: MIT Press.

Pinker, Steven. 1989. *Learnability and Cognition: The Acquisition of Argument Structure*. Cambridge, MA: MIT Press.

Pylkkänen, Liina. 2002. *Introducing Arguments*. Ph.D. thesis, MIT.

Richards, Norvin. 2001. An idiomatic argument for lexical decomposition. *Linguistic Inquiry* 32:183–192.

Sportiche, Dominique. 1988. A theory of floating quantifiers and its corollaries for constituent structure. *Linguistic Inquiry* 19:425–450.

Stowell, Timothy A. 1981. *Origins of Phrase Structure*. Ph.D. thesis, MIT.

Tremblay, Mireille. 1991. The syntax of possession. In K. Leffel and D. Bouchard, eds., *Views on Phrase Structure*, pages 57–81. Dordrecht: Kluwer.

15

Headless Relative Clauses and WH-Questions in Singapore Malay

NORHAIDA AMAN, PETER COLE AND GABRIELLA HERMON

15.1 Introduction

There are three types of WH-questions in the Educated Informal Malay (EIM) of Singapore.[1] In addition to WH in situ questions like (1), in which the question word fails to undergo movement, as in Chinese and Japanese,

(1) *Ali (mem)beli apa?*[2]
Ali buy what
'What did Ali buy?'

there are two types of questions in which the question word appears at the beginning of the clause over which it has scope. In (2) the word order of the WH-question is similar to that found in familiar languages like Dutch and English: The question word *apa* 'what' is fronted, and no complementizer follows the question word.

[1]In Singapore, Malaysia and much of the Malay/Indonesian speaking world, the colloquial language of native speakers differs greatly from the standard language. In addition to basilectal, colloquial Malay and the standard language as defined by official language planning bodies, there exists a near standard used by native speakers in contexts in which they view the standard language as being required. In many cases this semi-standard language is quite distant from the demands of the language planners, but this quasi-standard is shared by large numbers of speakers and appears to be surprisingly uniform within a fairly large geographic area. We refer to it as Educated Informal Malay (EIM) and, except where otherwise, it is the variety of Malay described in this paper.

[2]The prefix meN- is omitted for transitive verbs in informal Malay. It is optional in EIM.

Reality Exploration and Discovery: Pattern Interaction in Language and Life.
Linda Uyechi and Lian-Hee Wee (eds.).

(2) *Apa Ali beli?*
what Ali buy
'What did Ali buy?'

(3) *Apa yang Ali beli?*
what that Ali buy
'What did Ali buy?'

In contrast, in (3) the question word also appears in initial position, but in addition the complementizer *yang* 'that' appears immediately after the question word: Both (2) and (3) are well-formed in EIM, and appear to be used in the same grammatical and discourse environments.[3]

There are two potential analyses for (3). According to the first analysis, which we shall refer to as the Matrix Comp Hypothesis (MCH), (2) and (3) are both derived from the same structure:[4]

(4)

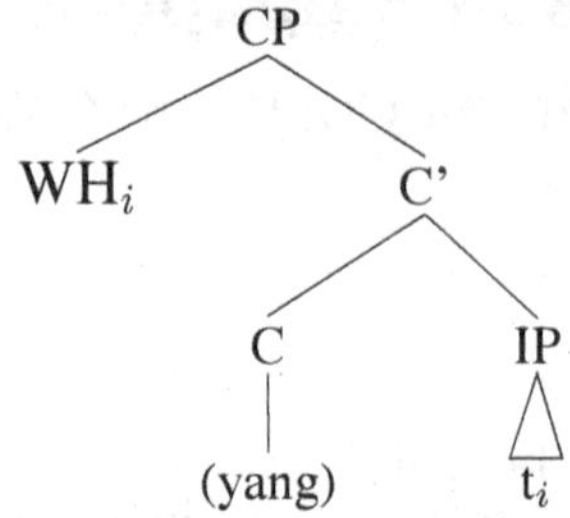

According to the MCH, in both (2) and (3), the question word *apa* has moved from its base generated position within IP to Spec of CP. The only difference between (2) and (3) is that in (2) the complementizer is null while in (3) it is filled by *yang*. Thus, according to the MCH, Malay WH-questions like (3) differ from those found in European languages like Dutch and English only in that Malay permits the comp position in main clauses to be filled while Dutch and English do not.

The second analysis, which we shall refer to as the Headless Relative Clause Hypothesis (HRCH), claims that while (2) does, in fact, have a structure like that of English WH-questions, sentences like (3) have a very different structure. According to the HRCH, questions like (3) are nominal (or null copula) sentences like (5):

(5) *Ali guru.*
Ali teacher
'Ali is a teacher.'

We assume that (5) is comprised of an IP or small clause containing two NPs, possibly related by an abstract verb 'be'. According to the HRCH, (3) consists of two NPs, a headless relative clause [yang Ali beli] 'what Ali bought' and

---

[3]Here EIM differs sharply from formal standard Malay. In formal Malay (2) is considered unacceptable. This, however, is not a fact of which the speakers of EIM that we encountered are aware.

[4]Kader (1976) is the first to consider a variant of the MCH.

apa 'what', which are related in the same way *Ali* and *guru* are related in (5), either as, roughly, (6) or (7).[5]

(6)

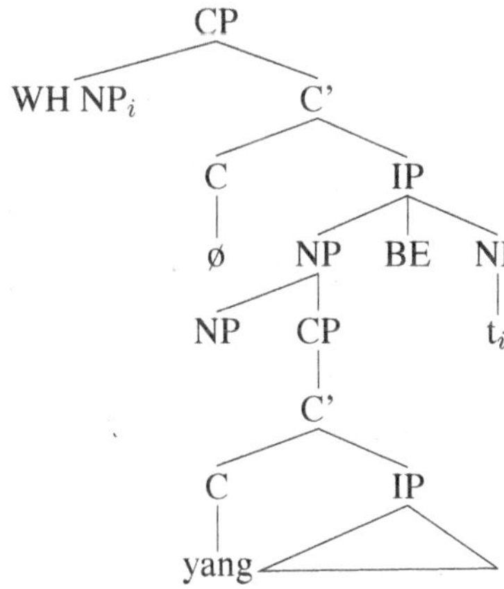

(7)

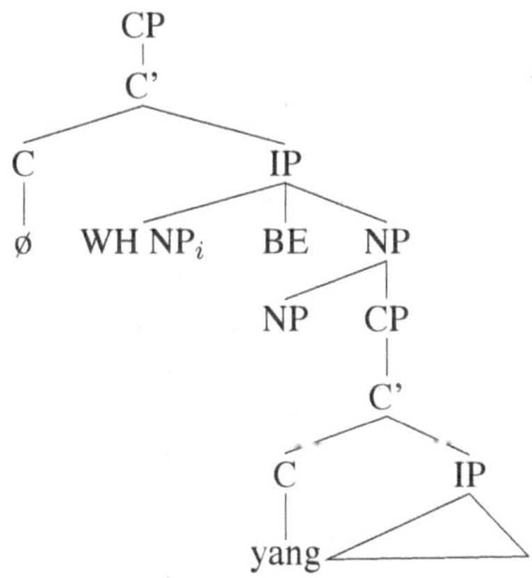

In both (6) and (7) *yang* is a complementizer introducing a headless relative clause rather than the complementizer of the matrix clause. In (6) it is claimed that the WH-word originates in predicate position and is moved to initial position by WH-movement, while in (7) it is claimed that the WH-word originates in subject position and does not undergo WH-movement.[6] In this note we shall abstract over the differences between (6) and (7), and will concentrate on determining whether the correct analysis is that of (4) or that of (6)/(7).

[5]Variants of the HRCH were first suggested by Kader (1976), and were later adopted by Alsagoff (1993) among others.

[6]Structure (6) was proposed by Kader (1976), who, as we noted above, originated the HRCH. Variants on (7) have been proposed by Alsagoff (1992), Cheng (1991) and Martohardjono (1993).

To the best of our knowledge, there has never been a systematic investigation of the arguments distinguishing between the MCH and the HRCH. In the discussion which follows, we shall present arguments that support the HRCH over the MCH. Thus, we argue that the apparent similarity between (2) and (3) is illusory, and that WH-questions employing *yang* have a structure quite different from those without *yang*, and also quite different from WH-questions in Dutch and English.

15.2 Restrictions on the Distribution of *Yang*

Our first argument will be based on restrictions on the distribution of *yang* in questions. For many speakers, questions without *yang* can be formed using the full range of question words:

(8) a. *Apa dibaiki Ali?*
what was.fixed Ali
'What was fixed by Ali?'

b. *Apa kau nak makan?*
what you want eat
'What do you want to eat?'

(9) a. *Siapa nampak kau?*
who see you
'Who saw you?'

b. *Siapa kau nampak?*
who you see
'Who do you see?'

(10) *Di mana kau tinggal?*
at where you stay
'Where do you live?'

(11) *Ke mana kau pergi?*
to where you go
'Where did you go?'

(12) *Bagaimana Ali baiki kereta itu?*
How Ali fix car that
'How did Ali fix that car?'

(13) *Macam mana awak buat itu?*
Kind which you do that
'How did you do that?'

(14) *Kenapa Ali dipecat?*
Why Ali was.fired
'Why is it that Ali was fired?'

Examples (8)-(9) are argument WH-questions (both subject and object questions). Examples (10)-(14) are different types of non-nominal WH-questions. In all questions the fronting of the WH-word without *yang* is well-formed in the colloquial language.

In contrast, when the question is formed with *yang* as in (3), only questions with *apa* and *siapa* are completely well-formed:

(8') a. *Apa yang dibaiki Ali?*
what that was.fixed Ali
'What was fixed by Ali?'

b. *Apa yang kau nak makan?*
what that you want eat
'What do you want to eat?'

(9') a. *Siapa yang nampak kau?*
who that see you
'Who saw you?'

b. *Siapa yang kau nampak?*
who that you see
'Who do you see?'

(10') *??Di mana yang kau tinggal?*
at where that you stay
'Where do you live?'

(11') *??Ke mana yang kau pergi?*
to where that you go
'Where did you go?'

(12') *??Bagaimana yang Ali baiki kereta itu?*
how that Ali fix car that
'How did Ali fix that car?'

(13') *??Macam mana yang awak buat itu?*
Kind which that you do that
'How did you do that?'

(14') *??Kenepa yang Ali dipecat?*
why that Ali was.fired
'Why is it that Ali was fired?'

Examples (8') and (9') show that it is well-formed to extract subjects and direct objects with *yang* present, employing *siapa* 'who' and *apa* 'what'. In contrast to (10)-(14), however, the extraction of non-nominal WH forms with yang is less than fully grammatical. Speakers vary with regard to their absolute judgements regarding (8')-(14'), but there is general agreement that while

(8')-(9') are perfect, (10')-(14') are of diminished grammaticality, ranging from odd for some speakers to ungrammatical for others.[7]

Let us consider the predictions of the MCH and the HRCH regarding (8')-(14'). According to the MCH, it is explicitly claimed that (8') and (9') differ from (10')-(14') only with respect to whether the WH-word is an NP or a non-nominal form (a prepositional phrase or adverb). The analysis, at least without auxiliary stipulations, provides no reason to expect that the grammatical category of the element filling the Spec of CP would affect whether it is grammatical to fill the complementizer position.[8] Thus, the MCH provides no explanation for the differences in well-formedness between (8')-(9') and (10')-(14').

Turning now to the HRCH, according to this analysis, *yang* is not the main clause complementizer but rather the complementizer introducing a headless relative clause. Thus, according to the HRCH, the restrictions on (8')-(14') should follow from the restrictions on which positions can be relativized in headless relative clauses. Speakers who find (10')-(14') ill-formed, should also find sentences like (15)-(19) ill-formed to roughly the same degree. This correlation would not be predicted to hold by the MCH. Examples (15)-(19) show that *yang* relativization of the adjunct positions in question is also ill-formed, as is claimed by the HRCH:[9]

(15) *??Yang aku tinggal (ialah) di K.L.*
that I stay is at K.L.
'The place I live is in K.L.'

(16) *??Yang aku pergi (ialah) ke K.L.*
that I go is to K.L.
'Where I am going is to K.L.'

(17) *??Yang Ali baiki kereta itu (ialah) dengan alatnya.*
that Ali fix car that is with tool-his
'The way that Ali fixed the car is with his tool.'

[7] We leave open the question of whether (8')-(9') may differ in meaning in subtle ways from (8)-(9). Since this question is tangential to the primary question we consider in this paper, we will not discuss it here.

[8] We do not argue that the element in spec of CP can never affect the choice of elements in C. See Rizzi (1996). Rather, we claim that there is nothing in the theory which would predict that a complementizer would be possible with a nominal WH form in spec of CP and not with a non-nominal form in that position. This would have to be stipulated to be the case under the MCH.

[9] The generalization regarding relativization is that *yang* relativization is possible for nominal arguments, and not for adjuncts. While the explanation of this generalization is interesting in its own right, this issue is not related directly to the subject of the present paper. What is important for our argument is which analysis predicts this correlation between questions and relative clauses.

(18) *??Yang Ali baiki kereta itu (ialah) dengan hati-hati.*
that Ali fix car that is with care
'The way that Ali fixed the car is with care.'

(19) *??Yang Ali dipecat (ialah) kerana dia cuai.*
that Ali was.fired is because he careless
'Why Ali was fired is because he was careless.'

The ungrammaticality of (15)-(19) is in sharp contrast to the grammaticality of the argument positions in (20)-(21):

(20) *Yang aku makan nasi goreng (-lah).*[10]
that I eat rice fried focus
'Fried rice is what I am eating.'

(21) *Yang aku nampak Siti (-lah).*
that you see Siti focus
'Siti is who you see.'

The generalization is that NP arguments can be relativized by headless *yang* relative clauses, but adverbial and prepositional phrases like 'location' (15), 'direction' (16), 'instrument' (17), 'manner' (18) and 'reason' (19) cannot.

Turning now to (8')-(14'), according to the HRCH, the sentences of (8')-(9') are based on headless relative clauses like (20)-(21), and, therefore, well-formed. Sentences (10')-(14'), however, are postulated to be based on headless relative clauses like those in (15)-(19), and, hence, are expected to be less than fully grammatical. Thus, the HRCH correctly predicts the ill-formedness of (10')-(14') without the need for additional stipulation.

15.3 Possible Replies to Questions

We will turn now to our second argument, one which is based on the possible replies to WH-questions with and without *yang*. The examples of (22)-(23) show the possible replies to (8)-(9), questions formed without *yang*. Note that in these examples we use the symbol "@" to indicate that the construct is "unsuitable as an answer to this question". In an appropriate context, the sentence is grammatical.

(22) **'What' Question without *yang***

a. *Apa kau nak makan?*
what you want eat
'What do you want to eat?'

[10]A pause is necessary after *makan* 'eat' if *-lah* is used. We introduce *-lah* in order to make the use of the NP NP structure more natural out of context. It is otherwise irrelevant to the discussion.

b. *Aku nak makan ayam buah keluak.*
I want eat chicken fruit keluak
'I want to eat chicken with keluak nuts.'

c. @ *Yang aku nak makan ayam buah keluak.*
that I want eat chicken fruit keluak
'What I want to eat is chicken with keluak nuts.'

(23) **'Who' Question without *yang***

a. *Siapa kau nampak?*
who you see
'Who do you see?'

b. *Aku nampak Fatimah.*
I see Fatimah
'I see Fatimah.'

c. @ *Yang aku nampak Fatimah*
that I see Fatimah
'The one that I see is Fatimah.'

While the appearance of a headless relative clause is infelicitous in replies to questions without *yang*, they are felicitous when *yang* appears in the question.

(24) **'What' Question with *yang***

a. *Apa yang kau nak makan?*
what that you want eat
'What do you want to eat? What is the thing that you want to eat?'

b. *Aku nak makan ayam buah keluak.*
I want eat chicken fruit keluak
'I want to eat chicken with keluak nuts.'

c. *Yang aku nak makan ayam buah keluak.*
that I want eat chicken fruit keluak
'What i want to eat is chicken with keluak nuts.'

(25) **'Who' Question with *yang***

a. *Siapa yang kau nampak?*
who that you see
'Who do you see? Who is the one that you see?'

b. *Aku nampak Fatimah.*
I see Fatimah
'I see Fatimah.'

c. *Yang aku nampak Fatimah*
that I see Fatimah
'The one that I see is Fatimah.'

To summarize, questions with *yang* can receive replies with headless relative clauses, but those without *yang* cannot.

Let us compare the predictions of the HRCH and the MCH regarding (22)-(25). According to the MCH, sentences with and without *yang* have the same structure except for the occurrence or nonoccurrence of an optional morpheme. Thus, it would be expected that answers with and without *yang* should be possible in reply to questions without *yang*, just as in English the absence of a complementizer in a question does not prevent its use in an answer:

(26) a. Who does Mary think Tom saw?
b. She thinks he saw Anne.
c. She thinks that he saw Anne.

Thus, the MCH fails to predict the contextual ill-formedness of the (c) sentences of (22)-(23).

In contrast, the HRCH provides an explanation for the ill-formedness of answers with *yang* in (22)-(23) and their well-formedness in (24)-(25). If questions like those of (24a)-(25a) have the structure [headless relative clause NP], it is unsurprising that headless relative clauses can be used in answers. The infelicity of *yang* in the replies to (22a)-(23a) is also predicted since answers are expected to preserve the overall structure of the question asked. Thus, the HRCH (but not the MCH) provides an explanation for the otherwise inexplicable differences in the sets of possible replies to questions with and without *yang*.[11] (Cf. Tham (this volume) for related ideas.)

15.4 The Distribution of *Yang* and *Bahawa*

We turn now to an argument suggested by the work of Kader (1976, 1980), based on the distribution of the complementizer *yang* versus that of the complementizer *bahawa*. Both *yang* and *bahawa* can be used to introduce complement clauses:

(27) *Ali memberitahu saya tadi yang Fatimah sakit semalam.*
Ali told me just now that Fatimah was sick yesterday
'Ali told me earlier that Fatimah was sick yesterday.'

[11]The question remains why questions employing headless relative clauses can be answered employing a structure that does not employ a headless relative clause. Note, however, that the same pattern is observed in English:

(i) a. Who bought the book?
b. Jon bought it.
c. @Jon is the one who bought it.

(ii) a. Who is the one that bought the book?
b. Jon bought it.
c. Jon is the one who bought it.

(28) *Ali memberitahu saya tadi bahawa Fatimah sakit semalam.*
Ali told me just now that Fatimah was sick yesterday
'Ali told me earlier that Fatimah was sick yesterday.'

Sentences (27) and (28) differ significantly in register, but both are well-formed (in their appropriate registers) and are part of the linguistic repertoire of speakers of EIM. (The use of *yang* to introduce complement clauses is ill-formed in formal Malay, but our informants were not aware of that fact.)

In the case of relative clauses, however, in all registers the modifying clause can be introduced with *yang* but not with *bahawa*:

(29) *perempuan* $\left\{ \begin{array}{c} yang \\ *bahawa \end{array} \right\}$ *telah diberi hadiah*
woman $\left\{ \begin{array}{c} \text{that} \\ \text{that} \end{array} \right\}$ already was given gift
'the woman that was already given a gift'

(30) *buku* $\left\{ \begin{array}{c} yang \\ *bahawa \end{array} \right\}$ *John beli*
book $\left\{ \begin{array}{c} \text{that} \\ \text{that} \end{array} \right\}$ John bought
'the book that John bought'

The same pattern seen in headed relative clauses is found in headless relative clauses:

(31) $\left\{ \begin{array}{c} yang \\ *bahawa \end{array} \right\}$ *Fatimah suka*
$\left\{ \begin{array}{c} \text{that} \\ \text{that} \end{array} \right\}$ Fatimah likes
'what Fatimah likes'

(32) $\left\{ \begin{array}{c} yang \\ *bahawa \end{array} \right\}$ *tinggal di Singapura*
$\left\{ \begin{array}{c} \text{that} \\ \text{that} \end{array} \right\}$ stays in Singapore
'the one that lives in Singapore'

To summarize, either the complementizer *bahawa* or the complementizer *yang* can be used to introduce complement clauses, but only *yang* can be used to introduce relative clauses, both headed and headless.

Let us turn now to the predictions regarding choice of complementizer made by the two hypotheses under consideration. The MCH claims that

Malay lacks the prohibition found in English blocking the presence of complementizers in main clauses. Thus, the MCH predicts that Malay main clauses should show the same range of complementizers found in complement clauses. Specifically, both *yang* and *bahawa* should be possible in questions.

In contrast, the HRCH claims that the complementizer found in *yang* questions is the complementizer introducing a headless relative clause. Since only *yang* and not *bahawa* can be used to introduce a relative clause, the HRCH predicts that only *yang* will be grammatical in forming WH-questions like (3).

The predictions of the HRCH are, in fact, correct. As (33) and (34) show, only *yang* can be used in the formation of WH-questions:

(33) *Siapa* { *yang* / **bahawa* } *kau nampak*

who { that / that } you see

'Who did you see?'

(34) *Semalan apa* { *yang* / **bahawa* } *Ali makan?*

Yesterday what { that / that } Ali eat

'What did Ali eat yesterday?'

Thus, the ungrammaticality of *bahawa* in the formation of WH-questions provides an additional argument in favor of the HRCH over the MCH.

15.5 Conclusions

We have presented three arguments that WH-questions employing overt WH-movement in Educated Informal Malay are derived from two very different structures. Those without the complementizer *yang* are similar to WH-questions in English and other European languages: The WH-word presumably moves successive cyclically to scopal Spec CP. Those with *yang*, however, are derived from a very different structure in which the matrix clause is a null copula sentence, the subject of which is a headless relative clause.

Acknowledgements

The research reported on in this paper was supported in part by the National Science Foundation (SBR-9122267, INT-9423291 and SBR-9729519 and (BCS-0444649)), a grant from the Netherlands Organization for Scientific Research (NWO) to the Utrecht Institute of Linguistics OTS, University of Utrecht and by the Max Plank Institute for Evolutionary Anthropology, Leipzig, Germany. We would like to thank David Gil, Uri Tadmor, Yassir Tjung and Ngee-Thai Yap for all their help with this topic. Thanks are also due to two anonymous reviewers, who made many helpful suggestions.

Our very special thanks, however, are due to K.P. Mohanan for his role in encouraging both this paper and our work on Malay in general. When Peter Cole and Gaby Hermon arrived in Singapore to spend the year of 1992-1993 as visiting professors, we discovered a rich community of linguists, with interests in all the local languages. The Mohanans were very much at the center of this community. The Singapore linguistic community was not a regimented group engaged in decorous discussion. Rather, each of us had a very different stance on every issue. Mohanan took obvious pleasure in the diversity of views and the spirited disagreements. Regardless of his personal beliefs, Mohanan would spend hours in discussion, following each idea to its logical conclusion, expected or not.

Mohanan was especially interested in encouraging research on local languages, ranging from Singlish (Singapore English) to local versions of Chinese dialects to all the many types of Malay spoken in Singapore and in the surrounding region. It was in this vibrant atmosphere that Peter and Gaby began to work on Singapore Malay.

Mohanan also strongly encouraged collaborative research among faculty and Singaporean students. It was only natural that during that time we began our collaboration with Norhaida Aman, now our colleague and co-author. It is, thus, especially appropriate that we dedicate this brief work to our dear friend and colleague, Mohanan.

References

Alsagoff, Lubna S. 1993. *Topic in Malay: The Other Subject*. Ph.D. thesis, Stanford University.

Cheng, Lisa. 1991. *On the Typology of Wh-Questions*. Ph.D. thesis, MIT.

Kader, Mashudi. 1976. *The Syntax of Malay Interrogatives*. Ph.D. thesis, Simon Fraser University.

Martohardjono, Gita. 1993. *Wh-Movement in the Acquisition of a Second Language: A Cross-Linguistics Study of 3 Languages With and Without Overt Movement*. Ph.D. thesis, Cornell University, Ithaca, NY.

Rizzi, Luigi. 1996. Residual verb second and the wh-criterion. In A. Belletti and L. Rizzi, eds., *Parameters and Functional Heads: Essays in Comparative Syntax*, pages 63–90. New York & Oxford: Oxford University Press.

16

Raising in a Unified Theory of Structure-Sharing in LFG

ALEX ALSINA

The goal of this paper is to present an analysis of raising as part of a more general theory of structure-sharing in LFG. Structure-sharing – the assignment of the same f-structure value to two (or more) different grammatical functions – is the way LFG captures the idea that a single constituent satisfies two or more grammatical functions, a phenomenon that is standardly assumed to occur at least in long-distance dependencies (the relation between a clause-initial phrase, such as a topicalized constituent or a wh-phrase, and the grammatical function it satisfies in the clause) and raising constructions. Specifically, the paper aims to derive the properties of raising from general principles eliminating the specifications (in the form of functional equations) in lexical entries that are needed in current LFG theories of raising.

An essential element of this theory is the idea that there are no functional annotations (the device standardly assumed in LFG for formalizing the correspondence between c-structure, or constituent structure, and f-structure, or functional structure, since Bresnan 1982a),[1] but general well-formedness constraints. It is fitting that this paper should be in honor of K.P. Mohanan, who made me aware of the need to dispense with annotations in the mid-nineties and with whom I have had many fruitful discussions about the issue.

The paper is organized as follows: first, I examine the current LFG treatment of raising and point out what appear to be shortcomings of the analysis; next, I outline a theory that accounts for structure-sharing through general

[1] See Dalrymple (this volume) for an example of the formalism standardly used in LFG for annotations.

Reality Exploration and Discovery: Pattern Interaction in Language and Life.
Linda Uyechi and Lian-Hee Wee (eds.).

constraints, minimizing lexical stipulations; finally, I show how this theory provides an account of raising that overcomes the problems noted earlier.

16.1 The Current LFG Treatment of Raising

The foundational work on raising in LFG is Bresnan (1982b) and the treatment proposed in this work has been adopted in practically all subsequent analyses within LFG with few minor adjustments. Recent overviews of LFG, such as Dalrymple (2001) and Falk (2001), show substantial agreement, both with each other and with previous work, regarding the treatment of raising.

It is standard to distinguish between two types of raising constructions depending on whether the controller is a subject, as in (1a), or an object, as in (1b):

(1) a. Freddy seemed to know the answer.
    b. I believed Freddy to know the answer.

In the raising-to-subject construction (1a), the NP *Freddy* maps onto the subject of the matrix clause and onto the subject of the embedded clause *to know the answer*. In the raising-to-object construction (1b), the NP *Freddy* maps onto the object of the matrix clause and onto the subject of the embedded clause. In both cases there is structure-sharing of a grammatical function (GF) of the matrix clause and the subject of the embedded clause: these two grammatical functions have the same f-structure as their value.

The following are some of the features of raising that one should hope to account for with a minimum of stipulations:

(2) a. One of the GFs of the raising verb is nonthematic: the subject of *seem* in (1a) and the object of *believe* in (1b) do not bear a thematic role to these verbs.[2]
    b. The nonthematic GF, and none other, (the subject of *seem* in (1a) and the object of *believe* in (1b)) is structure-shared with a GF of the embedded clause.
    c. The GF of the embedded clause that is involved in structure-sharing is always a subject.[3]
    d. The embedded clause out of which raising takes place is a complement, never a subject. (See ex. (16)–(17).)
    e. The embedded clause out of which raising takes place is an argument of the raising verb, never an adjunct. (See ex. (18).)

[2]Their thematic role, if any, comes from the embedded verb or, in the case of stacking of raising verbs, from a verb embedded in the embedded clause.

[3]Despite claims that there are languages that have raising constructions in which the raised GF is not a subject, the claim that raising can only involve a subject of an embedded clause is generally accepted and allows researchers to use raising as a subjecthood diagnostic: the GF that undergoes raising out of an embedded clause is a subject.

f. The embedded clause out of which raising takes place is a tenseless clause, never a tensed clause. (See ex. (19).)

Let us see how current LFG accounts for these properties of raising. It is fundamentally the lexical entries of raising verbs that carry the crucial information that accounts for these properties. Raising-to-subject verbs like *seem* are assumed to carry the information in (3a) and raising-to-object verbs like *believe* the information in (3b).

(3) a. *seem*: (↑PRED) = 'seem ⟨ (↑ XCOMP) ⟩ (↑ SUBJ)'
(↑ SUBJ) = (↑ XCOMP SUBJ)

b. *believe*: (↑ PRED) = 'believe ⟨ (↑ SUBJ) (↑ XCOMP) ⟩ (↑ OBJ)'
(↑ OBJ) = (↑ XCOMP SUBJ)

The first line of these lexical entries specifies the PRED feature of these verbs, which contains the array of grammatical functions that the verb requires. A distinction is made in this feature between the GFs that belong in the argument structure (or a-structure) of the verb and thus correspond to argument roles of the predicate and bear thematic roles and those that are not part of the a-structure and therefore do not bear thematic roles (i.e., are nonthematic). In (3a), for example, the only thematic GF required by the verb is the XCOMP and the subject is nonthematic. In (3b) the PRED feature of the verb *believe* indicates that it requires a nonthematic object. The second line of these lexical entries contains the control equation, which specifies that a particular GF required by the verb is identified with (has the same value as) a particular GF of the clausal argument of the verb. XCOMP is the name of the grammatical function whose subject is controlled by (i.e., structure-shared with) a GF external to it. Thus, the control equation of (3a) states that the subject of the verb is identified with the subject of its clausal complement, or XCOMP; likewise in (3b) regarding the object of the verb.

Whereas the analysis may appear to be simple enough, all of the properties of (2) are captured through stipulations embedded in the equations or annotations of (3) or of similar lexical entries or through principles (e.g., restricting XCOMP to tenseless clauses) that need to be stated anyway. A satisfactory analysis of raising should derive as many of the observations in (2) as possible from general principles, rather than stipulate them in the lexical entries.[4]

[4]Although general principles or constraints are stipulations, as noted by an anonymous reviewer, in the sense that they are statements of the theory, it is useful to distinguish between stipulations in lexical entries and "stipulations" that are independent of particular lexical entries. A theory that accounts for a certain phenomenon through stipulations in the lexical entry of each item that may be involved in the phenomenon is by far more complex than a theory that accounts for it through constraints (item-independent "stipulations") that apply to any item that may be involved. Furthermore, the former theory does not really explain the phenomenon, since nothing in principle prevents a lexical item from having a stipulation that contradicts what the latter theory stipulates as a general constraint.

16.2 A General Theory of Structure-Sharing

The theory of raising that I will present is part of a more general theory of structure-sharing, a feature common to the analysis of raising and long-distance dependencies. Instead of functional annotations on the c-structure, there are well-formedness conditions on each of the syntactic structures that model linguistic expressions (i.e., c-structure, f-structure, and a-structure) and on the correspondence among the various levels of structure. These well-formedness conditions are ranked in an Optimality Theoretic (OT) style hierarchy so that a given triplet of structures will be considered well-formed if it satisfies the hierarchy of constraints better than all other competing triplets of structure. In this section, I will summarize the main features of the theory developed in greater detail in Alsina (2008).

An important constraint of this theory is F-faithfulness, a faithfulness constraint requiring all features of the f-structure to be introduced by the c-structure, either because the lexical entries of the lexical items present in the c-structure contain the features in question or because the c-to-f-structure mapping constraints introduce the features in question. This will exclude the presence of features in the f-structure that are not licensed by lexical items or by mapping constraints, unless the presence of such features is required to satisfy a constraint that outranks the faithfulness constraint.

Structure-sharing arises simply because the GEN component generates f-structures in which two attributes in the f-structure have the same f-structure as their value, as well as generating f-structures in which no such structure-sharing occurs. On the assumption that all and only GF attributes, such as SUBJ or OBJ, take f-structures as their values, this will give rise to structures in which two different GFs, possibly in the same f-structure, possibly in different f-structures, may have the same value. However, not all conceivable instances in which two GFs have the same value (or are identified) are well-formed. In order to rule out illicit instances of structure-sharing, we need a set of constraints on the well-formedness of structure-sharing.

We can observe that the constructions standardly assumed in LFG to involve structure-sharing[5] have several properties in common. In the first place, all of these constructions involve a nonthematic function that is identified with a possibly thematic function. In the case of long-distance dependencies, the nonthematic function is the non-argument discourse function OP, short for "operator".[6] In the case of raising, the nonthematic function is the raising

[5]These constructions are raising and long-distance dependencies. Alsina (1995, 1996) additionally assumes that certain expletive subject constructions may also involve structure-sharing. I will ignore this latter type of construction in the present discussion, for simplicity of exposition.

[6]Most versions of LFG assume that non-argument discourse functions are TOP (topic) or FOC (focus). As it seems that the distinction between topic and focus is more of a discourse structure or information structure nature, than of a syntactic nature, I assume that there is only one non-

function, a subject or an object that does not bear a thematic role to the raising verb. We can define *nonthematic function* as follows, so as to include both types of situations:

(4) **Nonthematic function:** A GF is nonthematic iff it is not licensed by an A-to-f Mapping Principle or as an adjunct.

The A-to-f Mapping Principles associate arguments in the a-structure with GFs. In accusative languages like English, they associate the external argument with the subject function, an internal argument with a core function, and an indirect argument with an oblique function. Following Bresnan (2001), the class of core functions includes subject and object; consequently, the function linked to an internal argument may be either a subject or an object. The choice between these two options depends on the Subject Condition (see (5)). On the assumption that the a-structure only contains arguments with semantic content, that is, with a thematic role, a nonthematic function is a GF that is neither an adjunct nor an argument, in the sense that it is not introduced by an A-to-f Mapping Principle.

Nonthematic GFs are of two types: (i) the discourse function OP or (ii) a non-OP that, while neither an argument nor an adjunct, is required in order to satisfy the Subject Condition (5)[7] or a lexical stipulation.

(5) **Subject Condition**

Every verbal f-structure must have a SUBJ and no f-structure may have more than one SUBJ.

In the second place, in all constructions involving structure-sharing, the nonthematic function is always more prominent at f-structure than the possibly thematic function identified with it. When the two identified GFs are in different clauses, as in raising and many instances of long-distance dependencies, the nonthematic function is in a clause that contains the clause in which the possibly thematic function identified with it occurs. The relationship is never the reverse (i.e., with the nonthematic function in a clause embedded in the clause where the thematic function occurs) or any other such that the clause in which one of the two functions appears is not contained in,

argument discourse function, which I refer to as OP, and whatever syntactic distinctions can be found between topic and focus can be attributed to the discourse structure, where these concepts are represented. In any case, if the distinction between topic and focus is found to be needed at the level of f-structure, it can be made as subclasses of the class of non-argument discourse functions.

[7]This formulation of the Subject Condition includes (a) the obligatoriness of the subject function in all verbal f-structures, generally assumed in LFG since Bresnan and Kanerva (1989) (see also Dalrymple 2001:19), and (b) the uniqueness of the subject, under the assumption in Alsina (1993, 1996) that the subject is the only GF of which there cannot be more than one instance in any given f-structure. It has been claimed that some languages admit violations of the Subject Condition; this is consistent with an OT approach to constraint satisfaction.

and does not contain, the clause in which the other function appears. When the two identified GFs are in the same clause, as in some instances of long-distance dependencies, the nonthematic function is always more prominent in a hierarchy of GFs. For this, we need to define a notion of *f-prominence*, which appeals to both structural embeddedness at f-structure, or *f-command*, and to the hierarchy of grammatical functions, *GF Hierarchy*. F-command, in (6), follows the definition in Bresnan (1982b:334), and the GF Hierarchy, in (7), while based on many previous formulations of the hierarchy, including Bresnan (2001:96), differs from them in that it uses a smaller inventory of grammatical functions and, crucially, assumes that the GFs SUBJ and OP, grouped as the class of discourse functions, DF, proposed in Bresnan (2001), occupy the same position in the hierarchy.

(6) **F-command:** GF α f-commands GF β iff the value of α does not contain β and every f-structure that contains α contains β.

(7) **GF Hierarchy:** DF $\gg$ OBJ $\gg$ OBL

(8) **F-prominence:** GF α is more f-prominent than GF β iff α f-commands β and either β does not f-command α or α is higher than β in the GF Hierarchy.

The notions just defined allow us to formulate the following condition that holds on all instances of structure-sharing:

(9) **Nonthematic Condition on GF Identification**

Structure-sharing of GFs is well-formed only if, in the minimal f-structure containing two structure-shared GFs, one of them:

a) is nonthematic and

b) is more f-prominent than any GF identified with it.

In the third place, another similarity among constructions involving structure-sharing is that the relationship between the two GFs that share their value is, in fact, bounded: when structure-sharing spans more than one clause, the relation between the GFs involved is always one of immediate embedding; the relationship never skips a clause. That this is so in the case of raising is clear on the basis of well-known contrasts such as (10):[8]

(10) a. *Mary is likely for Kim to suggest to stay.

b. Mary appears to be likely to stay.

The subject of *stay* in (10a) cannot raise up to the matrix clause, even though the predicate of that clause is the raising predicate *likely*, because there is an intervening clause whose predicate does not allow raising. In (10b), on the

[8]The type of ungrammatical structure illustrated by (10a) is similar to examples such as **John seems that it is certain to win* (Chomsky 1986:18), known as super-raising.

other hand, the subject of *stay* does raise up to the matrix clause, because raising is allowed by the predicates of both the matrix clause and the immediately embedded clause. Thus, we can conclude that when raising appears to relate a GF with another GF at two levels of embedding, it is because the predicate at the first level of embedding is also a raising predicate and there is a chain of structure-sharing relations linking a GF at each level of embedding.

While this assumption is standard for raising in all syntactic frameworks, including LFG, it is not standardly made for long-distance dependencies (or extraction) in LFG, although it is in frameworks such as GB or the Minimalist Program, if we take movement to be the analogue of structure-sharing in these frameworks. I assume that the boundedness generally assumed for raising is, in fact, common to all structure-sharing relations, including long-distance dependencies. Thus, we need a locality condition on structure-sharing stating that if structure-sharing goes into an f-structure, it must involve a DF in the embedded structure:

(11) **Locality Condition on GF Identification**

$$\begin{bmatrix} \alpha & [\;]_1 \\ \beta & [\ldots\gamma\;]_2 \end{bmatrix} \rightarrow [\text{DF}\ [\;]_1\ ]_2$$

In this constraint, coindexing of f-structures signifies identity of f-structures. Coindexing is the standard device for expressing correspondence between levels: a c-structure node and an f-structure with the same index are in a mapping relation. Given the uniqueness condition on f-structures, each f-structure has a unique index. Thus, constraint (11) says that if an f-structure includes a GF γ structure-shared with a GF outside that f-structure, that f-structure must have a DF (a SUBJ or an OP) whose value is that of γ.

The DF required by (11) whenever structure-sharing spans more than one f-structure has to satisfy different "binding" conditions depending on whether it is a SUBJ or an OP. This requires defining the relevant notion of binding, which we can call *f-binding*, to distinguish it from anaphoric binding, and can state in (12):

(12) **F-binding:** α f-binds β iff α and β are different GFs with the same value, α f-commands β, and any γ that is equal to β or has β as a feature and is an argument in α's f-structure is not higher than α in the GF Hierarchy.

The binding condition on OPs can be stated as in (13):

(13) **OP Binding Condition:** Only an OP may bind an OP.

In long-distance dependencies, when the structure-sharing relation involves clauses at several levels of embedding, the locality condition, together with the OP Binding Condition, requires each intervening clause to include an OP with the shared value. Notice that the constraints on structure-sharing given so far allow for the possibility of a structure containing multiple gaps (or parasitic gaps), where by "gap" is meant a within-clause GF structure-shared with an OP. For example, a sentence like *Which book did you review __ without reading __ ?* is allowed by the theory.[9] However, the OP Binding Condition rules out multiple gap constructions in which one of the gaps (or an OP identified with it) is f-bound by the other gap, as in **Who did you tell __ that Kim would invite __ ?*, as shown in Alsina (2008).

In the case of raising, the combination of (11) and (13) entails that when a GF such as a SUBJ or an OBJ is structure-shared with a GF in an embedded clause, (a) the structure-sharing relation cannot involve a GF at two levels of embedding without also involving a GF at the first level of embedding (i.e., cannot skip a clause) and (b) the GF in the embedded clause must be a SUBJ. This explains the ungrammaticality of (10a): the SUBJ of *likely* would have to be structure-shared with a DF in the complement clause in order to satisfy the Locality Condition (11), but this DF cannot be the SUBJ (*Kim*), as it is not structure-shared with the matrix subject, and it cannot be an OP, as it would then violate the OP Binding Condition (13). The f-bound SUBJ in the complement clause of a raising predicate can, in turn, f-bind another GF in a more embedded clause, resulting in a chain of structure-sharing relations involving a GF in each of the clauses, as is the case in (10b).

Finally, the binding condition on SUBJs can be stated as follows:

(14) **SUBJ Binding Condition**

A subject that is structure-shared with a more f-prominent GF
(a) is f-bound in a non-subject GF of a clausal f-structure and
(b) is in a tenseless f-structure if its closest f-binder is a non-OP.

Clause (a) of this condition restricts both raising and subject extraction to structures in which the raised or extracted subject is in a complement of a clausal structure.[10] Thus, subject extraction is excluded out of a subject or out of an adjunct, as illustrated in (15):

(15) a. *Which politicians that __ spoke bothers you?
b. *Who did you enter the room while __ was talking on the phone?

Likewise, by clause (a) of this condition, raising is possible out of a complement, as in (16), but not out of a subject, as in (17),[11] or out of an adjunct, as

[9]In these and other examples, the empty underscore (__) represents the canonical position that a within-clause GF would occupy if it weren't identified with a more f-prominent GF.

[10]This is not valid for all languages. As pointed out by a reviewer, Kroeger (1993) claims that raising and extraction are only possible out of subjects in Tagalog. I leave it to further research to integrate the facts of such languages in the present theory.

[11]A reviewer suggests sentences like **Kim is [__ to drift] likely* and **We expected Kim [[__ to drift] to be likely]* as better examples than (17). However, these suggested examples are indepen-

in (18):

(16) a. Kim tends to drift.
b. We expected Kim to drift.

(17) a. *To drift tends Kim.
b. *To drift was expected Kim.

(18) *There seemed after being a storm that Mary would come.

For clause (b) of condition (14), we can define α as the closest f-binder of β iff α is an f-binder of β and there is no γ f-binder of β such that α is an f-binder of γ. This clause restricts raising to tenseless clauses, accounting for the contrast in (19):

(19) a. Kim seems to have missed the train.
b. *Kim seems (that) has missed the train.

16.3 Raising vs. Equi

Section 1.2 has outlined a theory of structure-sharing that is designed to explain the facts of long-distance dependencies and raising alike. It shows, among other things, that it is possible to dispense with control equations which, in addition to being highly specific, embody a great many stipulations. In the present section we deal with the difference between raising and equi (also known as control) regarding the null subject of the complement of the raising or equi predicate.

LFG has standardly assumed that the clausal complement to both raising and equi control verbs, when this complement is verbal, is a VP rather than an IP. A VP, like the other maximal projections of lexical categories, is generally defined as a category that does not include the c-structure realization of its subject. The subject of a VP is provided by some constituent external to the VP: the Spec of IP, the complement of the preposition *for* as in *I would like very much for Kim to stay*, through structure-sharing, and perhaps other devices. If we assume that in English the default subject position is the Spec of IP, it will follow that there is no subject position if the c-structure of the clause lacks the IP layer of structure (unless provided by some alternative mechanism). This can be captured by making the standard, although often implicit, assumption in LFG that tenseless clauses with a verbal predicate are just VPs and that only tensed clauses have the IP layer, embodied in the following condition:

(20) **Tensed IP Constraint:** $\text{IP}_1 \;\dot{\leftrightarrow}\; [\text{TENSE} +]_1$

dently ruled out because *to drift* occupies the subject position of a tenseless clause and tenseless clauses do not have a subject position (unless provided by some special construction such as the preposition *for*), as will be argued in connection with (20).

This is a biconditional constraint on the mapping between c-structure and f-structure that requires an IP to map onto an f-structure with the feature [TENSE +] and that requires an f-structure with the feature [TENSE +] to map onto an IP. While this constraint requires a tensed clause to map onto an IP, it prevents a tenseless clause from doing so. It can, however, map onto a VP. By this principle, it follows that tenseless verbal clauses are VPs.[12] A verb that takes a VP complement need only specify in its lexical entry that its complement is verbal (therefore, compatible with IP and CP, as well as VP, at c-structure) and [TENSE −] (or unspecified for tense).

The claim that a particular f-structure does not map onto an IP because it is tenseless, implies that it lacks a subject position, since there is no Spec-IP. However, the f-structure in question may require a subject because of the Subject Condition (5). There are two ways to satisfy the Subject Condition without having a phrase in Spec-IP: either by structure-sharing the SUBJ of the embedded clause with some GF in a position where it can be realized, or by having its features supplied by default. The first way yields a raising structure: structure when the SUBJ of an embedded f-structure is structure-shared with a non-OP in the matrix clause. The second way yields a structure in which the subject of the embedded clause is a null pronominal (as in equi control constructions and nonfinite adjunct clauses). Although no lexical item specifies any PRED feature for the subject, we can assume that this feature appears in the f-structure of the subject even if that violates F-faithfulness (see page 216), because of the completeness requirement that GFs that map onto an argument include the feature PRED. Following Mohanan (1981, 1983:650) (and also Austin and Bresnan 1996, Bresnan 1982b, Bresnan 2001:295, Hale 1983, Kuhn 2003:109, Simpson 1983, Simpson 1991, among others), we may assume that the feature [PRED 'pro'] is the least costly of the PRED features and therefore wins over competing specifications of this feature. In an OT framework where the completeness requirement ranks above F-faithfulness, a violation of the latter constraint will be required in order to satisfy the former if there is no way to satisfy both constraints and, among all the possible specifications for the feature PRED, the one that triggers the lowest ranked violation is [PRED 'pro'].

What determines the choice between the two ways just noted that an f-structure corresponding to a VP complement can satisfy the Subject Condition? F-faithfulness (page 216) provides the answer. If we compare two competing structures such that one satisfies the Subject Condition by structure-sharing the subject with a non-OP of the matrix clause and the other one satisfies it by having its necessary features (PRED at least, and possibly others)

[12] It also follows, as pointed out by a reviewer, that a construction like *for John to go* is not an IP. See Falk (2001:147) for a proposal compatible with this.

supplied by default, a violation of F-faithfulness will arise in the latter structure but not in the former.[13]

Suppose the ranking of the Subject Condition and F-faithfulness is as shown in (21):

(21) Subject Condition (5) $\gg$ F-faithfulness

By this ranking, if no other constraints are considered, satisfying the Subject Condition is required, even if that means that F-faithfulness is violated. In addition, since a given structure may accumulate several violations of F-faithfulness, the fewer violations of this constraint which are incurred in order to satisfy the Subject Condition, the better. If no other constraints were taken into account, this ranking would imply that the raising structure is always preferred over the structure with a null pronominal subject.

However, raising does not occur if any of the Conditions on GF Identification presented in section 1.2 are violated. For expository purposes, let us treat all those conditions as a cluster of constraints, which I will refer to as *GF ID*, and suppose the ranking of this group of constraints and F-faithfulness is as shown in (22):

(22) GF ID $\gg$ F-faithfulness

By this ranking, respecting GF ID is more important than incurring violations of F-faithfulness. Therefore, structure-sharing will not occur if any of the conditions included in GF ID is violated, for example, the Nonthematic Condition on GF Identification, (9). Thus, if the potential binder in a structure-sharing relation is thematic, the competition between a structure in which there is structure-sharing and another structure in which there is not, the second one wins out, because the former violates GF ID, whereas the second one only has one more violation of F-faithfulness.[14]

A consequence of the ranking just proposed in (22) is that structure-sharing does not occur between the SUBJ or OBJ of an equi verb and the unexpressed SUBJ of the nonfinite clausal complement of this verb. This is because the potential binder of the subject of this complement is thematic and therefore the structure-sharing relation of these two GFs would violate GF ID, specifically (9). The same will be true of adjunct clauses such as *for*-phrases, participial adjuncts, and the like, e.g., *don't sing, while driving*. Since a vi-

[13]Both structures will incur a violation of F-faithfulness because the subject is not licensed by a C-to-f-structure Mapping Principle in either case. Since they are equal with respect to this violation, a second violation of F-faithfulness in one of the structures will serve to distinguish the two with respect to EVAL.

[14]It is not possible to rank the Subject Condition and GF ID with respect to each other: they seem to allow no violations in English. In order to propose a relative ranking of these constraints we would need to find evidence that one of the two can be violated in order to comply with the other, and I am not aware of such evidence.

olation of GF ID is dispreferred compared to a violation of F-faithfulness, according to (22), the subject of such embedded clauses will not be structure-shared with a GF of the matrix clause, but will be a null pronominal which may be referentially dependent on that GF.

It is worth noting that the lexical entry of an infinitive (or any nonfinite verbal form) is not different for a structure in which the subject of the infinitive is structure-shared with a nonthematic GF of the matrix clause (a raising structure) and for a structure in which it is a null pronominal and therefore possibly anaphorically controlled by a GF of the matrix clause.

Given the theory presented so far, we can now consider what information needs to be specified in the lexical entry of a raising verb, distinguishing raising-to-subject verbs from raising-to-object verbs. A raising-to-subject verb like *seem* specifies in its lexical entry that it takes a propositional nonsubject argument as its sole argument. If we make the natural assumption that propositional-type arguments map onto clausal f-structures (i.e., f-structures with a SUBJ), it follows that this propositional argument may map onto a variety of categories in the c-structure, including CP and IP, as in (23a), and VP, AP, and PP, as illustrated in (23b–d).[15]

(23) a. It seems (that) Jan is a happy student.
b. Jan seems to be a happy student.
c. Jan seems happy as a student.
d. Jan seems in a hurry to go back to school.

The lexical entry of *seem* regarding its c-structure and f-structure information is as shown in (24). It specifies categorial information, namely verb, and f-structure information, which are coindexed. Its f-structure information includes the PRED feature, which is an a-structure consisting only of a propositional internal argument (notated as $[_{Prop}\,\text{Int}\,]$), and the restriction that this argument cannot map onto a subject.

(24) *seem*: $$\text{V}_1 \quad \left[\begin{array}{ll} \text{PRED} & \text{`seem}\,\langle\, [_{Prop}\,\text{Int}\,]_2\,\rangle\text{'} \\ \neg\text{SUBJ} & [\ ]_2 \end{array}\right]_1$$

If the propositional argument maps onto an IP, as in (23a), and optionally also onto a CP, as shown by the possibility of having the phrase introduced by a complementizer, the corresponding f-structure is tensed in compliance with (20). Since it is tensed, raising is excluded by the SUBJ Binding Condition (14), which only allows raising (structure-sharing of a GF in a clausal f-structure with a non-OP outside that clause) out of tenseless f-structures.

[15]Most varieties of English do not allow the propositional argument of *seem* to map onto an NP, as in **Jan seems a happy student*, a fact that can be accounted for through a categorial restriction. As pointed out by a reviewer, most PPs are bad with *seem* (**Jan seems in the garden*), a fact that probably needs to be accounted for through a semantic restriction.

Thus (23a) is, in fact, not an instance of raising, although the verb *seem* in this example is assumed to be the same verb (with the same lexical entry) that we find in the other examples of (23). It follows that the subject of *seem* in (23a) is not selected by the verb because its only argument is not the subject. Rather, the form *it* appears in the c-structure position of the subject licensing a subject in the f-structure in order to satisfy the Subject Condition.

If a tenseless verb form is chosen as the head of the phrase that maps onto the propositional argument of *seem*, as in (23b), that phrase cannot be IP in order to comply with (20), because the corresponding clausal f-structure will be tenseless. Thus, the clausal complement of *seem* will be a VP which lacks a subject position. Since this clausal complement needs to include a subject, its value can be provided either through identification with another GF or by default. As argued above, as long as the structure-sharing relation respects all of the GF ID constraints, structure-sharing is the preferred option. Consequently, the subject of the tenseless complement is identified with a GF outside this complement. This GF, in order to comply with the GF ID constraints, specifically (9), must be nonthematic as well as more f-prominent than the other GF it is identified with. Since the clause whose PRED is provided by the verb *seem* needs a subject in order to comply with the Subject Condition (5) and this subject is not an argument of the PRED, it is a nonthematic subject and therefore a candidate for GF identification. Thus, identifying this subject with the subject of the clausal complement allows the Subject Condition to be satisfied in both clauses, while respecting all of the GF ID constraints and having the fewest possible violations of F-faithfulness. Following are the c- and f-structures of (23b).

(25) a.

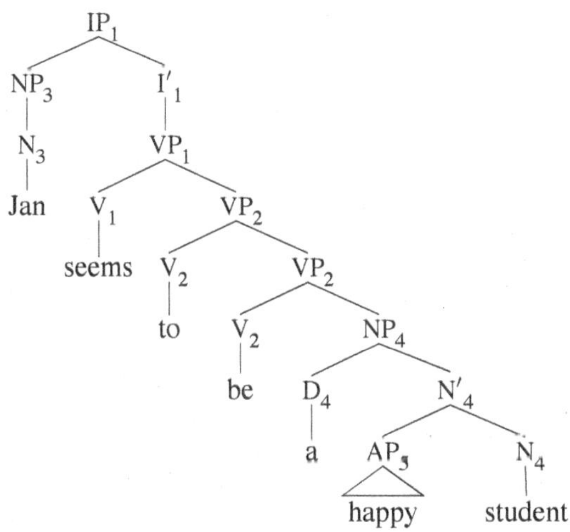

b. $$\left[\begin{array}{ll} \text{PRED} & \text{`seem} \langle [_{Prop}\,\text{Int}]_2 \rangle\text{'} \\ \text{TENSE} & + \\ \text{OBJ} & \left[\begin{array}{ll} \text{PRED} & \text{`be} \langle [_{Prop}\,\text{Int}]_4 \rangle\text{'} \\ \text{TENSE} & - \\ \text{OBJ} & \left[\begin{array}{ll} \text{PRED} & \text{`student} \langle [\text{Int}]_3 \rangle\text{'} \\ \text{SUBJ} & \end{array}\right]_4 \\ \text{SUBJ} & \end{array}\right]_2 \\ \text{SUBJ} & [\,\text{PRED `Jan'}\,]_3 \end{array}\right]_1$$

Examples (23c–d) are also instances of raising; only here the PRED of the clausal complement is provided by a nonverbal category, an adjective in (23c) and a preposition in (23d). The considerations that lead to a structure-sharing relation between the subject of the clausal complement and the subject of the matrix clause are the same for these examples as for (23b).

Nothing in the lexical entry of *seem* stipulates that there should be structure-sharing between its subject and a GF of its clausal complement. In fact, it doesn't even specify the presence of a subject. Both of these properties of a raising structure follow from the interaction of general constraints with a lexical entry that lacks an argument that maps onto the subject and takes a possibly tenseless propositional argument.

Whereas with raising-to-subject verbs we can rely on the Subject Condition to ensure the presence of a GF that is not required by the A-to-F Mapping Principles, this is not possible with raising-to-object verbs, as the nonthematic GF is the object and there is no general principle requiring an object. For such verbs, we simply have to stipulate in their lexical entry that they select a non-argument GF.[16] It is a lexically unspecified GF, as its further specification as a SUBJ or an OBJ depends on the Subject Condition and the other GFs of the structure. The lexical entry of a raising-to-object verb like *believe* would be as shown in (26):

(26) *believe*: $\text{V}_1 \quad \left[\begin{array}{ll} \text{PRED} & \text{`believe} \langle [\text{Ext}]_1\ [_{Prop}\,\text{Int}]_2 \rangle\text{'} \\ (\text{GF} & [\ ]_3) \end{array}\right]_1$

The propositional argument can map onto either a tensed or a tenseless clause, because its tense feature is not lexically specified. This allows both the raising and the non-raising use of *believe*, as illustrated in (27):

(27) a. I believe Jan to be a happy student.
b. I believe that Jan is a happy student.

[16]As suggested by a reviewer, the fact that the non-argument GF has to be stipulated for raising-to-object verbs can be seen as reflecting the relative rarity of raising to object compared to raising to subject.

If the propositional argument maps onto a tenseless clause, as in (27a), the subject of this clause is identified with the non-argument GF, for the reasons presented for raising-to-subject structures. Consequently, the f-structure of (27a) includes an OBJ (*Jan*), which is nonthematic, identified with the SUBJ of the complement clause. The reason why the non-argument GF of (26) is used obligatorily when the propositional argument is nonfinite is that not using it incurs more violations of F-faithfulness than using it, without avoiding the violation of a higher constraint. Consequently, *believe* is never an equi verb accounting for **I believe to be happy*, meaning either "I believe I am happy" or "I believe people are happy."[17] If the propositional argument maps onto a tensed clause, as in (27b), raising is blocked by (14) and the c-structure realization of this clause may include an overt subject. The optional non-argument GF in (26) cannot be used, if we assume some version of Economy of Expression (Bresnan 2001): given two structures that satisfy all syntactic constraints equally and do not differ in their semantic contribution, the one with fewer elements of structure is chosen. In (27b), the optional non-argument GF would make no semantic contribution and would not allow any syntactic constraint to be satisfied any better than if it weren't there.

16.4 Conclusions

The theory of raising proposed in this paper allows us to capture the main features of raising without stipulating them in the lexical entries of raising verbs. These properties are derived from general constraints, most of them not specific to raising constructions:

1. The claim that a raising verb has a nonthematic GF need not be lexically stipulated in the case of raising-to-subject verbs, but follows from the Subject Condition, (5).
2. The claim that the structure-sharing relation in a raising structure involves a nonthematic GF in the matrix structure is a consequence of the Nonthematic Condition on GF Identification, (9).
3. The claim that at most one clause boundary may separate the two structure-shared GFs in raising structures derives from the Locality Condition on GF Identification, (11).
4. The claim that it is always the subject (and not any other GF) of an f-structure f-commanded by the raising verb that is involved in structure-

[17]This means something special needs to be said about *expect* in order to allow this verb to be used either as a raising-to-object verb or as an equi verb. We can account for this duality by assuming that *expect*, in addition to an entry like (26), has another entry in which it takes a nonfinite complement clause and no non-argument GF. This second lexical entry allows *expect* to behave like other equi verbs such as *try*, *hope*, *want*, etc. whose subject controls the null pronominal subject of the nonfinite complement clause.

sharing is a consequence of the Locality Condition on GF Identification, (11), and the OP Binding Condition, (13).

5. The claim that the embedded clause out of which raising takes place is not a subject or an adjunct and is a tenseless clause is a consequence of the SUBJ Binding Condition, (14).
6. Structure-sharing across clauses, as a defining feature of raising, need not be stipulated in the lexical entry of raising verbs, but comes about in an OT model as the result of the interaction of constraints, specifically of the conditions on GF Identification (GF ID) and F-faithfulness, given the ranking in (22).
7. The observation that tenseless clauses have non-overt subjects, which may be null pronominals or structure-shared with a more prominent nonthematic GF, is captured by the Tensed IP Constraint, (20).

The majority of these constraints are needed independently of the facts of raising. This is the case of: (a) the Subject Condition, motivated on the basis of many different constructions; (b) the GF ID constraints ((9), (11), (13), and (14)), which are needed to account for long-distance dependencies; and (c) the Tensed IP Constraint, (20), which is needed to explain the absence of a subject position in all tenseless clauses, not only in those where raising is involved. Some of these constraints are assumed in equivalent form in alternative approaches to raising in LFG, such as the Subject Condition; others would have to be if the relevant facts were to be accounted for, as is the case with (20). The fact that there is no one principle equivalent to (20) in standard LFG is not a positive feature of this approach over the present one, because it means that the relevant facts are either not accounted for or accounted for through the accumulated effect of different constraints. Likewise with the GF ID constraints.

The only constraint that is exclusive to raising is clause (b) of the SUBJ Binding Condition, (14), which says that the f-structure out of which raising takes place must be a tenseless structure. Both this property and the claim that raising only takes place out of a complement (as opposed to a subject or an adjunct) are stipulated in standard LFG in ways that are much less economical than the present one. In standard LFG, the clausal f-structure out of which raising takes place is stipulated to be an XCOMP and XCOMP is stipulated to be a *governable grammatical function* (Kaplan and Bresnan (1982), Dalrymple (2001:11), also called *argument function* in Bresnan (2001:97) and Falk (2001:57)), the class of GFs that must be assigned to arguments in an a-structure. This is achieved at the cost of positing a GF (XCOMP) used only as the clausal complement of raising predicates. Following the arguments in Alsina, Mohanan, and Mohanan (2005) for dispensing with the GF COMP, the present theory dispenses with XCOMP as well, achieving a simplification of the formal framework and no loss in empirical adequacy. As for the restriction that raising occurs only out of tenseless clauses, it is not stated as a general constraint in standard LFG. Since it is not derived from any principle, we have to assume that it would be stipulated lexical item by lexical item, at a great cost to the grammar and loss of generality. Thus, the fact that this restriction is stated as part of the general constraint in (14) is a positive rather than a negative feature of the present theory.

To conclude, the theory of raising proposed in this paper is practically cost-free. Most of the properties of raising are derived from principles that are needed independently of raising. And the only constraint that is specific to raising achieves a significant simplification in the grammar in comparison with theories of raising that do not posit it.

Acknowledgments

I am grateful for the comments of two anonymous reviewers, which made me clarify some of the issues in this paper. All errors are mine. One of the reasons for developing the theory presented in this paper is the observation that raising and long-distance dependencies have similar patterns. Rather than assuming that these similarities are coincidental, this theory aims to explain them, thus underscoring the theme of this volume – *pattern interaction in language and life*.

References

Alsina, Alex. 1993. *Predicate Composition: A Theory of Syntactic Function Alternations*. Ph.D. thesis, Stanford Department of Linguistics, Stanford, CA.

Alsina, Alex. 1995. The fall of function-argument biuniqueness. In G. V. Morrill and R. T. Oehrle, eds., *Formal Grammar. Proceedings of the Conference of the European Summer School in Logic, Language and Information*, pages 1–16. Barcelona.

Alsina, Alex. 1996. *The Role of Argument Structure in Grammar: Evidence from Romance*. Stanford, CA: CSLI Publications.

Alsina, Alex. 2008. A theory of structure-sharing: Focus on long-distance dependencies and parasitic gaps. In M. Butt and T. H. King, eds., *The Proceedings of the LFG '08 Conference*, pages 5–25. Stanford, CA: CSLI.

Alsina, Alex, Tara Mohanan, and K. P. Mohanan. 2005. How to get rid of the COMP. In M. Butt and T. H. King, eds., *The Proceedings of the LFG'05 Conference*, pages 21–41. CSLI Online Publications.

Austin, Peter and Joan Bresnan. 1996. Nonconfigurationality in Australian aboriginal languages. *Natural Language and Linguistic Theory* 14:216–268.

Bresnan, Joan. 1982a. Control and complementation. *Linguistic Inquiry* 13:343–434. Reprinted in Bresnan (1982b), 282–390.

Bresnan, Joan. 1982b. *The Mental Representation of Grammatical Relations*. Cambridge, MA: MIT Press.

Bresnan, Joan. 2001. *Lexical-Functional Syntax*. Oxford: Blackwell.

Bresnan, Joan and Jonni Kanerva. 1989. Locative inversion in Chichewa: A case study of factorisation in grammar. *Linguistic Inquiry* 20:1–50.

Chomsky, Noam. 1986. *Barriers*. Cambridge, MA: MIT Press.

Dalrymple, Mary. 2001. *Lexical Functional Grammar*. San Diego, CA: Academic Press.

Falk, Yehuda N. 2001. *Lexical-Functional Grammar: An Introduction to Parallel Constraint-Based Syntax*. Stanford, CA: CSLI Publications.

Hale, Kenneth. 1983. Warlpiri and the grammar of non-configurational languages. *Natural Language and Linguistic Theory* 1:5–47.

Kaplan, Ronald M. and Joan Bresnan. 1982. Lexical-functional grammar: A formal system for grammatical representation. In J. Bresnan, ed., *The Mental Representation of Grammatical Relations*, pages 173–281. Cambridge, MA: MIT Press.

Kroeger, Paul. 1993. *Phrase Structure and Grammatical Relations in Tagalog*. Stanford, CA: CSLI Publications. Revised and corrected version of 1991 Stanford University doctoral dissertation.

Kuhn, Jonas. 2003. *Optimality-Theoretic Syntax – A Declarative Approach*. Stanford, CA: CSLI Publications.

Mohanan, K. P. 1981. On pronouns and their antecedents. Ms., National University of Singapore.

Mohanan, K. P. 1983. Functional and anaphoric control. *Linguistic Inquiry* 14:641–674.

Simpson, Jane. 1983. *Aspects of Warlpiri Morphology and Syntax*. Ph.D. thesis, MIT, Department of Linguistics and Philosophy, Cambridge, MA.

Simpson, Jane. 1991. *Warlpiri Morpho-Syntax: A Lexicalist Approach*. Dordrecht: Kluwer Academic.

17

Complex Predication: How Did the Child Pinch the Elephant?

MIRIAM BUTT, TRACY HOLLOWAY KING, GILLIAN RAMCHAND

17.1 Introduction

It is an acknowledged truth that some of the most productive linguistics is done in pubs or restaurants (cf. M.T. Mohanan, this volume). And that a linguist, when in the happy situation of being in the company of other linguists, might write on a paper napkin something like the Urdu sentence in (1) and triumphantly and expectantly turn to the other linguists and say: "And what do you make of that?!"

(1) tara=ne ɑmu=ko (bɑcce=se) hatʰi
Tara=Erg Amu=Dat child.Obl=Inst elephant.M.Sg.Nom
pɪnc kɑr-va le-ne di-ya
pinch do-Caus take-Inf.Obl give-Perf.M.Sg
'Tara let Amu have the elephant pinched (by the child).'[1]

In the particular situation we are reporting on here, the linguists around the table were all students of K.P. Mohanan during the late 1980s. This means they know quite a bit about the structure of Malayalam and South Asian languages in general and have all written papers at some point in their careers on the complex predicates of a South Asian language. And this means they can now delve immediately into a discussion on how to analyze (1). However,

[1]All examples in this paper were checked with native speakers of Urdu. Furthermore, no elephants were harmed in the writing of this paper. Anyone found pinching an elephant will be forced to write an Optimality Theory (OT) section of this paper for us.

Reality Exploration and Discovery: Pattern Interaction in Language and Life.
Linda Uyechi and Lian-Hee Wee (eds.).

the reader is presumably not necessarily in this enviable position and so some basic background knowledge is provided in section 17.2.

The three linguists, though all students of Mohanan at the same time, went on to pursue quite different frameworks. Miriam Butt (MB) and Tracy Holloway King (THK) have very firmly developed analyses within Lexical-Functional Grammar (LFG) and have both worked on large computational grammars. THK works almost exclusively in computational linguistics now, while MB continues to pursue both theoretical and computational perspectives. Gillian Ramchand (GR), on the other hand, works equally firmly within the Minimalist Program and shows no sign of finding computational linguistics even remotely interesting. All three are highly opinionated and all three see themselves as simply continuing the kinds of debates one used to have as a matter of course in any of Mohanan's classes, who encouraged lively discussions and used them to arrive at a high level of abstraction.

Sections 17.3 – 17.5 present the debate in the pub (minus the beer (MB), cider (THK), wine (GR) and insults (all)). Section 17.6 charts the morning after.

17.2 Language and Structural Background

South Asian languages are generally verb final. This is true for Urdu, which is structurally identical to Hindi and is spoken mainly in Pakistan and India. There are only about 500 simplex verbs in Urdu, so the language makes productive use of complex predication. The following combinations are possible: N+V, A+V, V+V. (2) is a noun-verb complex predicate (*pɪnc ki-ya*).

(2) bɑcce=ne hatʰi pɪnc ki-ya
child.Obl=Erg elephant.M.Sg.Nom pinch do-Perf.M.Sg
'The child pinched the/an elephant.'

There is no simplex verb for 'pinch' in Urdu.[2] If one did not press an English noun into service, as in (2), a different kind of N-V complex predicate would be used. Urdu has also borrowed extensively from Persian with respect to nouns for N-V complex predicates. For ease of exposition, we use the borrowed English noun here. As Mohanan (1994) has shown, these N+V predications are monoclausal and must be analyzed as complex predicates. Thus, (2) is equivalent to a simple transitive clause in terms of argument structure.

South Asian languages also generally have a morphological causative. Urdu has two: one with an *-a* morpheme and one with *-va*. The former is used for more direct causation, the latter for indirect causation, i.a., Saksena (1982), Butt (1998), Ramchand (2008). Almost any verb in Urdu can

[2] We leave aside the discussion of why Malayalam feels strongly enough about pinching that it encodes the notion via a simplex verb (*ṇulli*), whereas Urdu does not.

be causativized, as shown in (3), including N+V complex predicates, as they are predicationally essentially equivalent to a simplex verb.

(3) ɑmu=ne (bɑcce=se) hatʰi pɪnc kɑr-vɑ-ya
Amu=Erg child.Obl=Inst elephant.M.Sg.Nom pinch do-Caus-Perf.M.Sg
'Amu had the elephant pinched (by the child).'

(3) is an example of indirect causation (hence the English translation with 'have'). The pattern of causativization across verb classes is quite complex (see Butt (1998) for a summary and references). For our purposes it is sufficient to know that when a canonical transitive is causativized, the causee is instrumental. There is some question of whether this instrumental causee ('child' in (3)) is syntactically an adjunct or whether it is parallel to the oblique *by*-phrases found in passives. Bhatt (2003) and Butt (1998) suggest the latter (though in different ways); Ramchand (2008) treats the instrumental as a syntactic adjunct.

Beyond causativization, other types of complex predication exist in Urdu. The existence of light verbs that convey some kind of aspectual information, as shown in (4), is another feature of South Asian languages.

(4) a. nadya=ne xɑt lɪkʰ li-ya
Nadya=Erg letter.M.Nom write take-Perf.M.Sg
'Nadya wrote a letter (completely).'

b. nadya=ne mɑkan bɑna di-ya
Nadya=Erg house.M.Nom make give-Perf.M.Sg
'Nadya built a house (completely, for somebody else).'

These V+V predications can also be shown to be monoclausal (Butt 1995). The first verb is always the main content-bearing verb and is always in what appears to be the stem form, but is actually an old perfect participle (this becomes relevant in section 17.4). The second verb is always form-identical to a main verb in the language (e.g., 'take' and 'give' in (4)), but is 'light' in the sense that it does not add its full argument structure to the predication: instead it conveys semantic information as to the completeness of the action, benefaction, forcefulness, etc. (i.a. Butt and Gender 2001, Hook 1974).

Every simplex verb in Urdu can be used in a V-V complex predicate as in (4), though there are selectional restrictions. The same selectional restrictions (for example, light verbs based on (di)transitives select agentive predications) hold for N-V and causativized verbs when used as the main V in V-V complex predicates. Example (5) shows the N-V complex predicate in combination with an aspectual light verb; example (6) shows the causativized version of (5) in combination with the same aspectual light verb.

(5) bɑcce=ne hatʰi pɪnc kɑr li-ya
child.Obl=Erg elephant.M.Sg.Nom pinch do take-Perf.M.Sg
'The child pinched the/an elephant (completely).'

(6) ɑmu=ne (bɑcce=se) hatʰi pɪnc kɑr-va
Amu=Erg child.Obl=Inst elephant.M.Sg.Nom pinch do-Caus
li-ya
take-Perf.M.Sg
'Amu had the elephant pinched (by the child) (completely).'

Urdu also has a permissive, as shown in (7). This permissive is formed with the verb for 'give' (*de*). Again, 'give' here is functioning as a light verb (Butt 1995). Unlike the aspectual light verbs discussed above, however, it requires the main verb to carry oblique infinitive morphology. Permissives are also monoclausal. One piece of evidence for this is verb agreement: in (7) the finite verb 'give' agrees with the nominative object 'note', showing that this argument is not just an argument of 'write', but of the whole complex predicate and therefore also of the finite verb 'give'. See Butt (1995) and Butt and Ramchand (2005) for details and argumentation.

(7) hɑsɑn=ne ram=ko cɪṭṭʰi lɪkʰ-ne d-i
Hassan=Erg Ram=Dat note.F.Nom write-Inf.Obl give-Perf.F.Sg
'Hassan let Ram write a note.'

Again, permissives can be formed with any verb in the language and therefore also with any complex monoclausal verb. Example (8) shows the permissive in combination with the simple N-V complex predicate, (9) is the permissive of the causativized N-V complex predicate and, finally, (10) is the the example on our paper napkin: a permissive of a causativized N-V complex predicate that has been supplemented with an aspectual light verb.

(8) tara=ne bɑcce=ko hatʰi pɪnc kɑr-ne
Tara=Erg child.Obl=Dat elephant.M.Sg.Nom pinch do-Inf.Obl
di-ya
give-Perf.M.Sg
'Tara let the child pinch the/an elephant.'

(9) tara=ne ɑmu=ko (bɑcce=se) hatʰi pɪnc
Tara=Erg Amu=Dat child.Obl=Inst elephant.M.Sg.Nom pinch
kɑr-va-ne di-ya
do-Caus-Inf.Obl give-Perf.M.Sg
'Tara let Amu have the elephant pinched by the child.'

(10) tara=ne ɑmu=ko (bɑcce=se) hatʰi
Tara=Erg Amu=Dat child.Obl=Inst elephant.M.Sg.Nom

pɪnc kɑr-va le-ne di-ya
pinch do-Caus take-Inf.Obl give-Perf.M.Sg
'Tara let Amu have the elephant pinched (by the child) (completely).'

Tests from agreement, control and anaphora resolution show that (10) is a monoclausal predication (Butt 1995). So in (10) we have five predicational elements (the noun *pinch*, the light verb *kar*, the causative *-va*, the aspectual light verb *le-ne*, and the permissive light verb *di-ya*) that combine to form a monoclausal predicational structure. Having established this, the question is how to best analyze these combinatorial predicational possibilities.

17.3 Linking Theory

Linking Theory within LFG was developed to deal with regularities in the expression of case, arguments and grammatical relations (see Butt (2006), Chapter 5 on linking theories in general and LFG in particular). Linking theory does not assume a one-to-one or a strict hierarchical mapping between thematic roles and grammatical relations – rather, the theory allows just the right kind of flexibility to be able to account for argument alternations as well as non-canonical subjects (e.g., experiencer subjects or the non-canonical case marking of Icelandic) and objects. This stands in stark contrast to the Uniformity of Theta Assignment Hypothesis (UTAH) formulated as part of Government-Binding (GB), by which identical thematic relationships between items must be represented by identical structural/syntactic relationships (Baker 1988).

In the 1980's, linking theory was applied to complex predication in Bantu, Romance and South Asian languages. The basic system is pleasingly simple and yet powerful enough to deal with a large range of complex predicate types. It is therefore a prime candidate for dealing with (10).

LFG is a theory which assumes several distinct *projections*. The c(onstituent)-structure models constituency, linear order and hierarchical embedding. The f(unctional)-structure encodes the basic predicate-argument relations of the clause in terms of grammatical functions, adjuncts, etc. The f-structure, part of syntax and the grammatical functions encoded there, are related to a more semantically based predicate-argument structure that encodes just the core arguments required by the verb. A simple example based on Bresnan and Zaenen (1990) is given in (11).

(11)	a-structure:	*pinch* <	agent	theme	>
			[−o]	[−r]	
			|	|	
	f-structure:		SUBJ	OBJ	

Grammatical functions (GF) are related to thematic roles at argument-structure via just two features: [± r(estricted)] and [± o(bjective)]. The features reflect crosslinguistic tendencies as to the properties of the thematic roles. For example, agents tend not to be realized as objects and themes tend to be subject to few restrictions. Similarly, subjects are not objects and tend to be related to all kinds of thematic roles, hence a subject is characterized by the feature complex [−o, −r]. The full correspondences are given in (12).

(12)

Grammatical Functions	**Features**
SUBJ	[−r, −o]
OBJ	[−r, +o]
OBJθ	[+r, +o]
OBLθ	[+r, −o]

Approaches within LFG have differed with respect to how thematic roles are connected up with the [± o,r] features. Due to space constraints, we do not discuss these here, but assume the standard approach of Bresnan and Zaenen (1990), which formulates basic principles determining the unmarked choice of features for thematic roles: patient-like roles are [−r], secondary patient-like roles (e.g., goals) [+o] and all others are [−o]. On the basis of this feature assignment, a set of mapping principles connects thematic roles with grammatical functions. For our purposes, no distinctions will be made between themes and patients, both are [−r], and goals are [+r]. As in Bresnan and Zaenen (1990), the highest role classified as [−o] should be mapped to SUBJ; if that is not available, then the [−r] role is mapped to SUBJ. Deviating from Bresnan and Zaenen, all other thematic roles are mapped to grammatical functions according to a combination of the feature specification of thematic roles and constraints coming from case markers. For example, the dative case contributes the feature [+o], resulting in a mapping to OBJθ (rather than OBLθ, cf. (25)).

17.3.1 Argument merger

With respect to complex predicates, a few extra pieces are needed for the analysis. One is the idea that light verbs have a variable in their argument structure that calls for another predicate to be substituted in. For example, take the information associated with the light verb 'do' (as in 'pinch do').[3]

(13) DO < ag %Pred >

The %Pred signals that the argument structure is incomplete: the argument structure of another predicate must be substituted in before the predication is complete (cf. Alsina (1996), who first proposed this idea). In our example, the a-structure of *pinch* would be substituted in.

Linking Theory was originally intended to apply only within the lexicon. Alsina (1996) and Butt (1995) showed that for syntactically formed com-

[3] ag=agent, pt=patient, th=theme, go=goal.

plex predicates, argument structure combinations and linking also had to be allowed within the syntax. Alsina (1996) further argued that morphological and syntactic complex predication should be analyzed at the same abstract level of representation: at a-structure via a-structure merger.

Furthermore, when a-structures are combined, *argument identification* must take place. That is, one of the matrix arguments must be identified with one of the embedded arguments (Alsina and Joshi 1991, Mohanan 1994, Butt 1995, Alsina 1996). The assumption that argument identification exists and plays a significant role in the realization of grammatical functions and the distribution of case marking is not óne generally shared by work within GB or the Minimalist Program (MP). A recent exception is Ramchand (2008) (section 17.4, this paper) and it is to be suspected that some cross-theoretical cross-fertilization has taken place due to late night discussions over paper napkins.

Rather than spending more time on abstractly describing how argument structures are merged, the next few sections chart how the analyses work out within LFG's Linking Theory with respect to our paper napkin example. For presentational convenience, the analyses work outwards from the inside, i.e., by beginning with the N-V complex predicate 'pinch do'.

17.3.2 N-V complex predicates

That the noun contributes to the overall a-structure of a N-V complex predicate is shown by examples such as (14), where 'story' is licensed by the noun 'memory', not by the verb 'do'; see Mohanan (1994).

(14) bacce=ne kahani yad k-i
child=Erg story.F.Sg.Nom memory do-Perf.F.Sg
'The child remembered a/the story.'

There are thus two separate a-structures involved in the predication that are combined as part of argument merger. We assume, following Butt (1998) and Mohanan (1994) that argument identification functions in parallel to syntactic control in that the lowest matrix argument is always identified with the highest embedded argument. Thus, the a-structure for 'do', repeated in (15a), is combined with the a-structure for 'pinch' in (15b), resulting in the merged a-structure in (16). The sole matrix argument, an agent, is identified with the highest embedded argument, also an agent.

(15) a. DO < ag %Pred >
b. PINCH < ag th >

(16) DO < ag PINCH < ag th >>

[−o] [−r]

SUBJ OBJ

The complex a-structure thus provides two arguments to be linked into the syntax. This is done via the standard linking relations, as also shown in (16). Themes are classified as [−r] and the agent is classified as [−o] by default. The highest (and only) [−o] argument is linked to SUBJ by the mapping principles. The theme could in principle be linked to SUBJ or OBJ, but given that the clause already contains a subject (linked to the agent), the theme is linked to OBJ. There is thus exactly one subject ('child') and one object ('elephant') in the clause. The noun 'pinch' does not function as an object. This is illustrated more clearly with respect to (14), where the finite verb 'do' agrees with the object 'story', but not with 'memory'. The nouns 'memory' and 'pinch' must thus be analyzed as part of the predicate, not as syntactic arguments.[4]

A further nice aspect of Linking Theory is that it allows one to express generalizations in terms of the distribution of case marking. In Urdu (and in South Asian languages more generally), the ergative is generally associated with agents (selects for [−o]), the instrumental with 'demoted' agents (selects for [−o,+r]) and the dative with goals (selects for [+r]).[5] The ergative in (14) thus marks the merged agent argument; the nominative marks the theme.

17.3.3 Causativization

As first proposed by Mohanan (1988) and taken up by Alsina (1996) for Romance, a three-place causative is assumed for direct causation, as in (17). The causee is labeled pt/th (for the sake of simplicity, no distinction is made between these roles). The cause predicate, CS, requires another predicate.

(17) CS < ag pt/th %Pred >

This other predicate could be any simplex or any complex verb in the language. In (18), the complex a-structure of the previous section has been substituted in.

(18) CS < ag pt/th DO < ag PINCH < ag th >>>

[−o] [−o] [−r]

SUBJ OBL OBJ

[4]The wider set of data with respect to N-V complex predicates and agreement are more complex. See Mohanan (1994) for a detailed discussion.

[5]Direct objects can either be marked with *ko*, the dative/accusative marker, or carry no marking. The latter is glossed as nominative. The *ko*/∅ alternation correlates with definiteness/specificity; see Butt (2006) Chapter 7 for discussion of this phenomenon.

Via the rule of argument identification the lowest matrix argument (the pt/th causee) has been identified with the embedded agent argument. The new merged argument, namely the causee, has both the properties of a patient/theme and those of an agent. In our example, repeated in (19), the causee is realized in the instrumental. Given that the instrumental (among other things) selects for 'demoted', or in this case, merged agents, the case marking is consonant with the [−o] feature of the agent part of the merged argument.

(19) ɑmu=ne (bɑcce=se) hatʰi pɪnc kɑr-va-ya
Amu=Erg child.Obl=Inst elephant.M.Sg.Nom pinch do-Caus-Perf.M.Sg
'Amu had the elephant pinched by the child.'

However, the dual nature of a merged argument can result in different case marking across languages. With respect to some verbs, the causee in (19) can be realized alternatively in the instrumental or in the accusative/dative. An example from Urdu is shown in (20).

(20) a. ɑnjʊm=ne sɑddɑf=**ko** masala cɑkʰ-va-ya
Anjum=Erg Saddaf=**Acc** spice.M.Nom taste-Caus-Perf.M.Sg
'Anjum had Saddaf taste the seasoning.'

b. ɑnjʊm=ne sɑddɑf=**se** masala cɑkʰ-va-ya
Anjum=Erg Saddaf=**Inst** spice.M.Nom taste-Caus-Perf.M.Sg
'Anjum had the seasoning tasted by Saddaf.'

The different linking possibilities associated with merged arguments thus account for wider patterns associated with causatives.[6]

17.3.4 Aspectual light verbs

Aspectual light verbs give a sense of completion of the event. Additionally, Butt (1995) shows that while aspectual light verbs make only a very subtle contribution to the predication, they determine the case marking of the subject. Light verbs based on (di)transitive verbs like the 'take' in our example require an ergative subject in the perfect. Light verbs based on intransitives require a nominative in the perfect (see Butt (1995) for details).

(21) ɑmu=ne (bɑcce=se) hatʰi pɪnc kɑr-va
Amu=Erg child.Obl=Inst elephant.M.Sg.Nom pinch do-Caus

[6] There is more to be said here, of course. Alsina and Joshi (1991), for example, propose to capture the cross-linguistic variation found in causativization via two different causative predicates, one 2-place and one 3-place (based on original argumentation by Mohanan (1988)) combined with parameters on argument identification, where different arguments of the matrix and embedded a-structures can be combined with one another. The analysis here follows proposals by Butt (1998) which allow for only one type of argument identification: that of the lowest matrix argument with that of the highest embedded argument. In addition, only a three-place causative predicate is assumed here.

li-ya
take-Perf.M.Sg
'Amu had the elephant pinched by the child (completely).'

Within Linking Theory, this falls out from the effects of argument merger if the a-structure of an aspectual light verb consists of just one argument plus a variable standing for another predicate. In (23) the complex a-structure of (18) has been substituted in for the variable.

(22) TAKE < ag %Pred >

(23)

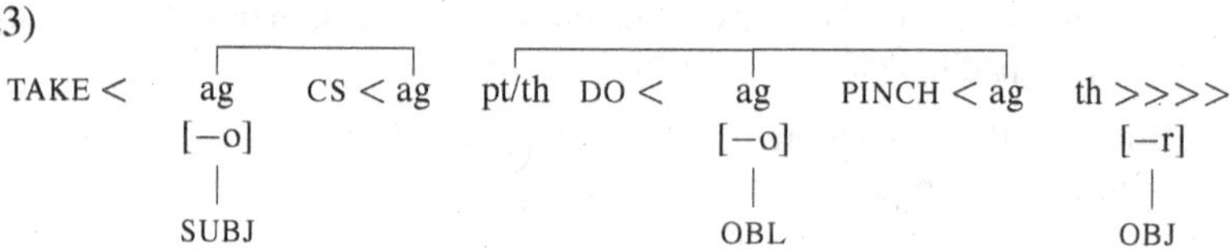

Because argument identification applies to merge the sole argument of 'take' with the highest argument of 'cause', there is no net increase in the number of GFs. The contribution of the aspectual light verb lies within the aspectual event semantics, which is not standardly part of Linking Theory. The linking in (23) confines itself to statements about morphosyntactic properties of a clause, such as the realization of GFs and the distribution of case marking. While some semantic properties are factored in via the semantic interpretation of thematic roles, Linking Theory per se is not about event semantics. This contrasts with the approach in section 17.4.

17.3.5 Permissive

The Urdu permissive is based on the verb 'give' and as such it is natural to assume a three-place predicate for the light verb as well, as in (24).

(24) GIVE < ag go %Pred >

In (25) the complex a-structure of (23) has been substituted in. Via argument identification, the lowest argument of the matrix a-structure (the goal) is identified with the highest argument of the complex embedded a-structure. This results in a net increase of one GF, the permitter. The goal is classified as [+r] by the basic classification principles and links to a dative object (OBJ_{go}). All other linkings have already been discussed.

(25)

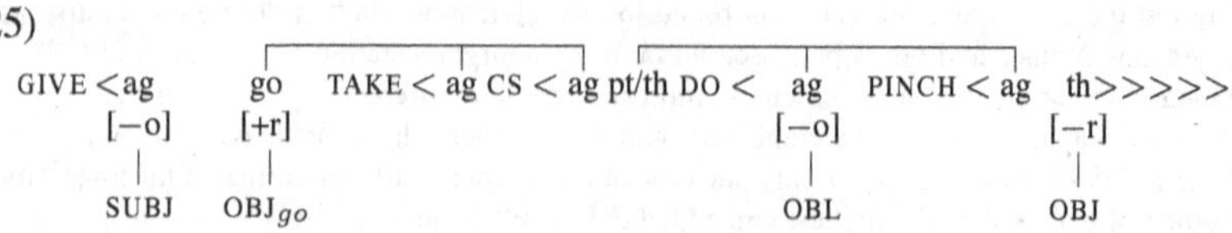

(26) tara=ne ɑmu=ko (bɑcce=se) hat^h^i
Tara=Erg Amu=Dat child.Obl=Inst elephant.M.Sg.Nom
pinch kɑr-va le-ne di-ya
pinch do-Caus take-Inf.Obl give-Perf.M.Sg
'Tara let Amu have the elephant pinched (by the child) (completely).'

Thus, even though we have eight arguments at the level of a-structure for (26), due to argument identification, these arguments correspond to only four GFs. Linking Theory makes exactly the right predictions as to the types of GFs involved and, furthermore, the case marking is consonant with the types of arguments linked at a-structure. In (26), the permittee 'Amu' has dative case because it is linked to a goal. The causee 'child' is analyzed as an oblique. In the following section, it is treated as an adjunct. If the instrumental causees indeed turn out to be syntactic adjuncts, rather than oblique agents like those found in passives, then this linking approach would need to be revised and the agent arguments would have to be suppressed rather than merged. However, argument suppression with respect to argument merger as part of complex predication is not predicted within Linking Theory.

17.4 First Phase Syntax

From the perspective of a minimalist architecture, complex predications are an important source of evidence for the internal structure of events and verbal lexical items. Ramchand's work on the syntactic decomposition of event structure makes a number of claims that distinguishes it from LFG (Ramchand 2008). Most importantly, it shares with a general minimalist approach the desire to have only one module in the grammar where systematic patterns and generalizations are stated.[7] This is called the 'narrow syntax' (Chomsky (1995) i.a.) and in particular, no rules or transformations can be stated in 'the lexicon'. In this theory, while the lexicon must exist in the sense of memorized associations between meaning and sound, and perhaps also syntactic features, it is not an encapsulated module and no rules can be stated to take place there. In this system, the equivalent of the argument structure module of LFG is an articulated syntax in the lowest portion of the clause. This architectural decision is justified by the fact that structures and mechanisms independently argued to be necessary for the narrow syntax are enough to account for the generalizations about argument structure relationships and predication.

Specifically, with regard to complex predications in a language like Urdu, independent lexical items and visible pieces of morphology give evidence of

[7]Here, we put aside generalizations that might have to be stated in a phonological module or at a discourse level; these can be handled at the interfaces between the computational system and the articulatory/perceptual or conceptual/intentional modules of the mind respectively.

the structure that must exist even for more morphologically stingy languages like English where one word lexicalizes highly complex meanings.

In Ramchand (2008), the event structure syntax contains three important subevental components: a causing subevent, a process denoting subevent and a subevent corresponding to result state. Each of these subevents is represented as its own projection, ordered in the hierarchical embedding relation in (27).

(27)

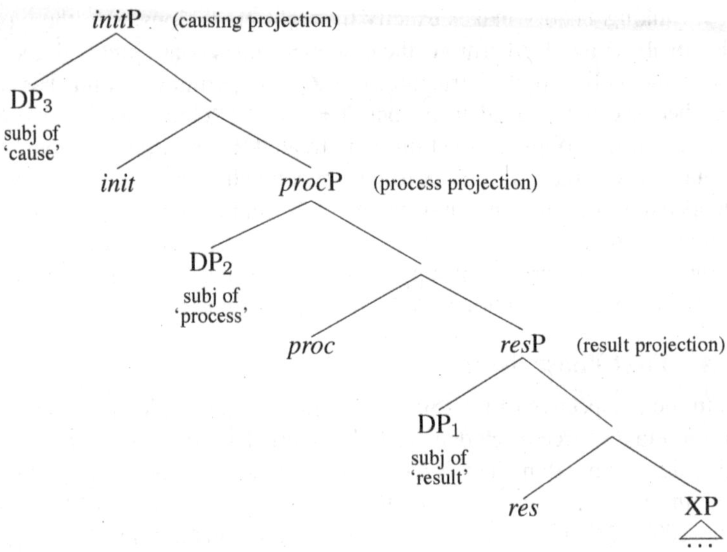

The label *init* (for initiation) represents the outer causational projection that is responsible for introducing the external argument; in many ways it is similar to the external argument introducing *v* (Hale and Keyser 1993, Harley 1995, Kratzer 1996). The central projection that represents the dynamic process is called *proc*P (for process phrase). The lowest projection has been labelled *res* for result. (27) represents the maximal possible decomposition, and a dynamic verbal projection may exist without either the *init* or *res* elements. Under this view, *proc*P is the heart of the dynamic predicate, since it represents change through time, and it is present in every dynamic verb. The *init*P exists when the verb expresses a causational or initiational state that leads to the process. The *res*P only exists when there is a result state explicitly expressed by the lexical predicate; it does not correlate with semantic/aspectual boundedness in a general sense.

In addition to representing subevental complexity, as motivated by work on verbal aktionsart (Vendler 1967, Parsons 1990, Pustejovsky 1991), this structure captures a set of core argument roles, as defined by the predicational relations formed at each level. In some sense, each projection forms its own core predicational structure with the specifier position filled by the 'subject' or 'theme' of a particular (sub)event, and the complement position filled by the phrase that provides the content of that event. The complement position is also complex and contains another mini-predication. In this way, the participant relations are built up recursively from successively embedded event descriptions and 'subject' predications.

- *init*P introduces the causation event and licenses the external argument ('subject' of cause = INITIATOR)
- *proc*P specifies the nature of the change or process and licenses the entity undergoing change or process ('subject' of process = UNDERGOER)
- *res*P gives the 'telos' or 'result state' of the event and licenses the entity that comes to hold the result state ('subject' of result = RESULTEE)

The other important thing is that DP arguments can move (or remerge) in more than one predicational position in the tree, accumulating relevant entailments as they do so. This means that thematic relations are often composite, and that the Theta Criterion as found in most versions of GB Theory is not in force (see Hornstein (2000) for arguments from control that the Theta Criterion in its original form should be dispensed with). The generalizations that the Theta Criterion was designed to account for are restated in terms of macro roles. This is one of the issues that lies at the heart of the problem of complex predications.

The challenge is to use this system to analyze the morphosyntactically complex monoclausal sentence on the paper napkin, namely (10). The tools are our disposal will be (i) the more finely decomposed structure of the event which separates the contributions of different lexical items to the larger predication and (ii) the possibility of phasal recursion. Recursion is generally available in syntactic organisation, provided we have a lexical item of the appropriate category that is syntactically specified to combine with something smaller than a fully tensed clause. In the cases considered here, causative recursion will obtain when an *init*P structure is selected for. Since the recursion is at the level of *init*P, before the case checking and tense-aspect functional structure of the clause is built, these complex predications are monoclausal from the point of view of LFG's grammatical functions or GB's Case theory.

Starting with the most deeply embedded piece of morphology, Ramchand (2008) analyses the causative morpheme in Urdu as the spell out of an *init* head that provides the semantics of generalized causation. When *-a* spells out the *init* head, the root spells out the *proc* and *res* portions of the event. The difference between the *-a* and *-va* causative marker lies in how much of the first phase is spelled out by the root. The *-va* causative marker spells out both the *init* and *proc* heads and the root identifies only the *res* portion. This gives the semantics of indirect causation because the processual subevent that the clause asserts is distinct from the lexical encyclopedic content of the root. Thus, the initiator exerts an act of will to initiate a process (which remains vague and open) to achieve the result of pinching.

Ramchand further argues that the existence of an instrumental marked adjunct interpreted as the causee is correlated directly with the suppression of a process subevent in the root. This always happens with *-va* causatives, because the root is forced into the *res* position. The lexically identified process of pinching remains implicit, since the *-va* causative simply asserts that some process (perhaps bribing a small child to do so) brought about the elephant's being pinched. The adjunct *-se* phrase is attached freely and its meaning describes information that is cotemporaneous with a process subevent; it must also be facilitating, and not in volitional control. Because of this analysis, the 'causee' is not placed within the argumental decomposition of a causative in *-va*. It is also assumed that it is an adjunct, freely adjoined at the *proc*P level.

Thus, (28) represents the *va* causative version of 'pinch-do' with 'Amu' as the subject and 'the elephant' as the holder of result. In the tree, the *-va* morpheme has been further decomposed into a *process* suffix *-v* and the already identified *init* suffix *-a*. However, nothing crucial hinges on this decomposition, as long as the combined suffix *-va* spells out both *init* and *proc*. The nominal complex predicate 'pinch do' is represented as a head complement structure. In addition to the specifiers, complement positions have a role in building up the event. Complement positions are 'rhematic': they co-describe the eventuality expressed by the eventive head, in this case *res*. The combinatoric semantics of the system thus accounts for the semantics of a N-V complex predicate in Urdu: provided that we merge the noun in complement position, the semantics will interpret the 'doing' event as one that was characterized by being a 'pinching' (Hale and Keyser (1993) propose much the same thing for their conflation verbs such as *dance* in English which is derived from DO-dance).

(28)

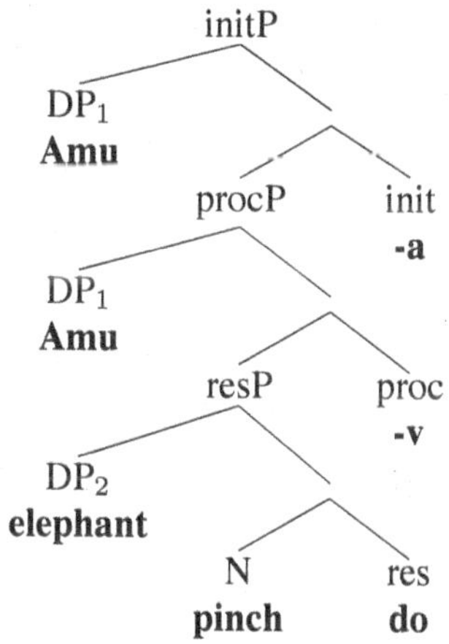

One final point should be made about (28). The DP_1 'Amu' is in Spec, procP in addition to Spec, initP. Ramchand (2008) argued that continuous dynamic involvement or psychological involvement allows causers to be interpreted as composite INITIATOR-UNDERGOERS, and DP_1 accounts for the volitionality associated with the *-va* causative.

(29)

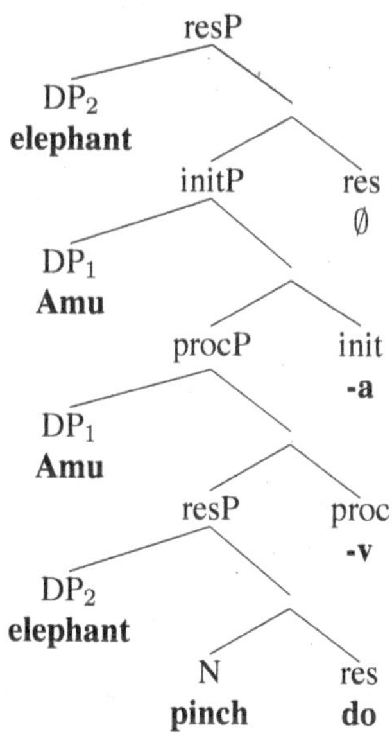

Once the causative of 'pinch-do' has been built, the next element in the structure turns the phrase into a perfect participle. This is our first use of recursion. There is no overt morphology for this, although the form in question is non-finite and is used in perfective non-finite adjunct clauses. In other South

Asian languages (e.g., Bengali), the morpheme is overt. The assumption here is that Urdu has a listed lexical item with the required categorial feature, but with null phonological exponence. In this system, null heads should be restricted to cases where such null lexical items are learnable in a particular language and are not freely available. The merging of the null *res* head is a required next step for convergence because the light verb *le* 'take' selects a verb in this form.

Since the semantics of this participle is perfective, the morpheme converts a full *init*P into a result projection, which predicates over the internal argument of the *initP*. This causes the internal argument 'the elephant' to move into the specifier of the newly created *res*P. The addition of the null result phrase creating morpheme is shown in (29).

Now we can combine this structure with the light verb *le*. Butt and Ramchand (2005) analyze complex predicates of this type within a Ramchandian decomposition structure and argue that the light verb *le* is a morpheme that identifies *init* and *proc*. This forces the root (in this case, the complex structure built up) to be a *resP* and gives the construction completive semantics. The lexical content of *le* only identifies the initiation and process vaguely since it has very abstract lexical semantics, but it says that the result state (of Amu having made the elephant be pinched) is brought about by somebody.[8]

(30)

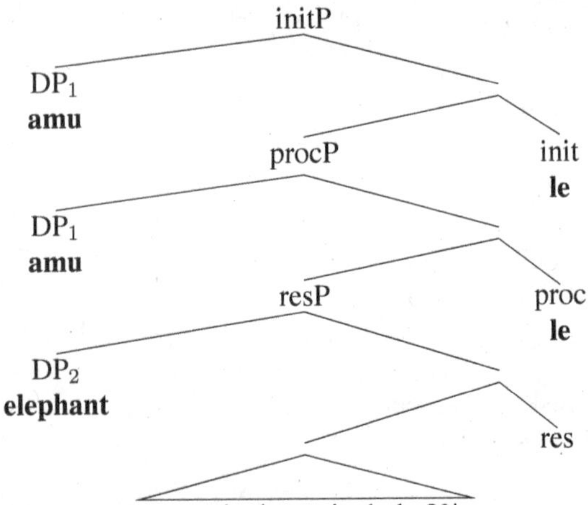

The light verb *le* creates new specifier positions for the subevents that it identifies. These must be filled. The argument in its specifiers must either be moved from a lower position or merged in from the lexical store. Merging in

[8]Different light verbs that select for a *res*P can also carry different nuances of meaning, such as suddenness, or forcefulness, but we assume that this is part of the lexical encyclopedic semantics of the individual light verb roots and should not be represented in the structure.

new DPs will cause trouble since only a maximum of three arguments can be licensed by the Case assigning functional structure in the next stage of sentence building. Attracting 'elephant' will also cause a crash because failing to move 'amu' will leave it too far down in the structure for Case licensing.[9] Thus, 'amu' is moved to fill the Spec, procP and Spec, initP positions.

It can be seen that the arguments are gradually accumulating entailments:

(31) 'elephant' RESULTEE of pinched state;
RESULTEE of someone's forceful action

'amu' INITIATOR-UNDERGOER of the willful causing of the elephant's pinched state;
INITIATOR-UNDERGOER of forceful action

The derivation is still not complete. The structure needs to be embedded under the permissive light verb *de* 'give' which requires a particular morphological form of the verb to combine with. Butt and Ramchand (2005) argued that the permissive complex predicate was like the *-a* causative in that the light verb only filled the *init* position, identifying an initiational state of giving permission. The lexical encyclopedic content of the 'give' light verb provides this content to the causing state, while the lexical encyclopedic content of the main verb identifies the content of the process that has been allowed. Before this can be done, the structure that has been built up must be converted into a *proc* category. This is the function of the *-ne* 'infinitival' morphology. The *-ne* morpheme takes a full blown verbal structure and creates a derived process out of it, one predicated crucially over the original external argument. The structure is now ready to combine with the light verb *de* to give the permission construction.

(32)

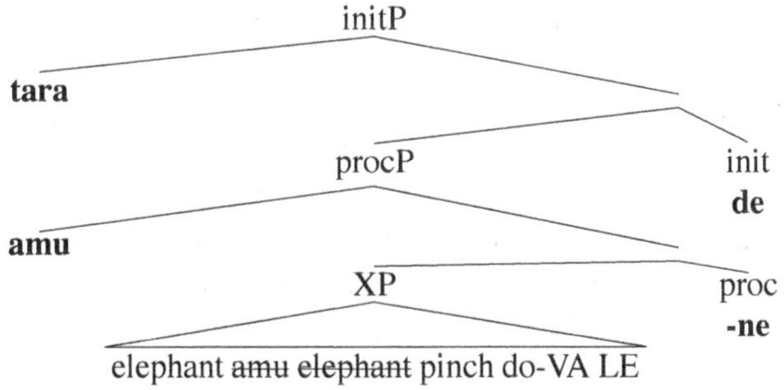

The light verb *de* introduces its own specifier which is filled by a new

[9]Elements are syntactically accessible within the same 'phase' or if they are at the edge of the previously constructed phase (cf Adger 2003). If we assume that *init*P is a phase, this allows us to move 'Amu' to the higher predicational positions.

merged argument, *tara*. Embedding under the Case assigning functional parts of the clause assigns ergative case to the argument in Spec, *init*P, dative/accusative to the argument in spec, *proc*P and accusative to 'elephant'. Since the Case properties of the complex predicate do not seem to be any different from those found in a normal ditransitive, the same mechanisms apply. Here we leave open whether Case can be assigned *in situ* via higher functional structure, or whether covert movement is required in this language for any of the three relevant arguments here. The strike-throughs in the diagram show copies of the DPs which will not be pronounced. Reading the tree from left to right (and assuming head movement in the case of the causative morphemes), we get the default word order in (10). The accumulated entailments after movement look like (33):

(33) 'elephant' RESULTEE of pinched state;
RESULTEE of someone's forceful action

'amu' INITIATOR-UNDERGOER of the willful causing of the elephant's pinched state;
INITIATOR-UNDERGOER of forceful action;
UNDERGOER of act of permission

'tara' INITIATOR of act of permission

This analysis has a number of advantages. It derives the correct word order and entailments over the argument positions, using a single syntactic mode of representation and operations that are independently attested in the grammar. In particular, it exploits the possibilities of recursion present in syntactic computation, and the hierarchy assumed on semantic grounds for subevent decomposition makes the right predictions for syntactic positioning of morphemes. The analysis also gives a concrete proposal for the interpretation and function of the morphemes *-ne* and *-va*, and for the null morpheme that creates perfect participles. Moreover, under a theory that has no lexical or argument structure module, no paradox arises from complex predications which behave as if they were embedded as a single clause under tense. The only difference between Urdu and other languages which do not exhibit the complex predicate phenomenon is that in Urdu there is more of a one-to-one correspondence between individual heads in the representation and lexical items/morphemes. In English, a single lexical item nearly always moves to identify more than one syntactic head in the structure, giving the illusion of simplicity. In fact, it is the English simple verb that is complex, in the sense of carrying more than one category feature in any particular structure.

17.5 A Computational Perspective

As was shown in section 17.3, the Urdu complex predication data fall out nicely within LFG's Linking Theory. The expectation would therefore be that this well-organized system of mapping between a-structure and GFs should be straightforward to implement given that LFG was designed with computation in mind. However, several problems present themselves. For one, from a computational linguistic perspective, *anything* involving complex argument composition is difficult. This is because information specified by the PRED(icate) is used to check that all and only the subcategorized arguments are present. Thus, operations which change the information specified by the PRED are difficult.[10] However, given the pervasive use of productive complex predicate formation, it is essential to find an efficient way to compose predicates, including the deeply nested compositions as in (10).

For another, computational accounts have generally shied away from implementing the linking relations posited by theoretical analyses of syntactically formed complex predicates such as those in sections 17.3 and 17.4. This is because when one looks closely, there is no standard version of Linking Theory, Theta-Assignment or Case Theory that is practiced. With respect to LFG, there is a core part of Linking Theory, described in Bresnan and Zaenen (1990); however, attempts to make it 'scale up', i.e., apply it to a large body of varied phenomena, has resulted in many differing versions of Linking Theory, rather than a steadily expanding body of common assumptions. The analyses presented in section 17.3, while containing a core of Linking Theory that everybody agrees on, is highly colored by ideas Butt has advanced on the basis of her work on Urdu, but which have not necessarily been widely adopted. In addition, some well-formedness checks, like Coherence and Completeness, have to be performed both at f-structure and at a-structure, thus duplicating these efforts (see also Dalrymple (2001) on how glue semantics accounts for completeness and coherence). Alsina (1996) therefore proposes to abandon checking at f-structure and to perform well-formedness checks only at a-structure (see also Alsina et al. (2005) for a discussion along these lines).

This state of affairs has led to a general perception among LFG computational linguists that a-structure and its relation to f-structure and c-structure are not theoretically well enough understood to warrant the effort of maintaining an extra projection; extra projections are computationally expensive and complex to maintain from the point of view of grammar engineering, see, e.g., Butt et al. (1999). Analyses of complex predicates thus reveal an

[10] In LFG, lexical rules are standardly used for simple argument deletions and renaming of grammatical functions (passives). However, they are not powerful enough to deal with complex predication because they do not provide complex ways of merging predicates. Even the addition of simple arguments to a predicate is complicated in that there must be a way of stating which argument slot is to be added and what happens to the existing arguments.

interesting tension between computational and theoretical approaches.

Eschewing the use of a separate projection for a-structure, Kaplan and Wedekind (1993) introduced an account of V-V complex predicates that employed the *Restriction Operator*, which manipulates f-structure representations and operates within the lexicon. However, Butt (1994) showed that this initial solution requires a large amount of undesirable lexical stipulation and cannot account for the full combinatorial power of complex predicate formation, which is a major drawback.

Subsequent developments then allowed the Restriction Operator to operate within the syntax as well as the lexicon. In particular, Butt et al. (2003) show that it is possible to implement the restriction analysis of complex predicates for Urdu in a way that seems to capture the original observations of Alsina and Butt satisfactorily. In light of the theoretical work showing the parallels between syntactic and morphological causatives, reflected in the data in section 17.2, Butt and King (2006) argue that the Restriction Operator can apply to morphologically formed complex predicates, such as the Urdu causative. Morphological causatives are usually assumed to comprise a single lexical item and hence a single constituent-structure node. The key to this analysis lies in the structure of the sublexical component and in the morphology-syntax interface assumed in computational grammars. In some ways this is similar to the analysis in section 17.4, but the morphemes are not identified as such, instead being features, and the posited structure is not as hierarchical. As with theoretical analyses, the output of one restriction operation can act as the input to another, allowing for exceedingly complex predication. The difference between theoretical LFG analyses of complex predicates and causatives and the one outlined here lies in the fact that the Restriction Operator analysis eschews any reference to a separate a-structure projection. The difference from the decompositional First-Phase Syntax account lies in less nesting, the positing of a separate functional-structure, and a different view of morphology.

The functional-structures for the relatively simple N-V complex predicate in (2), its causative in (3), and the permissive causative (9) are shown in (34). The core N-V complex predicate is represented here as a simple verb in the interests of space, however in the actual implementation, it is of course combined by means of the Restriction Operator in a manner very similar to what is described below for the other combinations.

Also note that the contribution of the aspectual light verb *le* 'take' has been abstracted away from. Again, combining this with the other predicates involves the Restriction Operator in the implementation, but the overall effect is not a valency changing and the aspectual contribution of the light verb is registered at f-structure, as shown in (34c).

(34) a. N-V: The child pinched the elephant.

PRED	‘pinch<SUBJ, OBJ>’
SUBJ	[PRED ‘child’]
OBJ	[PRED ‘elephant’]

b. N-V Caus: Amu had the elephant pinched by the child.

PRED	‘Cause<SUBJ, ‘pinch<OBL-AG, OBJ>’>’
SUBJ	[PRED ‘Amu’]
OBL-AG	[PRED ‘child’]
OBJ	[PRED ‘elephant’]

c. N-V Caus Asp Perm: Tara let Amu have the elephant pinched by the child.

PRED	‘Perm<SUBJ, ‘Cause<OBJ-GO, ‘pinch<OBL-AG, OBJ>’>’>’
SUBJ	[PRED ‘Tara’]
OBJ-GO	[PRED ‘Amu’]
OBL-AG	[PRED ‘child’]
OBJ	[PRED ‘elephant’]
TNS-ASP	[COMPLETION +]

So how are these functional-structures arrived at from the surface string, given that there is no lexical entry for the complex predicates: that is, how are the complex PRED values formed?

The Restriction Operator takes well-formed functional structures and allows them to be used for “restricting out” certain features. With complex predicates the structures are identical except for the grammatical functions of some of the arguments and the form of the predicate. For example, modifiers (e.g., *on Tuesday*, *silently*) are not affected, nor is the internal structure of the arguments, which may be quite complex.[11] Formally, this is done in LFG by annotated constituent-structure rules like in (35).

(35) Vcomplex $\rightarrow$

Vmain	Vlight
$\downarrow$\OLDGF\PRED=$\uparrow$\OLDGF\PRED ($\downarrow$OLDGF) = ($\uparrow$NEWGF) ($\uparrow$ PRED ARG2)=($\downarrow$ PRED)	$\uparrow$=$\downarrow$

The annotation $\downarrow$\OLDGF\PRED=$\uparrow$\OLDGF\PRED states that the f-structure corresponding to the complex predicate is identical to that of the heavy verb except for the argument that is not identical (often the subject) and the predicate itself. The annotation ($\downarrow$OLDGF) = ($\uparrow$NEWGF) allows the f-structure of the old argument to be used by the complex predicate as some new argument (e.g., the subject might be an oblique agent in the causative (section 17.2)).

[11]The arguments also differ in the case assignment. Case assignment is only done on non-restricted functional-structures. The rules of case assignment in the Urdu LFG implementation are similar to those described in section 17.3.

For rules like (35) to work, both the light verbs and the causative morphology need to have lexical entries which allow for the predicates to be composed, in particular to expect another predicate as an argument. For example, the entry associated with the causative morpheme is (↑ PRED) = 'Cause<(↑ SUBJ), %PRED2>'. This is very similar to the argument structure proposal in section 17.3. The annotation (↑ PRED ARG2)=(↓ PRED) in (35) provides this predicate argument to the causative, thereby creating a complex predicate.

The restriction analysis treats morphologically and syntactically formed complex predicates identically by associating the same kinds of a-structures with the light verbs and causative morphemes and by composing the complex predications in the syntax (c- and f-structure). This conforms to theoretical LFG analyses so that even though the location of the predicate manipulation is different (syntax for computational implementation and a-structure for theoretical analyses), the uniformity and, importantly, the productive formation and monoclausal nature of complex predicates are preserved.[12]

17.6 Beyond the Details: The Morning After

Complex predications are some of the most challenging constructions to account for. The purpose of this exercise has been to compare three distinct approaches that have taken the problem seriously. In doing so, certain lessons are learned. The first is that the tools available in each framework can be adapted to do the job, at least descriptively. One of the things Mohanan taught us is that in some cases, ideological rigidity can blind one to the commonalities across frameworks and obstruct general progress on substantive issues. Therefore, we begin by outlining the core discoveries that we all agree on.

Each framework needs to have a way of "composing" participant relations. In the case of LFG, this is done at a-structure by means of argument identification. In the syntactic decompositional account, participant role semantics are associated with particular positions, and entailments are accumulated by means of movement. In the computational approach, the Restriction Operator selectively modifies the f-structure of the composed predicate, keeping the other properties intact. In each of the three cases, there is evidence for constructional compositionality, where information does not get lost but is increasingly specified. The constraints on these processes (which arguments

[12]Joan Bresnan (p.c.) argues that the restriction operator raises questions about the status of the Principle of Direct Syntactic Encoding: one of the principles of LFG was to avoid the overly powerful transformation architecture of Transformational Grammar (and its successors) and to not allow for the change of grammatical functions in the syntax. However, restriction as used for complex predicate formation does not change syntactic functions. Rather it takes in new content at each level of the c-structure, i.e. as the complex predicate is built up, and uses this content to project an appropriate f-structure.

can merge with which) are a substantive point of grammatical description with empirical consequences.

Discussions at this level are an important area for crossfertilization and sharing of results. In each case, the fact of complex predication has given rise to changes in theoretical machinery, the most important of which is the highly constructional nature of the phenomenon. Modifications have to be made to the views of grammar that build in too much lexical autonomy to argument structure properties. The level of argument structure in LFG is forced to operate over and modify units that were previously seen as lexically autonomous, and that level as a whole is mapped to the f-structure. The computational approach has to develop a tool that will modify predicate argument information that is present in individual morphemes. The syntactic decompositional account has to argue that participant relations are a property of the way the syntax is built up and not directly of the individual units involved.

Differences remain, particularly at the level of overall architecture. The LFG account relies crucially on an extra level of representation: the argument structure, while the other two accounts prefer a slimmer architecture. Surprisingly then, the syntactic decompositional view advocated by Ramchand is closer architecturally to the computational approach and is much further away from the LFG account than other currently available theories within the Chomskian framework (particularly those with an argument structure level that precedes syntax). The LFG and the syntactic decomposition account, however, share an interest in the semantic properties of composed argument relations, while the computational approach manipulates grammatical structure information. The syntactic decompositional account differs from the other two in building in event structure information as part and parcel of defining participant relations, and in making no explicit statements about case.

The view here is that case is a property of the higher functional structure of the clause, thus introducing a kind of hierarchical modularity into the architecture. The modularization is justified if, as is claimed, the internal composition required at the event structure level is logically independent of (and opaque to) subsequent case assignment. The final structures proposed in section 17.4 do not differ formally from any normal clause, and the arguments are in recognisable positions. Whatever case assignment mechanisms account for case in a simplex Urdu verb should apply here, feeding off the composed structure. This architectural decision, as well as the decision to build in event structure correlates to the syntactic representation, are substantive points of difference, though not necessarily disagreement – crosstheoretical fertilization should lead to a consideration of event structure as part of the linking process (cf. Butt 1998).

In particular, because the syntactic decompositional approach includes a theory of event structure, the predictions with respect to the combinatorial possibilities of complex predicates are much more constrained. With the LFG approaches, especially the computational one, many more combinatorial possibilities are allowed than are actually possible. Within this framework, one could argue that these combinatorial possibilities are ruled out due to semantic factors governing the kinds of complex event predications one can build, but should not be ruled out by the syntax per se.

Beyond the factors discussed here, it is unclear whether the existing architectural differences have further empirical or explanatory bite, but it is possible that they will, given more research in this area. These are important issues to identify as areas of debate, central to the further development of all three frameworks.

Ramchand sees the construction of grammars as a theory of (a component of) the human mind and is not at all convinced that we know enough yet to demand computational implementability of our hypotheses, since the very structures being manipulated are still up for discussion. On the other hand, the computational linguists' goals are somewhat different from the pure theoreticians', and because of those more practical constraints, they are held to higher standards of rigour and consistency (something shared with LFG, which is highly consistent and implementable). All three approaches face the challenge of needing to achieve basic descriptive adequacy, and each approach has faced the basic challenges of complex predication head on.

In laying out the architectural differences with respect to one very complex phenomenon, we hope we have set the stage for new and productive debate.

References

Adger, David. 2003. *Core Syntax*. Oxford: Oxford University Press.

Alsina, Alex. 1996. *The Role of Argument Structure in Grammar: Evidence from Romance*. Stanford, CA: CSLI Publications.

Alsina, Alex and Smita Joshi. 1991. Parameters in causative constructions. In L. Dobrin, L. Nichols, and R. Rodriguez, eds., *Papers from the 27th Regional Meeting of the Chicago Linguistic Society (CLS)*, pages 1–16.

Alsina, Alex, Tara Mohanan, and KP Mohanan. 2005. How to get rid of the COMP. In M. Butt and T. H. King, eds., *Proceedings of the LFG05 Conference*, pages 21–41. Stanford, CA: CSLI Publications. University of Bergen.

Baker, Mark. 1988. *Incorporation: A Theory of Grammatical Function Changing*. Chicago: The University of Chicago Press.

Bhatt, Rajesh. 2003. Topics in the syntax of modern Indo-Aryan languages: Causativization. Class Handout.

Bresnan, Joan and Annie Zaenen. 1990. Deep unaccusativity in LFG. In K. Dziwirek, P. Farrell, and E. Mejías-Bikandi, eds., *Grammatical Relations: A Cross-Theoretical Perspective*, pages 45–57. Stanford, CA: CSLI Publications.

Butt, Miriam. 1994. Machine translation and complex predicates. In H. Trost, ed., *Proceedings of the Conference Verarbeitung Natürlicher Sprache (KONVENS)*, pages 62–71. Vienna.

Butt, Miriam. 1995. *The Structure of Complex Predicates in Urdu*. Stanford, CA: CSLI Publications.

Butt, Miriam. 1998. Constraining argument merger through aspect. In E. Hinrichs, A. Kathol, and T. Nakazawa, eds., *Complex Predicates in Nonderivational Syntax*, pages 73–113. Academic Press.

Butt, Miriam. 2006. *Theories of Case*. Cambridge: Cambridge University Press.

Butt, Miriam and Tracy Holloway King. 2006. Restriction for morphological valency alternations: The Urdu causative. In M. Butt, M. Dalrymple, and T. H. King, eds., *Intelligent Linguistic Architectures: Variations on Themes by Ronald M. Kaplan*, pages 235–258. CSLI Publications.

Butt, Miriam, Tracy Holloway King, and John T. Maxwell III. 2003. Complex predicates via restriction. In M. Butt and T. H. King, eds., *The Proceedings of the LFG '03 Conference*, pages 92–104. Stanford, CA: CSLI Publications.

Butt, Miriam, Tracy Holloway King, María-Eugenia Niño, and Frédérique Segond. 1999. *A Grammar Writer's Cookbook*. Stanford, CA: CSLI Publications.

Butt, Miriam and Gillian Ramchand. 2005. Complex aspectual structure in Hindi/Urdu. In N. Ertischik-Shir and T. Rapoport, eds., *The Syntax of Aspect*, pages 117–153. Oxford: Oxford University Press.

Chomsky, Noam. 1995. *The Minimalist Program*. Cambridge, MA: MIT Press.

Dalrymple, Mary. 2001. *Lexical Functional Grammar*. New York: Academic Press.

Hale, Kenneth and Samuel Jay Keyser. 1993. On argument structure and the lexical expression of syntactic relations. In K. Hale and S. J. Keyser, eds., *The View from Building 20: Essays in Linguistics in Honor of Sylvain Bromberger*, no. 24 in Current Studies in Linguistics, pages 53–109. Cambridge, MA: MIT Press.

Harley, Heidi. 1995. *Subjects, Events, and Licensing*. Ph.D. thesis, MIT.

Hornstein, Norbert. 2000. *Move! A Minimalist Theory of Construal*. Oxford: Blackwell Publishers.

Kaplan, Ronald M. and Jürgen Wedekind. 1993. Restriction and correspondence-based translation. In *Proceedings of the 6th Conference of the Association for Computational Linguistics European Chapter (EACL)*, pages 193–202.

Kratzer, Angelika. 1996. Severing the external argument from the verb. In J. Rooryck and L. Zaring, eds., *Phrase Structure and the Lexicon*, pages 109–137. Dordrecht: Kluwer.

Mohanan, Tara. 1988. Causatives in Malayạlam. Unpublished ms, Stanford University.

Mohanan, Tara. 1994. *Argument Structure in Hindi*. Stanford, CA: CSLI Publications.

Parsons, Terence. 1990. *Events in the Semantics of English: A Study in Subatomic Semantics*. Cambridge, MA: MIT Press.

Pustejovsky, James. 1991. The syntax of event structure. *Cognition* 41:47–81.

Ramchand, Gillian. 2008. *Verb Meaning and the Lexicon: A First Phase Syntax*. Cambridge: Cambridge University Press.

Saksena, Anuradha. 1982. *Topics in the Analysis of Causatives with an Account of Hindi Paradigms*. University of California Press.

Vendler, Zeno. 1967. *Linguistics in Philosophy*. Ithaca, NY: Cornell University Press.

18

Constraints on Operator Binding in Malayalam

MARY DALRYMPLE

Mohanan (1984) presents evidence from Malayalam that 'operator binding' of in-situ relativized phrases in co-relative clauses, or of wh-phrases in wh-questions, patterns differently from 'gap binding' in an alternative relative clause construction involving a gap rather than a relativized phrase. In this paper, I review the data presented by Mohanan (1984), and provide a new treatment which preserves the crucial intuitions of the original analysis.

18.1 Relative Clause Formation Strategies

The 'co-relative construction' involves the appearance of a relativized phrase instead of a gap in the relative clause. The following sentence exemplifies the co-relative construction in Malayalam:[1]

(1) Co-relative construction:

[[kuṭṭi eeṯə aanaye nuḷḷiyoo] aa aanaa] uraŋŋi
child REL elephant-ACC pinched that elephant-NOM slept

'The elephant such that the child pinched it slept.' (372)
('The elephant, such that the child pinched said elephant, slept.'/
'[[The child pinched which elephant], that elephant] slept.')

The co-relative clause is 'the child pinched REL elephant', in which a head noun is modified by the relative determiner *eeṯə*, glossed REL. The same head noun appears in the main clause, modified by the demonstrative determiner

[1]Except where noted, all data are from Mohanan (1984), and are annotated with the page number on which the example appears.

Reality Exploration and Discovery: Pattern Interaction in Language and Life.
Linda Uyechi and Lian-Hee Wee (eds.).

aa. The co-relative construction in Malayalam is different from its counterpart in Hindi or Marathi in that the co-relative clause appears adjacent to the noun it modifies and forms a constituent with it, as indicated by the brackets in (1), rather than adjoining to the main clause.[2]

The other relative clause formation strategy in Malayalam is the gap relative strategy, exemplified in (2).

(2) Gap relative construction:

[[kuṭṭi ___	ṉuḷḷiya] aanaa]	uraŋŋi
child	pinched elephant-NOM	slept

'The elephant that the child pinched slept.' (360)

In this construction, the relative clause contains a gap rather than a relativized phrase, and is analogous to English relative clauses with no relative pronoun or complementizer ('the man [I met ___]').

Mohanan (1984) uses the term 'operator binding' to describe the co-relative construction: in operator binding, a non-overt element higher in the tree (the operator) is scopally related to a lower overt element (the relativized phrase) by means of a path through the tree connecting the operator to the lower element. Binding in wh-questions is similar, with a non-overt operator binding the in-situ wh-phrase. 'Gap binding', in contrast, involves binding of a non-overt element, the gap. Mohanan (1984) shows that syntactic constraints on operator binding and gap binding differ, and provides an explanation for the differences which appeals to paths from the operator to the bound position, and to Pesetsky's (1982) Path Containment Condition. In the next section, I review some of the data presented by Mohanan (1984) as a basis for the discussion in the following sections.

18.2 Constraints on Relativization

Mohanan (1984) shows that operator binding in the co-relative construction does not obey island constraints which are often associated with relative clause formation. The relativized phrase can appear inside a complex NP, a sentential subject, a coordinate structure, an adjunct, or a gap relative clause:

[2] For discussion of the syntax and semantics of the clause-adjoined co-relatives found in Hindi and Marathi, see Srivastav (1991) and Dayal (1996).

(3) Relativized phrase in complex NP:

[[[[kuṭṭi eeṯə aanaye ṉuḷḷi] eṉṉə kaar̄yam] amma
child-NOM REL elephant pinched that fact-NOM mother-NOM
paraññuwoo] aa aana] uraŋŋi
said that elephant-NOM slept

'The elephant such that [mother stated [the fact that the child pinched it]] slept.' (373)
('[Mother stated [the fact that the child pinched which elephant]], that elephant slept.')

(4) Relativized phrase in sentential subject:

[[[kuṭṭi eeṯə aanaye ṉuḷḷi] eṉṉə ṉaaṭaake
child-NOM REL elephant-ACC pinched that land-LOC
par̄aṉṉuwoo] aa aana] uraŋŋi
spread that elephant-NOM slept

'The elephant such that [[that the child pinched it] spread throughout the land] slept.' (373)
('[[That the child pinched which elephant] spread throughout the land], that elephant slept.')

(5) Relativized phrase in coordinate structure:

(?) [[[[kuṭṭi eeṯə aanaye ṉuḷḷi eññum] [amma
child-NOM REL elephant-ACC pinched COMP mother-NOM
acchane aṭiccu eṉṉum]] jooṇ paraññuwoo] aa
father-ACC beat COMP John-NOM said that
aana] uraŋŋi
elephant-NOM slept

'The elephant such that [John said that [the child pinched it] and [mother beat father]] slept.' (373)
('John said that [[the child pinched which elephant] and [mother beat father]], that elephant slept.')

(6) Relativized phrase in adjunct:

[[[kuṭṭi eeṯə aanaye ṉuḷḷiyappooḷ] amma
child-NOM REL elephant-ACC pinched-then mother-NOM
cir̃iccuwoo] aa aana] uraŋŋi
smiled that elephant-NOM slept

'The elephant such that mother smiled when the child pinched it slept.' (373)
('[Mother smiled [when the child pinched which elephant]], that elephant slept.')

(7) Relativized phrase in gap relative:

[[[[eeṯə kuṭṭi ___ ṉuḷḷiya] aana] uraŋŋiyoo] aa kuṭṭi]
REL child-NOM pinched elephant slept that child
kar̃aññu
cried

'The child such that [the elephant that it pinched slept], cried.' (376)
('[[The elephant that which child pinched] slept], that child cried.')

In Malayalam wh-questions, wh-phrases do not appear in a displaced position, but remain in situ, like the relativized phrase in a co-relative clause. With respect to island constraints, the distribution of the wh-phrase in a wh-question is exactly the same as that of the relativized phrase: a wh-phrase can scope out of a complex NP, a sentential subject, a coordinate structure, an adjunct, or a gap relative clause. In contrast, the gap in a gap relative clause does obey island constraints, and the gap relative counterparts of all of these examples are ungrammatical. See Mohanan (1984) for discussion and details.

However, the distribution of the relativized phrase is not completely unconstrained. In particular, the relativized phrase cannot appear as the nonclefted constituent in a cleft construction, or internal to a nonclefted constituent:[3]

(8) Relativized phrase as nonclefted constituent in a cleft:

* [[kuṭṭi aaṇə [eeṯə aanaye] ṉuḷḷiyat] aa aana]
child-NOM is REL elephant-ACC pinched-it that elephant-NOM
uraŋŋi
slept

'The elephant such that it was the child that pinched it slept.' (378)
('[It was the child that pinched which elephant], that elephant slept.')

[3]Thanks to Tara Mohanan for discussion of example (9).

(9) Relativized phrase embedded within nonclefted constituent:

* [[kuṭṭi aaṇoo [[[eeṯə aana] walarṯiya puuccaye]
child-NOM is REL elephant-NOM brought.up cat-ACC
ṉuḷḷiyaṯə] aa aana] uraŋŋi
pinched-it that elephant-NOM slept

'The elephant such that it was the child that pinched the cat that the elephant brought up slept.'
('[It was [the child that pinched [the cat that which elephant brought up]]], that elephant slept.')

In contrast, it may appear as the clefted constituent or internal to the clefted constituent:

(10) Relativized phrase as clefted constituent:

[[kuṭṭi [eeṯə aanaye] aaṇoo ṉuḷḷiyaṯə] aa aana]
child-NOM REL elephant-ACC is pinched-it that elephant-NOM
uraŋŋi
slept

'The elephant such that it was it that the child pinched slept.' (378)
('[It was which elephant that the child pinched], that elephant slept.')

(11) Relativized phrase embedded within clefted constituent:

[[kuṭṭi [[[eeṯə aana] walarṯiya puuccaye] aaṇoo
child-NOM REL elephant-NOM brought.up cat-ACC is
ṉuḷḷiyaṯə] aa aana] uraŋŋi
pinched-it that elephant-NOM slept

'The elephant such that it was the cat that it brought up that the child pinched slept.' (378)
('[It was [the cat that brought up which elephant] that the child pinched], that elephant slept.')

Interestingly, the example in (10) seems to counterexemplify Bresnan and Mchombo's (1987) proposed constraints on the relation between clefting and relativization. They analyze the relativized constituent in a relative clause as bearing the TOPIC role and the clefted constituent in a cleft construction as bearing the FOCUS role, and they claim that the same constituent cannot be both FOCUS and TOPIC at the same level of clause structure. This correctly rules out unacceptable English examples such as *??I met the person who it was ___ that Marilyn suspected* (Bresnan and Mchombo's example 37b), in which the clefted constituent is also the target of relativization, but also incorrectly rules out example (10). I return below to a discussion of constraints on the distribution of the relativized phrase in cleft constructions.

Again, the distribution of the wh-phrase exactly mirrors the distribution of the relativized phrase. In contrast, either the clefted or the noncleft constituent can be gapped in a gap relative clause (Mohanan 1984, 377-378).

Additionally, the relativized phrase may not appear within a co-relative clause:

(12) Relativized phrase in embedded co-relative clause:

* [[[[[eeṯə kuṭṭi] [eeṯə aanaye] ṉuḷḷiyoo] aa
REL child-NOM REL elephant-ACC pinched that
aana] uraŋŋiyoo] aa kuṭṭi] kar̃aññu
elephant-NOM slept that child cried

'The child such that the elephant such that he pinched it slept, cried.' (376)

('[[[[Which child pinched which elephant], that elephant] slept], that child] cried.')

Similarly, wh-phrases cannot scope out of an embedded co-relative clause. Finally, neither the relativized phrase nor a wh-phrase may appear in an embedded question:

(13) Relativized phrase in embedded question:

* [[[aar̃ə eeṯə aanaye ṉuḷḷi eṉṉə] amma
who-NOM REL elephant-ACC pinched COMP mother-NOM
cooḏiccuwoo] aa aana] uraŋŋi
asked that elephant-NOM slept

'The elephant such that mother asked who pinched it slept.' (374)

('[Mother asked who pinched which elephant], that elephant slept.')

The gap in a gap relative clause is not constrained in this way, and may appear in an embedded question.

TABLE 1 summarizes constraints on the syntax of gap relatives, co-relatives, and wh-questions.

	complex NP	sent. subject	coord. structure	adjunct	gap relative
gap	no (8a)	no (8b)	no (8c)	no (8d)	no (32c)
relativized phrase	yes (28a) [3]	yes (28b) [4]	yes (28c) [5]	yes (28d) [6]	yes (32a) [7]
wh-phrase	yes (9a)	yes (9b)	yes (9c)	yes (9d)	yes (30b)

	co-rel	clefted const.	nonclefted const.	emb. question
gap	no (32d)	yes	yes (33)	yes (30a)
relativized phrase	no (32b) [12]	yes (34a,b) [10,11]	no (35a,b) [8]	no (29a) [13]
wh-phrase	no (29b)	yes (11b,13)	no (12)	no (23)

TABLE 1 Distribution of gap in gap relative clauses, relativized phrase in co-relative clauses, and wh-phrase in wh-questions. Numbers in parentheses refer to example numbers in Mohanan (1984); numbers for examples that are also provided in this paper are given inside square brackets.

18.3 Wh- and Relative Clause Paths

Mohanan (1984) analyzes Malayalam wh-questions and co-relatives in terms of the relation between an in-situ overt element and an empty operator in a c-commanding position. The relation between those two elements is expressed in terms of a path connecting them, in the manner of Pesetsky (1982). Thus, for example, a wh-phrase in an embedded clause which has scope over a higher clause is analyzed as bound by an unpronounced operator Q in the higher clause and connected to that operator by means of a path through the tree:

(14)

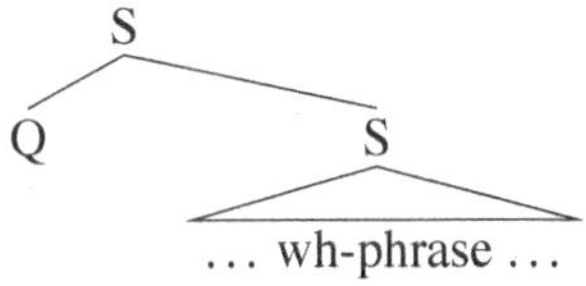

The difference between constructions of this type and their counterparts in languages like English is that there is no displacement of the wh-phrase. Under this analysis, English is similar to Malayalam in that a position higher in the tree is related to a lower position; the difference is that in English the relation is between a displaced wh-phrase and a gap, while in Malayalam the relation is between an unpronounced operator and a wh-phrase in situ.

Mohanan (1984) proposes that constraints on the distribution of wh-phrases and relativized phrases can be explained by reference to Pesetsky's (1982) Path Containment Condition:

(15) Path Containment Condition: If two paths overlap, one must contain the other.

This attributes the ungrammaticality of example (8) to the presence of two operator paths in the tree, one connecting the focus operator F to the focused element 'child', and the other connecting the co-relative operator R to the relativized phrase 'REL elephant'.

(16) Disallowed:

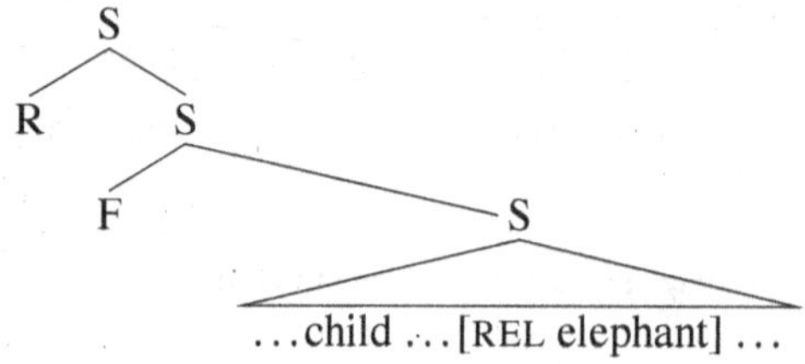

The co-relative operator R binds 'REL elephant', and the focus operator F binds 'child'. These two paths do not obey Path Containment (the paths overlap, but neither contains the other, since each path includes some nodes not included in the other), and the example is ruled out.

Crucial to the analysis is the distinction between paths associated with operator binding and those associated with gap binding. In particular, the analysis requires that gap binding is *invisible* to operator binding when Path Containment is applied. If this is not assumed, then example (7), in which a relativized phrase appears in a gap relative clause, would be incorrectly ruled out, as illustrated in (17). Here, the co-relative operator R binds 'REL child', while the gap operator G binds the gap. If the path from G to the gap were visible to Path Containment, a violation would ensue: again, the paths overlap, but neither contains the other. If we assume that the path from G to the gap is invisible or ignored in operator binding, we can explain why the configuration in (17) is allowed.

(17)

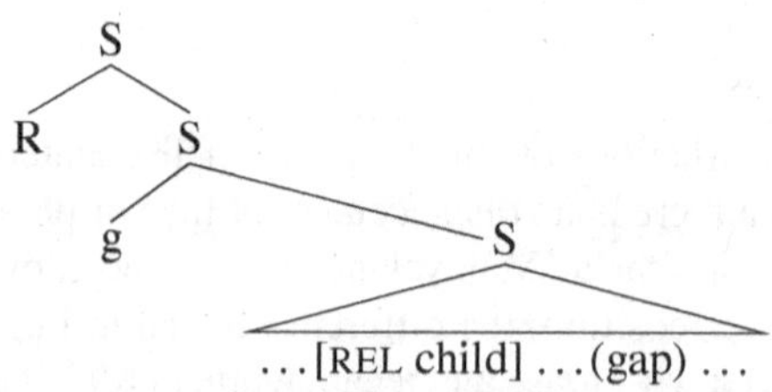

Thus, the analysis entails that the relativized phrase and the wh-phrase can appear anywhere in the clause, including within islands, except when another operator-bound in-situ constituent is present. Relativized phrases cannot appear in embedded questions, where there is a wh-phrase bound by the operator Q; in an embedded co-relative clause, where another relativized phrase is bound by the operator R; or as a non-clefted constituent in a cleft, where another constituent is bound by the operator F. The relativized phrase can appear in a cleft clause as the clefted constituent, however: even though the relativized phrase is bound by two operators, R and F, the path from R contains the path from F, and Path Containment is obeyed.

18.4 Gap Relatives and Co-relative Binding

As Mohanan (1984) notes, the pattern of grammaticality shown in TABLE 1 for gap relative clauses, including the inability of gaps to appear in co-relative clauses, can be fully explained by requiring that gap relatives obey island constraints. Kaplan and Zaenen (1989) show that long-distance dependencies such as are found in Malayalam gap relative clauses are best characterized in terms of abstract grammatical functions rather than phrase structure configuration, at a level of grammatical representation such as LFG's functional structure. This contrasts with Mohanan's (1984) analysis, which is stated in terms of constraints on the constituent structure tree, though it is in line with the speculative discussion in Mohanan (1984, sec. 11). In the analysis of gap relative clauses, a path is defined through the functional structure which ends in the grammatical function of the gap. Island constraints are imposed by preventing the path from including attributes which define an island; for example, the adjunct island constraint can be imposed by requiring the path not to contain the attribute ADJ(unct). In (18), island constraints on gap relatives are imposed in the definition of the path RELPATH through the functional structure. No TOPIC function is introduced in this relative clause rule; even so, the meaning constructor **rel** given below the phrase structure rule in (18) allows the meaning of the relative clause to be derived, as explained below.

(18) Gap relative clauses:

NP →	S	N′
	$\downarrow \in (\uparrow \text{ ADJ})$	$\uparrow = \downarrow$
	$(\downarrow \text{ RELPATH}) = \%\text{rel}$	
	$(\%\text{rel PRED}) = \text{`PRO'}$	
	rel	

$$\text{RELPATH} = [\text{GF} - \{\text{SUBJ}, \text{ADJ}, \in\}]^{*}\ \text{GF}$$

rel $\lambda P.\lambda Q.\lambda X.P(X) \wedge Q(X):$

$[\%\text{rel}_\sigma \multimap \downarrow_\sigma] \multimap$

$[[(\uparrow_\sigma \text{ VAR}) \multimap (\uparrow_\sigma \text{ RESTR})] \multimap$

$[(\uparrow_\sigma \text{ VAR}) \multimap (\uparrow_\sigma \text{ RESTR})]]$

I assume that the Malayalam clause is best analyzed in terms of the exocentric category S, as proposed by Bresnan (2001), and that the gap relative clause appears in the specifier position of NP. Nothing hangs on these assumptions about the phrase structure of gap relatives in Malayalam, however; the annotations on the relative clause node are what is at issue here.

The rule in (18) follows the standard treatment of long-distance dependencies in relative clauses in LFG by means of functional uncertainty, as proposed by Kaplan and Zaenen (1989).[4] The first line of the functional annotations on the clausal constituent S requires the functional structure of the relative clause (↓) to be a modifier, appearing as a member of the ADJ(uncts) set of the modified NP. The second line introduces a functional metavariable %rel, the functional structure corresponding to the gap in the relative clause, and requires it to appear at the end of the path RELPATH in the relative clause. RELPATH delineates the syntactic domain in which the gap can occur, and is defined in terms of the regular expression given below the rule in (18). In the definition of RELPATH, the GFs in the first part of the path range over the grammatical functions within which the gap may felicitously appear, and the final GF is the grammatical function of the gap itself: the gap may be embedded arbitrarily deeply inside any grammatical function (GF) *except* SUBJ (the sentential subject condition) or ADJ (adjunct islands and the complex NP[5]), and may not appear as an element ∈ of a coordinate structure (the coordinate structure constraint). The third line of the annotations on S ensures that the relative clause is syntactically complete by providing the gap with a pronominal PRED value.

Finally, the fourth line introduces a meaning constructor **rel**, whose definition appears below the definition of RELPATH in (18). This meaning constructor provides a way of deriving the meaning of the relative clause within the glue semantics approach of LFG (Dalrymple 1999, 2001, Asudeh 2004). Essentially, the meaning of the relative clause is obtained by abstracting on the position corresponding to the gap, as proposed for Irish by Asudeh (2004). Unlike relative clauses in English, no TOPIC function is introduced into the relative clause functional structure of gap relative clauses: since there is no overt material in the relative clause corresponding to the relativized position, the position is not syntactically prominent. With this meaning constructor, the proper interpretation for relative clauses can be obtained even when no

---

[4]See Dalrymple (2001), Chapter 14 and Falk (2001), Chapter 6 for more discussion, and Asudeh (2004) for discussion of an alternative, successive-cyclic means of characterizing long-distance dependencies.

[5]This assumes that the clausal constituent in (3) is an appositive modifier of *kaar̃yam* 'fact'. If this constituent is analyzed instead as a clausal complement COMP, RELPATH would be defined so as to disallow paths through the COMP of a typically nominal grammatical function such as SUBJ or OBJ, but to allow paths through a COMP contained within a typically clausal grammatical function such as COMP or XCOMP.

TOPIC is introduced. The absence of a TOPIC in gap relative clauses reflects Mohanan's observation that gap binding is invisible for application of the Path Containment Condition, and is crucial for the treatment of co-relatives in the next section.

18.5 Co-relative Binding

We have seen that the distribution of the relativized phrase in the co-relative clause is not syntactically constrained in the usual sense, since the relativized phrase can appear within constituents that behave as islands for the gap relative construction. This is in contrast to the co-relative construction in other languages: for instance, Dalrymple and Joshi (1986) show that the distribution of the Marathi relativized phrase is syntactically constrained.

The phrase structure rule for gap relative clauses given in (18) is not applicable to co-relatives, which are adjoined to a full noun phrase which must contain a demonstrative determiner; a different phrase structure rule for co-relatives is needed. The constraints associated with this rule are different from those associated with the gap relative rule in that island constraints are not imposed. Instead, the co-relative path is constrained by the presence of a TOPIC or FOCUS function in the f-structures on the path, capturing Mohanan's intuition that an intervening binder interferes with co-relative binding.

(19) Co-relative clauses:

$$\text{NP} \rightarrow \begin{array}{c} \text{S} \\ \downarrow\in(\uparrow \text{ADJ}) \\ (\downarrow \text{TOPIC}) = \%\text{rel} \\ (\downarrow \text{CORELPATH}) = \%\text{rel} \\ (\%\text{rel PRONTYPE}) =_c \text{REL} \end{array} \quad \begin{array}{c} \text{NP} \\ \uparrow = \downarrow \end{array}$$

$$\text{CORELPATH} = \begin{array}{c} \text{GF}^* \\ \{\neg(\leftarrow \{\text{TOPIC}|\text{FOCUS}\}) \\ \mid (\leftarrow \{\text{TOPIC}|\text{FOCUS}\}\ \text{GF}^*) = \%\text{rel}\} \end{array} \quad \text{GF}$$

As in the rule in (18), the first line in the annotations on S ensures that the co-relative clause is a member of the ADJ set. The second line provides the co-relative clause with a TOPIC, referred to by the functional metavariable %rel; this is crucially different from the rule for gap relative clauses, which do not contain a relative pronoun or other overt binder, and so do not have a TOPIC. The third and fourth lines provide additional information and constraints on %rel: the third line identifies %rel with the embedded relativized phrase within the co-relative clause, accessible by the path CORELPATH, and the fourth line ensures that %rel is a relativized phrase with PRONTYPE REL.

The path CORELPATH through the co-relative clause to the functional structure of the relativized phrase is required to consist of any number of grammatical functions GF* followed by the grammatical function GF of the relativized phrase. No island constraints are imposed; instead, the annotations on GF* are *off-path constraints* (see Dalrymple (2001), Chapter 6 for more discussion) which impose the equivalent of the Path Containment Condition. According to the definition of off-path constraints, the left arrow ← in an annotation on an attribute name refers to the functional structure which has that attribute. Thus, the annotation on GF* requires that each functional structure through which the path passes either (1) contains no TOPIC or FOCUS function, or (2) contains a TOPIC or FOCUS function which is identical to the co-relative TOPIC, or which contains it.

The inability of a relativized phrase to appear as the nonclefted constituent in a cleft (8), in a co-relative clause (12), or in an embedded question (13) follows from the definition of CORELPATH: for each functional structure in the path, either there is no TOPIC or FOCUS (the functional structure is not a co-relative clause or an embedded question), or the FOCUS or TOPIC contains the relativized phrase. In the second case, the functional structure is a co-relative construction or a cleft construction, and the relativized phrase is the TOPIC of the co-relative clause or the clefted FOCUS constituent in a cleft (10).

The lexical entry for the relative determiner *eeṯə* marks its phrase as relativized:

(20) eeṯə (↑ SPEC) = eeṯə
(↑ PRONTYPE) = REL

It is also associated with a meaning constructor to derive the meaning of the relative clause, which we will not provide here; it is similar to the meaning constructor for the English relative pronoun 'whose' given in Dalrymple (2001, Chapter 14).

This analysis of gap relatives and co-relatives is an explicit instantiation of the research program outlined in Section 11 of Mohanan (1984), where what Mohanan calls 'sentential grammatical functions' like TOPIC and FOCUS govern the behavior and distribution of the relativized phrase. It captures Mohanan's insight that the TOPIC and FOCUS roles associated with relativized phrases and wh-phrases are crucial to determining the distribution of the relativized phrase in the co-relative construction, and also explains why gap relative clauses seem to be invisible to the Path Containment Condition: since they do not have an overt relative pronoun, they do not contain a TOPIC. Even without a TOPIC, the rules for gap relatives ensure that island constraints on relative clause formation are enforced, and the proper meaning for the relative clause is obtained.

Acknowledgments

This paper is (loosely) based on a term paper I wrote in 1987 for Mohanan's *Structure of Malayalam* class at Stanford University. I had been lucky enough to attend Mohanan's class in Lexical Functional Grammar at the University of Texas in 1982, which was a life-transforming experience; when Mohanan arrived at Stanford to teach syntax, I was overjoyed. His teaching built a solid foundation in thinking about syntax and doing syntactic argumentation that has served me well ever since. I am grateful to Smita Joshi, K.P. Mohanan, and Tara Mohanan for helpful discussion of the original paper, and to Ash Asudeh, Miriam Butt, Tara Mohanan, and an anonymous reviewer for comments on the current version.

References

Asudeh, Ash. 2004. *Resumption as Resource Management*. Ph.D. thesis, Stanford University.

Bresnan, Joan. 2001. *Lexical-Functional Syntax*. Oxford: Blackwell Publishers.

Bresnan, Joan and Sam A. Mchombo. 1987. Topic, pronoun, and agreement in Chicheŵa. *Language* 63(4):741–782.

Dalrymple, Mary, ed. 1999. *Semantics and Syntax in Lexical Functional Grammar: The Resource Logic Approach*. Cambridge, MA: The MIT Press.

Dalrymple, Mary. 2001. *Lexical Functional Grammar*, vol. 34 of *Syntax and Semantics*. New York, NY: Academic Press.

Dalrymple, Mary and Smita Joshi. 1986. Relative clause linking in Marathi. Presented at the 1986 Annual Meeting of the Linguistic Society of America, New York.

Dayal, Veneeta. 1996. *Locality in WH Quantification: Questions and Relative Clauses in Hindi*. Dordrecht: Kluwer Academic Publishers.

Kaplan, Ronald M. and Annie Zaenen. 1989. Long-distance dependencies, constituent structure, and functional uncertainty. In M. Baltin and A. Kroch, eds., *Alternative Conceptions of Phrase Structure*, pages 17–42. Chicago University Press. Reprinted in Dalrymple, Kaplan, Maxwell and Zaenen (1995):137–165.

Mohanan, K. P. 1984. Operator binding and the path containment condition. *Natural Language and Linguistic Theory* 2(4):357 – 396.

Pesetsky, David. 1982. *Paths and Categories*. Ph.D. thesis, MIT.

Srivastav, Veneeta. 1991. The syntax and semantics of correlatives. *Natural Language and Linguistic Theory* 9(4):637–686.

19

Evidence for the Linearization-Based Theory of Long-Distance Scrambling in Japanese

SHÛICHI YATABE

19.1 Introduction

On a purely descriptive level, it can be said that scrambling is clause-bound in some languages but not in others. Scrambling in German is more or less clause-bound; apparent exceptions arguably involve clause union and are to be dealt with in terms of function composition (in Combinatory Categorial Grammar parlance) or argument composition (in Head-Driven Phrase Structure Grammar parlance). Likewise, it has been noted that scrambling in Malayalam is clause-bound (Mohanan 1982). On the other hand, scrambling in languages like Japanese and Korean does not seem to be clause-bound, at least at first blush. The Japanese sentence in (1) is one example involving long-distance scrambling, i.e. scrambling that seems not to be clause-bound. (The numbers in angle brackets here and in (10) refer to the result of questionnaire studies described in section 19.3.)

(1) ?[Sono dôbutsuen ni], Tarô ga panda ga iru to itta
[that zoo DAT] Tarô NOM panda NOM are COMP said
rashii no desu. <12, 17, 10, 1>
it seems
'It seems that Tarô said that there are pandas at that zoo.'

There have been two fundamentally different theories of long-distance scrambling in languages like Japanese and Korean: the movement-based the-

Reality Exploration and Discovery: Pattern Interaction in Language and Life.
Linda Uyechi and Lian-Hee Wee (eds.).

ory, according to which long-distance scrambling is an operation that induces filler-gap dependency (Harada 1977, Saito 1985), and the linearization-based theory, according to which long-distance scrambling alters the linear order of expressions without altering the syntactic structure involved (Yatabe 1996, 2003). The movement-based theory views long-distance scrambling as something analogous to *wh*-movement in a language like English; the linearization-based theory, on the other hand, views long-distance scrambling as something analogous to extraposition out of NP in a language like English.

The purpose of this paper is to present some evidence for the linearization-based theory of long-distance scrambling in Japanese. First, in Section 19.2, the outline of the linearization-based theory will be described and its predictions will be delineated. Then, in Section 19.3, the result of several questionnaire studies regarding those predictions will be presented and its implications will be discussed.

19.2 Extraposition and Long-distance Scrambling

The linearization-based theory of long-distance scrambling is based on the view that long-distance scrambling in a language like Japanese is analogous to extraposition out of NP in languages like English and German, and it builds on Kathol and Pollard's analysis of extraposition in German (Kathol and Pollard 1995). Thus, in this section, Kathol and Pollard's theory of extraposition will be described in section 19.2.1, before the linearization-based theory of long-distance scrambling in Japanese is presented in section 19.2.2.

19.2.1 The Kathol-Pollard theory of extraposition

Extraposition out of NP in English has the following three properties which set it apart from canonical instances of filler-gap dependency. First, a string α can be extraposed out of a phrase β only if α constitutes the right periphery of β, as shown by (2). In these examples the words that have been extraposed are shown in italics.

(2) *It appears I have given the assignment to a fool after all(,) *complete and utter*. (from Stucky 1987)
(Cf. There may be somebody here *more technically oriented than I*.)

Second, when two or more constituents are extraposed out of a phrase, the linear order between those constituents must be preserved, as shown by (3).

(3) (from Dowty 1996)
a. Can you give me the names of any newcomers as soon as possible *from Finland who may have programming experience*?
(Cf. newcomers from Finland who may have programming experience)

b. *Can you give me the names of any newcomers as soon as possible *who may have programming experience from Finland*? (Cf. *newcomers who may have programming experience from Finland)

And third, extraposition violates some of the island conditions that constrain canonical instances of filler-gap dependency such as topicalization. For instance, extraposition out of a subject NP always violates the condition that bans extraction out of a grammatical subject. Likewise, a sentence like (4) indicates that extraposition is also allowed to violate the Coordinate Structure Constraint.

(4) ?She was comparing Kyoto University today *and Tokyo University*. (from Yatabe 2003)

This example is a result of dislocating the conjunct *and Tokyo University* out of the coordinate structure *Kyoto University and Tokyo University*, and it is nevertheless only awkward, unlike an example like (5), which is completely unacceptable.

(5) *[And John]$_i$, I saw [Bill t_i]

The theory of discontinuous constituency proposed in Kathol and Pollard (1995) offers one way to explain why extraposition has these properties.[1] In Kathol and Pollard's theory, the portion of a syntactic structure that determines grammatical dependency relations is represented by means of an unordered tree, that is, a tree with no specifications as to the ordering of its constituents. The information concerning the linear order between the constituents is contained in what are called *order domains*, each of which is associated with a node in the unordered tree. An order domain is a list of *domain objects*, and is given as the value of the DOM feature. A domain object is very much like a sign; unlike a sign, however, it does not carry any information as to its internal morphosyntactic structure.

Let us take a concrete example. Figure 1 shows part of the structure assigned to the English sentence *The man bought it*. What is shown in this figure is an unordered tree; there is no linear precedence relation between the VP node and the NP node. The order domain (i.e. the DOM value) of the VP node consists of two domain objects, one that is pronounced *bought*, and the other one that is pronounced *it*. The order between these two domain objects is significant; it indicates that this VP is to be pronounced *bought it*, rather than *it bought*. Likewise, the order domain of the NP node tells us that this NP is to be pronounced *the man*, and the order domain of the S node tells us that the S node is to be pronounced *The man bought it*.

[1]Due to space limitation, other theories of discontinuous constituency, such as those that make use of LFG mechanisms, will not be considered in this article.

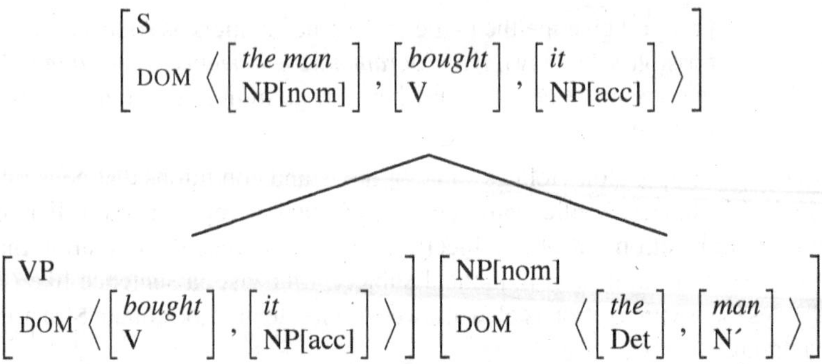

FIGURE 1 Total compaction of an NP

Let us take a closer look and see how the order domain of the S node is related to the order domains of the NP node and the VP node in Figure 1. The two domain objects in the order domain of the VP node are both integrated, unaltered, into the order domain of the S node.[2] Notice that the domain object that is pronounced *bought* precedes the domain object that is pronounced *it* in the order domain of the S as well as in the order domain of the VP. This is a consequence of the constraint given in (6) (Kathol 1995).

(6) The Persistence Constraint
Any ordering relation that holds between domain objects α and β in one order domain must also hold between α and β in all other order domains that α and β are members of.

Next, let us see how the order domain of the NP is related to the order domain of the S in Figure 1. The order domain of the NP node contains two domain objects, but this NP node contributes only one domain object, pronounced *the man*, to the order domain of the S node. What is at work here is an operation called "total compaction". (7) illustrates the way the total compaction operation takes a sign and turns it into a single domain object.

(7) $$\begin{bmatrix} \alpha_0 \\ \text{DOM} \left\langle \begin{bmatrix} \beta_1 \\ \alpha_1 \end{bmatrix}, \ldots, \begin{bmatrix} \beta_n \\ \alpha_n \end{bmatrix} \right\rangle \end{bmatrix} \Rightarrow \begin{bmatrix} \beta_1 \circ \cdots \circ \beta_n \\ \alpha_0 \end{bmatrix}$$

What is shown on the left of the arrow is the input to the operation; the input is a sign. The first line of a sign ("α_0" in this case) is its SYNSEM value; the second line ("DOM ...") shows what its order domain looks like. On the right of the arrow is shown the output of the operation; the output is a domain object. The first line of a domain object, in this case "$\beta_1 \circ \cdots \circ \beta_n$", is its

[2]The exposition here employs procedural terms in order to enhance readability, although a purely constraint-based theoretical framework is presupposed throughout.

PHON value where the small circle is an operator that concatenates strings. The second line of a domain object ("α_0" in this case) is its SYNSEM value.

The domain object created by totally compacting a sign X is placed in the order domain of the mother of X. In Figure 1, the domain object created by totally compacting the subject NP is placed in the order domain of the S.

The order between the domain object that comes from the subject NP and the domain objects that come from the VP is determined by a linear precedence statement that states that a V must follow its subject in English. Although domain objects coming from two or more daughter nodes can be strung together in any order as long as they do not violate any constraints explicitly stated in the grammar, the order of the three domain objects is completely determined in this case, due to the Persistence Constraint and the linear precedence statement concerning subject NPs.

So far, we have seen two processes whereby the order domain of a given node is integrated into that of its mother. First, a node can be totally compacted. Second, a node may undergo no compaction whatsoever. Henceforth the latter situation is going to be described by saying that the node in question has been *liberated*. The VP in Figure 1 has been liberated.

There is a third process allowed by the theory: a given node can be *partially compacted*. Partial compaction takes a sign and turns it into one or more domain objects, as opposed to total compaction, which always produces a single domain object. (As will become clear shortly, total compaction can be seen as a special case of partial compaction.) (8) and (9) illustrate how the partial compaction operation takes a sign and turns it into one or more domain objects to be placed in the order domain of the mother of that sign.

(8) Partial compaction for head-first languages:

$$\begin{bmatrix} \alpha_0 \\ \text{DOM} \left\langle \begin{bmatrix} \beta_1 \\ \alpha_1 \end{bmatrix}, \ldots, \begin{bmatrix} \beta_n \\ \alpha_n \end{bmatrix} \right\rangle \end{bmatrix} \Rightarrow \begin{bmatrix} \beta_1 \circ \cdots \circ \beta_i \\ \alpha_0 \end{bmatrix}, \begin{bmatrix} \beta_{i+1} \\ \alpha_{i+1} \end{bmatrix}, \ldots, \begin{bmatrix} \beta_n \\ \alpha_n \end{bmatrix}$$

(9) Partial compaction for head-last languages:

$$\begin{bmatrix} \alpha_0 \\ \text{DOM} \left\langle \begin{bmatrix} \beta_1 \\ \alpha_1 \end{bmatrix}, \ldots, \begin{bmatrix} \beta_n \\ \alpha_n \end{bmatrix} \right\rangle \end{bmatrix} \Rightarrow \begin{bmatrix} \beta_1 \\ \alpha_1 \end{bmatrix}, \ldots, \begin{bmatrix} \beta_{i-1} \\ \alpha_{i-1} \end{bmatrix}, \begin{bmatrix} \beta_i \circ \cdots \circ \beta_n \\ \alpha_0 \end{bmatrix}$$

In (8), the DOM value of the sign fed to the operation as the input has n domain objects. Of those, the first (i.e. leftmost) i are bundled together and turned into a single domain object, while the remaining ones, if any, are left out of the bundle and continue to be separate domain objects. (9) is a mirror image of (8). Roughly speaking, partial compaction of a sign α is achieved by first obtaining a sign α' by deleting a certain number of domain objects in the DOM value of α (the rightmost n–i domain objects in the case of (8) and the leftmost i–1 domain objects in (9)) and then totally compacting α'.

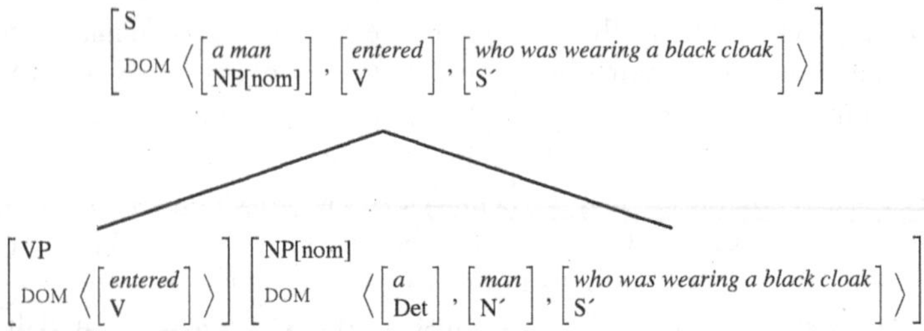

FIGURE 2 Partial compaction of an NP

Various types of extraposition constructions result when an expression is partially compacted and surfaces as a discontinuous constituent. Figure 2 shows how the English extraposition construction can be generated via partial compaction. Here, the subject NP has been partially compacted. The relative clause has been left out of the bundle and appears in the sentence-final position. What puts the relative clause in this particular position is an English-particular linear precedence statement, which is not formulated in this paper.

In this theory, the fact that only things that constitute the right edge of a phrase can be extraposed out of it is a consequence of the Persistence Constraint.[3] The fact that the linear order between two or more extraposed constituents must be preserved is also a consequence of the Persistence Constraint. And the fact that extraposition violates some of the island conditions is unsurprising, as extraposition is assumed not to induce filler-gap dependency.

The putative fact noted in Guéron (1980) that extraposition sometimes has an effect on semantic scope relations remains unexplained in Kathol and Pollard's theory. In Yatabe (2001), however, a variant of their theory is proposed which provides an explanation for Guéron's observation.

19.2.2 The linearization-based theory of long-distance scrambling

The linearization-based theory of long-distance scrambling is based on the idea that long-distance scrambling in a language like Japanese is the mirror image of extraposition in a language like English. This idea is not as farfetched as it might appear at first. First, examples like (10), whose resemblance to familiar English extraposition constructions is evident, lend plausibility to the view that the Japanese equivalent of extraposition shifts expressions to the left rather than to the right. Note that this example involves leftward dislocation of the phrase *Yoshino san kara no* out of an NP meaning

[3]The definition of partial compaction alone does not ensure this consequence. Without the Persistence Constraint, it might be possible to extrapose β_{i+1} in (8) without also extraposing β_n, for instance.

'the last letter from Yoshino san'. (The numbers in angle brackets here and in (1) refer to the result of questionnaire studies described in section 19.3.)

(10) [Yoshino san kara no], tabun kore ga saigo no tegami ni
[Yoshino from GEN] probably this NOM last GEN letter DAT
naru n darô na. <13, 13, 2, 0>
become NML I suspect
'This will probably be the last letter from Yoshino san, I suspect.'

Second, the fact that long-distance scrambling in Japanese can dislocate expressions out of an S is not a problem for the proposed theory, as extraposition in English is likewise capable of dislocating an expression out of an S, as in the following sentence. Notice that this example involves extraposition of the innermost S out of the second innermost S.

(11) I had hoped that it was true for many years that Rosa Luxemburg had actually defected to Iceland. (Gazdar 1981)

Finally, the fact that long-distance scrambling in Japanese is arguably unbounded and not subject to a constraint analogous to the so-called Right-Roof Constraint[4] does not pose a problem for the linearization-based theory either, because constraints on extraposition are known to vary from language to language. For instance, Müller (2004) shows that, unlike English, German allows relative clauses and complement clauses to be extraposed over an indefinite number of NP boundaries. It will therefore not be particularly surprising if the Japanese counterpart of extraposition turns out to be capable of dislocating an expression over an indefinite number of S boundaries.

The theory of long-distance scrambling proposed in Yatabe (1996) is based on the assumption that the compaction operation is applied in accordance with the constraints given in (12a-e).[5]

(12) a. In a head-complement structure whose head is verbal, the head is liberated and the non-head is partially compacted.
b. In a head-adjunct structure whose head is verbal, the head and the adjunct are both partially compacted.
c. In a headed structure whose head is nominal and whose non-head is not a marker, the head is totally compacted[6] and the non-head is partially compacted.

---

[4]It is in fact quite difficult to demonstrate that long-distance scrambling in Japanese is not bounded, but see Yatabe (1996) for an attested example in which an expression seems to have been long-distance-scrambled over two S boundaries.

[5]Another assumption is that head-complement structures and head-adjunct structures in Japanese are strictly binary. See Yatabe (1996) for more details.

[6]Without this requirement, it would be possible in a language like Japanese to extrapose Y in a structure like $[_{N'_1}\ X\ [_{N'_2}\ Y\ Z]]$ out of N'_1 by first extraposing it to the left of X, despite the fact that Y does not constitute the left edge of N'_1.

d. In a head-marker structure, the head and marker are both liberated.
e. In a coordinate structure, each of the conjuncts is totally compacted.

Let us also assume that complementizers and case particles are markers and thus subject to (12d) in Japanese. Given these assumptions, sentences involving long-distance scrambling are automatically generated, unless we posit in the grammar of Japanese a linear precedence statement that specifically prohibits long-distance scrambling. In what follows it will be assumed, for the sake of simplicity, that Japanese syntax has only two linear precedence statements: one that requires heads to follow their dependents (i.e. complements and adjuncts), and another one that requires markers to follow what they mark.

Figure 3 (facing page) shows how part of sentence (1) is generated in this theory. At the bottom of the unordered tree shown in Figure 3, there is a head-marker structure with a VP functioning as a head and a complementizer functioning as a marker. (Note that what is called a VP here is in fact a complete clause; the term *VP* is used here to refer to all phrases in Japanese that are headed by a verb.) The VP and the complementizer are both liberated, and the order domain of the VP[to] ends up containing four domain objects. When this VP[to] then combines with the V *itta* to produce a VP, the V is liberated while the VP[to] is partially compacted; the first element in the order domain of the VP[to] escapes the compaction and continues to be a separate domain object. The topmost local subtree in the figure is a head-complement structure that combines this VP and a subject NP. The VP is liberated, and the subject NP is partially (in fact, totally) compacted. The domain object that comes from the subject is allowed to be anywhere in the order domain of the topmost VP, as long as it does not follow the domain object corresponding to the V *itta*. Hence it is perfectly legitimate for that domain object to be immediately preceded by the domain object corresponding to the phrase *sono dôbutsuen ni*, which is syntactically a part of the embedded clause.

This theory of long-distance scrambling makes the following predictions. First, it predicts that a string α can be long-distance-scrambled out of a phrase β only if α constitutes the left periphery of β. The second prediction is that, when two or more constituents are long-distance-scrambled out of a phrase, the linear order between those constituents must be preserved. And the third prediction is that long-distance scrambling should be allowed to violate some of the island conditions that constrain canonical instances of filler-gap dependency such as topicalization in English. Specifically, long-distance scrambling is predicted to be capable of dislocating a conjunct, in violation of the Coordinate Structure Constraint (as in (4)).

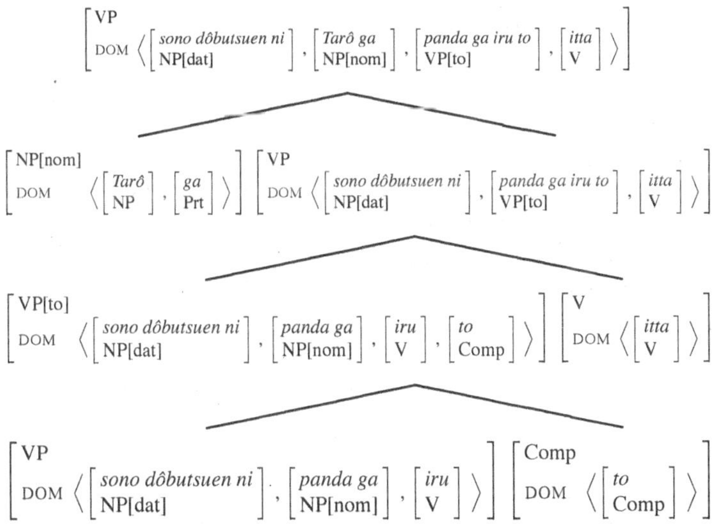

FIGURE 3 Long-distance scrambling via partial compaction

19.3 Questionnaire Studies

In this section, the results of several questionnaire studies whose purpose was to test the three predictions of the linearization-based theory of long-distance scrambling will be presented in section 19.3.1, and the implications of those results will be discussed in section 19.3.2. The respondents in these studies, conducted in 2006 and 2007, consisted of students at the University of Tokyo who were not linguists, and who were compensated for their time. When the relative acceptability of two or more examples was of interest, the order between those examples was randomized for each respondent. In what follows, the four figures immediately following example sentences show the number of speakers who found the sentence 'completely natural under the intended reading', 'slightly unnatural under the intended reading', 'considerably unnatural under the intended reading', and 'completely impossible under the intended reading', respectively. The *average rating* for a linguistic material L, which will be represented as $r(L)$, is defined here as $(1a + 2b + 3c + 4d)/(a + b + c + d)$, when the questionnaire result for L is $<a, b, c, d>$. A linguistic material L that is associated with a questionnaire result is shown here with no diacritic if $1 \leq r(L) < 2$, with '?' if $2 \leq r(L) < 2.5$, with '??' if $2.5 \leq r(L) < 3$, with '?*' if $3 \leq r(L) < 3.5$, and with '*' if $3.5 < r(L) \leq 4$.[7]

[7] The notion of average rating is only intended as an expedient; the way it is defined and used here is arbitrary to a certain extent.

19.3.1 Questionnaire results

(13) and (14) form a minimal pair that tests the first prediction of the linearization-based theory, i.e. the prediction that an expression α can be scrambled out of another expression β only if α constitutes the left edge of β. (14) is a sentence obtained by exchanging the two expressions in (13) that both modify the noun *kutsu*. The relative clause *sono toki o-shiro ni ita*, which is long-distance-scrambled to the sentence-initial position in both sentences, originates at the left edge of the NP meaning 'the glass shoe of the person called Cinderella, who was at the castle at the time' in (13) (as shown in (15a)), but not in (14) (as shown in (15b)).

(13) ??[Sono toki o-shiro ni ita], kore ga, [Shinderera to yû]
[that time castle DAT was] this NOM [Cinderella COMP call]
hito no garasu no kutsu na n desu. <2,9,5,6>
person GEN glass GEN shoe COP I say politely
This is the glass shoe of the person called Cinderella, who was at the castle at the time.'

(14) ?*[Sono toki o-shiro ni ita], kore ga, garasu no, [Shinderera
[that time castle DAT was] this NOM glass GEN [Cinderella
to yû] hito no kutsu na n desu. <0,4,6,12>
COMP call] person GEN shoe COP I say politely

(15) a. [[[sono toki o-shiro ni ita] [Shinderera to yû] hito] no]
[[[that time castle DAT was] [Cinderella COMP call] person] GEN]
garasu no kutsu
glass GEN shoe
'the glass shoe of the person called Cinderella, who was at the castle at the time'

b. garasu no [[[sono toki o-shiro ni ita] [Shinderera to yû]
glass GEN [[[that time castle DAT was] [Cinderella COP call]
hito] no] kutsu
person] GEN] shoe

The Wilcoxon signed-rank test showed that the rating for (13) was significantly higher than the rating for (14) ($T = 7, n = 15, p < 0.001$), as predicted by the theory.

(16) and (17) are another minimal pair that tests the prediction that an expression α can be scrambled out of another expression β only if α constitutes the left edge of β. As shown in (18), the NP *ude ni* must be at the left edge of the phrase whose literal meaning is 'to give a twist to one's arms', in order for the phrase to have the idiomatic meaning 'to make extra efforts'. There-

fore it can be said that the scrambled phrase originates at the left edge of the embedded clause in (16) but not in (17), as long as the embedded clause is to be interpreted in its idiomatic sense.

(16) ?*[Ude ni] aitsu ga yori o kaketai tte itteta yo.
[arm DAT] that guy NOM twist ACC want to give COMP was saying
<0, 7, 10, 13>
'That guy was saying that he wants to make extra efforts.'
('That guy was saying that he wants to give a twist to his arms.' (Lit.))

(17) *[Yori o] aitsu ga ude ni kaketai tte itteta yo.
[twist ACC] that guy NOM arm DAT want to give COMP was saying
<0, 0, 5, 25>

(18) a. Ude ni yori o kaketai. <20, 8, 1, 1>
arm DAT twist ACC want to give
'(I) want to make extra efforts.'
('(I) want to give a twist to my arms.' (Lit.))
b. *Yori o ude ni kaketai. <0, 0, 9, 21>
twist ACC arm DAT want to give

Again, as predicted by the proposed theory, (16) was found to be significantly better than (17) ($T = 0, n = 15, p < 0.0001$).

Next, (19) and (20) form a minimal pair that tests the second prediction of the linearization-based theory, i.e. the prediction that, when two or more constituents are long-distance-scrambled out of a phrase, the linear order between those constituents must be preserved. In both sentences, two phrases (*Ken no koto o* and *hannin to*) have been long-distance-scrambled out of the embedded clause. As shown in (21) and (22), the phrase *Ken no koto o* must precede the phrase *hannin to*, when the two phrases are co-arguments of the verb *shinjikonde*; (21) was indeed found to be significantly better than (22) ($T = 0, n = 14, p < 0.0001$). Therefore it can be said that (19) preserves the pre-scrambling order between the two scrambled phrases and that (20) does not.

(19) ??[Ken no koto o] [hannin to], Tanaka ga keisatsu ga
[Ken GEN matter ACC] [culprit COMP] Tanaka NOM police NOM
shinjikonderu tte itteta. <1, 8, 4, 3>
believe COMP said
'Tanaka said that the police firmly believed Ken to be the culprit.'

(20) *[Hannin to] [Ken no koto o], Tanaka ga keisatsu ga
[culprit COMP] [Ken GEN matter ACC] Tanaka NOM police NOM
shinjikonderu tte itteta. <0, 1, 4, 11>
believe COMP said

(21) [Ken no koto o] [hannin to] keisatsu ga shinjikonde
[Ken GEN matter ACC] [culprit COMP] police NOM believe-GER
iru. <11, 5, 0, 0>
be-PRES
'The police firmly believe Ken to be the culprit.'

(22) ?*[Hannin to] [Ken no koto o] keisatsu ga shinjikonde
[culprit COMP] [Ken GEN matter ACC] police NOM believe-GER
iru. <0, 4, 3, 9>
be-PRES

As predicted by the theory, (19) was found to be significantly better than (20) ($T = 8, n = 14, p < 0.01$).

Finally, (23) and (24) test whether Japanese scrambling obeys the Coordinate Structure Constraint. (23) involves scrambling of a conjunct, whereas (24) involves scrambling of part of a conjunct out of that conjunct.[8]

(23) ?[Kyôdai to], kanojo ga [Tôdai to] o kurabeteru tte,
[Kyoto U. and] she NOM [Tokyo U. and] ACC is comparing COMP
shitteta? <2, 14, 9, 3>
did you know
'Did you know that she is comparing Kyoto University and Tokyo University?'

(24) *[Tanaka sensei no], kore wa, [saisho no chosho to]
[Prof. Tanaka GEN] these TOP [first GEN book and]
[Suzuki sensei no saigo no chosho] da. <0, 0, 6, 6>
[Prof. Suzuki GEN last GEN book] are
'These are Prof. Tanaka's first book and Prof. Suzuki's last book.'

As indicated above, the average rating for (23) was in the '?' range, and the average rating for (24) was in the '*' range.

[8](23) becomes structurally ambiguous when the second occurrence of *to* is omitted. In order to ensure that the respondents notice the presence of the second *to* in this example, a variant of the sentence without the second occurrence of *to* was also included in the questionnaire.

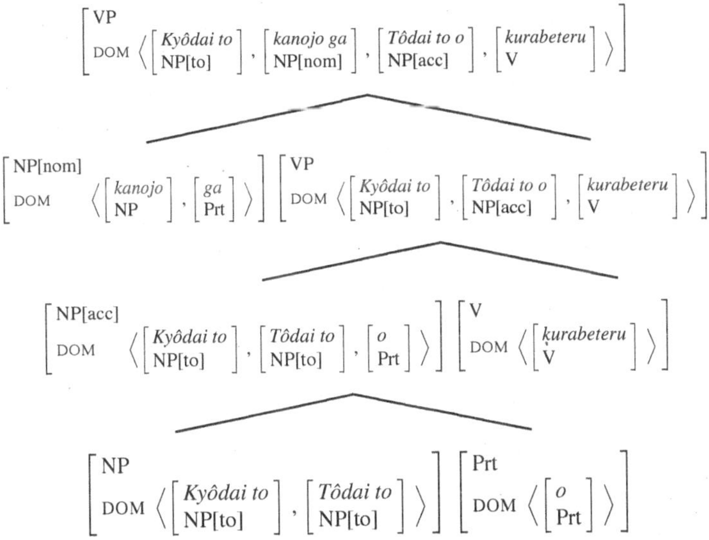

FIGURE 4 Scrambling of a conjunct

19.3.2 Discussion

The results of the questionnaire studies invariably confirm the predictions of the linearization-based theory of long-distance scrambling. (23) is predicted to be grammatical, because the embedded clause in the sentence can be assigned the structure shown in Figure 4. On the other hand, (24) is predicted to be ungrammatical; no well-formed structure can be assigned to it, due to the requirement, stated in (12e), that a conjunct must be totally compacted.

On the other hand, the questionnaire results above do not make sense in the standard, movement-based theory of long-distance scrambling. In the movement-based theory, there is no grammar-internal reason why long-distance scrambling should be possible only from the left edge of an expression, although there could be a processing-related reason why that must be so. Likewise, in the standard theory, there is no grammar-internal reason why the linear order between two scrambled expressions must be preserved, although, again, there could be a processing-related reason why that must be so. The fact that long-distance scrambling in Japanese does not obey the Coordinate Structure Constraint (CSC), as shown by (23), is particularly problematic for the movement-based theory; the theory seems to make it impossible to explain how learners could come to know that dislocation of a conjunct is allowed in Japanese but not in the case of leftward movement in English.

The awkwardness of (13), (16), and (19) is not predicted by the proposed theory, but it is not predicted by the movement-based theory either. It appears that both theories need to be augmented with "soft constraints" (see Bresnan and Nikitina's contribution to this volume) against dislocating an expression across more than one NP boundary, dislocating an idiom chunk, and dislocating more than one constituent out of a single clause, although it is not clear at this point whether such constraints would have to be viewed as part of the grammar.

As has been noted by Harada (1977), scrambling in Japanese does appear to obey the Complex NP Constraint, just like topicalization and relativization in English. This, however, does not mean that the movement-based theory of scrambling is on the right track; there are reasons to believe that the Complex NP Constraint is not a syntactic constraint and hence is irrelevant in the present context (Kluender 1998). In fact, there are attested examples in which long-distance scrambling violates the Complex NP Constraint. One example is sentence (21) in Yatabe (1996), and another example is the following sentence,[9] in which the dative argument of the verb *fitto shita* 'fit' has been long-distance-scrambled out of a relative clause.

(25) Dakara, hontô ni, [[sô iu Nihon no wakamono no kenzen na,
so really [[such Japanese young people's wholesome

nan to iu ka, kibô to iu mono ni] wareware ga fitto shita
what shall I say thing called hope DAT] we NOM fit

seisaku o dashite iku to iu koto ga] hijô ni daiji da
policy ACC produce NML NOM] very important

to iu fû ni omotte iru tokoro desu.
that think

'So, really, I think it is very important that we should produce policies that fit Japan's young people's such wholesome hope.'

On the other hand, the constraint that bans movement of a conjunct seems to be a purely syntactic one. Some authors have argued that the part of the CSC that prohibits extraction out of a conjunct should be taken to be non-syntactic, but even those authors regard that part of the CSC that prohibits extraction of a whole conjunct as a syntactic constraint (Lakoff 1986, p. 161; Kehler 1996, p. 220).

19.4 Conclusion

In this article, the results of some questionnaire studies regarding long-distance scrambling in Japanese were presented, and it was argued that they provide some reasons to favor the linearization-based theory over the movement-based theory. The findings presented here indicate that there are at least two distinct kinds of dislocation in natural language syntax and that an

[9]From the original Japanese text: http://www.mhlw.go.jp/kaiken/daijin/2007/02/k0206.html

analysis in terms of complex domain formation involving partial compaction is an adequate description of one of them.

Acknowledgments

I would like to thank Mohanan for various memorable remarks that have provided me with food for thought over the years. On one occasion, he told me that you need to have a lot of "ammunition" when you publish a paper which argues for an unconventional view such as the view that long-distance scrambling in Japanese does not give rise to filler-gap dependency. In writing this paper, I hope I am being a good rebel, packing a reasonable amount of ammunition.

References

Dowty, David R. 1996. Toward a minimalist theory of syntactic structure. In H. Bunt and A. van Horck, eds., *Discontinuous Constituency*, pages 11–62. Berlin: Mouton de Gruyter.

Gazdar, Gerald. 1981. Unbounded dependencies and coordinate structure. *Linguistic Inquiry* 12:155–184.

Guéron, Jacqueline. 1980. On the syntax and semantics of PP extraposition. *Linguistic Inquiry* 11:637–678.

Harada, S.-I. 1977. Nihongo ni "henkei" wa hitsuyô da. *Gengo* 6:88–95 (in no. 11) and 96–103 (in no. 12).

Kathol, Andreas. 1995. *Linearization-Based German Syntax*. Ph.D. thesis, Ohio State University, Columbus.

Kathol, Andreas and Carl Pollard. 1995. Extraposition via complex domain formation. In *33rd Annual Meeting of the Association for Computational Linguistics*, pages 174–180. San Francisco: Morgan Kaufmann.

Kehler, Andrew. 1996. Coherence and the coordinate structure constraint. In J. Johnson, M. L. Juge, and J. L. Moxley, eds., *BLS 22*, pages 220–231. Berkeley: Berkeley Linguistics Society.

Kluender, Robert. 1998. On the distinction between strong and weak islands: A processing perspective. In P. Culicover and L. McNally, eds., *The Limits of Syntax (Syntax and Semantics 29)*, pages 241–279. San Diego: Academic Press.

Lakoff, George. 1986. Frame semantic control of the coordinate structure constraint. In A. M. Farley, P. T. Farley, and K.-E. McCullough, eds., *CLS 22 Part 2: Papers from the Parasession on Pragmatics and Grammatical Theory*, pages 152–167. Chicago: Chicago Linguistic Society.

Mohanan, K. P. 1982. Grammatical relations and clause structure in Malayalam. In J. Bresnan, ed., *The Mental Representation of Grammatical Relations*, pages 504–589. Cambridge, Massachusetts: MIT Press.

Müller, Stefan. 2004. Complex NPs, subjacency, and extraposition. *Snippets* 8:10–11.

Saito, Mamoru. 1985. *Some Asymmetries in Japanese and Their Theoretical Implications*. Ph.D. thesis, Massachusetts Institute of Technology, Cambridge, Massachusetts.

Stucky, Susan U. 1987. Configurational variation in English: A study of extraposition and related matters. In G. J. Huck and A. E. Ojeda, eds., *Discontinuous Constituency*, pages 377–404. Orlando: Academic Press.

Yatabe, Shûichi. 1996. Long-distance scrambling via partial compaction. In M. Koizumi, M. Oishi, and U. Sauerland, eds., *Formal Approaches to Japanese Linguistics 2 (MIT Working Papers in Linguistics 29)*, pages 303–317. Cambridge, Mass.: MITWPL.

Yatabe, Shûichi. 2001. The syntax and semantics of left-node raising in Japanese. In D. Flickinger and A. Kathol, eds., *Proceedings of the 7th International Conference on Head-Driven Phrase Structure Grammar*, pages 325–344. Stanford: CSLI Publications. http://cslipublications.stanford.edu/HPSG/.

Yatabe, Shûichi. 2003. Does scrambling in Japanese obey the Coordinate Structure Constraint? In *Nihon Gengogakkai Dai-126-kai Taikai Yokôshû (Proceedings of the 126th Meeting of the Linguistic Society of Japan)*, pages 262–267. Kyoto: Linguistic Society of Japan.

20

Aspects of the Semantics of Logophoricity: Comparison of Malayalam with Yoruba and Japanese

YO MATSUMOTO

20.1 Introduction

Logophoric pronouns are pronouns that characteristically refer to the person whose speech or thought is being reported. Since Hagège (1974) and Clements (1975) first examined them in West African languages three decades ago, there has been increasing interest in expressions coding logophoricity. Their grammatical properties (e.g., the grammatical environments in which logophoric pronouns and other markers occur) have been examined extensively in the literature (see Culy 1994, Huang 2000). This paper focuses on their semantics (Kuno 1978, Sells 1987, Schlenker 2003, Safir 2004a, b, Oshima 2007, 2009). I first establish two major semantic properties of logophoric pronouns on the basis of data from Japanese and Yoruba. I will then show that Malayalam reflexive *t̠aan* has those properties, but in slightly different ways. I will argue that the differences can be captured by parameterizing the two proposed constraints.[1]

[1]This paper goes back to the term paper that I wrote in 1987 for K.P. Mohanan's Structure of Malayalam class at Stanford University. An earlier, unpublished version of this paper has often been cited as Matsumoto (1990), whose contents are summarized in Kay (1992). In the present version I have included discussions of works published after 1990, but my basic claims remain the same.

Reality Exploration and Discovery: Pattern Interaction in Language and Life.
Linda Uyechi and Lian-Hee Wee (eds.).

20.2 Semantic Properties of Logophoric Pronouns

Many West African languages have typical logophoric pronouns, which are used in the complement clause of the verbs of speech and mental activities and refer to the subject of the verbs. An example from Yoruba is given in (1) (see Bamgbose 1966, Adesola 2005).

(1) $ó_i$ ní {$ó_{*i}$/$\grave{o}un_i$} fẹ́ẹ́ lọ
He say he/self like go
'He said that he wanted to go.'

In this example the pronoun *òun* is used to refer to the person whose speech is represented. In contrast, the pronoun *ó* (for third person singular), often called a weak pronoun or a clitic pronoun (Bamgbose 1966, Pulleyblank 1986), cannot have such a referent.

It has also been suggested that long-distance reflexives in languages such as Japanese, Chinese and Icelandic also have logophoric properties. Take Japanese reflexive pronoun *zibun*, whose discourse properties have been discussed much in the literature (Kuno 1972, 1978, 1986a, Kameyama 1984, Iida 1996, Oshima 2007, etc.). Unlike Yoruba *òun*, Japanese *zibun* can have as an antecedent not just the subject of the verb of speech or thought, but any subject (or some other argument in some cases), as in (2).

(2) $Zyon_i$ wa $Taro_j$ ga $zibun_{i,j}$ o hihan shitato itta.
John Top Taro Nom self Acc criticize did Comp said.
'John said that Taro criticized him/himself.'

It has been argued that *zibun* entails that the antecedent's "point of view" is taken in the discourse, at least in some cases (e.g., Kuno 1978). This has been related to logophoricity (e.g., Sells 1987), though some have doubted a real connection (Culy 1997).

In this paper, I argue that logophoric pronouns (including "point-of-view reflexives") tend to have the following two properties—properties that they share with first person pronouns (see also Schlenker 2003): they represent (a) a primary deictic center, and (b) a source of identification. I will show that differences among languages can be captured by parameterizing the constraints coming from these properties.

20.2.1 Logophoricity and the primary deictic center

Events that are linguistically described can crucially involve a deictic center or a location of the person from whose standpoint events are observed. I call such a person PIVOT, after Sells (1987). One obvious PIVOT is the speaker at the time of utterance, whose location is described by the adverb *here*. I call this PIVOT the primary PIVOT (P-PIVOT). PIVOT can be someone other than the first-person speaker, in which case I will use the term the secondary PIVOT

(S-PIVOT). One type of S-PIVOT is the logophoric PIVOT (L-PIVOT), defined as the reported speaker or cognizer whose speech or thought is reported in the complement clause of a verb of speech or thought.

The uses of deictic expressions crucially involve PIVOT, though the way they make reference to it differs from expression to expression. For example, in its basic use the verb *come* requires that the speaker or the hearer be at the goal of motion at the time of utterance or at the time of the motion event; *go* requires the speaker not be present at the goal of motion at the time of utterance (Fillmore 1997). Due to these restrictions the goal of *come* can be the location of P-PIVOT, but that of *go* cannot, as shown in (3).

(3) John {came/#went} here.

The situation is more complicated when *come* and *go* appear in the complement clause of a verb of speech or thought. These verbs differ in their S-PIVOT sensitivity. Consider (4).

(4) Of course John knows that I {came/went} to him.

In the event described by the complement clause, the person described as cognizing the event, in this case *John*, functions as S-PIVOT (L-PIVOT in this case). The verb *come* readily allows the goal to be the location of S-PIVOT, so *came* is possible in (4). The verb *go*, in contrast, does not necessarily prohibit the goal from being the location of S-PIVOT, as shown by the use of *went* in (4) (see Ohye 1980 for a complex set of data).[2]

Other PIVOT-sensitive expressions include demonstratives like *this* and *that*. English demonstratives are always used in reference to the location of the first-person speaker at the time of utterance (P-PIVOT). Consider the phrases *on this side of* and *on that side of*, used in the sense of 'on my side of' and 'on the far side of'.

(5) There is a cat on this/that side of John.[3]

These expressions crucially involve three participants: an object whose location is indicated (e.g. a cat above), called FIGURE; an object or place in reference to which the location of FIGURE is described (e.g. John above), called GROUND; and finally, the syntactically unexpressed first-person speaker, from whose point of observation the choice of *this* and *that* is determined. This first-person speaker must be distinct from the GROUND, since the GROUND

[2] P-PIVOT incompatibility of *go* is still maintained when the verb is embedded in a complement clause. For this reason the absence of S-PIVOT at the goal alone does not license the use of *go*; the absence of P-PIVOT is required, as shown in (i).
(i) John said that his daughter would {come/#go} here (from where he was then).

[3] Here I am considering the reading in which *this* and *that* are interpreted as showing a difference in distance from the speaker. Different readings are possible if finger pointing is involved, or if a demonstrative is interpreted anaphorically.

provides the dividing line between the *this* side and the *that* side, which must lie at some distance from the speaker. For this reason the speaker cannot be the GROUND, as in (6).

(6) #There is a cat on that side of me.

This means that the GROUND of *on this/that side of* is P-PIVOT-incompatible.

Demonstratives like *this* and *that* are not interpreted in reference to S-PIVOT (except in free indirect speech). In the following sentence, the point of observation can only be that of P-PIVOT; it cannot be interpreted with respect to the S-PIVOT, *John*.

(7) John didn't know that there was a cat on that side of Bill.

Logophoric pronouns have PIVOT-sensitivity. I argue that logophoric pronouns in general tend to be sensitive to the constraint in (8).

(8) P-PIVOT constraint:
The referent of a logophoric pronoun is treated as P-PIVOT, and therefore it must be compatible with P-PIVOT requirements of other expressions.

I illustrate this constraint by using Japanese *zibun* (drawing on works such as Kuno 1976, 1986a, Sells 1987, Iida 1996). First, consider the *iku* 'go'/*kuru* 'come' contrast with respect to *zibun*. In the complement clause in (9), Taro is only an S-PIVOT (L-PIVOT), and therefore he can be at the goal of *kuru* and he is not prohibited from being at the goal of *iku*.

(9) Taro$_i$ wa boku no ko ga kare$_i$ no tokoro ni {itta/kita} to iu.
Taro Top I Gen child Nom he Gen place Go went/came Comp say
'Taro$_i$ says that my child {went/came} to him$_i$.'

However, if *zibun* is used, Taro is treated as P-PIVOT. Therefore he can be at the goal of *kuru* only, as in (10); the goal of *iku* is P-PIVOT-incompatible, and therefore this verb is ruled out if the referent of *zibun* is at the goal.

(10) Taro$_i$ wa boku no kodomo ga zibun$_i$ no tokoro ni {*itta/kita} to itta.
Taro Top I Gen child Nom self Gen place Go went/came said
'Taro$_i$ said that my child {went/came} to him$_i$.'

Other evidence comes from the use of *kotira/atira gawa* 'this/that side'. Note the contrast in (11).

(11) Zyon$_i$ wa [{*zibun$_i$/kare$_i$} no atira gawa ni
John Top {self/he} Gen that side Loc
neko ga iru] no o sir-anai.
cat Nom exist Nmlz Acc know-Neg
John$_i$ does not know that there is a cat on that side of him$_i$.

Zibun is excluded in (12) because the referent of *zibun* is at the P-PIVOT-incompatible location. Such P-PIVOT-sensitivity is not limited to the complement of verbs of speech or thought. *Zibun* has to respect the P-PIVOT constraint even when it has an intra-clause antecedent, as shown in (12).

(12) Zyon$_i$ wa sibaraku ima no {karc$_i$/*zibun$_i$} no atira-gawa ni ita.
John Top for.a.while now Gen he/self Gen that-side Loc was.
'For a while, John was on that side of him (=his position) now.'

Relevance of P-PIVOT to logophoric pronouns in West African languages has not been well-explored (Huang 2000). Culy (1997) even claims that logophoric pronouns in these languages do not represent "point of view" as in Japanese. In fact, Yoruba *òun* is also sensitive to the P-PIVOT constraint. (13) shows that the referent of *òun* cannot be at the goal of the verb *lọ* 'go'; the nonlogophoric *ó* creates no problem. (See below for the circumstances under which *ó* is used in complement clauses.)

(13) Jónù$_i$ ko rántí pé Olú lọ sí ìhí tí {ó$_i$/#òun$_i$} wà.
John Neg remember Comp Olu go at city Rel he/self exist
'John$_i$ does not remember that Olu went to the city where he$_i$ was.'

20.2.2 Logophoricity and the source of identification

Second, consider the notion of the source of identification. The first person speaker is usually the source of expressions used to describe an entity. Consider the sentences in (14).

(14) a. Judah kneeled to a minister of Egypt.
b. Judah kneeled to his brother Joseph.

In a situation where a speaker can say (14a), s/he can choose to use (14b) if s/he believes or knows that the minister of Egypt that Judah kneeled to was his own (younger) brother Joseph. Note that such a description is possible irrespective of the belief/knowledge on the part of the referent of the pronoun *his* (Judah); (14b) can be used even when Judah did not know the identity of the minister, as in the story of Joseph in the Old Testament.

The first person pronoun is different in this respect. The first-person pronoun refers to the speaker himself/herself, whose description/identification is reflected in the wording of the utterance. Therefore whenever this pronoun is used, it refers to the person that its referent identifies as himself/herself. In (15), if the referent of the first person pronoun did not believe/know that the minister is his/her own brother, s/he would not (or could not) say (15b).

(15) a. I kneeled to a minister of Egypt.
b. I kneeled to my brother Joseph.

Things are a little more complicated, however, since what one says can be different from what one believes or knows. Suppose someone, say Abraham, has a wife named Sarah, but for some reason he wants to hide the fact she is his wife, and tells a lie, as in (16).

(16) Abraham: “Sarah is my sister.”

Here *my sister* does not reflect his belief. He has presented or described Sarah as his sister to the hearer (he wants the hearer to believe this is the case). This means that *my* in (16), or the first person pronoun in general, can be more accurately regarded as referring to the person who its referent (speaker) *presents* as identical with himself/herself.

Logophoric pronouns, I claim, can be similar to the first-person pronoun in this respect: they tend to be sensitive to the constraint in (17).

(17) Self-identification Constraint: A logophoric pronoun must represent a person whom its referent a) believes to be himself/herself, or b) verbally presents as identical with himself/herself.

Note the use of disjunction in this constraint. I will show that logophoric pronouns can differ in the contexts in which belief or presentation counts.[4]

A claim similar to this one has been made by Schlenker (2003) and Safir (2004a, b). For example, based on Adesola's (2005) observation concerning Yoruba *òun* in a complement of a verb of thought, Safir claims that logophoric pronouns are interpreted under the *de se* reading, or self-conscious self-reference on the part of a reported speaker. The present claim differs from these studies in that a possible discrepancy between what one believes and what one says is recognized. It also differs in that (17) applies not just to the complement of the verbs of speech or thought.

The Yoruba pronoun *òun* is sensitive to a version of the Self-identification Constraint. First, consider (18).

(18) Júdà$_i$ {sọ/rò} (wí)pé òun$_i$ pàdé àbúrò {(#)òun$_i$/rẹ̀$_i$}.
Judah say/think that self meet sibling self/his
‘Judah$_i$ says/thinks that he$_i$ met his$_i$ brother.’

In (18), *òun* is acceptable with a verb of thought only if Judah in fact believes/knows that he met his brother, and, with a verb of speech, only if Judah in fact says so. Under the Joseph/Judah scenario in which he did not know it and did not say so, *òun* is not acceptable (the judgment given in parentheses in (18) indicates the acceptability in the intended scenario). The nonlogophoric rẹ̀ (the genitive form of *ó*) creates no problem.

An important feature of Yoruba *òun* is that when it occurs in the complement of a verb of speech, it is what is presented, and not what is believed, that counts. This can be shown in sentences like (19).

---

[4]The disjunction here is reminiscent of Sells' (1987) distinction between SOURCE (speech source) and SELF (the person whose “mind” is reported) as elements of logophoricity.

(19) Abraham said that his wife Sarah was his sister.

I consider two major readings of this sentence. In one case, Abraham said that he had married his own sister (i.e., he said, "my wife is my sister"). In the other case, he lied (the Abraham/Sarah scenario above). Most importantly, in the lying scenario, *his wife* matches his belief, but not what he said (i.e., what he presented as his belief); *his sister* does not match his belief but matches what he said.[5]

Yoruba expresses this situation in the following way.

(20) Ábúráámù$_i$ sọ (wí)pé àbúró {òun$_i$/#rẹ̀$_i$} ni ìyàwó {(#)òun$_i$/rẹ̀$_i$}.
Abraham say Comp sibling self /his Cop wife self/his
'Abraham$_i$ said that his$_i$ wife was his$_i$ sister.'

In (20), in the Abraham/Sarah scenario 'his' in 'his wife' cannot be *òun* but 'his' in 'his sister' must, suggesting that *òun* represents what the speaker presents and not what s/he in fact believes. (If Abraham said he had married his sister, both must be *òun*.)

Irrelevance of belief in the speech complement can also be shown in the situation like the following (McCawley 1970).

(21) a. John: "I didn't kiss Mary."
b. John says that he didn't kiss the girl that he kissed.

In reporting the utterance like (21a), the first-person speaker can say (21b) if s/he believes that Mary is in fact the person John kissed. Now, there are two major situations in which (21b) might be used. In one case John has a memory problem: he somehow believes that he didn't kiss Mary, and he says so. In this case, the phrase *the girl that he kissed* neither reflects John's belief about the girl nor does it match his verbal presentation of her. In the other case he is telling a lie: he in fact believes (or knows) he kissed Mary but makes a statement to the contrary. In this case, the phrase does match his belief, but not his verbal presentation.

The Yoruba version of (21b) is given in (22).

(22) Jónù$_i$ sọ (wí)pé òun$_i$ ò-pàdé ọmọbìrin tí {#òun$_i$/ó$_i$} pàdé
John say that self Neg-meet girl that self/he meet
'John$_i$ says that he$_i$ didn't meet the girl that he$_i$ met.'

Here, *ó* is acceptable but *òun* is not. Most importantly, *òun* is unacceptable both in the memory problem scenario and the lying scenario, suggesting that *òun* must match the described speaker's verbal presentation. (One informant said that (22) might be interpreted as John saying that he does not feel like he in fact met the girl, a reading compatible with the constraint above.)

[5]Another reading is that he had a recognition problem (he mistook his wife to be his sister). I will ignore this reading to avoid unnecessary complication.

So, in Yoruba, *òun* must refer to the person whom its referent (as a speaker) presents as identical with himself/herself when used in the complement of a verb of speech (as in (22)), and to the person whom its referent believes to be identical with himself/herself when used in the complement of a verb of thought (as in (18)).

Not all logophoric pronouns are sensitive to this constraint. Consider Japanese *zibun* in (23).

(23) a. Yuda$_i$ wa zibun$_i$ no otooto ni hizamaduita.
Judah Top self Gen younger.brother Dat kneeled
'Judah kneeled to his younger brother.'

b. Zyon$_i$ wa [PRO$_i$ [zibun$_i$ ga kisu sita] hito ni
John Top self Nom kiss did person Dat
kisu shite i-nai] to {itte/omotte} iru yooda
kiss do Asp-Neg Comp say/think Asp seem
'John$_i$ seems to be saying/think that he$_i$ hasn't kissed the girl that he$_i$ kissed.'

Unlike *òun*, Japanese *zibun* is fully acceptable in (23a) under the Joseph/Judah scenario. It is also fully acceptable in (23b), both in the memory problem scenario and the lying scenario (with *itte* 'say'). These observations suggest that *zibun* does not intrinsically involve a *de se* reading.[6]

20.3 Malayalam *t̠aan*

In this section I show that a Malayalam reflexive *t̠aan* has properties similar to, but slightly different from, Japanese *zibun* and Yoruba *òun*.

---

[6]Oshima (2009) claims that *zibun* in (i) is interpreted in a *de se* reading.

(i) Zyon$_i$ wa [zibun$_i$ ga boku o tasuke-ta] to omotte i-ru.
John Top self Nom I Acc help-Pst Comp think Asp-NPst
'John thinks that he helped me.'

He claims that this sentence is not acceptable when amnestic John happened to read in his biography that someone called John helped the speaker without knowing that this was in fact himself. In my judgment such a reading is certainly not readily available, but this appears to be due in part to the nature of the complement of the verb of believing, which appears to favor a *de se* interpretation. The following sentence, in which *shitta* 'came to know' is used instead, can be more naturally interpreted in a non *de se* reading.

(ii) Zyon wa [zibun ga kanozyo o tasuketa] koto o shitta.
John Top self Nom she Acc helped Comp Acc came.to.know
'John came to know that he helped her.'

The present analysis is at odds with Oshima's claim that *kare* 'he', if used in place of *zibun* in (i), does not have a *de se* reading. My judgment, however, is that *kare* in the embedded subject position cannot have the upper subject as an antecedent in any reading, the judgment shared by Kuno (1986b).

20.3.1 A previous analysis: Syntactic conditions

Malayalam has two reflexives *t̲aan* and *swa-* (Mohanan 1982a). *t̲aan* is a Dravidian reflexive that is shared by other Dravidian languages, while *swa-* is Sanskrit in origin. In this paper I will focus on *t̲aan*, and refer to *swa-* only in passing for comparison, since the former is the one that has logophoric properties. Some dialectal differences are known as to the use of *t̲aan* as a reflexive (Asher & Kumari 1997). In this paper I will examine this reflexive as used by the two speakers I consulted, K.P. Mohanan and Tara Mohanan.

The syntactic conditions of *t̲aan* have been discussed by Mohanan (1982a, b), Asher & Kumari (1997), and Jayaseelan (1999a, b). In Mohanan's analysis of his own dialect, *t̲aan* must satisfy the following conditions.

(24) a. C-commanding Subjecthood Condition: *t̲aan* must be bound by a c-commanding subject.

b. Disjoint Reference Condition (Anti-Locality Condition): *t̲aan* must be free in the minimal NP or S that contains it.

These are supported by the following sentences. (25a) and (25b) show that *t̲aan* (as an argument of a verb) must be free in the S that contains it, while (25c) shows that it can have an antecedent within the minimal clause if it is an NP contained in an NP. Note that the antecedent has to be a subject, but does not have to be the subject of verbs of speech or thought, like Japanese but unlike Yoruba, as in (25b, c).

(25) a. jooṇ$_i$ [meeri$_j$ t̲anne$_{i,*j}$ n̲uḷḷi] en̲n̲ə paraɲɲu.
John Mary self.Acc pinched Comp said
'John$_i$ said that Mary$_j$ pinched {him$_i$/*herself$_j$}.'

b. r̲aajaawə$_i$ [t̲anne$_{i,*j}$ aar̲aadhik'k'unna] aaḷe$_j$ kaṇṭu.
king.Nom self.Acc worship.Rel person.Acc saw
'King$_i$ saw a person$_j$ who worships him$_{i,*j}$.'

c. jooṇ$_i$ meeriye$_j$ t̲ante$_{i,*j}$ wiiṭṭl weccə umma weccu.
John Mary.Acc self.Gen house.Loc at kiss placed
'John$_i$ kissed Mary$_j$ at {his$_i$/*her$_j$} house.'

There are certain counterexamples to the subjecthood condition, however (see Mohanan 1982a, b, Jayaseelan 1999a, b). Examples include those in (26), in which *t̲aan* has a non-subject antecedent who believes, or is at least aware of, what is represented by the clause that contains *t̲aan*, though acceptability varies according to speakers.[7]

---

[7]In Yoruba and some other West-African languages the source argument of the verb 'hear' can be an antecedent of a logophoric pronoun (see Culy 1994). This is not (easily) possible in Malayalam.

(26) a. %Moohanante$_i$ abhipraayattil tante$_i$ kuṭṭi dhiiran-aaṇə.
Mohanan.Gen opinion.Loc self.Gen child brave.one-Cop
'In Mohanan's$_i$ opinion, his$_i$ child is brave.'

b. %[tante$_i$ kuṭṭik'k'ə praisə kiṭṭiyaṭə] joonne$_i$ santoosippiccu.
self.Gen child.Dat prize get.Nm John.Acc happy.Caus.Pst
'That his$_i$ child won the prize made John$_i$ happy.'

These examples suggest that Malayalam *taan* has logophoric uses. In fact Jayaseelan (1999b) claims that *taan* can sometimes have an antecedent outside the sentence that contains it, and claims that such uses are logophoric in nature. In this paper, I claim that even clause-bound, "normal" uses of this reflexive have the semantic properties of logophoric pronouns seen above.

20.3.2 Logophoric properties of *taan* I: Deixis

Malayalam *taan* has the P-PIVOT constraint as a necessary condition. Malayalam has several P-PIVOT-sensitive expressions. The P-PIVOT constraint above predicts that unacceptability occurs when *taan* conflicts with the P-PIVOT compatibility requirement of other such expressions.

An example can be seen in the verbs *waruka* 'come' and *pookuka* 'go' (Asher & Kumari 1997: 349). Consider (27).

(27) jooṇ iwiṭe {wannu/*pooyi}.
John here came/went
'John {came/*went} here.'

As can be seen from (27), the Goal argument of *waruka* can be the location of P-PIVOT, while that of *pookuka* cannot. Consider now (28).

(28) [tanne$_i$ kaaṇan {wanna/*pookunna}] kuṭṭikaḷeyum jooṇ$_i$ karayippiccu.
self see-ing came.Rel/went.Rel children.Acc John cry.Caus.Pst
'John$_i$ made the children who {came/*went} to see him$_i$ cry.'

In (28), the referent of *taan* cannot be at the goal of *pookuka*, which is P-PIVOT incompatible, as predicted by the P-PIVOT constraint.

Other PIVOT-sensitive expressions in Malayalam include the verbs of giving *koṭukkuka* and *taruka* (Asher & Kumari 1997), which are somewhat similar to Japanese verbs of giving *ageru* and *kureru* (see Kuno 1986a). The verb *koṭukkuka* requires its recipient (Dative Object) to be the third person, whereas there is no restriction on the agent (Subject). The verb *taruka*, in contrast, requires the recipient to be the first or the second person, while there is no restriction on the subject. These are seen in the following examples.

(29) a. ɲaan/nii/jooṇ meerik'k'ə pustakam {koṭuttu/*tannu}.
I/You/John Mary.Dat$_1$ book gave$_{to3}$/gave$_{to\,1,2}$
'I/You/John gave a book to Mary.'

b. n̲ii/meeri enik'k'ə pust̲akam {*koṭut̲t̲u / t̲an̲n̲u}.
you/Mary I.Dat$_1$ book gave$_{to3}$/gave$_{to\,1,2}$
'You/Mary gave a book to me.'

c. ɲaan/meeri ninak'k'ə pust̲akam {*koṭut̲t̲u / t̲an̲n̲u}.
I/Mary you.Dat$_1$ book gave$_{to3}$/gave$_{to\,1,2}$
'I/Mary gave a book to you.'

Thus, the recipient argument of *koṭukkuka* is P-PIVOT-incompatible, while that of *t̲aruka* is P-PIVOT-compatible.

Now consider the following.

(30) a. joon̩$_i$ [meeri tannik'k'ə$_i$ {*koṭut̲t̲a / t̲an̲n̲a }
John Mary self.Dat$_1$ gave$_{to3}$.Rel/gave$_{to\,1,2}$.Rel
kaarə rippeyar ceyt̲u.
car.Acc repair did
'John$_i$ repaired the car that Mary gave to him$_i$.'

b. joon̩$_i$ [meeri t̲annik'k'ə$_i$ pust̲akam {*koṭut̲t̲u/t̲an̲n̲u}] en̲n̲ə
John Mary self.Dat book gave$_{to3}$/gave$_{to\,1,2}$ Comp
paraɲɲu.
say-Past
'John$_i$ said that Mary gave a book to him$_i$.'

(30a, b) show that *t̲aan* cannot occur as the recipient argument of *koṭukkuka*, but can occur as the same argument of *t̲aruka* (the regular third person pronoun *awanə* behaves in the opposite way). This is predicted if *t̲aan* behaves as P-PIVOT.

The next pair of P-PIVOT-sensitive expressions in Malayalam to be discussed is *i-ppurat̲t̲ə* 'on this side of' and *a-ppurat̲t̲ə* 'on that side of'. As in the English and Japanese equivalents, the GROUND argument of these expressions is P-PIVOT-incompatible.

(31) {joon̩nte/*ente} a-ppurat̲t̲ə puccay-untə.
John.Gen/I.Gen that-side.Loc cat-Cop
'There is a cat on that side of {John/*me}.'

The example in (32) shows that *t̲aan* is not acceptable as the GROUND, as predicted.

(32) *[t̲ante$_i$ a-ppurat̲t̲ə puccay-untə en̲n̲ə] joon̩nə$_i$ ariyilla.
self.Gen that-side.Loc cat-Cop Comp John.Dat know.Neg
'John$_i$ doesn't know that there is a cat on that side (=the far side) of him$_i$.'

20.3.3 Logophoric properties of *t̲aan* II: Self-identification

I propose the following constraint for Malayalam *t̲aan*.

(33) *t̲aan* must represent a person whom its referent believes to be himself/herself or, in the complement of a verb of speech, a person whom its referent presents as identical with himself/herself.

This formulation in Malayalam differs from that in Yoruba in that the referent's belief counts in all contexts. This is seen in sentences like the following, in which *t̲aan* has an intra-clausal antecedent.

(34) iidipus$_i$ {(#)t̲ante$_i$/swant̲an$_i$} ammaye kaḷyaaṇm kaziccu.
Oedipus self.Gen/self.Gen mother marriage did
'Oedipus$_i$ married his$_i$ mother.'

In (34) *t̲ante* is acceptable only if Oedipus knew/believed that he had married his own mother; it is unacceptable in the scenario where Oedipus, as in the Greek myth, did not know the identity of his wife.

The referent's belief also counts in the complement of a verb of speech. Consider the following sentence, in the Abraham/Sarah scenario above.

(35) awan$_i$ [t̲ante$_i$ bhaarya saar̲a t̲ante$_i$ sahoodari aan̲ə] en̲n̲ə (nun̲a)
he self's wife Sarah self's sister Cop Comp lie
paraɲɲu.
said
He$_i$ said (lied) that his$_i$ wife Sarah was his$_i$ sister.

In (35) *t̲aan* can be used both for 'his (wife)' and 'his (sister)' in this scenario, suggesting that both the speaker's knowledge/belief and his/her presentation count in the speech complement clause.

This is also confirmed by the following sentence.

(36) jooṇ$_i$ [PRO$_i$ [t̲aan$_i$ at̲icca] kuṭṭiye at̲iccilla] en̲n̲ə paraɲɲu.
John self hit.Rel child.Acc hit.Neg Comp said
'John$_i$ said that he$_i$ did not hit the girl that he$_i$ hit.'

T̲aan in (36) is judged as acceptable in the lying scenario, but as unacceptable or almost unacceptable in the memory problem scenario, where *t̲aan* does not refer to the person whom John believes to be himself or presents as identical with himself.

When the matrix verb of (36) above is changed to a verb of belief, the lying interpretation is no longer possible, and so (37) is unacceptable.

(37) # jooṇ$_i$ [PRO$_i$ [t̲aan$_i$ at̲icca] kuṭṭiye at̲iccilla] en̲n̲ə wiswasikkunnu
John self hit.Rel child.Acc hit-Neg Comp believe
'John$_i$ believes that he$_i$ did not hit the girl that he$_i$ hit.'

One consequence of both the P-PIVOT constraint and the Self-identification constraint is that the referent of *taan* has consciousness, and consequently, is a living person (cf. the first person pronoun always refers to a living person). This prediction is borne out, as shown in (38), in which *taan* refers to a person after his death. The use of the pronoun *awan*, in contrast, creates no problem.

(38) jooṇ$_i$ [{*t̲aan$_i$/awan$_i$} leekhanannaliluute maranattinu seesam
John self/he writings-through death-Gen after
influuens ceyt̲a] vidwaanmaar wali prasiddhi neet̲i.
influence did.Rel scholars through fame gained
'John$_i$ became famous through the scholars that he$_i$ influenced after his death through his writings.'

20.4 Concluding Remarks

In this paper I have argued that logophoric pronouns tend to respect the (1) P-PIVOT Constraint and the (2) Self-identification Constraint. Logophoric pronouns in the three languages examined vary in (a) whether they respect one or both of these conditions, and (b) in which contexts belief (as opposed to verbal presentation) counts in self-identification. The three languages examined do not exhaust the logical possibilities that this parameterization allows. Examination of other languages might reveal examples of remaining possibilities.

Acknowledgements

In writing this paper I would like to express my deepest thanks to the Mohanan family. This paper would have never existed without them; it grew as I kept asking Mo and Tara questions at their home, while Ammu (see M.T. Mohanan, this volume) was playing (and waiting) around us. I would also like to thank Pullattu Abraham George for his help on the Malayalam sentences, Desola Amos and Femi Opadiji for the Yoruba data, and David Oshima for helpful discussion.

In one class Mohanan once proclaimed that the acknowledgment section of a paper should say "all of the remaining errors found in this paper should be attributed to my teachers, because they educated me." I leave it to Mohanan to see if that is true of this paper.

References

Adesola, Oluseye. 2005. *Pronouns and Null Operators: A-bar Dependencies and Relations in Yoruba*. Ph.D. thesis, State University of New Jersey.

Asher, Ronald E. and T. C. Kumari. 1997. *Malayalam*. Abingdon, Oxon: Routledge.

Bamgbose, Ayo. 1966. *A Grammar of Yoruba*. Cambridge: Cambridge University Press.

Clements, George N. 1975. The logophoric pronoun in Ewe: Its role in discourse. *Journal of Western African Language* 10(2):141–177.

Culy, Christopher. 1994. Aspects of logophoric marking. *Linguistics* 32:1055–1094.

Culy, Christopher. 1997. Logophoric pronouns and point of view. *Linguistics* 35:845–859.

Fillmore, Charles. 1997. *Lectures on Deixis*. Stanford: CSLI Publications.

Hagège, Claude. 1974. Les pronoms logophoriques. *Bulletin de la Societé de Linguistique de Paris* 69:287–310.

Huang, Yan. 2000. *Anaphora: A Cross-linguistic Study*. New York: Oxford University Press.

Iida, Masayo. 1996. *Context and Binding in Japanese*. Stanford: CSLI Publications.

Jayaseelan, K. A. 1999a. Lexical anaphors and pronouns in Malayalam. In B. Lust, K. Wali, J. Gair, and K. V. Subbarao, eds., *Anaphors and Pronouns in Selected South Asian Languages*. Berlin: Mouton de Gruyter.

Jayaseelan, K. A. 1999b. *Parametric Studies in Malayalam Syntax*. Mumbai, India: Allied Publishers.

Kameyama, Megumi. 1984. Subjective/logophoric bound anaphor *zibun*. Papers from the Regional Meeting of Chicago Linguistic Society.

Kay, Paul. 1992. The inheritance of presupposition. *Linguistics and Philosophy* 15:333–381.

Kuno, Susumu. 1972. Pronominalization, reflexivization, and direct discourse. *Linguistic Inquiry* 3:161–195.

Kuno, Susumu. 1978. *Danwa no Bunpoo [Discourse Grammar]*. Tokyo: Taishuukan.

Kuno, Susumu. 1986a. *Functional Syntax. Anaphora, Discourse and Empathy*. Chicago: University of Chicago Press.

Kuno, Susumu. 1986b. Anaphora in Japanese. In S.-Y. Kuroda, ed., *Papers from the First SDF Workshop in Japanese Syntax*, pages 11–70. San Diego: University of California at San Diego, Department of Linguistics.

Matsumoto, Yo. 1990. Logophoric conditions on reflexives in Malayalam. Manuscript, Department of Linguistics, Stanford University.

McCawley, James. 1970. Where do noun phrases come from? In R. Jacobs and P. Rosenbaum, eds., *Readings in English Transformational Grammar*, pages 166–183. Waltham, Massachusetts: Ginn.

Mohanan, Karuvannur P. 1982a. Grammatical relations and anaphora in Malayalam. In A. Marantz and T. Stowell, eds., *Papers in Syntax (MIT Working Papers IV)*. Cambridge: Department of Linguistics and Philosophy, MIT.

Mohanan, Karuvannur P. 1982b. Pronouns in Malayalam. *Studies in the Linguistic Sciences* 11:67–75.

Oshima, David Y. 2007. On empathic and logophoric binding. *Research on Language and Computation* 5:19–35.

Oshima, David Y. 2009. Perspective, logophoricity, and embedded tense in Japanese. In Y. Takubo, ed., *Japanese/Korean Linguistics*, vol. 16. Stanford: CSLI Publications.

Pulleyblank, Douglas. 1986. Clitics in Yoruba. In H. Borer, ed., *The Syntax of Pronominal Clitics (Syntax and Semantics 19)*, pages 43–64. Orlando: Academic Press.

Saburo, Ohye. 1980. *Nichi-eigo no Hikaku Kenkyuu: Shukansei o Megutte [A Comparison of Japanese and English: Concerning Subjectivity]*. Tokyo: Nan'undo.

Safir, Ken. 2004a. *The Syntax of Anaphora*. Oxford/New York: Oxford University Press.

Safir, Ken. 2004b. Person, context and perspective. *Rivista di Linguistica/Italian Journal of Linguistics* 16.

Schlenker, Philippe. 2003. A plea for monsters. *Linguistics and Philosophy* 26:29–120.

Sells, Peter. 1987. Aspects of logophoricity. *Linguistic Inquiry* 18:445–479.

21

Unpredicated Particles

BETH LEVIN AND PETER SELLS

21.1 Introduction

In their introduction to the volume *Grammatical Semantics*, Mohanan, Mohanan, and Wee lay out a research program of that name "which seeks to explore grammatically relevant aspects of meaning" (1999:1). This paper is intended to further this research program by addressing the analysis of the (b) examples in (1) and (2) and others like them:

(1) a. He hosed the dirt off.
    b. He hosed the window off.

(2) a. He rinsed the dirt out.
    b. He rinsed the cloth out.

Although the same particle appears in both members of each pair of examples, its relation to the object is different. In the (a) examples, intuitively the particle is predicated of the object, which refers to what we call the 'material' argument of the verb; thus, the (a) examples have resultative meanings, e.g., 'the dirt is off' and 'the dirt is out', with respect to some understood, but unexpressed location. In the (b) examples, where the object expresses the location (of the material), there is no such predication: the window is not off, nor is the cloth out. The acceptability of the (b) examples is yet more intriguing in the context of the existence of related examples as in (c) and (d):

(1) c. He hosed the dirt off the window.
    d. He hosed the window off (*the dirt/*of the dirt/*with the dirt).

(2) c. He rinsed the dirt out of the cloth.
    d. He rinsed the cloth out (*the dirt/*of the dirt/*with the dirt).

Reality Exploration and Discovery: Pattern Interaction in Language and Life.
Linda Uyechi and Lian-Hee Wee (eds.).

In the (c) examples, both material and location are expressed; the examples are related to the (a) examples, as they have the material as the object, with the location apparently being part of a PP headed by a preposition analogous to the particle in the (a) and (b) examples. We refer to these as 'full expression' examples. However, there are no examples which have the location as object (as in the (b) examples) which include the particle, and yet also express the material; none of the attempts to construct such examples as in the (d) sentences works. We refer to the particles in the (b) examples as 'unpredicated'.

Other verbs with the same behavior include *wipe*, *sweep*, *scrub* and *scrape*.

(3) a. She wiped the crumbs off. (cf. The crumbs are off.)
b. She wiped the table off. (cf. *The table is off.)

(4) a. She scraped the paint off. (cf. The paint is off.)
b. She scraped the windowsill off. (cf. *The windowsill is off.)

These are all removing type surface contact verbs—or *wipe* verbs—discussed in Levin and Rappaport Hovav (1991) and Rappaport Hovav and Levin (1998; hereafter RH&L98). They are surface contact verbs as they describe an action involving making contact with a surface in some manner; they are of the removing type as they describe actions usually performed to remove stuff from a surface or container.

In addition, there is an interesting restriction on the particles with unpredicated uses. The particles exemplified so far involve a notion of not being at a location, or movement away from a location: *off* and *out*. These particles have 'opposites', *on* or *in*, which are found with certain *spray/load* verbs—the surface contact verb subclass whose members describe actions intended to put stuff on a surface or in a container. However, these verb-particle combinations lack unpredicated uses.

(5) a. He smeared the ointment on (his hands).
b. *He smeared his hands on.

(6) a. He stuffed the laundry in (the basket).
b. *He stuffed the basket in.

(7) a. He packed the clothes in (the suitcase).
b. *He packed the suitcase in.

The relevant behavior is determined by the particle, not the verb, for the same verb can tolerate unpredicated uses of some particles, but not others, as the contrast between (8b) and (9b) shows:

(8) a. She sprayed the paint on (the wall).
b. *She sprayed the wall on.

(9) a. She sprayed the dirt off (the wall).
b. She sprayed the wall off.

Our analysis of when unpredicated particles are possible is based closely on observations on English resultative constructions with a subcategorized NP. Previous work has shown that a verb in a resultative construction has differential tolerance for which adjectives can head the result phrase: some adjectives are possible and some are not (*wipe the counter clean/*dirty*). Hay (1997) and Wechsler (2005) explicate the restriction in terms of the scale structure of the adjectives: only so-called 'maximal endpoint closed-scale' adjectives can give rise to a telic sentence, which the resultative construction requires. Our account of the particle constructions is that *wipe the table off* is analogous to *wipe the table clean*, while **wipe the table on* is analogous to **wipe the table dirty*.

The paper is organized as follows. In section 21.2, we present some basic facts about English unpredicated particle constructions. Section 21.3 briefly addresses previous literature on the topic. We present our analysis in section 21.4, relating the unpredicated particle construction to the resultative construction, and then focus on the precise aspectual properties of the relevant examples. We conclude with a brief summary and an overview of areas for future research.

21.2 Properties of the Unpredicated Particle Construction

The verbs appearing in the relevant constructions typically take just the location argument as object, as with *wipe* in the examples below (see RH&L98, Zeller 2001). The verbs can be augmented with one of the allowable particles (as in the (b) example), retaining the location as object; alternatively, the verbs can take the material as object and the location as a PP, as discussed above. They cannot, however, be found with the material alone, except in the presence of a particle.

(10) a. wipe the mirror b. wipe the mirror off
(11) a. *wipe the fingerprints b. wipe the fingerprints off (the mirror)

In *wipe the mirror*, typically there is material (to be wiped off) implied; our world knowledge of mirrors is such that we assume that we wipe a mirror so that it can carry out its intended function better—in other words, by removing from it foreign substances that occlude or blur its surface. However, it is certainly possible to wipe a surface without anything being on it. Thus, the presence of some material on a surface is probably not part of the core meaning of *wipe* or comparable surface contact verbs (RH&L98). Similarly, consider *spray*, which also allows the unpredicated particle construction, though only with *off*. The verb itself just means putting liquid (drops) into motion, and surely the default interpretation of *spray the wall* involves spraying something—the drops that are set in motion—*onto* the wall.

Both types of verb-particle construction (as in (3) or (4) above) have one overt internal argument and one unexpressed argument, but there is an asymmetry in the interpretation of the unexpressed argument. In those instances where the material is the direct object and the location is unexpressed, as in *wipe the fingerprints off*, the location must be understood as what Fillmore (1986) calls a definite null argument, better described as an unexpressed argument having a contextually determined interpretation (cf. Condoravdi and Gawron 1996, Lambrecht and Lemoine 2005).[1] Thus, (12a) is odd as the context does not allow a particular location to be inferred for the material, the fingerprints; in contrast, (12b), which includes enough context for the location to be inferred, is felicitous.

(12) a. The maid said that whenever she goes in to clean a room,
#she has to wipe the fingerprints off.
b. If the maid sees that the mirror is dirty,
she has to wipe the fingerprints off (= 'off it').

Now in the unpredicated examples, the location is expressed and the material is unexpressed. Here the material is interpreted like an indefinite null argument in Fillmore's terms, comparable to the unexpressed object in *She just ate*. That is, some material is understood to be at the location, but the exact nature and quantity of the material can only be inferred using knowledge of what might be prototypically be found at such a location. These properties are illustrated in (13), where that material might be dust, fingerprints, toothpaste, water spots or anything else that might turn up on the surface of a mirror.

(13) The maid said that whenever she goes in to clean a room,
she has to wipe the mirror off.

Importantly, the interpretation of the unexpressed material, unlike that of the unexpressed location, does not depend on context. Examples with unexpressed material are felicitous even in the absence of (adequate) context, unlike examples with unexpressed locations. The contrasting felicity of the sentences in (14) makes this point.

(14) a. Before you drink, you need to wipe the glass off.

[1] Condoravdi and Gawron's characterization of the interpretation as contextually dependent seems most accurate to us. Although it is true that unexpressed locations are often understood as definite, we suggest that this is a consequence of the more general oddness of non-quantized locations in such PPs (*#She wiped the fingerprints off glass; #She rinsed a spot out of silk*). Furthermore, the need to determine the unexpressed location from context strongly favors its being definite and, hence, referential, perhaps enhancing the bias against indefinite locations.

b. #Before you drink, you need to wipe any/the fingerprints off.
(cf. Before you drink from a glass, you need to wipe any/the fingerprints off.)

The understood contextually determined location in *wipe the fingerprints off* is one manifestation of a more general phenomenon: even simple 'intransitive' expressions with particles such as *She ran off/out/in* show the same interpretive properties. With *run* and other motion verbs, the unexpressed location again receives a contextually determined interpretation. In the absence of a specific context, this location is determined deictically with motion verbs, being understood as the location of the speaker. As far as we can tell, all unexpressed locations—whether static locations, sources, goals, or paths—receive a contextually determined interpretation. Consider the examples in (15).

(15) a. We squeezed the toothpaste out [ ].
b. We stuffed the feathers in [ ].
c. We pushed the needle through [ ].
d. We pushed the cart across [ ].
e. We crossed [ ] at the light.
f. All the employees left [ ] for home at 5pm today.
g. As soon as they open the office, the first customers telephone [ ].

We include the (e) and (f) examples here as their unexpressed path- and source-like arguments pattern in the same way as the others, although strictly speaking they would not be expressed syntactically as a complement of a particle or preposition in these examples; and we include the last example since the unexpressed argument is notionally a goal PP. We have no explanation for the observation that unexpressed locations receive a contextually determined interpretation, but the generality of the facts suggests that we should not seek an explanation for this interpretation as it is found in say (15b) just within that type of example; thus, we will set this question aside.

Finally, we mention the contribution of the particles *off* and *out* to the meaning of the construction. Each by its very nature defines a particular spatial relation between a Figure, the material, and a Ground, the location, borrowing the terms used by Talmy (1975).[2] In so doing, a particle imposes certain restrictions on possible materials and locations. Consider the differences in interpretation of the examples in (16).

(16) a. wipe the suitcase
b. wipe the suitcase off
c. wipe the suitcase out

[2]Some particles have acquired additional non-spatial uses as with *up* and *on* in *cut the meat up* or *talk on*. We leave such uses aside.

The (a) sentence is vague as to what part and how much of the surface of the suitcase is being wiped; it could be some or all of it. The other two examples contrast with (a) in implying that some material is present at the location, presumably because the particle by its nature relates a Figure (the material) to a Ground (the location); furthermore, they describe a different kind of event: the removal of the material from the location, due to the 'removal' facet of meaning introduced by the particles. However, along with the difference in particle in the (b–c) examples, there is a difference in how the location is conceptualized: in the *off* example it is conceptualized as 2-dimensional, a surface, while in the *out* example it is conceptualized as 3-dimensional, a container. This conceptual difference plays out according to whether the wiping is understood as involving the exterior of the suitcase (the suitcase as a surface) or the interior of the suitcase (the suitcase as a container).

21.3 Previous Literature

The unpredicated uses of particles have not gone unnoticed in the literature. Svenonius (1996:31) presents the examples in (17), which are also considered in Zeller (2001), McIntyre (2003), and Svenonius (2003), among others.

(17) a. The waiter wiped the dust off the table.
b. The waiter wiped {off} the dust {off}.
c. The waiter wiped {off} the table {off}.

The alternation is found to some degree in all Germanic languages, as extensively surveyed by Svenonius. In German, for instance, the verb *spülen* 'wash' in conjunction with the particle *ab* 'off' gives a familiar pattern (examples from Zeller (2001)):

(18) a. Peter spülte den Teller.
'Peter washed the plate.'
b. Peter spülte den Teller ab.
'Peter washed the plate off.'

(19) a.*Peter spülte das Fett.
'Peter washed the grease.'
b. Peter spülte das Fett ab.
'Peter washed the grease off.'

In Zeller's account, all the internal arguments in a verb-particle construction are licensed by the particle, and not by the verb (more specifically, not *only* by the verb).[3] Zeller makes the important observation that in washing a plate, as in (18), the grease (theme) is what is removed; and that washing off the grease

[3]It seems to be a necessary but not sufficient condition on the unpredicated uses that the location be an argument of the verb itself; see our discussion of (48) below.

from a plate as in (19) implies that the plate (source) thereby becomes clean. He locates these properties in the semantics of the particle *ab*; *spülen* has a default argument structure of agent and source, and the theme is only linked through the particle. Once *ab* is added, either internal argument (source or theme) may be the object, giving the facts in (18)–(19) above.

Broadly speaking, German and English seem quite similar in the types and interpretations of unpredicated particle examples which intuitively alternate with predicated particle variants (as in (19)). For example, in terms of the interpretation of unexpressed arguments, the two languages are the same; an unexpressed location must be contextually determined, while an unexpressed material argument need not be and receives an unspecified interpretation (cf. 12 above):[4]

(20) Jedes Mal wenn ich in die Küche gehe
     Each time when I in the kitchen go
  a. ??... muss ich das Fett ab-spülen.
     ... must I the grease off-wash
  b. ... muss ich die Teller ab-spülen.
     ... must I the plates off-wash

Using the notions of Figure and Ground, McIntyre (2007) also discusses our unpredicated examples under the notion of 'Ground promotion': "suppression of the Figure and promotion of the Ground to direct argument" (2007:353), presenting German examples such as those shown in (21):

(21) a. Er hat den Tee (mit heißem Wasser) auf-gegossen.
        he has the tea (with hot water) on-poured
     b. Sie schmierte meinen Rücken (mit Sonnencreme) ein.
        she smeared my back (with sun-cream) in

The 'promotion' idea draws on the analysis of prepositions in Svenonius (1996, 2003), in which they are considered notionally transitive but syntactically decomposed into two parts, *p* licensing an 'external' argument, Figure, and *P* licensing an 'internal' argument, Ground. Svenonius' analysis of the alternation is that the canonical construction with a Figure object involves *p*-*P*, while the unpredicated variant only involves *P*. (22) illustrates with Dutch examples from Svenonius (2003); the promotion in the second case is evident from the syntactic derivation:

(22) a. Ingrid smeert henna in haar haar.
                    Figure   Ground
        'Ingrid smears henna in her hair.'

[4]We are grateful to Magdalena Schwager for assistance with the German examples.

b. Ingrid smeert [haar haar]$_i$ in t$_i$.
Ground
'Ingrid smears up her hair.'

In (22a), the form *in* corresponds to *p-P*, licensing both arguments, the higher of which (Figure) is the verb's surface object. In (22b), only *P* is projected, giving an unaccusative-like structure. The object of *P* (Ground) moves to the verb's object position to be licensed on the surface (e.g., for case reasons).

Svenonius posits that German and Dutch have very flexible patterns of argument alternation, as suggested by the examples above and the derivation in (22b); he takes English to be somewhat restricted in comparison, essentially having only the *off*/*out* type of unpredicated example, derived in a different way from the general alternations found in German and Dutch. The existence of a real asymmetry between German and English, for example, might not seem surprising given that prepositions, particles, and (inseparable) verbal prefixes provide German with considerable potential resources for licensing argument alternations; we might indeed expect English to show fewer options. However, as McIntyre comments, the difference between German and English is only a tendency, and not a qualitative or parametric difference; examples as in (21) are not fully productive in German. McIntyre observes that "we should be mindful of two qualitative similarities between the languages: (i) the vast bulk of particle verbs disallow Ground promotion, and (ii) Ground promotion is not fully productive" (2007:355). To illustrate with one of his examples, Ground promotion in (23) is as bad in German as in English:

(23)	Ich	habe	{die	Bettwäsche	/*das	Bett}	ab-gerissen.
	I	have	{the	bedsheets	/*the	bed}	off-ripped

In summary, it seems likely that a full account of apparently unpredicated particle examples will involve careful consideration of specific types of verbs, with respect to the kind of action they denote. The semantic properties of the verbs will interact with the various argument-extension and argument-alternation resources in particular languages. We undertake such an enterprise in a limited way with respect to English in the analysis part of this paper. We take the previous literature to have shown that the unpredicated particle construction is a fact of all Germanic languages, only underscoring the importance of presenting an analysis of its core properties.

21.4 The Interpretation of Particle Constructions and Telicity

We now need to further elucidate why the unpredicated particle construction is possible with *off* and *out*, but not *on* and *in*. For example, there is a clear contrast in acceptability between (8b) and (9b), repeated in (24), yet there is no obvious, concomitant sense in which the semantics of *on* and *off* differ.

(24) a. *She sprayed the wall on.
b. She sprayed the wall off.

Hence, the next step is to identify the property that distinguishes complex events of removing described by *off/out* verb-particle examples from the complex events of putting described by *in/on* examples.

We first examine the aspectual properties of surface contact verbs outside the verb-particle construction. We then discuss the aspectual analysis of resultatives, as result phrases have the same roles as particles; they make it possible to telicize the event denoted by the verb and they provide additional licensing options for arguments. With this context, we return to the unpredicated particle examples and discuss their aspectual analysis. In turn, this provides the basis for our explanation of why certain particles are excluded from the unpredicated particle construction.

21.4.1 The basic (a)telicity of surface contact verbs

Surface contact verbs like *scrub, sweep* and *wipe* describe actions usually performed to remove stuff from a surface or container. They contrast with the putting type surface contact verbs, such as as *dab, smear* and *stuff*, which describe actions usually performed to put stuff on a surface or in a container. (There are also a few surface contact verbs which describe actions that can be used for either putting or removing, such as *shovel* and *spray*.)

As discussed by Rappaport Hovav and Levin (2005), a hallmark of verbs such as *sweep* and *wipe* is that they allow either telic or atelic interpretations in their simple transitive uses with a definite location object. The atelic interpretation arises when the specific pattern of motion and contact characteristic of the verb is understood as repeated indefinitely over the surface (or container). The telic interpretation arises when the spatial extent of the surface is taken to bound the action, which still involves multiple instances of the characteristic pattern of motion and contact. In this instance, the event is over when the action has been carried out with respect to the entire surface. Specifically, on this interpretation the location serves as an incremental theme (Dowty 1991), with its spatial extent measuring out the event's progress.[5]

(25) a. She wiped the counter for five minutes. (Atelic)
b. She wiped the counter in 30 seconds flat. (Telic)

Surface contact verbs, which exemplify what might be called potential—or 'latent' (Tenny 1992:20)—incremental theme verbs, contrast with canonical

[5]In the absence of context, simple past examples such as *She wiped the counter* tend to receive a telic interpretation (and, in fact, some work does not even recognize the existence of an atelic interpretation; cf. Dowty's (1991:567) use of *mow the lawn* to illustrate the notion of incremental theme). Rappaport Hovav (2008) proposes that such telic interpretations are the result of conversational implicature, noting that pragmatic considerations govern their availability.

incremental theme verbs (e.g., *build, eat, translate*), which are necessarily telic when they take a definite object; their object is almost always understood as an incremental theme, with its spatial extent necessarily serving as a measure for the event.

21.4.2 Determining telicity in resultative examples

Telic predicates denote events with inherent terminal points. Most current approaches to telicity take such predicates to have a designated argument which plays a crucial role in determining whether this terminal point has been attained. Specifically, this argument has a property that in some sense 'measures out' the event, defining a homomorphism between a change in this property and the event's temporal progress (e.g., Beavers 2007, Borer 2005, Hay, Kennedy and Levin 1999, Krifka 1992, 1998, Ramchand 1997, Tenny 1992). Incremental themes are arguments that define the homomorphism via the spatial extent of their referent.

The homomorphism can also be defined in events of 'scalar' change: a change along a scale consisting of a set of degrees—points or intervals indicating measurement values—ordered on a particular dimension (e.g., cost, height, temperature; Kennedy (2001)). This dimension represents an attribute of an argument of the event, with the degrees indicating the possible values of this attribute. A scalar change involves a change in the value of the relevant attribute in a particular direction along the associated scale. The change along the scale also determines the time course of the event: there is a homomorphism between the scale of change and the event's temporal progress. Specifically, when the scale is bounded, it provides a natural bound for the event, and the event is telic.

Some verbs, such as *ascend* and *widen*, denote events of scalar change in that they lexically entail a scale. Other verbs, such as incremental theme verbs, do not lexicalize a scale of change (Rappaport Hovav 2008). Surface contact verbs also do not lexicalize a scale of change; however, in combination with a particle or a result phrase, they may form a complex event of removal or putting, and a scale of change is necessarily introduced via the particle, a PP or a result phrase. To show this, we start with resultative constructions based on surface contact verbs.

As Hay (1997) and Wechsler (2005) point out, an examination of naturally-occurring resultatives with subcategorized objects reveals that only so-called 'maximal endpoint closed-scale' gradable adjectives, such as *flat* or *clean*, can head the result phrase. 'Open-scale' gradable adjectives, such as *long* or *wide*, and 'minimal endpoint closed-scale' gradable adjectives such as *dirty* or *wet* cannot. That is, there are resultatives such as *hammer the metal flat* or *wipe the shelf clean*, but not **hammer the metal long* or **wipe the shelf wet*.

To understand what defines these three classes of gradable adjectives, it is important to understand two properties: their associated scale and standard. An essential property of a gradable adjective is the existence of an associated attribute whose values can be ordered to form a scale. For example, *long* is associated with the attribute 'length', with the possible values of this attribute ranging from 0 to infinity (on some measurement system). Consequently, things possessing this attribute can be ordered, and thus compared, according to their lengths. When a gradable adjective is predicated of an object, as in *The new kitchen counter is long*, an implicit comparison is made between the length of the kitchen counter and a contextually determined 'standard' of length, with this particular counter exceeding this standard. Maximal endpoint closed-scale adjectives, as their name implies, are associated with a closed scale, a scale with a maximal value; this value is used as the default standard, so the adjective is only applicable when this value is reached. In contrast, the scale associated with 'open-scale' adjectives lacks a minimum or maximum value;[6] these adjectives necessarily have a contextually determined standard. Minimal endpoint closed-scale adjectives such as *dirty* and *wet* also have a bounded scale, but it is bounded by a minimum value: that is, the relevant adjective can be applied as soon as an entity has the property to even a minimal degree. For instance, a towel is dirty as soon as there is a speck of dust on it or wet as soon as there is a drop of liquid on it. However, what makes these adjectives like open-scale adjectives is that when evaluating their applicability to an entity, the standard of dirtiness or wetness that is used is often contextually determined and assigned a value above the minimal degree, as Wechsler discusses.

Since maximal endpoint closed-scale adjectives are associated with a scale with a maximal value, this value can serve as a bound on the scalar change denoted by a resultative, thus making the event temporally bounded. In contrast, the scale associated with open-scale adjectives lacks a maximum value; such adjectives do not provide a natural bound on a scalar change, so there is no clear temporal bound for the event denoted by a resultative. The same applies to the minimal endpoint closed-scale adjectives: apparently, there is no clear natural bound for the scalar change.

The distribution of adjectives in resultatives, then, suggests that result phrases can serve to telicize events. However, this statement is not sufficiently nuanced, as sentences with appropriate result phrases are not always telic.

---

[6]Occasionally, an adjective whose associated scale is typically open may be associated with a closed scale when applied to a particular argument (Kennedy and McNally 2005:265ff.). It is interesting that the few examples cited of open-scale adjectives heading result phrases show exactly such shifts. Thus, Hay (1997:12) cites *her nails were clipped short*, due to the way nails grow, *short* here has a maximal endpoint (contrasting, for example, with *short* applied to dresses). Open-scale adjectives may also be found with pseudo-resultatives, as in *open one's mouth wide* (see Levinson 2006). Here we focus solely on the types of scales relevant to our concerns and ignore further subtypes that may be otherwise important, such as scales closed at one vs. both ends.

Again, we make this point with surface contact verbs, though it holds more generally. It is more accurate to say that examples such as *Sam wiped the table* or *Phil pounded the scrap metal*, which may receive either telic or atelic interpretations with a definite object (see section (21.4.3)), become necessarily telic with a result phrase, as shown in (26).

(26) a. Sam wiped the table clean in one minute flat.
b. Phil pounded the scrap metal flat in an hour.

However, if the object of the resultative is not quantized, then the sentence is nevertheless atelic, as in these examples with mass noun objects:

(27) a. Sam wiped furniture clean for an hour.
b. Phil pounded scrap metal flat for an afternoon.

These examples show that in resultatives maximal endpoint closed-scale adjectives define a scalar change that is necessarily bounded, and that change is predicated of some entity, which is an incremental theme in its own right by virtue of its spatial extent. In other words, for each part of this entity, the boundedness of the change of state denoted by the resultative is being assessed. The entire event is bounded only if the spatial extent of this entity is bounded: in resultatives the scale of change has no affect on telicity, for the only possible result phrases guarantee that the scale of change is bounded. Thus, resultative constructions are telic or atelic depending precisely on whether the object is quantized.

Thus, two interacting 'measures' must be recognized in resultatives, and as we show in sections 21.4.3 and 21.4.4, both figure in the interpretation of verb-particle examples. It is the nature of the scale of change, whose importance has not been fully appreciated in previous studies, which distinguishes the predicated and unpredicated particle examples. In this paper we describe these two measures informally, focussing on why both must be identified.[7]

21.4.3 Determining telicity when the material argument is expressed

Now we return to the constructions of interest. In the full expression and acceptable verb-particle examples, the PPs or particles do not telicize across the board, but only under precisely the same circumstances as result phrases: that is, they must provide a bound to the scale of change and the argument that changes, as an incremental theme, must have a bounded spatial extent. What differentiates these constructions from resultatives is that the scale of change involves a change in the material's location.

The telicity of the putting type surface contact verbs, often referred to as *spray/load* verbs, has received considerable discussion (Dowty 1991, Jack-

[7]Based mainly on other data, Beavers (2007) recognizes that the computation of telicity frequently involves these two types of measure and proposes a way to formalize these observations.

endoff 1996), and the analyses of these verbs can be extended to the full expression examples. In these examples, the material is expressed as the object and contributes to the delimitation of the event. Compare an example with a quantized material NP to one with a non-quantized material NP: only if this NP is quantized is the example telic; contrast (28) with (29).[8]

(28) a. She swept dirt off the floor for/*in 2 minutes.
b. He wiped toothpaste out of the sink for/*in 5 minutes. (Atelic)

(29) a. She swept the dirt off the floor *for/in 5 minutes.
b. He wiped the toothpaste out of the sink *for/in 5 minutes. (Telic)

Furthermore, the progressive entails the perfect with atelic predicates, but not with telic predicates (Dowty 1979, among others). Thus, the availability of perfect entailments only in (30b), where the material is non-quantized, also indicates that such sentences are atelic; in contrast, the examples in (31b), where the material is quantized, lack these entailments, consistent with telicity.

(30) a. She is sweeping dirt off the floor.
⇒ She has swept dirt off the floor.
b. He is wiping toothpaste out of the sink.
⇒ He has wiped toothpaste out of the sink.

(31) a. She is sweeping the dirt off the floor.
⇏ She has swept the dirt off the floor.
b. He is wiping the toothpaste out of the sink.
⇏ He has wiped the toothpaste out of the sink.

As previous work notes, what matters to the determination of telicity is that the object, i.e. the material, is an incremental theme. The spatial extent of the material provides a measure of the progress of the event. Only when the material is quantized is this measure bounded, and the event telic.

Such accounts focus on the spatial extent of the material, that is, a measure as incremental theme; however, there is more to the determination of the telicity of the event than this. As in resultatives, all parts of the material as a direct object are involved in an event of scalar change: from being located on some surface, or in some container, to no longer being located on or in it. This

[8]The location argument does not contribute to the basic telicity of full expression sentences where both material and location are expressed. When the location is a singular NP there is a strong preference that it be quantized; examples like *She wiped the spot off stainless steel* or *She rinsed the grease off velvet* are rather odd, but if acceptable are telic (due to the quantized material argument). Examples of this type improve in acceptability in habitual contexts: consider *When you rinse a spot off velvet, it leaves a stain*, which also receives a telic interpretation. If there is a plural location (e.g., *She wiped the jam off (the) counters*), then it is irrelevant to our concerns, as atelicity arises from iteratively carrying out the action with respect to the location.

change is characterizable by a two-point scale, necessarily bounded (on–off, in–out). Hence there is also bounded change, predicated of an argument and holding of that argument's spatial extent, just as with the resultatives. While the overall telicity of the sentence is determined by whether the spatial extent is bounded or not, the contribution of the boundedness of the scalar change to the overall telicity, though not usually commented on, cannot be ignored.

Predicated particle examples work just like the full expression examples, except that the location is not expressed, but contextually determined (see (15) above). The scale of change is once again from *on* to *off* (or from *in* to *out of*) the location, and thus necessarily bounded, so that the overall telicity is determined by whether the material is quantized or not. So, as we expect, the examples in the first pair below with non-quantized material NPs are atelic, while those in the second pair with quantized NPs are telic.

(32) a. He rinsed dirt out for/*in 30 seconds.
 b. She wiped jam off for/*in just a minute.

(33) a. He rinsed the dirt out in just 30 seconds.
 b. She wiped the jam off in one minute flat.

Specifically, in (33a), the dirt is understood to have been removed from its location to some acceptable degree, while in (33b) the jam is removed from its location to some acceptable degree (see note 9).

21.4.4 Determining telicity in unpredicated particle examples

The full expression and predicated particle examples can be thought of as describing removing events. Importantly, unpredicated particle examples are conceptually different, and are better characterized as involving clearing or emptying events brought about by the relevant form of surface contact, depending on whether the location is a surface or a container. As in non-particle examples like *I cleared the table* or *I emptied the tub*, what matters in the unpredicated examples is the state of the location: it starts off in a state of having material on or in it and ends up in a state of not having material on or in it. There is a scale between these two states, defined by the loss of material (see section (21.4.3)). The location argument has a spatial extent which also determines the progress of the event up to the change of state, and the particular particle gives more information about the nature of the surface or container.

As the examples below show, the unpredicated particle examples are telic, only when the location NP is quantized.

(34) a. She wiped the counter off in/*?for 10 minutes.
 b. He rinsed the cloth out in/*?for 30 seconds.

(35) a. She wiped glass off *in/for 2 hours.

b. He rinsed rice out *in/for 10 minutes.

(36) a. She was wiping the counter off. $\not\Rightarrow$ She had wiped the counter off.
b. He was rinsing the cloth out. $\not\Rightarrow$ He had rinsed the cloth out.

In this respect they are like the predicated particle examples: it appears that the spatial extent of the object provides a measure whose boundedness determines the telicity of the example.

Yet how can examples such as (34) be telic given that their unexpressed material argument receives an unspecified interpretation? The availability of the telic interpretation makes sense in the context of our world knowledge. In the presence of the particles *off* or *out*, surface contact verbs are being used in the description of events of clearing or emptying, and such events are over when the surface is bare or the container empty to an acceptable degree.[9]

As the unpredicated particles examples have a location object, the amount of material is not and can not be a determining factor: 'is not', because it is unexpressed, by hypothesis, and 'can not' as we know that only properties of the direct object enter into the determination of telicity. Just as our intuitions tell us, the events in (36) are over when the counter is bare and the cloth has nothing unwanted in it; we have no interest in what was on the counter or in the cloth, or how much of it there was. This is due precisely to the fact that the particles define closed-scale changes in such clearing or emptying uses: the event simply involves a location changing from a state where it has stuff on or in it to one where it does not. Given the bounded nature of the change, the overall telicity of the sentence is then determined by the spatial extent of the location, which serves as an incremental theme, as shown above in (34)–(36).

21.4.5 The difference between *off/out* and *on/in*

The remaining issue is why *off* or *out*, but not *on* or *in*, have unpredicated uses:

(37) a. We smeared (the) lotion on (the baby).
b.*We smeared the baby on.

(38) a. We sprayed (the) paint on (the wall).
b.*We sprayed the wall on.

In events of clearing or emptying, if the location is spatially bounded, then it imposes a natural bound on the event: the event is over when everything is removed from it. That is, there is a salient point of transition to a result state

[9]By acceptable degree, we mean that if any material remains, the remaining amount is so little as not to count (cf. Lasersohn (1999) on 'pragmatic halos' and Kennedy and McNally (2005) on imprecision in adjective uses). Due to this imprecision, speakers vary as to how acceptable they find examples like *He wiped the counter off (#but he left some crumbs)* or *He rinsed the cloth out (#but it still had some dye in it).*

at the end of the process of clearing or emptying the location. In contrast, the unacceptable unpredicated particle examples involve *on* and *in* and describe filling or covering events, crucially, a different relation between the location and the event. It is true that as soon as even a little bit of material is placed on or in a location, the predicate *on* or *in* could be said to hold of that location; in this sense, these particles are just like the minimal endpoint closed-scale adjective *dirty*, which can be applied as soon as a minimal amount of dirt is on a surface. However, as Wechsler discusses, *dirty* is treated as a 'de facto' open-scale adjective, with a standard that is somewhere above the minimum (see section 21.4.2); we propose that the same holds of *on* and *in*. Therefore, an unpredicated particle construction with one of them will involve an open scale of change (applied over the spatial extent of the location, as an incremental theme), and, for this reason, the telicity of the whole construction cannot be guaranteed simply by the boundedness of the location argument; yet, the well-formedness of the construction rests on this guarantee.

The predicated particle constructions involving *in* and *on* are quite straightforward. The telicity of (38a), for example, is determined by the volume of paint, which serves as a measure of the event, and the overall interpretation is atelic or telic, according to whether the object is the mass *paint* or the count *the paint*, as only the latter has a quantized spatial extent.

21.4.6 Filling in: An apparent exception

Our discussion suggests that only *off* and *out* permit unpredicated particle uses, specifically in describing clearing or emptying events. Surprising, then, is an apparent exception to this generalization: *in* seems to have an unpredicated use with *fill*, as in (39b).

(39) a. We filled the hole (with plaster).
b. We filled the hole in. (cf. *The hole is in.)

We attribute this use to *fill*'s being a change of state verb: for instance, it shows the causative alternation, the hallmark of such verbs: *We filled the tub/The tub filled*. We have already pointed to parallels between particles and result phrases, and we propose that the unpredicated particle in (39b) further specifies the result state lexicalized by *fill*, just as result phrases do with change of state verbs (e.g., *break the bag open*; RH&L98).

As a change of state verb, *fill* lexicalizes a scalar change: a positive change along a scale of fullness. This scale represents the occupied volume of a container—an entity with a 3-dimensional spatial extent—and it has a maximal endpoint, representing a state in which the container has no empty volume. In this respect, *fill* is different from the surface contact verbs found in the unpredicated *off* and *out* examples. As noted in section 21.4.2, surface contact verbs are not lexically associated with a scale of change, but such a scale is contributed by the unpredicated particle. In isolation, surface contact verbs with a definite object may be interpreted as atelic, contrasting with the telic *fill the hole*. In contrast, an unpredicated particle with *fill* is not contributing telicity; rather, it simply further specifies the result state lexicalized by the verb.

Unlike simple uses of *fill*, the unpredicated particle uses are best with objects which denote holes or other 'negative' spaces. Such examples describe a decrease in the unoccupied volume defined by the negative space—a change which occurs as this space is filled. The contrasting interpretations of the pair in (40) reinforce this point.

(40) a. We filled the glass (up). b. We filled the glass in.

While the (a) sentence just describes the action of gradually filling the space inside the glass, (b) is odd precisely because it forces the glass to be treated as a negative space. To the extent it is interpretable, it describes a process which leaves the glass in a state in which it lacks interior usable space, depriving it of its intended function. Underscoring this point, the unpredicated particle use in *We filled the form *(in)* is acceptable because, abstractly, the form is 'filled' when the necessary amount of information is entered onto it—once again, the maximal endpoint of a scale.

We argued in section 21.4.5 that *in* resists unpredicated uses as it can not introduce a bounded scale of change, yet such a scale is necessary to ensure that the telicity of a verb-particle construction could be determined by properties of its object. However, the verb-particle constructions discussed so far involved surface contact verbs, which do not lexicalize a scalar change, let alone a bounded change of state. In contrast, *fill* already lexicalizes such a change, which we assume is why it can combine with *in*, while maintaining the constraint that the telicity of the overall verb-particle construction depends on its object. Furthermore, since *in* describes a containment relation between a Figure and a Ground, it is compatible with the change *fill* lexicalizes, and it is apparently exploited in the description of a subclass of filling events. We leave open for now an explanation for precisely why this specialization in meaning occurs.

fill's 'antonym' *empty* also lexicalizes a scalar change involving a closed scale with a maximal endpoint that involves a change in the occupied volume of a container, but this time a negative change. Again, it allows unpredicated particle uses, as does the semantically similar verb *clear*.

(41) We emptied the bucket (out).

(42) The waiter cleared the table off/away.

(43) The police cleared the room out.

The unpredicated particles in these examples include the familiar *out* and *off*, as well as *away*. All three represent spatial relations between a Figure and

Ground that are compatible with the removing nature of the events described by these verbs, again supporting the proposal that with change of state verbs unpredicated particles further specify the lexicalized change of state.

Given that filling is the opposite of emptying, the verb *cover*, roughly the opposite of a verb of clearing, might be expected to allow unpredicated particle uses with *on*—the opposite of *off*. However, *cover* allows such uses with *over* and *in*, but not *on*:[10]

(44) a. He covered the table (*on).

b. Crew members quickly covered in the hole, where the box had been ...

c. I picked up the blanket and covered myself over with it.

As with *fill*, simple uses of *cover* as in *cover the table* are telic with a quantized object, indicating that the verb itself is associated with a maximal endpoint closed scale of change, a change that involves the gradual occlusion of a surface. The subtle differences in meaning in the unpredicated particle examples are, as we would expect, nuanced by the underlying spatial meanings of the particles. (44b) resembles the comparable *in* examples with *fill*: a negative space in a surface is being filled in as part of the covering process. In (44c), *over* is licensed due to the spatial dispersal facet of covering actions, which involves precisely the type of spatial configuration that can be described by this particle. Thus, the particle reinforces the verb's own meaning. Again, the particles do not introduce bounded scales of change, but refine the nature of the bounded scalar change lexicalized in *cover* itself.

We return now to *on*'s exclusion with *cover* and attribute it to the nature of the spatial relation it names. This relation has been characterized in naive physics terms as a relation of support (often against gravity). When a Figure and a Ground are in such a relation, the Ground does not impose any limitation on the spatial extent of the Figure; it contrasts with a Ground in the *in* or *over* relation, which can impose such a limitation on its Figure due to the nature of the containment and dispersal relations. For instance, in **cover the table on*, the fixed area of the table is irrelevant to *on*, which simply cares about the table as a support. Since the scale of change associated with *cover* involves occlusion of a surface, the spatial relation described by *on* is incompatible with it and can not combine with the verb to further specify it.

The previous sections showed that unpredicated particles are only possible if they can be associated with a scale of change with a maximal endpoint. The examples discussed in this section demonstrate that in the absence of such an endpoint, such particles are possible if they can combine with a predicate which lexicalizes a bounded scale of change, which is compatible with the

---

[10] The (b–c) examples were found via internet searches.

scale of change associated with the particle by virtue of the spatial relation it denotes. It is only in these two instances that the overall telicity of an event can depend on just the object.

21.5 Conclusion

Only some particles allow unpredicated uses with surface contact and change of state verbs. From our observations so far, these include *off*, *out*, in limited ways *away*, *over* and *in*, but not *on*. Although the canonical unpredicated particle examples involve removing events, the correct generalization is that such examples are acceptable only if their telicity can be determined solely from the properties of the expressed location object. We have shown that this requirement imposes a constraint on possible unpredicated particle examples: the event must be associated with a bounded scale of change. We have further suggested that this requirement holds more generally: it is manifested in predicated particle constructions, full expression constructions, and subcategorized NP resultative constructions. This observation might provide new insights into the nature of secondary predication in English.

More work is also needed in the domain of unpredicated particles. Even particles which allow unpredicated uses with surface contact verbs resist such uses with other verbs:

(45) a. I broke the branch off (the tree).
b.*I broke the tree off. (on the intended interpretation)

(46) a. I cut the flower out (of the paper).
b.*I cut the paper out.

(47) a. I pushed the box off (the table).
b.*I pushed the table off. (on the intended interpretation)

Rapappport Hovav and Levin (1998, 2005) and Rappaport Hovav (2008) have argued that change of state verbs like *break* lexically specify a scale of change, and that the argument that this scale is predicated of must be expressed; this might limit the argument realization options available to such verbs. Although *break the branch* and *break the branch off* have somewhat different interpretations, it is a property of the branch that determines telicity in both: the event is over when the branch is either broken or separated from the tree. It is possible that the unpredicated *break* example is out precisely because what is separated from the tree (i.e. the branch) is not 'in the picture': there is no sense in which the 'amount of branch' is inferable from the 'amount of tree'. We hypothesize that the *cut* example might have a comparable explanation. Here the particle construction has a creation sense, and the nature and extent of the created object (i.e. the flower) can not be inferred from the raw material (i.e. the paper). The key to the *push* example may be that the location is not an underlying argument of the verb, as it is in the surface contact verb examples. In its simple use, *push* takes a theme, as in (48), in contrast to surface contact verbs, which take a location.

(48) a. I pushed the cart (up the hill).
b.*I pushed the hill.

These are just a few of the many examples we have encountered where two internal arguments of a verb are not equally possible in the NP position of the V⌒NP⌒Prt construction.

We hope that this paper provides a basis for future studies into the distribution of unpredicated particles, and that these and related studies of argument realization and interpretation will further contribute to our understanding of the nature and breadth of Grammatical Semantics.

Acknowledgements

We are very pleased to present this paper to Mohanan, addressing a puzzling phenomenon which became apparent to us while we were teaching a syntax class, and which neither one of us could solve in front of the other. We hope that it will be seen as a contribution to the 'Grammatical Semantics' program that Mohanan and his colleagues have laid out, and we invite Mohanan himself to solve the remaining problems.

The present version of this paper owes much to comments from John Beavers, Chris Kennedy, Shin-Sook Kim, Maria Polinsky, Malka Rappaport Hovav and two anonymous reviewers.

References

Beavers, John. 2007. Measurability, multiple incremental themes, and figure/path relations. Abstract from Workshop on the Syntax and Semantics of Measurability, CASTL, University of Tromsø.

Borer, Hagit. 2005. *Structuring Sense II: The Normal Course of Events*. Oxford: Oxford University Press.

Condoravdi, Cleo and Jean Mark Gawron. 1996. The context-dependency of implicit arguments. In M. Kanazawa, C. J. Piñón, and H. de Swart, eds., *Quantifiers, Deduction, and Context*, pages 1–32. Stanford, CA: CSLI Publications.

Dowty, David R. 1979. *Word Meaning and Montague Grammar*. Dordrecht: Reidel.

Dowty, David R. 1991. Thematic proto-roles and argument selection. *Language* 67:547–619.

Fillmore, Charles J. 1986. Pragmatically controlled zero anaphora. In V. Nikiforidou, ed., *Proceedings of the Berkeley Linguistics Society*, vol. 12, pages 95–107. Berkeley: Berkeley Linguistics Society.

Hay, Jen. 1997. The long and short of adjectival scales: Putting things straight. Unpublished ms, Northwestern University, Evanston, IL.

Hay, Jen, Christopher Kennedy, and Beth Levin. 1999. Scalar structure underlies telicity in 'degree achievements'. *SALT* 9:127–144.

Jackendoff, Ray S. 1996. The proper treatment of measuring out, telicity, and perhaps even quantification in English. *Natural Language and Linguistic Theory* 14:305–354.

Kennedy, Christopher. 2001. Polar opposition and the ontology of 'degrees'. *Linguistics and Philosophy* 24:33–70.

Kennedy, Christopher and Louise McNally. 2005. Scale structure, degree modification, and the semantic typology of gradable predicates. *Language* 81:345–381.

Krifka, Manfred. 1992. Thematic relations as links between nominal reference and temporal constitution. In I. A. Sag and A. Szabolcsi, eds., *Lexical Matters*. Stanford, CA.: CSLI Publications.

Krifka, Manfred. 1998. The origins of telicity. In S. Rothstein, ed., *Events and Grammar*, pages 197–235. Dordrecht: Kluwer.

Lambrecht, Knud and Kevin Lemoine. 2005. Definite null objects in (spoken) French: A construction-grammar account. In M. Fried and H. C. Boas, eds., *Grammatical Constructions: Back to the Roots*, pages 13–55. Amsterdam: John Benjamins.

Lasersohn, Peter. 1999. Pragmatic halos. *Language* 75:522–551.

Levin, Beth and Malka Rappaport-Hovav. 1991. Wiping the slate clean: A lexical semantic exploration. *Cognition* 41:123–151.

Levinson, Lisa. 2006. Arguments for pseudo-resultative predicates. Unpublished ms, New York University, New York. (lingBuzz/000315).

McIntyre, Andrew. 2003. Preverbs, argument linking and verb semantics. *Yearbook of Morphology* pages 119–144.

McIntyre, Andrew. 2007. Particle verbs and argument structure. *Language and Linguistics Compass* 1:350–367.

Mohanan, K. P., Tara Mohanan, and Lionel Wee. 1999. Introduction. In T. Mohanan and L. Wee, eds., *Grammatical Semantics: Evidence for Structure in Meaning*, pages 1–21. Stanford, CA.: CSLI Publications.

Ramchand, Gillian C. 1997. *Aspect and Predication*. Oxford: Clarendon Press.

Rappaport Hovav, Malka. 2008. Lexicalized meaning and the internal temporal structure of events. In S. Rothstein, ed., *Crosslinguistic and Theoretical Approaches to the Semantics of Aspect*, pages 13–42. Amsterdam: John Benjamins.

Rappaport Hovav, Malka and Beth Levin. 1998. Building verb meanings. In M. Butt and W. Geuder, eds., *The Projection of Arguments: Lexical and Compositional Factors*, pages 97–134. Stanford, CA: CSLI Publications.

Rappaport Hovav, Malka and Beth Levin. 2005. Change of state verbs: Implications for theories of argument projection. In N. Erteschik-Shir and T. Rapoport, eds., *The Syntax of Aspect*, pages 274–286. Oxford: Oxford University Press.

Svenonius, Peter. 1996. The verb-particle alternation in the Scandinavian languages. Unpublished ms, University of Tromsø.

Svenonius, Peter. 2003. Limits on P: Filling in holes vs. falling in holes. In *Nordlyd (Tromsø Working Papers in Linguistics)*, vol. 31, pages 431–445. University of Tromsø.

Talmy, Leonard. 1975. Semantics and syntax of motion. *Syntax and Semantics* 4:181–238.

Tenny, Carol L. 1992. The aspectual interface hypothesis. In I. A. Sag and A. Szabolcsi, eds., *Lexical Matters*, pages 1–27. Stanford, CA: CSLI Publications.

Wechsler, Stephen. 2005. Resultatives under the 'event-argument homomorphism' model of telicity. In N. Erteschik-Shir and T. Rapoport, eds., *The Syntax of Aspect*, pages 255–273. Oxford: Oxford University Press.

Zeller, Jochen. 2001. How syntax restricts the lexicon: Particle verbs and internal arguments. *Linguistische Berichte* 188:459–492.

22

The Discourse Mode of Mandarin Verbal *-le* Sentences

SHIAO WEI THAM

This paper investigates the discourse effects of the Mandarin aspectual particle *-le*, in particular when it occurs in post-verbal position: henceforth verbal *-le*. I propose that verbal *-le* sentences have a discourse category, or discourse mode (Smith 2003) specification. In particular, verbal *-le* sentences by default constitute Narratives, unless there is evidence to the contrary. As discussed below, the particle *-le* in Mandarin may occur in two positions: post-verbally (verbal *-le*) or sentence-finally (sentential *-le*). Studies of *-le* have largely been focused on the complex temporal interpretations of *-le* sentences, especially their interactions with situation type (see e.g. Shi 1988, 1990, Ross 1995, Klein et al 2000, Lin 2003, Wu 2004, 2005, Soh and Gao 2007, to name just a few) and interpretations for *-le* in its different positions (Chao 1968, Li and Thompson 1981, Shi 1988, 1990, Soh and Gao 2004, Soh 2008).

Aspectual categories, however, are known to interact with temporal interpretation in discourse (Dowty 1986, Partee 1984), and recently they have been argued to play in the definition of so-called discourse modes (Smith 2003). Not surprisingly, then, interaction with discourse has always been part of the characterization of *-le*. For instance, Li and Thompson (1981) note that *-le* occurs infrequently in formal written discourse but is used frequently in spoken discourse. They also observe when that *-le* occurs post-verbally, "there is often something strange and 'unfinished' about a sentence containing *-le* and a simple unquantified direct object noun" (p. 200). Sentence-final *-le* is called a marker of "currently relevant state": [sentence-final] "*-le* claims that a *state of affairs has special current relevance with respect to some partic-*

Reality Exploration and Discovery: Pattern Interaction in Language and Life.
Linda Uyechi and Lian-Hee Wee (eds.).

ular situation" (ibid. p. 240; emphasis theirs). The current relevance effect of sentence-final *-le* has been characterized in terms of a presupposition triggered by sentence-final *-le* (Soh 2008). The infelicity of post-verbal *-le* has rarely been directly accounted for, but recent studies by Wu (2004, 2005) have attributed this effect to a requirement by verbal *-le* to identify some kind of endpoint (called a 'significant point' or SigP) to the eventuality being described. The requirement for a SigP may be satisfied across clauses, thus bringing out the relevance of discourse for this phenomenon.

The current study proposes that the felicity of activity verbal *-le* sentences is related to the kind of discourse which the sentence corresponds to. I suggest that a verbal *-le* sentence always specifies a discourse category, which is usually only specified by chunks of discourse. Moreover, unless evidence to the contrary is present, the discourse category of a verbal *-le* sentence is assumed to be that of Narrative. The paper is organized as follows: section 22.1 compares and contrasts sentences containing verbal and sentential *-le*, and provides the semantics assumed for verbal *-le*; section 22.2 describes discourse-related properties of verbal and sentential *-le*; sections 22.3 and 22.4 introduce discourse modes, and apply them to an analysis of verbal *-le* sentences; 22.5 provides the conclusion.

22.1 Mandarin *-le*: Some Background

Mandarin *-le* may occur in two positions: post-verbally (1a) or sentence-finally (1b).[1]

(1) a. Sānmáo zhòng-le tóu jiǎng
Sanmao get-LE head prize
Sanmao (has) won first prize!

b. Sānmáo zhòng tóu jiǎng le
Sanmao get head prize LE
Sanmao (has) won first prize!

Researchers differ on whether *-le* in both positions should be treated as the same morpheme (see Chao (1968), Li and Thompson (1981), Ross (1995), Smith (1997), Sybesma (1999)) for the distinct morphemes approach; and Shi (1990), Lin (2003), Huang and Davis (1989), Soh (2008), for the single morpheme approach). Since this paper is mainly concerned with verbal *-le* sentences, the following discussion will focus on the differences between verbal and sentential *-le*. The issue is orthogonal to current purposes, however, and the reader should feel free to assume either approach.

Common to both approaches, though, is the understanding that both verbal and sentential *-le* interact with the situation type of the predicate complex they attach to. The following discussion, which will be concerned with non-

[1] *-le* may also occur simultaneously in both positions, see Soh and Gao (2004) for discussion on the 'double *-le*' construction.

stative situation types only,[2] will demonstrate that the eventualities described by verbal *-le* sentences are interpreted as past relative to some reference time, whereas sentential *-le* is often associated with current effects of an eventuality.

22.1.1 Verbal *-le*

In this section, I discuss the interpretations of verbal *-le* sentences and lay out my assumptions on the semantics for verbal *-le*. Verbal *-le* is associated with readings of completion and termination. A completion interpretation arises with telic (achievement and accomplishment) predicates; a termination reading with non-telic (activity) predicates.

Verbal *-le* with accomplishment predicates indicates that the eventuality is completed prior to a certain time, call it the reference time. The reference time is assumed to be speech time if not otherwise specified. (2), taken from an essay set before World War II about a deceased grandfather, encodes an event long past.

(2) zǔfù **mǎi-le** yí dòng zhái-zi ...
grandfather buy-LE one CL house ...
Grandfather bought a house ...[3]
(http://spku.org/dlu/bookclub/YuanJZ_011305.doc)

The example in (3) describes an achievement. Again, the event described is understood to have occurred. The resultative compound *shōu-dào* 'collect/keep-arrive = receive' can be assumed to describe an achievement. It is incompatible with the progressive marker *zài* 'be.at'.

(3) Hé Zhīshuǐ guī duì xùnliàn de dì wǔ tiān, Zhāng Yún
NAME return team train Assoc ORD five day NAME
yìwai-de **shōu-dào-le** yì fēng xìn.
unexpectedly receive-LE one CL letter
On the fifth day of He Zhishui's return to her team for training, Zhang Yun unexpectedly received a letter.
(http://shuku.net/novels/dangdai/jiejxianxi/jiejxianxi.html)

With the activity verbs *jǔxíng* 'hold' and *fǎngwèn* 'visit, interview', *-le* indicates that the relevant event is terminated. So (4) indicates that the meetings and the Amman visit took place and, at the time of the news story, are over.

---

[2]There is controversy over whether verbal *-le* occurs with stative predicates. I follow Soh (2008) in assuming that verbal *-le* occurs only with bounded stative predicates, and not with unbounded ones, but do not discuss them in this paper.

[3]Abbreviations: Assoc = associative marker; CL = classifier; ORD = ordinal numeral marker; Redup = reduplication

(4) Měiguó guówùqīng Làisī zài liǎng tiān de Zhōng-dōng
US secretary.of.state Rice be.at two day Assoc Middle.East
fǎngwèn zhōng **jǔxíng-le** mìjí de huìtán, hái
visit within hold-LE densely-packed Assoc conference and
fǎngwèn-le Yuēdàn shǒudū Amàn
visit-LE Jordan capital Amman
US Secretary of State Rice held densely packed conferences in her two-day visit to the Middle East, and visited the Jordanian capital Amman. (http://www.cnd.org/HXWZ/CM07/cm0703e.gb.html)

I assume a version of the realization semantics for verbal *-le* proposed in Lin (2003) (which draws on the approach in Liu (1988)) reproduced in (5) below, slightly modified. τ is the temporal trace operator in Krifka (1989); τ applied to an eventuality e yields τ(e), the runtime of e. This semantics adopts Klein's (1994) analysis of aspect as a relationship between topic time (a time about which an assertion is made) and situation time (the time of the eventuality). It follows Klein's analysis of perfectivity as situation time being contained in topic time.

(5) $[\![le]\!] = \lambda P \, \lambda t_2 \, \lambda e \, \exists e' \, [P(e) \wedge P(e') \wedge e' \leq_E e \wedge \tau(e') \subseteq t_2 \wedge t_2 < t_{pro}]$

The representation above says that a verbal *-le* clause entails an eventuality *e* described as P, which contains a subevent *e'* (e' is a part of ($\leq_E$) e) also describable as P. For a telic eventuality e described as P, any subpart of e also describable as P can only correspond to the entire event e. For instance, if John ate two fish between 10:00 a.m. and 10:30 a.m., and at 10:05 a.m. he had eaten half a fish, the eventuality between 10:00 a.m. and 10:05 a.m. cannot be described as John ate two fish. In contrast, an atelic predicate can be applied to any subpart of the eventuality it describes (as long as it contains a large enough interval to identify the activity taking place). So in the fish eating example above, it is true of any time between 10:00 a.m. and 10:30 a.m. that John ate fish. This is how the analysis captures the completion reading for achievement and accomplishment predicates versus the termination reading for activity predicates.[4]

In addition, the runtime of this subevent falls within the topic time (t_2). The topic time occurs prior to (<) a reference time, here represented as a

[4]A reviewer notes that the realization analysis does not in fact entail termination for activity verbal *-le* clauses, a point actually raised by Lin as a plus for the system, as it allows for continuative readings given by some *-le* sentences. See Lin (2003:271), and Soh and Gao (2007) for relevant discussion. It does, however, allow for the possibility that the subevent corresponds to the entire activity, as monoclausal verbal *-le* sentences do seem to entail that the activity has ended, as suggested by the contradictory (i) below, adapted from (4).

(i) Měiguó guówùqīng Làisī… fǎngwèn-le Yuēdàn shǒudū Amàn, #xiànzài hài
US secretary.of.state Rice visit-LE Jordan capital Amman now still

free variable t_{pro}, which is by default set to speech time unless otherwise specified.[5] This captures the relative anteriority reading of verbal *-le* clauses discussed above.

22.1.2 Sentential *-le*

Sentential *-le* may give rise to the same readings as verbal *-le*, but it also allows for other readings. In particular, sentential *-le* gives rise to inchoative readings that verbal *-le* does not yield.

With accomplishment predicates, in addition to a completion reading, sentential *-le* may indicate that the event described is now habitually true. So in different contexts (6) has two possible interpretations, (i) and (ii).

(6) wǒ chī liǎng zhǒng yào le
 1sg eat two type medicine LE
 (i) I have taken two types of medicine.
 (ii) I have started taking two types of medicine.

The current relevance interpretation associated with sentential *-le* also shows up clearly in achievement sentences such as (7a) below, which can be uttered upon approaching one's doorstep. In vivid contrast, the corresponding verbal *-le* version (7b) is infelicitous in this context.

(7) a. (wǒ-men) dào jiā le!
 1-pl arrive home LE
 We're home!

 b.#(wǒ-men) dào-le jiā!
 1-pl arrive-LE home
 Intended: We're home!

Of course, the current relevance effect need not be present, given the right context, as we see in the examples in (8). The context for (8a) is a brief telling of an event during the Sino-Japanese war, about two Japanese soldiers who were beating up a pious Chinese scholar, but who during the beating were

---

jìxù zài Amàn jìnxíng fǎngwèn.
continue be.at Amman hold visit
US Secretary of State Rice visited the Jordanian capital Amman, and now is still there continuing her visit.

On the other hand, activity predicates such as *jǔxíng* 'hold' with *in an hour*-type adverbials show variability in interpretation, suggesting a degree of flexibility.

(ii) Bái-gōng fā-yán-rén yì xiǎoshí nèi jǔxíng-le jìzhě zhāodài huì
 White.House spokesperson one hour within hold-LE reporter reception meeting
 The White House spokesperson held (began) a meeting in an hour.

(iii) tāmen yì nián nèi jǔxíng-le hūnlǐ
 3pl one year within hold-LE wedding.ceremony
 They held (completed) their wedding ceremony within one year.

To allow for these different interpretations, I adopt the more flexible system provided by Lin's analysis, with the caveat that for non-modified verbal *-le* clauses, the subevent is interpreted as corresponding to the entire event.

[5] In Lin's original formula, reference time is defined using the runtime of an eventuality e_{pro}, resolvable to an event described in a matrix clause in which the verbal *-le* clause may be embedded. Topic time is also allowed to overlap reference time.

moved to tears by the scholar's appeals to a divine authority for their forgiveness. The first instance of sentential *-le* occurs with the achievement predicate *zhù shǒu* 'to stay one's hand, to stop'. The stopping is understood to have taken place. The second instance of *-le* (in boldface) occurs with the activity predicate *liú lèi* 'weep' (*lit.* 'flow tears'). The weeping is interpreted as having just begun. This contrasts with the activity verbal *-le* sentences we saw earlier, where the eventuality described is understood to be over.

(8) a. tūrán, tāmen **zhù shǒu le, liú lèi le** …
suddenly 3pl stay hand LE flow tears LE …
Suddenly they stopped (beating) (and) started weeping …
(http://www.cnd.org/HXWZ/CM07/cm0704d.gb.html)

b. xǐ-chuāng gàn-le sān nián hòu, **dài túdi le,** …
mill work-LE three years after, bring disciple LE …
After three years of working at the mill, (I) had started training my disciple(s), …
(http://spku.org/dlu/bookclub/MengY_040705.doc)

In (8b), the activity predicate *dài túdi* 'train disciple' with *-le* yields a continuative reading: the situation of training an apprentice had begun recently relative to the time of the accident that almost occurred, and was an ongoing activity at the time of reference.

The different readings produced by verbal and sentential *-le* in eventive sentences are summarized in the table below. Verbal and sentential *-le* also show contrasts in their interaction with negation (see Soh and Gao 2004) and with downward entailing quantifiers (see Soh 2008).

(9) Interpretational contrasts between verbal and sentential *-le*

Situation type	**Verbal *-le***	**Sentential *-le***
Achievement	completion	completion
Accomplishment	completion	completion, inchoative habitual
Activity	termination	inchoative, inchoative habitual

While verbal *-le* and sentential *-le* may produce the same kinds of interpretation, their effects are far from being identical. Sidestepping the issue of whether they are the same morpheme, the data discussed should present at least a prima facie case for treating their discourse effects separately.

22.2 Discourse Properties of *-le*

In this section, I discuss the discourse-related properties of *-le*, in particular verbal *-le*. I show that verbal *-le* sentences are sensitive to the situation type of the predicate complex, and to the genre of discourse they occur in, setting the scene for the analysis based on discourse modes proposed in section 22.3.

22.2.1 Verbal *-le* sentences in discourse

The sensitivity of verbal *-le* to discourse was mentioned at the beginning of the paper. One illustration of this point is the 'unfinished' or incomplete quality evoked by activity verb *-le* sentences with a non-quantified object NP, such as (10a) (Li and Thompson 1981). The infelicity disappears if the sentence is followed by some other material, e.g. (10b).

(10) a.? wǒ hē le chá
1sg drink LE tea
I drank tea.

b. wǒ hē-le chá ránhòu xǐ-le bēi-zi
1sg drink-LE tea then wash-LE cup
I drank the tea then washed the cup.

Some speakers (Ji Fang, p.c.) find that in general, verbal *-le* sentences are less felicitous than sentences with final *-le*, and this may not be directly related to situation type. I suggest, however, that infelicities associated with verbal *-le*, fall into two categories. The first, more general, type cuts across situation type. It is an infelicity associated with vague time reference of the sentence. The eventuality described by the verbal *-le* sentence is understood to be over, but exactly when it took place is unclear. I hypothesize that, absent further evidence, e.g. temporal adverbials or prior context, the addressee interprets the eventuality time as closely to speech time as possible.

In general, however, utterances that describe immediately past eventualities fall into the province of sentential *-le*, since they satisfy the current relevance condition (see section (22.1.2) and example (7); also see discussion of sentential *-le* in Lin (2003)). The infelicity of verbal *-le* sentences for which eventuality time is not clear, would reflect a default strategy of speakers to interpret the eventualities described as having taken place as recently as possible, and to employ the typical sentential *-le* option for such cases.

The relative felicity of sentential over verbal *-le* is, interestingly, reversed when the object is realized by a quantified NP. In this case, the verbal *-le* sentence, (11a), is the felicitous one in most cases. Even if one has just bought three books, (11b) would be a very strange way to announce it to the world. Rather, the most likely interpretation of (11b) is either (i) the habitual interpretation, irrelevant here since verbal *-le* cannot encode it, or (ii) the speaker feels three books is a large amount of books to have bought (see also example (6)).

(11) a. wǒ mǎi-le sān běn shū
1sg buy-LE three CL books
I bought three books.

b. wǒ mǎi sān běn shū le
1sg buy three CL books LE
I have bought three books.

I suggest this reversal of felicity patterns is because the quantified NP evokes a scale on which the quantity represents a value high on the scale (giving us reading (ii)). In the current example this is a subjective scale evaluating the number of books bought (see Soh (2008) for relevant discussion, based on different assumptions). This scalar effect is available with both verbal and sentential *-le* if intonational prominence falls on the numeral, but I speculate it is more obvious with sentential *-le* precisely because of the current relevance effect: utterances such as (11b) are typically used by the speaker to protest against increasing this number, in this case, against buying more books. The current relevance of the eventuality is "set" to the scale evoked by the numeral – we can treat the current relevance of the sentence as an open variable that is filled by some contextually given value. Sentential *-le* with the numeral object thus takes on a special meaning based on the presence of the numeral. The sentence implicates more than the simple occurrence of an event of buying three books. In Gricean terms, then, unless this additional interpretation for the utterance is intended, the speaker will use the verbal *-le* sentence in (11a).

22.2.2 Aspectually-based felicity conditions

Setting sentential *-le* aside at this point, I show here that verbal *-le* sentences among themselves exhibit relative felicities conditioned by situation type. The previous subsection argued that verbal *-le* sentences in isolation are infelicitous because temporal reference is unclear. This suggests that when temporal reference can be concluded from the content of the sentence, verbal *-le* sentences should be improved. This prediction is, indeed, borne out, but only partly. In particular, verbal *-le* sentences with an activity predicate complex remain infelicitous out of context, but accomplishment and achievement sentences are felicitous. For instance, in the examples in (12), world knowledge tells us that the events related are long past. Therefore, it is clear that the reference time is not in the immediate past, and it should be safe to use verbal *-le*. This expectation is fulfilled for the achievement and accomplishment sentences in (12a, b) respectively. The activity sentence in (12c), however, still yields the 'incomplete' intuition noted by Li and Thompson.

(12) a. Jūlǐ fūren huò-dé-le Nuòbèiěr jiǎng
Curie lady win-get-LE Nobel prize
Madame Curie won the Nobel Prize.

b. Gēlúnbù de chuánzhī héng-kuà-le Dà-xī-yáng
Columbus Assoc ships horizontal-straddle-LE Atlantic
Columbus' ships crossed the Atlantic.

c.? Yǎlìshāndà dà dì zhǐhuī-le qiān-jūn-wàn-mǎ
Alexander big king command-LE 1000-troop-10,000-horse
Alexander the Great commanded a huge military force.

This judgement is quite fine, and the distinction may not be easily available to speakers, who tend to accommodate by supplying the necessary context for interpreting the sentence, which is otherwise grammatical.

That some aspectually-based distinction between different kinds of verbal *-le* sentences does exist, however, is further implied by frequency patterns in discourse. Preliminary results of a pilot corpus study of verbal *-le* clauses I have conducted suggest that activity verbal *-le* clauses are special in some way. First, activity verbal *-le* sentences rarely occur in narrative discourse such as stories, biographies, and the like, that relate events in an order that largely respects chronology. The language sample for narrative discourse was obtained from the first three chapters of an online novel (Du 2001). Out of 170 verbal *-le* clauses in the text, I found at most one that could be said to contain an activity predicate, and this clause clearly did not form a sentence on its own, but was linked to a following clause which expressed a following eventuality.

Interestingly, activity verbal *-le* clauses show up frequently in news articles. A preliminary investigation based on items from the People's Daily, obtained via the Peking University Center for Chinese Linguistics online corpus, showed that of the first 500 lines of text containing the character *-le*, there were 494 instances of verbal *-le*.[6] Among these, a conservative count yielded 34 instances of activity verbal *-le* clauses, approximately 7%.

Converging with the greater frequency of verbal *-le* in news articles, if an activity verbal *-le* sentence comprises proper names that refer to well-known individuals such as political figures, or describes eventualities in which such individuals typically participate, such as state visits (e.g. (4)) and summit meetings, the sentence is quite felicitous in isolation. This discussion strongly suggests that type of discourse plays an important role in felicity conditions manifested by verbal *-le* sentences.

22.3 The Discourse Mode of Verbal *-le* Sentences

In this section, I propose an explanation for the felicity conditions on verbal *-le* sentences based on the theory of DISCOURSE MODES advanced in recent work by Smith (2001, 2003, 2005). Specifically, I propose that verbal *-le* sentences are by default interpreted as Narratives. When a verbal *-le* sentence does not meet the criteria of Narrative discourse, to be discussed below, it may be infelicitous. This, I claim, is the case for most activity verbal *-le* sentences in isolation. I then account for the felicity of isolated activity verbal *-le* sentences in news articles as a result of their being compatible with another discourse mode interpretation, namely that of Report.

Smith proposes that passages fall into linguistically identifiable categories of discourse, identifying five discourse modes: Narrative, Report, Description, Informative/Information, and Argument. These modes are distinguished by the types of linguistic entities that constitute them (as determined by aspectual type), and in how the texts progress. Smith draws on the following

[6] Some lines contained more than one *-le*. Sentential *-le*, and the character *-le* in disyllabic verbs and prepositions were removed from the count.

linguistic entities: Events, States, General Statives, Facts, and Propositions. Events and States coincide with conventional use of the terms to indicate sentences describing temporally located eventualities. General Statives correspond to what are often called generic sentences. Facts and Propositions are the linguistic entities (in English, typically *that* clauses and gerundives) that occur with factive and propositional predicates such as those pertaining to knowledge, thinking, and belief. The Description mode is temporally static, while the Information and Argument modes are atemporal (Smith 2003: 19-20). The Narrative and Report modes are temporally dynamic, in that they often describe specific events, and they are the modes we will be most concerned with below.

22.3.1 Sequencing in narratives

I first discuss the notion of Narrative discourse. A Narrative passage from Smith (2003) is provided below in (13). The defining characteristic of Narrative that will feature a great deal in the following discussion is the notion of a sequence of eventualities. According to Smith, in a Narrative, "the text advances as narrative advances. This advancement is based on sequence: we interpret the events of a narrative as occurring in sequence, one after another". This sequentiality is illustrated in the example below. The italicized portions describe Events (as identified in Smith (2003:14(6))), and they are understood to be occurring in order.

(13) A few days later *I called on Dr P and his wife at home*, with the score of the Dichterliebe in my briefcase and a variety of odd objects for the testing of perception. *Mrs P showed me into a lofty apartment*, which recalled fin-de-siècle Berlin. A magnificent old Bösendorfer stood in state in the centre of the room, and all around it were music stands, instruments, scores. There were books, there were paintings, but the music was central. *Dr P came in*, a little bowed, and *advanced with outstretched hand to the grandfather clock*, but, hearing my voice, *corrected himself*, and *shook hands with me*. We *exchanged greetings* and *chatted a little of current concerts and performances*. Diffidently, *I asked him if he would sing*.

The sequentiality of events in Narratives is also recognized in other approaches to discourse, e.g. at the level of genre (Labov and Waletzky 1967/1997)[7] , in studies of discourse relations (Asher 1999), etc. It should

[7]Even though the notion of Narrative in Labov and Waletzky (1997/1972) applies to the level of genre (what Polanyi (1981) calls 'story'), and is thus quite different from either Smith's Narrative passages or Asher and Lascarides' Narration relation, the notion of sequence is still crucial to Labov and Waletzky's definition of Narrative. For them, a Narrative contains at least two independent "narrative clauses" (Labov and Waletzky 1997: 20-22, Labov 1972: 360-361). A narrative clause is crucially ordered relative to a companion narrative clause; changing the order of two narrative clauses would represent a different order of occurrence for the events described.

also be added that the eventualities in sequence should form (part of) a coherent knowledge schema (van Dijk and Kintsch 1983).

22.3.2 Sublexical sequencing

With this background, I now return to the infelicity of activity verbal *-le* sentences described earlier, and to a distinction between activity versus achievement and accomplishment sentences. It is agreed among various authors that accomplishments and achievements are events of change (Pustejovsky 1991, Smith 1997, Rothstein 2004). Putting this idea in terms closer to the current discussion, they consist of two sub-eventualities in a lexically specified sequence (Tham and Soh 2006). Accomplishments typically consist of an activity sub-event followed by a change of state, while achievements encode the change into a state from a situation when the state did not hold. In contrast, activities do not specify such a change. That is, a clause describing an accomplishment or an achievement entails that two (sub)eventualities occurred, whereas a clause describing an activity entails only the occurrence of one eventuality. Now, a Narrative passage consists of a sequence of eventualities. To form a sequence, it seems reasonable that at least two eventualities would be involved. That is, accomplishment and achievement clauses actually share a property of Narratives in entailing this point.

We can propose a rule for inferring a Narrative based on this sequencing property, employing von Wright's (1963) operator T 'and next' which encodes a "transition" (p.28) from one state of affairs to another. Dowty (1979, p.144) (citing von Wright (1968)) suggests an interval-based semantics for the T operator, as in (14) below.

(14) [ϕ T ψ] is true at an interval I iff
  (1) there is an interval J containing the lower bound of I such that ϕ is true at J and ψ is false at J,
  (2) there is an interval K containing the upper bound of I such that ψ is true at K and ϕ is false at K, and
  (3) there is no non-empty interval I' such that I' is a proper subinterval of I and such that (1) and (2) hold for I' as well as for I.

Employing this definition of the T operator, I propose an enabling condition for inferring a Narrative, where 'Role' ranges over the possible thematic roles for a predicate. According to (15), a series of clauses which share a topic referent that is a participant in the eventualities described by each clause, or which describe eventualities within a knowledge schema, can be interpreted as a Narrative. Note however, that (15) is an enabling condition only, and meeting either or both conditions in (15) does not immediately mean interpretation as a Narrative.

(15) A string α comprising at least one monoclausal sentence can be inferred as a Narrative if, for an interval i, the topic time of α,

$$[\![\alpha]\!] \models \exists\, e_1, e_2, [P(e_1) \wedge Q(e_2) \wedge [\, [e_1 \; T \; e_2] \in i]]$$

and at least

(i) $\exists\, x\, [Role(x, e_1) \wedge Role(x, e_2) \wedge Topic(x,\alpha)]$, or

(ii) P and Q describe sub-eventualities of a knowledge schema.

Following Smith, discourse modes are assumed to be properties of text passages, and not in general of individual sentences. Given the discourse-sensitive properties of verbal *-le* laid out above, however, I assume further that verbal *-le* sentences in isolation, out of context, are also assigned a discourse mode specification, although this specification is absent when the verbal *-le* sentence is found within a passage, where the discourse mode specification is assigned to the passage itself.

22.3.3 V-*le* clauses as minimal narratives

Returning to verbal *-le* sentences, we can describe their entailments using the T operator, showing that accomplishment and achievement verbal *-le* sentences describe two sub-eventualities occurring in sequence, whereas their activity counterparts do not. According to the semantics for verbal *-le* assumed earlier, two sub-eventualities occur during the topic times of (16) and (17).

(16) zǔfù **mǎi-le** yí dòng zhái-zi
grandfather buy-LE one CL house
Grandfather bought a house.
$\exists\, e_1, e_2, x, i\; [house(x) \wedge Act(g)(e_1)\; T\; Own(g,x)(e_2) \in i]$

(17) Zhāng Yún **shōu-dào-le** yì fēng xìn.
name receive-LE one CL letter
Zhang Yun received a letter.
$\exists\, e_1, e_2\; x, i\; [letter(x) \wedge (\neg Poss(z,x))(e_1)\; T\; Poss(z,x)(e_2) \in i]$

With activity verbal *-le* sentences such as (18a), however, we know that in the topic time no change is entailed to have occurred. Only one kind of eventuality has taken place. This does not meet the enabling condition for Narratives in (15). In contrast, when continued by a clause depicting a following eventuality as in (18b), the enabling condition for a Narrative is met. The verbal *-le* sentence is interpreted as part of a Narrative, and the sequence is felicitous.

(18) a.? wǒ hē le chá
1sg drink LE tea
I drank tea.

b. wǒ hē-le chá ránhòu xǐ-le bēi-zi
1sg drink-LE tea then wash-LE cup
I drank the tea then washed the cup.

The Narrative analysis of telic verbal *-le* sentences receives support from a study of discourse relations embodied by *-le*. In his study of verbal *-le* examples retrieved from the Sinica Corpus, Wu (2004) found that verbal -le sentences (which he calls perfective *-le*) can be connected by any rhetorical relation, e.g. Narration, Elaboration, Background, Parallel, Result, Contrast, etc, to another clause. Among these, however, examples of the Narration relation outnumber examples of the other rhetorical relations, supporting the idea that verbal *-le* clauses bear a strong affinity with Narratives. The interpretational differences discussed above, and the convergence with participation of verbal *-le* sentences in discourse relations supports the treatment of verbal *-le* sentences as (default) Narratives. Achievement and accomplishment verbal *-le* sentences meet the enabling conditions for Narratives, but activity verbal *-le* sentences do not, hence their infelicity and 'incomplete' interpretation out of context.

22.4 Verbal *-le* Clauses in Reports

If activity verbal *-le* sentences do not make felicitous Narratives, what is it that licenses them in news articles? In this section, I propose they are interpreted as Reports, and that is why isolated monoclausal verbal *-le* sentences are relatively so much more numerous in news articles than in novels and stories. Smith (2003:16) observes that although like Narratives, Reports are also made up of Events and States, "situations are related to the time of the report, Speech Time, rather than to each other". Moreover, "[t]he time talked about moves back and forth from past to present". An excerpt from an example in Smith (2003) is given in (19) (italics mine –tsw). The italicized temporal adverbs show that time in the report is related to speech time.

(19) *A week after* Ethiopia started an offensive that it says is aimed at ending the two-year-war, it is *now* clear that the whole of Eritrea could become a battlefield. With hundreds of civilians fleeing the region, Colonel Kidane said Ethiopian soldiers continue to skirmish with Eritrean soldiers on the run here in western Eritrea.

Tonight, Ethiopian officials said planes bombed the main Eritrean military training center at Sawa, an American-built base 100 miles west of Amara, the capital ...

An example of an activity verbal *-le* sentence in a news brief is given in (20a) below. The verb *tǎolùn* 'discuss' describes an atelic situation, but the verbal *-le* sentence is quite normal in the context. But the same verbal *-le* sentence out of such a context, as in (20b) still seems incomplete.

(20) a. Měiguó zǒngtǒng Bùshí zài Luómǎ tóng jiàozōng Běndú
US president Bush be.at Rome with Pope Benedict
shí-liù shǒu-cì jiànmiàn. Fándìgāng chēng, liǎng rén
sixteen first-time meet Vatican state two people
tǎolùn-le ... Yīlākè júshì.
discuss-LE ... Iraq situation
US President Bush met Pope Benedict XVI for the first time in Rome. The Vatican stated that the two of them discussed the Iraq situation.
(http://www.cnd.org/HXWZ/CM07/cm0706c.gb.html)

b.? wǒmen zuótiān tǎolùn-le Yīlākè de júshì.
1pl yesterday discuss-LE Iraq DE situation
We discussed the Iraq situation yesterday.

I propose that the verbal *-le* sentence in (20b) is infelicitous because it does not have a discourse specification. This is due to two reasons. First, as discussed above, it does not exhibit Narrative properties: the activity verbal *-le* sentence in isolation encodes only one eventuality. Second, unlike (20a), it cannot be interpreted as a Report either. That is, certain linguistic and external cues found in (20a), allow a reader to assign a verbal *-le* sentence to the category of Report. In this case, names of political and religious leaders and the typical public events they create, such as summit meetings, conferences, etc. provide some of the cues. The use of "news language" in a formal, semi-classical register such as *shǒu-cì* 'initial time' (instead of the more colloquial *dì-yī cì* 'ORD-one time = the first time') as in (20a), also adds to this interpretation. Because a Report does not require a sequence of eventualities to be described, an activity verbal *-le* sentence, if interpreted as a Report, is felicitous. The prototypical Report is found in news articles. Certain lexical items, proper names of individuals and places, even the kinds of eventualities reported, provide cues as to the genre of the text, allowing certain conclusions about discourse mode to surface.[8]

[8]One reviewer suggests that Reports might perhaps be a special kind of Narrative. While many Reports are indeed very similar to Narratives in relating eventualities in sequence, I would argue that they cannot be subsumed under the Narrative category. This is because a Report could be made up mostly, and possibly entirely, by States, as shown in (i), which is taken verbatim from a news outline in an online news digest. It contains a final sentence which is non-stative, but its absence does not make it any less of a legitimate news item. It might further be argued that the first sentence contains a relative clause that is eventive, but the relative NP could just as well be replaced by a modifier such as *zùi-xīn (shùjù)* 'most-new, i.e. the latest (statistics)', without any deterioration. Therefore, we cannot simply treat Reports as a subtype of Narratives.

22.5 Discussion and Conclusion

Preferences for particular forms in different contexts often arise from the interaction of multiple factors (see e.g. Fong and Anttila (this volume), Bresnan and Nikitina (this volume)). Besides the well-known contribution of situation type, the current study identifies discourse as a major strand of the verbal *-le* thread. Studies of discourse have been approached from widely different directions ranging from computational (Grosz and Sidner 1986, Marcu 1997) to cognitive (Chafe 1980) to cultural (Polanyi 1985). Much of the linguistically-oriented research into discourse structure is concerned in particular with relationships between discourse constituents, often known as *coherence relations* (Halliday and Hasan 1976, Hobbs 1985, Asher and Lascarides 2003). Smith's investigation of discourse modes is relatively recent.

The current study can be seen as providing further motivation for recognizing the existence of discourse modes as a form of discourse representation distinct from discourse relations. This is because monoclausal verbal *-le* sentences display properties sensitive to discourse, and if the proposal here is correct, sensitive to discourse mode. Although discourse relations may hold between discourse constituents smaller than the clause (Marcu 1997), discourse mode should not be reduced to a configuration of discourse relations, since the same discourse relations may hold between discourse constituents that still form passages of different modes. This is especially the case for the current proposal, since a simplex clause offers limited options for the kinds of discourse relations that may hold within the relevant discourse constituents.

More importantly, activity verbal *-le* sentences should be able participate in the same kinds of narrative relations with surrounding clauses independently of the discourse mode of the larger passage in which they occur. Yet a contrast still shows up between verbal *-le* sentences that exhibit newswire properties and their more colloquial counterparts. I suggest this contrast comes about because these sentences do not provide the same cues concerning genre, and furthermore, certain genres are more strongly associated with certain discourse modes and relations. For instance, one might expect fiction to consist mostly of narrative passages and narrative relations. Sim-

(i) Zhōngguó zhèngfǔ jīntiān gōngkāi de shùjù xiǎnshì, Zhōngguó wǔyuè-fen
China government today publicise Assoc statistics show China May-period
gōngyè chǎn chū bǐ qù-nián tóngqī zēngzhǎng 18.1%.
industry product output compare last.year same.period grow 18.1%
Statistics made public today by the Chinese government show that industrial output in May was 18.1% higher than the same period last year.
Zhè gè zeng-fú yuǎnyuan gāo yú yùqī de 17% ...
This CL increase-degree far-Redup higher of projected Assoc 17%
This increase is far higher than the projected 17%.
(http://www.cnd.org/HXWZ/newcm.gb.html)

ilarly, news articles would correspond largely to the Report mode. Verbal *-le* sentences that are news-like indicate a news report and can be assigned the Report mode. Those activity verbal *-le* sentences without news story-like characteristics cannot be assigned this mode. Their semantic entailments do not allow them to be inferred as Narratives. These sentences have no discourse mode specification and are infelicitous.

The distinction between discourse category and discourse relation is reminiscent of the distinction between grammatical category and grammatical function or grammatical relations, and it is suggestive of a multidimensionality in the representation of discourse. That natural language phenomena should be organizable along independent but related dimensions is a theme that permeates much of K.P. Mohanan's work (often in collaboration with Tara Mohanan: Mohanan and Mohanan 1998, Mohanan et al. 1999). In showing that both category and relation are relevant in the analysis of discourse structure, this paper hopes to present yet another area where the multidimensional nature of natural (language) phenomena manifests itself.

Acknowledgments

This paper arose as a direct response to comments by Mohanan in November 2006 on an earlier joint paper I cowrote with Hooi Ling Soh[9] (Tham and Soh 2006) on the discourse characteristics of verbal *-le* clauses, a very new project for both of us. With his usual methodical approach of providing empirical motivation to clarify every kind of claim, Mohanan suggested that texts from different genres could provide a way to solidify our intuitions about discourse mode and verbal *-le*. It is my hope that this paper reflects at least some of the sense of adventure, respect for data, and conviction that complex phenomena can be simply described (among other things) that Mohanan (and Tara Mohanan) teach, both explicitly and by example.

References

Asher, Nicholas. 1999. *Discourse Structure and the Logic of Conversation*. Elsevier.

Asher, Nicholas and Alex Lascarides. 2003. *Logics of Conversation*. Cambridge: Cambridge University Press.

Asher, Nicholas and L. Vieu. 2003. Subordinating and coordinating discourse relations. *Lingua* 115:591–610.

Chafe, Wallace L., ed. 1980. *The Pear Stories: Cognitive, Cultural, and Linguistic Aspects of Narrative Production*. Norwood, NJ: Ablex Publishing Corporation.

[9]Who, with two anonymous reviewers is due a special note of thanks for valuable comments on a previous draft. Errors or omissions here are solely my responsibility.

Chao, Yuan-Ren. 1968. *A Grammar of Spoken Chinese*. Berkeley, CA: University of California Press.

Dong, Shumin. 2007. Jièxiàn "dividing line". Online at http://shuku.net/novels/dangdai/jiejxianxi/jiejxianxi.html.

Dowty, David. 1986. The effects of aspectual class on the temporal structure of discourse: Semantics or pragmatics? *Linguistics & Philosophy* 9:37–61.

Dowty, David R. 1979. *Word Meaning and Montague Grammar*. Dordrecht: Holland: Reidel.

Du, Liang. 2001. Xuèsè làngmàn "Bloodstained Romance". Online at: http://book.sina.com.cn/nzt/1088402496_xuselangman/index.shtml. Originally a script for a drama serial.

Grosz, B. and C. Sidner. 1986. Attentions, intentions, and the structure of discourse. *Computational Linguistics* 12:175–204.

Halliday, M.A.K. and Ruqaiya Hasan. 1976. *Cohesion in English*. London, UK: Longman.

Heim, Irene. 1982. *The Semantics of Definite and Indefinite Noun Phrases*. Ph.D. thesis, University of Massachussetts, Amherst.

Hinrichs, E. 1986. Temporal anaphora in discourses of English. *Linguistics and Philosophy* 9:63–82.

Hobbs, Jerry E. 1985. *On the Coherence and Structure of Discourse, Report no. CSLI-85-37*. Stanford, CA: CSLI Publications.

Huang, L. and P.W. Davis. 1989. An aspectual system in Mandarin Chinese. *Journal of Chinese Linguistics* 17(1):128–166.

Klein, Wolfgang. 1994. *Time in Language*. London: Routledge.

Klein, Wolfgang, Ping Li, and Henriette Hendriks. 2000. Aspect and assertion in Mandarin Chinese. *Natural Language and Linguistic Theory* 18:723–770.

Krifka, Manfred. 1989. Nominal reference, temporal constitution and quantification in event semantics. In R. Bartsch, J. van Benthem, and P. van Emde Boas, eds., *Semantics and Contextual Expressions*, pages 75–115. Dordrecht: Foris Publications.

Labov, William and Joshua Waletzky. 1967. Narrative analysis: Oral versions of personal experience. In J. Helm, ed., *Essays of the Verbal and Visual Arts*, pages 12–44. Seattle, WA: University of Washington Press.

Labov, William and Joshua Waletzky. 1997. Narrative analysis: Oral versions of personal experience. *Journal of Narrative and Life History* 7:3–38.

Li, Charles N. and Sandra Thompson. 1981. *Mandarin Chinese: A Functional Reference Grammar*. Berkeley, CA: University of California Press, 2nd edn.

Lin, Jo-Wang. 2003. Temporal reference in Mandarin Chinese. *Journal of East Asian Linguistics* 12:159–311.

Liu, Xunning. 1988. *Xiandai Hanyu ciwei le de yufa yiyi* 'The grammatical meaning of post-verbal *le* in modern Chinese. *Zhongguo Yuwen* 5:321–330.

Marcu, D. 1997. The rhetorical parsing of unrestricted natural language texts. In P. Cohen and W. Wahlster, eds., *Proceedings of the 31st Annual Meeting of the Association for Computational Linguistics and Eighth Conference of the European Chapter of the Association for Computational Linguistics*, pages 96–103. Association for Computational Linguistics, New Jersey.

Mohanan, K.P. and Tara Mohanan. 1998. Strong and weak projection: Lexical reflexives and reciprocals. In M. Butt and W. Geuder, eds., *The Projection of Arguments*. Stanford, CA: CSLI Publications.

Mohanan, K.P., Tara Mohanan, and Lionel Wee. 1999. Introduction. In T. Mohanan and L. Wee, eds., *Grammatical Semantics: Evidence for Structure in Meaning*. Stanford, CA: CSLI Publications.

Parsons, Terence. 2002. Eventualities and narrative progression. *Linguistics and Philosophy* 25:681–699.

Partee, Barbara. 1984. Nominal and temporal anaphora. *Linguistics and Philosophy* 7:243–286.

Polanyi, Livia. 1985. *Telling the American Story: A Structural and Cultural Analysis of Conversational Storytelling*. Norwood, New Jersey: Ablex.

Polanyi, Livia. 1988. A formal model of the structure of discourse. *Journal of Pragmatics* 12:601–638.

Polanyi, Livia, Martin van den Berg, and David Ahn. 2003. Discourse structure and sentential information structure: An initial proposal. *Journal of Logic, Language and Information* 3:337–350.

Portner, Paul. 2003. The (temporal) semantics and (modal) pragmatics of the perfect. *Linguistics and Philosophy* 26:459–510.

Pustejovsky, James. 1991. The syntax of event structure. *Cognition* 41(1-3):47–81.

Ross, Claudia. 1995. Temporal and aspectual reference in Mandarin Chinese. *Journal of Chinese Linguistics* 23(1):87–135.

Rothstein, Susan. 2004. *Structuring Events*. Malden, MA: Blackwell.

Shi, Ziqiang. 1988. *The Present and Past of the Particle LE in Mandarin Chinese*. Ph.D. thesis, University of Pennsylvania.

Shi, Ziqiang. 1990. Decomposition of perfectivity and inchoativity and the meaning of the particle LE in Mandarin Chinese. *Journal of Chinese Linguistics* 18(1):95–123.

Smith, Carlota. 1997. *The Parameter of Aspect*. Dordrecht, Holland: Kluwer Academic Publishers.

Smith, Carlota. 1999. Activities: States or events? *Linguistics and Philosophy* 22(5):479–508.

Smith, Carlota. 2001. Discourse modes: Aspectual entities and tense interpretation. *Cahiers de Grammatique* 26:83–206.

Smith, Carlota. 2003. *Modes of Discourse: The Local Structure of Texts*. Cambridge: Cambridge University Press.

Smith, Carlota. 2005. Aspectual entities and tense in discourse. In P. Kempchinsky and S. Poumyana, eds., *Aspectual Inquiries*, pages 223–237. Dordrecht: Springer.

Soh, Hooi Ling. 2008. The syntax and semantics of change/transition: Evidence from Mandarin Chinese. In S. Rothstein, ed., *Theoretical and Cross-linguistic Approaches to the Semantics of Aspect*. Philadelphia: John Benjamins.

Soh, Hooi Ling and Meijia Gao. 2004. Perfective aspect and transition in Mandarin Chinese: An analysis of double *-le* sentences. In P. Denis, E. McCready, A. Palmer, and B. Reese, eds., *Proceedings of the 2004 Texas Linguistics Society Conference: Issues at the Semantics-Pragmatics Interface*, pages 107–122. Somerville, MA: Cascadilla Proceedings Project. Available online at http://www.lingref.com/cpp/tls/2004/index.html.

Soh, Hooi Ling and Meijia Gao. 2007. It's over: Verbal *-le* in Mandarin Chinese. In N. Hedberg and R. Zacharski, eds., *Topics on the Grammar-Pragmatics Interface: Essays in Honour of Jeanette K. Gundel*. Philadelphia: John Benjamins.

Soh, Hooi Ling and Jenny Chun-Yi Kuo. 2005. Perfective aspect and accomplishment situations in Mandarin Chinese. In A. van Hout, H. de Swart, and H. Verkuyl, eds., *Perspectives on Aspect*, pages 199–216. Dordrecht: Springer.

Sybesma, Rint. 1997. Why Chinese verb *-le* is a resultative predicate. *Journal of East Asian Linguistics* 6(3):215–261.

Sybesma, Rint. 1999. *The Mandarin VP*. Dordrecht: Kluwer Academic Publishers.

Tham, Shiao Wei and Hooi Ling Soh. 2006. Discourse effects of lexical specification: The case of the Mandarin aspectual particle *-le*. In M. Butt, ed., *Proceedings of KONVENS 2006 (Konferenz Verarbeitung Natürlicher Systeme)*, pages 181–188. Universität Konstanz, Konstanz.

van Dijk, T. and W. Kintsch. 1983. *Strategies of Discourse Comprehension*. Florida: Academic Press.

von Wright, Georg Henrik. 1963. *Norm and Action: A Logical Enquiry*. London: Routledge and Keagan Paul.

von Wright, Georg Henrik. 1968. *An Essay in Deontic Logic and the General Theory of Action*. Acta Philophica Fennica. North Holland Pub. Co.

Wu, Jiun-Shiung. 2004. *Modifying Temporal Progression in Mandarin*. Ph.D. thesis, University of Texas, Austin.

Wu, Jiun-Shiung. 2005. The semantics of the perfective *le* and its context dependency. *Journal of East Asian Linguistics* 14(4):299–336.

Yuan, Jingzhen. 2005. Zǔmǔ jiā de shìzi shù 'The Persimmon Tree at Grandmother's'. Online at http://spku.org/dlu/member_works.html.

23

Variation and Ambiguity

VIVIENNE FONG AND ARTO ANTTILA

23.1 Introduction

Variation and ambiguity abound in natural language. One construction that exhibits both phenomena simultaneously is the English possessive. One meaning can be expressed as multiple forms, (1), and one form may have multiple interpretations, (2):

(1) my parents' house ~ the house of my parents
'the house owned by my parents'

(2) my picture
a. 'a/the picture representing me'
b. 'a/the picture drawn/owned/etc. by me'

Variation and ambiguity are often accompanied by preferences. It is not uncommon to find cases of variation where one variant is preferred over the other. Consider the following examples (cf. Grimshaw 1990: 87): pronouns are preferred in the Specifier position and full NPs in the Complement position.[1]

(3) a. its removal ~ ?the removal of it
b. ?the tree's removal ~ the removal of the tree

Similar preferences are also found in ambiguity. Examples like *Aida's performance* are at least four-ways ambiguous, as in (4). While all four readings seem possible, some of them appear more easily accessible than others.

[1]A Google search (29 August 2007) returned the following results: 2,010,000 hits for *its removal* versus 17,300 for *the removal of it*; 524 for *the tree's removal* versus 34,900 for *the removal of the tree*.

Reality Exploration and Discovery: Pattern Interaction in Language and Life.
Linda Uyechi and Lian-Hee Wee (eds.).

(4) Aida's performance
   a. 'the performance by Aida'
   b. 'a performance by Aida'
   c. 'the performance of Aida'
   d. 'a performance of Aida'

The patterns of variation and ambiguity in the English possessive are sensitive to multiple factors, including topicality, animacy, and the semantic type of possession (Barker 1995, Taylor 1996, Rosenbach 2003, O'Connor et al. 2004, among others). In this paper, we focus on the interaction of two factors: the relationality of the possessum (Barker and Dowty 1993) and the pronominality of the possessor (e.g. O'Connor 2003, Anttila and Fong 2004). First, it has been noted that relational nouns (e.g. *picture*) tend to prefer the *of*-genitive more than non-relational nouns (e.g. *cat*) (Barker and Dowty 1993). This emerges in two ways: (i) if the possessor is pronominal, variation is possible with relational nouns (*my picture* ~ *the picture of me*), but not with non-relational nouns (*my cat*/**the cat of me*); (ii) if the possessor is non-pronominal, variation is possible with both types of nouns, but the *of*-genitive is more common with relational nouns than with non-relational nouns (*the picture of Mrs. Clinton* / ?*the cat of Mrs. Clinton*). Here, the relationality of the noun finds its expression in the grammatical system of English through variation in syntactic constituency and word order.[2] Second, as noted above, pronominal possessors are preferred in the specifier position (*'s*-genitive); non-pronominal possessors are preferred in the complement position (*of*-genitive).

In an earlier paper (Anttila and Fong 2004, henceforth A&F), we developed an optimality-theoretic analysis of English possessives using multiple constraint rankings to derive both variation and ambiguity from the same grammar. We hypothesized that the probability of an expression or interpretation is proportional to the number of constraint rankings that derive it.[3] The A&F analysis posited a specific partial ranking of constraints that approximated the variation frequencies in the Brown corpus. In this paper, we outline a generalization of the A&F approach. We show that the constraints derive a set of IMPLICATIONAL UNIVERSALS that are predicted to emerge quantitatively in variation (preferences in expression) and ambiguity (preferences in interpretation) independently of rankings.

---

[2]See Mohanan and Mohanan (1999:24) for other examples of grammatically expressible meanings.

[3]Other approaches to unifying gradient and categorical effects include stochastic OT (e.g. Bresnan and Nikitina, this volume), and the variable rule paradigm (e.g. Paolillo, this volume).

23.2 The A&F OT Grammar

We first spell out the main points of the A&F analysis. An optimality-theoretic grammar defines a set of possible mappings between inputs (= meanings) and outputs (= forms). In A&F, the input meanings relevant for relational and non-relational nouns are represented as in (5) and (6) respectively, following Barker (1995).

(5) λx(child$_{[specific]}$(**john**, x))
'a child of John' (*Internal relation*)

(6) λx(π(**john**, x) $\wedge$ **cat**$_{[specific,definite]}$(x))
'the cat in some extrinsic relation with John' (*External relation*)

Below, we will simplify the notation to facilitate comparisons across inputs.

(7) Simplified notation:

a. Re / Ri	Relation is external ('e') or internal ('i')
b. a / the N	The possessum is specific ('a') or specific and definite ('the').
c. PRO / NP	The possessor is a pronoun ('PRO') or a non-pronoun ('NP').[4]

(8) Sample inputs:

a. Possessum is specific, definite, and non-relational; possessor is pronominal (e.g. 'the cat belonging to him'): Re (the N, PRO)

b. Possessum is specific and relational, possessor is non-pronominal (e.g. 'a picture representing John'): Ri (a N, NP)

The task is to find a grammar that successfully maps every semantic input to the correct syntactic outputs (see e.g. Bresnan 2001). A syntactic output contains at least two kinds of material: (i) lexical items that correspond to the semantic predicates and constants (e.g. *cat*, *child*, *John*), and (ii) grammatical morphemes that express functional information such as definiteness and specificity. Given the observation that possessives pattern like definites in several respects (e.g. Woisetschlaeger 1983, Barker 1995, Taylor 1996), A&F assume that the morphemes *the, my, your, his/her/its, our, their* and *'s* express a definite, specific meaning, while the morpheme *a(n)* only expresses a specific meaning.[5] Two types of output candidates are shown in (9), the

[4]We use 'PRO' to stand in for the semantic properties shared by all personal pronominals, which include shifting reference and anaphoricity (see e.g. Bresnan 2000), and which distinguish pronominals from other nominals ('NP', e.g. *John*).

[5]*A(n)* may be non-specific in examples like *I'm looking for a dictionary*. Following A&F, we treat such cases as faithfulness violations where the presence of *a(n)* is forced for reasons independent of meaning. For a parallel example involving an indefinite use of *my*, see (15).

's-genitive and the *of*-genitive.[6]

(9) a. John's $cat_{[specific,definite]}$ (*'s*-genitive)
John's $child_{[specific,definite]}$

b. the cat of $John_{[specific,definite]}$ (*of*-genitive)
a cat of $John_{[specific]}$

The analysis assumes two Faithfulness constraints, (10a,b)[7], and two general Markedness constraints, (10c,d).

(10) a. MAX Express meaning present in the input.
b. DEP Do not express meaning not present in the input.
c. *C No Complement
d. *S No Specifier

The more specific markedness constraints relate the expression type of the possessor (pronoun/non-pronoun), its argument status (external/internal), and its structural position (Specifier/Complement). The constraints are derived from the harmonic alignment of elements on prominence scales (Prince and Smolensky 1993/2004, Ch. 8). From the universal prominence scales in (11), harmonic alignment derives the set of partially ranked constraint hierarchies in the rightmost columns of Tables 1 and 2.

(11) a. NP Form Hierarchy: Pronoun > Non-pronoun
(O'Connor 2003, cf. Silverstein 1976, Aissen 1999)

b. Argument Hierarchy: External > Internal
(Grimshaw 1990)

c. Structural Hierarchy: Specifier > Complement

[6]We will not discuss the construction *a/the cat of mine/John's*, which has been dubbed the 'double genitive' or 'possessive partitive'. According to Barker (1998), the *of* in the possessive partitive is not a genitive, but rather a partitive *of*. While a genitive *of* cannot co-occur with a prenominal possessive (**Mary's child of John*), suggesting that there can only be one syntactic possessor per nominal, nothing prevents the co-occurrence of a partitive *of* and a prenominal possessive (*Mary's most recently published book of John's*).

[7]In OT, MAX constraints require input elements to have corresponding output elements, and DEP constraints require output elements to have corresponding input elements (McCarthy and Prince 1995).

Scales	Harmonic Alignment	Constraint Alignment
Pronoun > Non-Pronoun	S/P $>_H$ S/NONP	{*C/P, *S/NONP} >> {*S/P, *C/NONP}
Specifier > Complement	C/NONP $>_H$ C/P	

TABLE 1 Alignment of NP form and structural prominence

Scales	Harmonic Alignment	Constraint Alignment
External > Internal	S/E $>_H$ S/I	{*S/I, *C/E} >> {*S/E, *C/I}
Specifier > Complement	C/I $>_H$ C/E	

TABLE 2 Alignment of argument structure and structural prominence

In the actual analysis, only the following three constraints are active:

(12) a. *C/P — No Complement with a pronoun
b. *S/I — No Specifier with an internal argument
c. *S/NONP — No Specifier with a non-pronoun

Ranking is the Optimality-theoretic way of resolving conflicts among constraints. By hypothesis, systematic variation among languages reduces to different constraint rankings. Here we assume that variation within a language reduces to different constraint rankings as well (e.g. Anttila and Fong 2000, A&F, Fong 2005).

We now illustrate how categorical and variable patterns are predicted. Pronominal possessors show a categorical pattern when the possessum is a non-relational noun: *my cat* versus **the cat of me*/**a cat of me*. A&F posit an English-specific ranking *C/P >> *S to capture this asymmetry. As the tableau shows, *my cat*, (13a), always beats *the cat of me*, (13b), if we assume the ranking *C/P >> *S. Moreover, *a cat of me*, (13c), is harmonically bounded by (13b), meaning that it incurs all of (13b)'s violations and more, and can never emerge as a winner.

(13) 'the cat owned by me' ⟶ *my cat*

Re (the cat, PRO)	MAX	*C/P	*C	*S
☞ a. my cat$_{[specific,definite]}$				*
b. *the cat of me$_{[specific,definite]}$		*	*	
c. *a cat of me$_{[specific]}$	*	*	*	

The tableaux in (14) show that variation is possible when the possessum is a relational noun, e.g. 'the picture representing me': some of the possible rankings predict *the picture of me*, and others predict *my picture*.

(14) 'the picture representing me' ⟶ *the picture of me*
⟶ *my picture*

Ri (the picture, PRO)	MAX	*S/I	*C/P	*C	*S
a. my picture$_{[specific,definite]}$		*!			*
☞ b. the picture of me$_{[specific,definite]}$			*	*	
c. a picture of me$_{[specific]}$	*!		*	*	

	MAX	*C/P	*S/I	*C	*S
☞ a. my picture$_{[specific,definite]}$			*		*
b. the picture of me$_{[specific,definite]}$		*!		*	
c. a picture of me$_{[specific]}$	*!	*		*	

If we assume that the number of total rankings that generate each output is proportional to the probability of occurrence of this output (Anttila 1997), we predict that *my picture* should be preferred over *the picture of me*. In this case, *my picture* is optimal by 80% and *the picture of me* by 20% of the total rankings. This quantitative bias comes from the ranking *C/P >> *S which prefers *my picture* over *the picture of me*. This same ranking gave us the earlier categorical contrast *my cat/*the cat of me*. This illustrates the fact that the same ranking may yield both categorical and quantitative effects, depending on the input.

A&F also note that the constraint prohibiting a pronoun in complement position may override semantic faithfulness. The meaning 'a cat owned by me' is not expressible as *a cat of me*, but only as *my cat*. This is despite the fact that *my* carries a 'definite' meaning. In (15), a further ranking *C/P >> DEP categorically rules out **a cat of me*. Notice that **the cat of me* is harmonically bounded. This gives *my cat* as the only possible output.

(15) 'a cat owned by me' ⟶ *my cat*

Re (a cat, PRO)	*C/P	DEP	*C	*S
☞ a. my cat$_{[specific,definite]}$		*		*
b. *the cat of me$_{[specific,definite]}$	*!	*	*	
c. *a cat of me$_{[specific]}$	*!		*	

In this way, the A&F system with seven constraints and two language-specific rankings derives a range of possible possessive expressions. In cases of variation, it also derives quantitative preferences in expression that depend on the input.

23.3 Typology and T-orders

In this section we will take a more general look at A&F's grammar. We will show how a set of optimality-theoretic constraints places strict limits on the possible quantitative patterns derivable from the grammar. The fundamental observation is that every set of optimality-theoretic constraints defines a set of implicational universals that holds among pairs of input-output pairs. These implicational universals are predicted to emerge quantitatively in variation data.

In our examples we will use the A&F constraint set without assuming any language-specific rankings. With seven constraints, we have a factorial typology of 7! (=5,040) total rankings, or grammars. The typology yields 14 distinct output patterns, shown on the next page, in Table 3. There are eight distinct inputs, which differ in terms of the relationality and definiteness of the possessum, and the pronominality of the possessor. The *'s*-genitive outputs are indicated by italics, and the *of*-genitive outputs by boldface.

By examining these 14 languages, we can find several implicational universals that hold true for all of the 14 languages. A sample implicational universal is given in (16).

(16) If a pronoun possessor is possible in the complement position, then so is a non-pronoun, all else being equal.

This corresponds to four more specific implicational universals stated as pairs of <input, output> pairs:

(17) <Re(the N, PRO), the N of PRO> ⟶ <Re(the N, NP), the N of NP>
<Re(a N, PRO), a N of PRO> ⟶ <Re(a N, NP), a N of NP>
<Ri(the N, PRO), the N of PRO> ⟶ <Ri(the N, NP), the N of NP>
<Ri(a N, PRO), a N of PRO> ⟶ <Ri(a N, NP), a N of NP>

These implicational universals hold true no matter how the constraints are ranked. We call the set of all implicational universals in a factorial typology a TYPOLOGICAL ORDER, or T-ORDER (Anttila et al. in press, Anttila and Andrus 2006).

	Input	Output #1	Output #2	Output #3	Output #4
1	Re(the N,PRO)	*PRO's N*	*PRO's N*	*PRO's N*	*PRO's N*
2	Re(the N, NP)	*NP's N*	*NP's N*	*NP's N*	*NP's N*
3	Re(a N, PRO)	*PRO's N*	*PRO's N*	*PRO's N*	*PRO's N*
4	Re(a N, NP)	*NP's N*	*NP's N*	*NP's N*	**a N of NP**
5	Ri(the N, PRO)	*PRO's N*	*PRO's N*	**the N of PRO**	*PRO's N*
6	Ri(the N, NP)	*NP's N*	**the N of NP**	**the N of NP**	*NP's N*
7	Ri(a N, PRO)	*PRO's N*	*PRO's N*	**a N of PRO**	*PRO's N*
8	Ri(a N, NP)	*NP's N*	**a N of NP**	**a N of NP**	**a N of NP**

	Input	Output #5	Output #6	Output #7	Output #8
1	Re(the N,PRO)	*PRO's N*	*PRO's N*	*PRO's N*	*PRO's N*
2	Re(the N, NP)	*NP's N*	*NP's N*	*NP's N*	*NP's N*
3	Re(a N, PRO)	*PRO's N*	**a N of PRO**	**a N of PRO**	**a N of PRO**
4	Re(a N, NP)	**a N of NP**	**a N of NP**	**a N of NP**	**a N of NP**
5	Ri(the N, PRO)	*PRO's N*	**the N of PRO**	*PRO's N*	*PRO's N*
6	Ri(the N, NP)	**the N of NP**	**the N of NP**	*NP's N*	**the N of NP**
7	Ri(a N, PRO)	*PRO's N*	**a N of PRO**	**a N of PRO**	**a N of PRO**
8	Ri(a N, NP)	**a N of NP**	**a N of NP**	**a N of NP**	**a N of NP**

	Input	Output #9	Output #10	Output #11
1	Re(the N,PRO)	*PRO's N*	*PRO's N*	*PRO's N*
2	Re(the N, NP)	*NP's N*	**the N of NP**	**the N of NP**
3	Re(a N, PRO)	**a N of PRO**	*PRO's N*	*PRO's N*
4	Re(a N, NP)	**a N of NP**	**a N of NP**	**a N of NP**
5	Ri(the N, PRO)	**the N of PRO**	*PRO's N*	**the N of PRO**
6	Ri(the N, NP)	**the N of NP**	**the N of NP**	**the N of NP**
7	Ri(a N, PRO)	**a N of PRO**	*PRO's N*	**a N of PRO**
8	Ri(a N, NP)	**a N of NP**	**a N of NP**	**a N of NP**

	Input	Output #12	Output #13	Output #14
1	Re(the N,PRO)	*PRO's N*	*PRO's N*	**the N of PRO**
2	Re(the N, NP)	**the N of NP**	**the N of NP**	**the N of NP**
3	Re(a N, PRO)	**a N of PRO**	**a N of PRO**	**a N of PRO**
4	Re(a N, NP)	**a N of NP**	**a N of NP**	**a N of NP**
5	Ri(the N, PRO)	*PRO's N*	**the N of PRO**	**the N of PRO**
6	Ri(the N, NP)	**the N of NP**	**the N of NP**	**the N of NP**
7	Ri(a N, PRO)	**a N of PRO**	**a N of PRO**	**a N of PRO**
8	Ri(a N, NP)	**a N of NP**	**a N of NP**	**a N of NP**

TABLE 3 Factorial Typology

To find all the implicational universals in the factorial typology, we used T-ORDER GENERATOR, an open-source Python program, which takes a factorial typology as input and returns the T-order as a directed graph (Anttila and Andrus 2006).[8] The T-order for the A&F grammar is given in (18). The nodes are <input, output> pairs. An arrow pointing from node A to node B is an implicational universal: if mapping A is possible, so is mapping B.

(18) The A&F grammar (without language-specific rankings)

a. *'s*-genitives

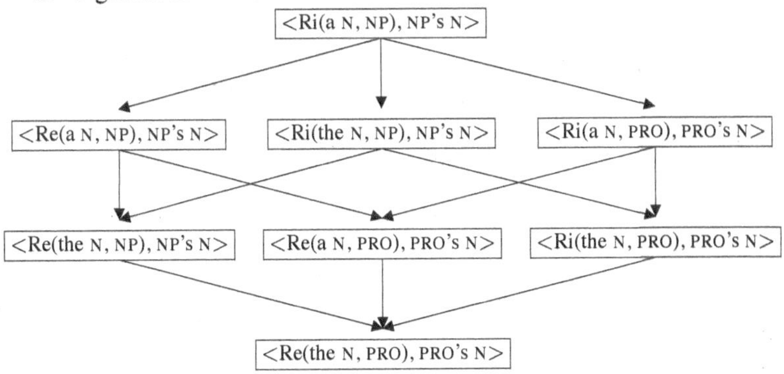

b. *of*-genitives

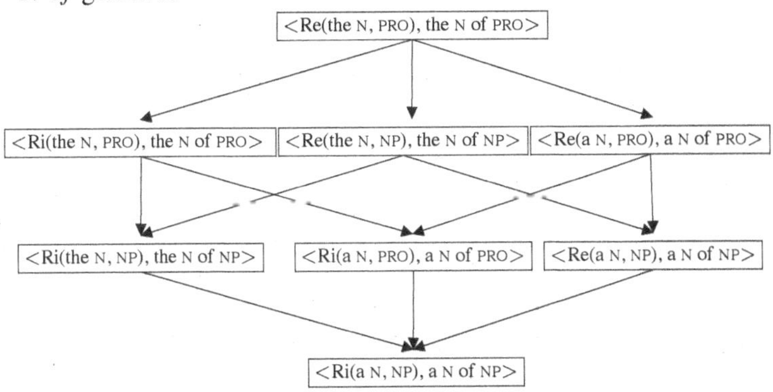

T-orders are relevant for quantitative variation in the following way. Suppose that variation (one input, multiple outputs) implies the existence of multiple constraint rankings within an individual's competence (e.g. Kiparsky 1994, Anttila 1997). Suppose further that the number of total rankings that generate each output is proportional to the probability of occurrence of that output. It follows that the proportion of *'s*-genitives/*of*-genitives should remain the same or increase in the direction of the arrows in the T-order.

[8]See Prince (2006) for a different approach where implicational universals are computed directly based on violation patterns.

We tested this quantitative prediction on A&F's data extracted from the Brown Corpus (Francis and Kučera 1982). The data consist of 17 relational nouns (1,116 tokens) based on Barker and Dowty (1993), listed in (19a), and 37 non-relational nouns (1,147 tokens), listed in (19b), all of which occurred at least 20 times in the relevant environments in the corpus. Only definite noun phrases (e.g. *the street's corner/the corner of the street*) were included in the count.

(19) a. 17 relational nouns (1,116 tokens): *hand, head, heart, leg, nose* (body part nouns); *friend, wife* (kinship nouns); *color, length, shape* (function nouns); *corner, edge, middle, point, side, surface, top* (topological properties).

b. 37 non-relational nouns (1,147 tokens): *body, boy, business, car, city, church, country, day, fact, field, god, law, life, line, man, moment, money, night, number, office, place, power, problem, program, public, school, system, thing, voice, war, water, week, woman, word, world, work, year*.

In (20), we show a T-order graph where each <input, output> node with a definite possessum is annotated with a number. This number is the observed percentage of this particular output out of all the outputs for this particular input. As predicted, the proportion of *'s*-genitives/*of*-genitives increases from top to bottom in the T-order.

(20) The A&F grammar (without language-specific rankings)

a. *'s*-genitives

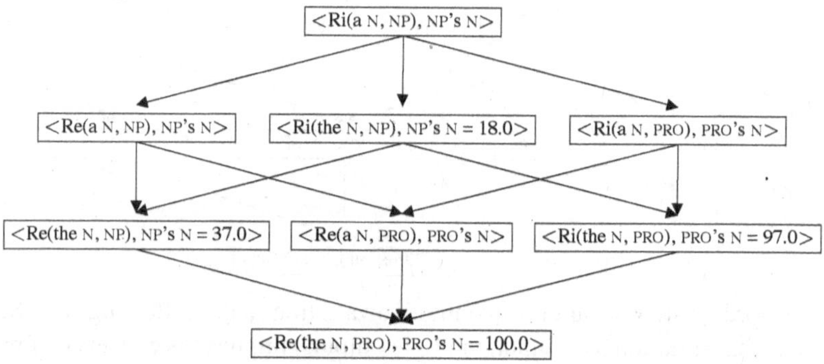

b. *of*-genitives

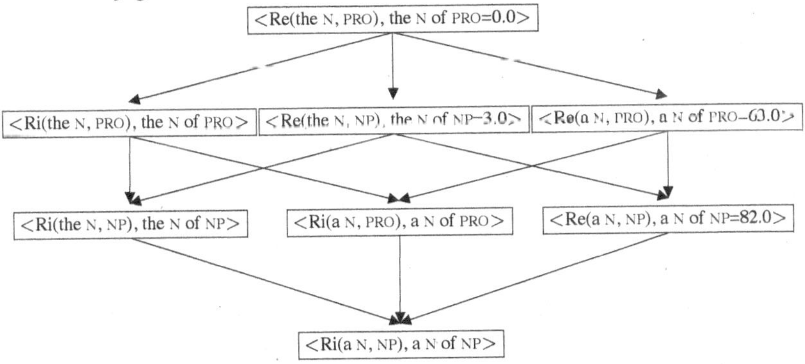

Similar predictions are made in the direction of ambiguity, where one output corresponds to several inputs. In this case, the T-order imposes a preference ordering on alternative readings. For a given expression with alternative readings, the preferred reading is the one lowest down in the T-order. To verify these predictions, one could either conduct an experimental study, or use corpora to establish preferred readings. We will leave this for future work. The ambiguities and preferences among readings predicted by A&F's constraint set are shown in (21).

(21) Predicted Preferences

1. *the N of NP*:
   Ri(the N, NP) $\geq$ Re(the N, NP)
2. *NP's N*:
   Re(an NP, NP) $\geq$ Ri(an NP, NP)
   Re(the N, NP) $\geq$ Ri(an NP, NP)
   Re(the N, NP) $\geq$ Ri(the N, NP)
   Ri(the N, NP) $\geq$ Ri(an NP, NP)
   Re(the N, NP) $\geq$ Re(an NP, NP)
3. *PRON's N*:
   Re(an NP, PRO) $\geq$ Ri(an NP, PRO)
   Re(the N, PRO) $\geq$ Ri(an NP, PRO)
   Re(the N, PRO) $\geq$ Ri(the N, PRO)
   Ri(the N, PRO) $\geq$ Ri(an NP, PRO)
   Re(the N, PRO) $\geq$ Re(an NP, PRO)
4. *the N of PRON*:
   Ri(the N, PRO) $\geq$ Re(the N, PRO)
5. *a N of NP*:
   Ri(an NP, NP) $\geq$ Re(an NP, NP)
6. *a N of PRON*:
   Ri(an NP, PRO) $\geq$ Re(an NP, PRO)

To summarize, we have shown how a set of optimality-theoretic constraints places strict limits on the possible quantitative patterns, both in the direction of variation as well as ambiguity. At present, this is a blueprint of a research program: testing and validating the model on large empirical data sets remains a task for the future.

23.4 Conclusion

We have shown how variation and ambiguity, as well as preferences among alternative expressions and alternative interpretations follow from one and the same optimality-theoretic grammar. We described a structure that reveals the intricate and almost completely unexplored quantitative predictions hidden in OT grammars, and called this structure a T-order. Because T-orders reflect the factorial typology, they hold true under several OT-based theories of variation, including the Multiple Grammars Theory (Kiparsky 1994), Partially Ordered Grammars (Anttila and Cho 1998), and Stochastic Optimality Theory (Boersma and Hayes 2001). This is because the factorial typology is the same in all these theories, given the same constraints. Paolillo (this volume) notes that the relationship between the OT and Variable Rule probabilistic models is one where VR subsumes OT as a special case. As we have shown, OT provides a restrictive theory that places strict limits on the possible quantitative patterns in expression and interpretation. It is precisely this restrictiveness that makes OT an attractive framework for exploring variation and ambiguity.

Acknowledgments

When we first started work on this topic, we benefited from sitting Mohanan down and telling him our ideas.[9] He can always be trusted to engage wholeheartedly in a discussion in a way that will enormously clarify your thinking. Mohanan and Tara Mohanan have taught us a lot about linguistics, modes of inquiry, and what it means to be good people. We hope that one day Mohanan will make good of his promise to teach us how to stand on our heads.

References

Aissen, Judith. 1999. Markedness and subject choice in Optimality Theory. *Natural Language and Linguistic Theory* 17:673–711.

Anttila, Arto. 1997. Deriving variation from grammar. In F. Hinskens, R. van Hout, and W. Wetzels, eds., *Variation and Change in Phonological Theory*. John Benjamins.

[9]This paper has also benefited from questions and comments from the audience at the 8th Semantics Fest 2007, Stanford University, and the detailed comments of an anonymous reviewer on a draft.

Anttila, Arto and Curtis Andrus. 2006. T-orders. http://www.stanford.edu/ anttila/research/software.html.

Anttila, Arto and Young-mee Yu Cho. 1998. Variation and change in Optimality Theory. *Lingua* 104:31–56.

Anttila, Arto and Vivienne Fong. 2000. The partitive constraint in Optimality Theory. *Journal of Semantics* 17:281–314.

Anttila, Arto and Vivienne Fong. 2004. Variation, ambiguity and noun classes in English. *Lingua* 114(9-10):1253–1290.

Anttila, Arto, Vivienne Fong, Stefan Benus, and Jennifer Nycz. In press. Variation and opacity in Singapore English consonant clusters. *Phonology* 25(2).

Barker, Chris. 1995. *Possessive Descriptions*. Stanford, CA: CSLI Publications.

Barker, Chris. 1998. Partitive, double genitives, and anti-uniqueness. *Natural Language and Linguistic Theory* 16:679–717.

Barker, Chris and David Dowty. 1993. Non-verbal thematic proto-roles. In A. Shafer, ed., *Proceedings of NELS 23*. GLSA.

Boersma, Paul and Bruce Hayes. 2001. Empirical tests of the gradual learning algorithm. *Linguistic Inquiry* 32:45–86.

Bresnan, Joan. 2000. Pidgin genesis and Optimality Theory. In J. Siegel, ed., *Processes of Language Contact: Case Studies from Australia and the Pacific*. Les Editions Fides.

Bresnan, Joan. 2001. Explaining morphosyntactic competition. In M. Baltin and C. Collins, eds., *The Handbook of Contemporary Syntactic Theory*. Blackwell

Fong, Vivienne. 2005. Unmarked *already*: Aspectual expressions in two varieties of English. In H. Verkuyl, H. de Swart, and A. van Hout, eds., *Perspectives on Aspect*. Springer.

Francis, W.N. and H. Kučera. 1982. *Frequency Analysis of English Usage*. Houghton Mifflin.

Grimshaw, Jane. 1990. *Argument Structure*. MIT Press.

Kiparsky, Paul. 1994. An OT perspective on phonological variation. Handout from Rutgers Optimality Workshop 1993 and the 23rd Conference on New Ways of Analyzing Variation 1994, Stanford University. Available at http://www.stanford.edu/ kiparsky/Papers/nwave94.pdf.

McCarthy, John J. and Alan Prince. 1995. Faithfulness and reduplicative identity. In J. Beckman, L. Dickey, and S. Urbanczyk, eds., *University of Massachusetts Occasional Papers 18: Papers in Optimality Theory*. GLSA.

Mohanan, Tara and K.P. Mohanan. 1999. On representations in grammatical semantics. In T. Mohanan and L.-H. Wee, eds., *Grammatical Semantics: Evidence for Structure in Meaning*. Stanford, CA: CSLI Publications.

O'Connor, Mary Catherine. 2003. Differential possessor expression: Are pair-wise comparisons ever required? In M. Butt and T. King, eds., *Proceedings of the LFG03 Conference*. Stanford, CA: CSLI Publications.

O'Connor, Mary Catherine, Arto Anttila, Vivienne Fong, and Joan Maling. 2004. Differential possessor expression in English: Re-evaluating animacy and topicality effects. Annual Meeting of the Linguistic Society of America, January 9–11, 2004. Boston, MA.

Prince, Alan. 2006. Implication and impossibility in grammatical systems: What it is and how to find it. ROA 880-1006.

Prince, Alan and Paul Smolensky. 1993/2004. *Optimality Theory: Constraint Interaction in Generative Grammar*. Blackwell.

Rosenbach, Anette. 2003. Aspects of iconicity and economy in the choice between the s-genitive and the of-genitive in English. In G. Rohdenburg and B. Mondorf, eds., *Determinants of Grammatical Variation in English*. Mouton de Gruyter.

Silverstein, Michael. 1976. Hierarchy of features and ergativity. In R. Dixon, ed., *Grammatical Categories in Australian Languages*. Australian Institute of Aboriginal Studies.

Taylor, John R. 1996. *Possessives in English*. Oxford University Press.

Woisetschlaeger, Erich. 1983. On the question of definiteness in 'An old man's book'. *Linguistic Inquiry* 14:137–154.

24

Now We See It, Now We Don't: Agreement Puzzles in ASL

CAROL NEIDLE

24.1 Introduction

As American Sign Language (ASL) came to be recognized as a full-fledged language only in the last half-century or so (following Stokoe et al. (1965)), the linguistic study of ASL is a relatively new enterprise. Although much is known about how language manifests in this modality—exhibiting striking structural parallels to spoken languages, albeit with interesting and important modality-specific differences—some rather fundamental aspects of ASL grammar remain either unexplored or disputed.

The visual-gestural modality offers rich possibilities for expression of agreement. Referents are associated with locations in the signing space that constitute a kind of spatial instantiation of person/reference/number features. The feature matching characteristic of agreement is manifested visually through incorporation of a particular 'locus' of agreement features into the articulation of agreeing signs. For example, a subject pronoun and a verb exhibiting subject agreement will be produced in such a way as to include, as part of both signs, the location associated with the subject referent.

Despite considerable attention to manifestations of person/number features, the literature surprisingly contains no comprehensive description of the pluralization of nouns. In fact, only a limited set of nouns can be overtly inflected for number. The distribution of overt plural marking even on those nouns that can be so marked remains puzzling. As in other instances, to be discussed in section 24.2, where the overt expression of agreement features in ASL exhibits variability, this raises questions about the grammatical status

Reality Exploration and Discovery: Pattern Interaction in Language and Life.
Linda Uyechi and Lian-Hee Wee (eds.).

of number features. These questions are raised in section 24.3 of this squib. It is suggested that the variability in distribution and appearance of plural morphology on nouns is due to complex interactions of syntax, semantics, morphology, and phonology, which determine the expression of plurality.

24.2 Background on Agreement in ASL

We begin with a (necessarily very brief and simplified) overview of agreement in ASL. This will be followed by a short discussion of the fact that overt expression of subject/object agreement occurs with some verbs but not others. In section 24.3, we turn to the morphological marking of plurality on nouns and the issue of when we see it, and when we don't.

24.2.1 Expression of agreement features

Compared with spoken languages, the visual-gestural modality allows for a richer agreement system, with distinctions among 3rd person entities based on reference.[1] Referents are assigned to distinct '*phi*-locations', as we have called them (Neidle and Lee 2006).[2] In ASL, the *phi*-location associated with a given referent is accessed for expression of coreferential (a) determiners and pronouns, (b) possessive markers, and (c) emphatic reflexives. Particular hand shapes are used for each of these functions, as illustrated in Figure 1: (a) generally the index finger, (b) an open palm, and (c) a closed fist with the thumb pointing upward with the fleshy part of the thumb directed toward the *phi*-location. The definite determiner and the 3rd person pronoun are indistinguishable in articulation. These same *phi*-locations are used, as seen in (d), as subject and object agreement affixes on those verbs that manifest such agreement, although not all verbs can do so.

(a) Determiner or Pronoun (b) Possessive (c) Emphatic reflexive (d) the verb GIVE: start / end = subject / object agreement

FIGURE 1 Spatially instantiated *phi*-features in agreeing constructions

[1]There is a long history of debate about whether, as we have argued (Neidle and Lee 2006), 1st, 2nd, and 3rd persons are all grammatically distinct in ASL (Friedman 1975, Lillo-Martin and Klima 1990, Lillo-Martin 1995, Meier 1990).

[2]In part on the basis of such differences between signed and spoken languages, Liddell disputes that this is actually agreement at all (Liddell 2000a, Liddell 2000b, Liddell 2003), but see Neidle and Lee (2006) for counterarguments.

Whereas a singular referent is associated with a point in space, an arc is used to express plurality. A sweeping movement marks plurality for third person pronouns, definite determiners, possessives, and emphatic reflexives, articulated with the same hand shapes as singulars (shown in Figure 1).[3] Verbs that can display number agreement with their subjects or objects[4] similarly incorporate an arc in their articulation, as illustrated in Figure 2.[5]

Plural definite determiner or pronoun: arc movement of index finger.

Object agreement on GIFT (motion completing the articulation)

FIGURE 2 A few frames from video sequences showing these sweeps

FIGURE 3 Start and end of the verb LOVE

24.2.2 Verbs that do not overtly inflect for agreement

The start/end points of agreeing verbs, such as GIVE, illustrated in Figure 1, example (d), normally correspond to the *phi*-locations of the subject/object.[6] However, not all verbs allow overt spatial marking of subject and object agreement.[7] In particular, 'body-anchored' verbs (articulated on the body rather than in the signing space) such as LOVE, in Figure 3, cannot so alter the start and end points of articulation and have been called *plain* verbs.

---

[3]This is a simplification. Pluralities when considered as collectives behave like singulars with respect to their spatial representation for purposes of agreement (Padden 1983, 1990).

[4]See Brentari (1988), Padden (1988) for details about differences among classes of verbs.

[5]For further discussion of plural inflection and its interaction with aspectual inflection, see MacLaughlin et al. (2000).

[6]However, there are exceptions, referred to a 'backwards' verbs (Baker and Cokely (1980), Brentari (1988), and Padden (1983, 1988).

[7]There is an extensive literature on agreement in ASL, much of it building on Padden (1983, 1988), who distinguishes among several subclasses of verbs, not all of which display spatial subject and object agreement.

24.2.3 Is syntactic agreement missing from some sentences in ASL?

The theoretical interpretation of these facts has been the subject of some controversy. According to Lillo-Martin (1986, 1991), sentences with plain verbs occur exclusively in syntactically nonagreeing clauses. Bahan et al. (2000) argue, to the contrary, that all main clause sentences in ASL are syntactically tensed and agreeing, and that the question of how such agreement is realized on particular lexical items is a matter of morphology. The English sentence, "They hit Bill" is tensed and agreeing, even though the form of that particular verb happens to be the same for both present and past tense, and, in the past, the same for 1st, 2nd, and 3rd person singular and plural subjects. We argued that this is equivalent to ASL sentences with verbs like LOVE: The lack of overt expression of agreement is a fact about the morpho(-phono)logical properties of that verb, not about the type of clause in which it occurs.[8] Evidence in favor of the existence of abstract syntactic agreement even in sentences with plain verbs was adduced from the possible *nonmanual* realization of subject and object agreement features.

24.2.4 Nonmanual expressions as realizations of syntactic features

ASL uses expressions of the head and upper body such as raised or lowered brows; head movement or position; eye aperture or gaze (Baker and Padden 1978, Baker-Shenk 1983, Coulter 1979, for example) to express essential syntactic features such as negation [+neg] and question status (e.g., [+wh]). These nonmanual markings co-occur with manual signs in the node associated with the relevant features and can spread over signs within its c-command domain. Intensity of these markings is greatest at the source (the node containing the relevant feature) and diminishes as distance from that node increases (e.g., Neidle and MacLaughlin 2002).

24.2.5 Existence of nonmanual expressions of agreement features

We observed (Bahan 1996, Bahan et al. 2000, MacLaughlin 1997, Neidle et al. 2000) that the *phi*-locations used for manual expression of clausal subject and object agreement features are also relevant for non-manual expressions of syntactic agreement via head tilt and eye gaze. In transitive constructions, either head tilt or eye gaze to the *phi*-location of the unique argument can mark agreement. In transitive constructions, head tilt (to the *phi*-location of the subject) can express subject agreement; eye gaze (to the *phi*-location of the

[8] Lillo-Martin further claimed that different mechanisms license null arguments in these two types of sentences. On her analysis, agreeing sentences pattern with Italian: null arguments are licensed by agreement. In contrast, sentences with plain verbs are considered to be syntactically like Chinese sentences, in which null arguments are licensed by topic. For arguments against this analysis, see Neidle et al. (1998); Bahan et al. (2000). One critical problem with this proposal was that Lillo-Martin did not distinguish *topicalization* (i.e. syntactic movement, leaving a trace) from the licensing of empty categories not associated with movement.

object) can express object agreement. This is shown in (1) with the agreeing verb VISIT, and the plain verb LOVE, in (2) (also in Figure 3). Interestingly, similar nonmanual expressions of agreement can be found within determiner phrases (DP). Possessives pattern with transitive clauses, and nonpossessive DP's with intransitives, as shown in (3). (The dotted lines with diamonds above and below mark the portions of the sentence that correspond to the video frames shown.)

(1) $\overline{\text{head tilt}}_i$

$\overline{\text{eye gaze}}_k$

JOHN$_i$ WILL VISIT$_k$ MARY$_k$

'John will visit Mary.'

a. b.

(1)-a.

(1)-b.

(2) $\overline{\text{head tilt}}_{i-}$

$\overline{\text{eye gaze}}_{k-}$

JOHN$_k$ IX$_k$ THINK MARY$_i$ LOVE e$_k$

'John thinks Mary loves (him).'

a. b.

(2)-a.

(2)-b.

Neutral position (a), followed by head tilt and eye gaze to *phi*-locations of subject and object, respectively (b) for ASL sentences glossed above.[9]

(3) $\overline{\text{head tilt}}_i$

$\overline{\text{eye gaze}}_k$

JOHN$_i$ POSS$_i$ FRIEND$_k$ HAVE CANDY

'John's friend has candy.'

a. b.

(3)-a.

(3)-b.

Neutral position (a), followed by head tilt and eye gaze to *phi*-locations of possessor and possessee, respectively (b)

[9]The subscripts are referential indices. The head tilts and the eyes gaze toward the *phi*-location associated with the NP with the same referential index. The subscript *k* on the verb VISIT indicates verb agreement with the object. Sentence (2) has a null object.

Of course, eye gaze has a myriad of functions in ASL and other signed languages, which interact in complex ways. It is certainly not the case that this is the sole, or even the principal, function of eye gaze.[10]

The main point for now is that these expressions provide evidence for the presence of syntactic agreement features in all types of main clause sentences, including those that happen to contain plain verbs. The variability in overt expression of these agreement features on verbs is a function of the morphological properties of particular lexical items (signs).

Bahan et al. (2000) observed from the outset that such nonmanual expressions of agreement, although possible, are not always present, which is again something of a mystery if these were to be interpreted merely as reflexes of syntactic agreement. Why should syntactic agreement be expressed nonmanually in *some* clauses and DP's, but not others? As discussed in Neidle and Lee (2006), it subsequently became apparent that there is a semantic difference between clauses and DP's that do and do not include such nonmanual expressions of agreement. In particular, the presence of these expressions is associated with focus.

Consider (4), containing two signs: the name J-O-H-N (fingerspelled) and the verb BATHE, meaning 'John is bathing.' (ASL signs are represented using conventional English glosses, in capital letters)

(4) J-O-H-N BATHE

(a) head tilt (b) eye gaze (c) both

FIGURE 4 The verb BATHE with non-manual marking of subject agreement

[10]Our observations about the distribution of non-manual expressions of agreement, as well as our analysis and the predictions that follow from it, are totally mischaracterized by Thompson et al. (2006), who present a statistical analysis of the distribution of eye gaze in relation to different classes of verbs in a sample of ASL story-telling that had been collected using an eye tracker, which is claimed to refute our analysis.

Our initial observation of *optional* non-manual realization of subject and object agreement is subsequently revisited in Neidle and Lee (2006), which argues (based on interactions with other focus constructions) that this is a reflex of focus, as discussed on the next page. In any case, we have been describing one particular construction in which non-manual agreement is manifested; we made no predictions whatsoever about the statistical frequency of either this construction (within ASL narratives or discourse) or, more generally, eye gaze in ASL.

This sentence can – but need not – be signed with nonmanual marking of agreement (head tilt, eye gaze, or both, to the *phi*-location of 'John'). If that agreement marking co-occurs with the VP – and the possibilities are illustrated in Figure 4 – this correlates with predicate focus.[11] Such focus would be expressed intonationally in English, as in (5).

(5) John *is bathing*. (English)

In this case, bathing is contrasted with other things that John is not doing. Alternatively, this nonmanual agreement marking can co-occur not with the predicate, but rather with the subject, the DP 'JOHN'. Such narrow focus (in the sense of Lambrecht (1994)) would likewise be expressed through prosody in English, as in (6), which could be used to contrast John with others who are not bathing.

(6) *John* is bathing. (English)

Thus the overt expression of syntactic agreement by head tilt and eye gaze correlates with focus; it is not uniformly present in all sentences. Nonetheless, the fact that such nonmanual expression of syntactic agreement features can appear even in sentences that include plain verbs supports the claim that such sentences are not devoid of agreement, syntactically. Verb classes differ, however, with respect to overt expression of agreement.

In the next section, it will be suggested that variability in overt realization of plurality on nouns is likewise due, in part, to lexical differences. Overt morphological realization of plural marking is possible for some noun classes, but not others. However, there is more to the story about nouns.

24.3 Pluralization of Nouns in ASL

ASL has a variety of syntactic devices for conveying information about quantity and spatial disposition of objects, e.g. using so-called classifier constructions (Emmorey 2003, Supalla 1986). It is also the case that nouns can be inflected for number, through a type of reduplication.[12] As with agreement marking on verbs, it turns out that only some nouns have a plural form distinct

[11]This analysis is consistent with the distribution of these non-manual agreement markings in constructions that have other constituents in focus. Examination of wh-constructions (Neidle 2003) and constructions involving an ASL focus particle (Conlin et al. 2003) yields the correct predictions: These non-manual expressions of agreement can only co-occur with the constituent that is understood to be in focus (Neidle and Lee 2006).

[12]Reduplication is also used to mark plurality in British Sign Language (Kyle et al. 1988: 132-133, Sutton-Spence and Woll 1999: 106), Estonian Sign Language (Miljan 2003), German Sign Language, and many others (Pfau and Steinbach 2006)). Within ASL, reduplication has a wide range of linguistic uses, of which number inflection is only one. It is also used, for example, to convey aspectual distinctions (Klima and Bellugi 1979) and to form deverbal nominals (Supalla and Newport 1978).

from the singular; in fact, for nouns, this is a highly restricted set. Consider this account from Baker and Cokely (1980: 377):

> Another way to indicate that a referent is plural is to repeat the noun itself (usually once). However, such repetition is only possible with a small number of nouns (such as SENTENCE, LANGUAGE, RULE, MEANING, SPECIALTY-FIELD, AREA, ROOM/BOX, HOUSE, STREET/WAY, STATUE) and in a limited set of contexts... We do not yet know the rules in ASL concerning where repetition of the noun is required or is not appropriate... [T]he separate articulations of nouns tend to have different spatial locations. (However in rapid conversation, they are sometimes made in the same place.)

24.3.1 Given a singular noun, how do you form the plural?

No precise phonological description has been offered in the literature of the relationship between the stem and reduplicated plural forms (which in fact often do not consist of two exact productions of the stem), although Wilbur (1987) pointed out a few generalizations about pluralization (which she attributed to unpublished work by Jones and Mohr (1975)).

Perry (2005) looked at the articulation of reduplicated plurals formed from mono- and bi-syllabic stems that are or are not body-anchored and found some variants in the pluralized forms, as well as systematic differences in the allowable phonological forms of the plurals for these four classes of nouns. She also observed some phonological restrictions on the class of singular nouns that can be pluralized in this way.

For example, the singular and plural of WAY are illustrated in Figure 5. The singular involves a single forward movement of the hands. The plural has two forward movements, with a lateral displacement between the two.

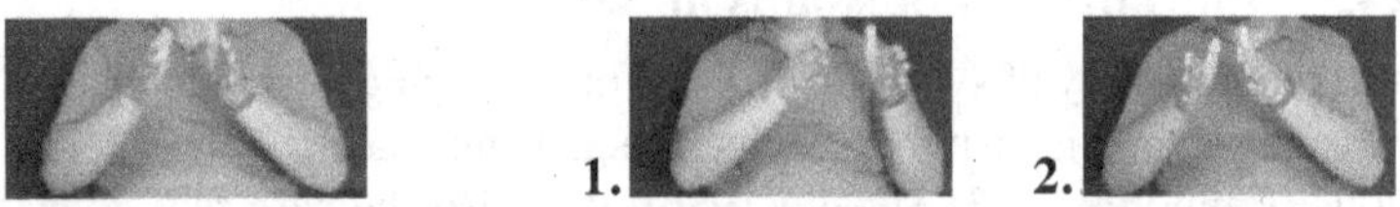

1. 2.

Singular – 1 movement Plural –sequence of 2 movements

FIGURE 5 Singular (monosyllabic) and plural (bisyllabic) forms of sign WAY

Figure 6 illustrates the pluralization of POSTER.[13] The singular has two forward movements of the hands (as if pushing in thumbtacks at the top and bottom of a poster). The plural is also bisyllabic, but involves downward movements, both essentially between the start and end points of the singular (although the vertical distance is reduced a bit), with a lateral translation between the two vertical movements. This translation, seen also with WAY, is characteristic of reduplicated plurals of non body-anchored signs.

[13]There are dialectal and idiolectal differences with respect to which nouns can be inflected for plurality. For example, not all signers use an overtly marked plural form for POSTER.

1.

2.

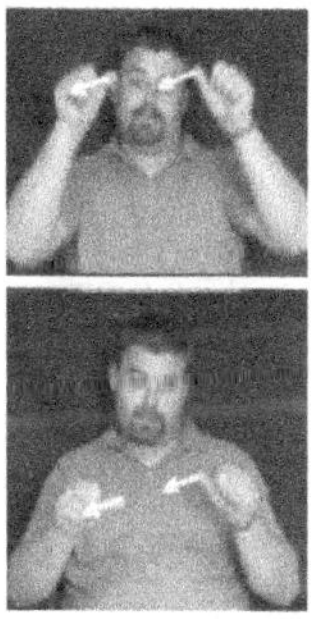

Singular – 2 forward movements of hands

1. 2.

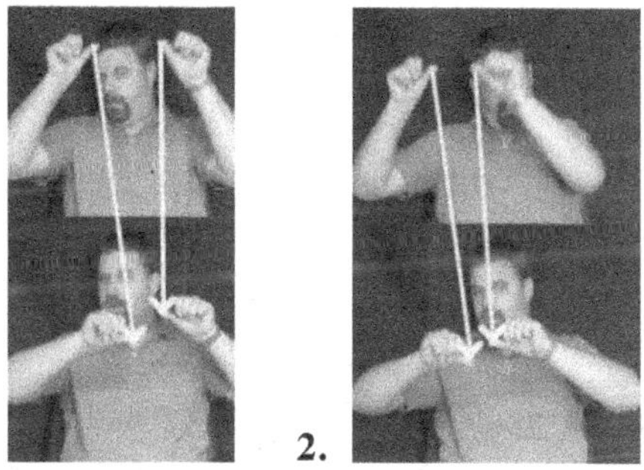

Plural – 2 downward movements, laterally displaced from one another

FIGURE 6 Singular and plural forms of sign POSTER, both bisyllabic

Perry proposes an optimality-theoretic approach to predicting well-formed outputs for reduplicated plurals, which includes constraints on syllabic structure. Specifically, what Brentari (1998) calls 'inherent features,' i.e. hand shapes, locations, and orientations, are more likely to be retained in the reduplicated plurals than 'prosodic features' of paths and movements. In any case, ASL appears to be like German Sign Language in having phonological conditions on pluralization of nouns by reduplication (Pfau and Steinbach 2006).

24.3.2 Why should it be optional to use the plural form of a plural noun?

There is, however, a puzzle. Even those nouns that *can* be inflected for plurality through reduplication do not always appear as reduplicated in plural contexts. If we are really dealing with a systematic grammatical marking of plurality, why should plural marking (for morphological classes of nouns for which a plural form *exists*) be optional? It might be suggested that ASL simply lacks grammatical marking for plurality within noun phrases. However, plural marking is found on pronouns, possessives, and emphatic reflexives (as discussed above), and there are distinct plural forms for at least some ASL nouns.

24.3.3 One possible reason for lack of visible plural morphology: Variability in phonological realization of morphologically 'reduplicated' forms

Consideration of reduplicated forms in ASL more generally suggests that at least part of the explanation may be phonological. There is a small set of singular nouns in ASL that have a reduplicated variant. Like plurals with the potential for reduplication, these singular signs can also be produced with or without the allowed reduplication.

An example of a reduplicable singular is COP, which involves either a single or double movement of the hand, in the shape of the letter 'C', against the chest. Another example is BOY, which is formed with the dominant hand near the forehead; the fingers open or close, either once or twice. Signs with similar alternations in the realization of singular forms include DOCTOR, BOSS, COMPUTER, and GIRL.

There are some differences in the form of the reduplicant for singular nouns and plural inflection. The singular forms with reduplicated variants all involve monosyllabic stems, and their reduplicated versions do not have the lateral translation described earlier as characteristic of non body-anchored plurals. Perry observed a contrast for the sign WORD, which can be articulated in the singular with either a single or double articulation. There is a difference between the singular and plural reduplicated forms in that only the latter involves horizontal translation.

The reduplicated form is more likely to surface in positions of greater prosodic prominence. Consider the examples shown in Figure 7, excerpted from a narrative by Ben Bahan. The first, with relatively neutral prosody, has COP in its reduplicated form. The second, with phrasal prominence on the preceding sign OTHER, is followed by a brief and reduced articulation of COP, without reduplication.

- - - COP (1st articulation) - - - | - - - - - (reduplication) - - - - -

From a sentence meaning: 'The *cop* pulled behind the car…'

- - - - - - - - - - - OTHER - - - - - - - - -   - - - - - - COP - - - - - - -

From a sentence meaning: '*Another* cop pulled the car over.'

FIGURE 7 COP signed with (above) and without (below) reduplication.

The conditions under which potentially reduplicated forms surface with and without reduplication remain to be studied carefully. However, it may well be that the same phonological processes are involved for both singular and plural forms that potentially involve reduplication. In both cases, phonological prominence appears to be relevant. With respect to plurals, it would be odd to have the presence of a morpho-syntactic feature such as number conditioned by phonological environment, although the realization (with or without reduplication) of a specific plural form certainly could be.

It should be noted that prosodic context is not completely determinative. There are, as alternatives to reduplication, other articulatory strategies to allow nonreduplicated forms to fill larger prosodic slots. For a few specific signs, like MOTHER, the reduplicated movement often found with the singular form (in this case, the thumb contacts the chin twice) can be replaced by finger wiggling[14] (while the hand is held in place with the thumb touching the chin); this is another type of movement that contributes to syllabic weight. Perry found similar variants for the plural forms of BOOK and LANGUAGE (two-handed symmetrical signs) involving a kind of trilled articulation of the dominant hand.

As another alternative to reduplication, a sign like COP can be produced with a single articulation accompanied by an up and down head nod.[15] Liddell (1980) observed that head nods in ASL frequently occur with constructions like gapping that contain instances of null syntactic structure. To the extent that ellipsis sites such as this are associated with lengthening of preceding material, head nods can be seen to correlate with phonological lengthening. It is also noteworthy that, although the possessives meaning 'my' 'your' 'his/her' etc. (shown in Figure 1) and glossed as POSS have no reduplication, the pronominal possessives meaning 'mine', 'yours', 'hers', etc. – occurring with a null head noun – are reduplicated: POSS+.

Perhaps signs that allow reduplication in the singular and/or plural contain a specification for a heavier prosodic template. Reduplication would be the normal result of mapping the stem to a template of the appropriate size. Such prosodic structure, however, would only be licensed in positions with sufficient prosodic prominence. In less prominent positions, the stem can only appear in the unmarked, unreduplicated form.

How could we tell the difference between a noun that is simply unmarked for number (and therefore surfaces without the reduplication that typically marks plurality for nouns that can be so marked) and one that has been marked [+plural] but which has been inserted into a prosodic position where that mor-

[14]There is idiolectal variation as to which of these variants (reduplication vs. finger-wiggling) is typically used. Some signers associate the two forms with differences in meaning.

[15]MacLaughlin (1997: 98-99) briefly discusses effects of constituent-final lengthening on the realization of such signs, and association with either reduplication or head nod.

phological marking cannot be overtly realized, for phonological reasons? In other words, how do we know whether the lack of plural marking on a noun is due to the absence of a morpho-syntactic specification of plurality, or to the phonological invisibility of that feature in a particular context? These both seem to amount to the same thing.

It seems in any case that the systematic number distinction in ASL is between unmarked and [+plural], with no forms explicitly marked as exclusively singular. Although nouns pluralized by reduplication are restricted to positions of phonological prominence, it is possible, in all positions, to find (potentially reduplicable) nouns with a plural interpretation that lack reduplication. Furthermore, as mentioned in footnote 3, even for signs that are otherwise rich in agreement (pronouns, determiners, possessives, emphatic reflexives), it is possible to use the non overtly plural, unmarked (=singular) form in reference to pluralities considered as collectives.

Where does this leave us? ASL nouns of the relevant class, when marked as [+plural], have a morphological instantiation with the potential for reduplication, although the realization of the plural form is subject to more general prosodic constraints that also affect other potentially reduplicated forms in the language. Forms not explicitly marked as plural are nonetheless compatible with a plural interpretation, even in cases where a marked plural form exists.

24.3.4 Another limitation on the morphological expression of plurality: Lack of concord internal to DP

Pfau and Steinbach (2006) report that for German Sign Language (DGS), plural inflection will not appear on the noun if it is modified by a numeral or quantifier. They observe that, as in Hungarian and Turkish, the marking of plurality in DGS can occur only once within the noun phrase, and that all these languages lack number concord. The same is true of ASL, and this has been reflected in the numerous descriptions in the literature that list use of a numeral or quantifier as a strategy for pluralizing a noun phrase. If a numeral or quantifier is used, the noun will not be reduplicated to mark plurality. In (7) and (8), the + indicates reduplication.

(7) a. MANY WOMAN ‘many women’ b. FIVE WOMEN ‘five women’

(8) a. *MANY WOMAN+ b. *FIVE WOMEN+

Similarly, there is a very limited set of adjectives in ASL that allow reduplication to mark plurality, including DIFFERENT. It is possible to have either DIFFERENT or the noun it modifies in a reduplicated plural form, but not both. The one likely to be reduplicated is the one that is phonologically more prominent. This is also true for plural DPs that include a determiner. If a plural form of the determiner is used, the noun would not normally be reduplicated. This, then, is a significant syntactic difference between ASL and languages in which all plural elements within the noun phrase (with the potential for overt number distinctions) will be marked as such.

24.4 Summary

This squib has considered two cases of variability in the overt manifestation of person/number features: (a) subject/object agreement on verbs, and (b) plural number on nouns. Part of the explanation in both cases resides in the lexical properties of the verbs and nouns in question. The absence of plural inflection on plural nouns with the potential to be so inflected is explained in part by the fact that reduplication is subject to prosodic constraints that may either exclude or obscure this morphological marking of plurality in certain contexts. Plural marking, even when a distinct plural form is available, is not grammatically obligatory, since forms *not* marked as plural are unmarked for number and compatible with plural readings. Thus, multiple marking of plurality within a noun phrase is superfluous and does not normally occur.

There is still much left to be explored with respect to the expressions of number and person agreement in ASL. If anything is clear, however, it is that the answers cannot be found without consideration of the complex interactions of phonology, morphology, syntax, semantics, and prosody, i.e., that one must pay attention to the wide range of topics that have been the focus of Mohanan's interests and publications!

Acknowledgements

This research involved collaboration with many people, especially Ben Bahan, Robert G. Lee, Dawn MacLaughlin, Deborah Perry, Mike Schlang, Lana Cook, and Norma Tourangeau, though they bear no responsibility for any errors. Thanks also to Jonathan Barnes, Quinn Duffy, and Paul Hagstrom. The data were annotated with SignStream (http://www.bu.edu/asllrp/SignStream), and collected with technical assistance from Stan Sclaroff and Vassilis Athitsos. Annotated data and video files are available from the National Center for Sign Language and Gesture Resources at http://www.bu.edu/asllrp/cslgr/. This research has been supported in part by grants from the National Science Foundation (#CNS-04279883 and #IIS-0329009).

References

Bahan, Benjamin. 1996. *Non-manual Realization of Agreement in American Sign Language*. Ph.D. thesis, Boston University, Boston, MA.

Bahan, Benjamin, Judy Kegl, Robert G. Lee, Dawn MacLaughlin, and Carol Neidle. 2000. The licensing of null arguments in American Sign Language. *Linguistic Inquiry* 31:1–27.

Baker, Charlotte and Dennis Cokely. 1980. *American Sign Language: A Teacher's Resource Text on Grammar and Culture*. Silver Spring, MD: T.J. Publishers.

Baker, Charlotte and Carol A. Padden. 1978. Focusing on the nonmanual components of American Sign Language. In P. Siple, ed., *Understanding Language Through Sign Language Research*, pages 27–57. New York, NY: Academic Press.

Baker-Shenk, Charlotte. 1983. *A Micro-analysis of the Nonmanual Components of Questions in American Sign Language*. Ph.D. thesis, University of California, Berkeley, CA.

Brentari, Diane. 1988. Backwards verbs in asl: Agreement re-opened. In G. L. D. Brentari and L. MacLeod, eds., *Chicago Linguistics Society Volume 24, Part 2: Agreement in Grammatical Theory*, pages 16–27.

Brentari, Diane. 1998. *A Prosodic Model of Sign Language Phonology*. Cambridge, MA: MIT Press.

Conlin, Frances, Paul Hagstrom, and Carol Neidle. 2003. A particle of indefiniteness in American Sign Language [2003]. In *Linguistic Discovery 2*.

Coulter, Geoffrey R. 1979. *American Sign Language Typology*. Ph.D. thesis, University of California, San Diego, CA.

Emmorey, Karen. 2003. *Perspectives on Classifier Constructions in Sign Languages*. Mahwah, NJ: Lawrence Erlbaum.

Friedman, Lynn A. 1975. Space, time and person reference in ASL. *Language* 51:940–961.

Jones, N. and K. Mohr. 1975. A working paper on plurals in ASL. University of California, Berkeley.

Klima, Edward S. and Ursula Bellugi. 1979. *The Signs of Language*. Cambridge, MA: Harvard University Press.

Kyle, Jim G., Bencie Woll, Gloria Pullen, and Frank Maddix. 1988. *Sign Language: The Study of Deaf People and Their Language*. Cambridge: Cambridge University Press.

Lambrecht, Knud. 1994. *Information Structure and Sentence Form: Topic, Focus, and the Mental Representation of Discourse Referents*. Cambridge: Cambridge University Press.

Liddell, Scott K. 1980. *American Sign Language Syntax*. The Hague: Mouton.

Liddell, Scott K. 2000a. Blended spaces and deixis in sign language discourse. In D. McNeill, ed., *Language and Gesture: Window into Thought and Language Discourse*. Cambridge: Cambridge University Press.

Liddell, Scott K. 2000b. Indicating verbs and pronouns: Pointing away from agreement. In K. Emmorey and H. Lane, eds., *The Signs of Language Revisited: An Anthology to Honor Ursula Bellugi and Edward Klima*. Mahwah, NJ: Lawrence Erlbaum.

Liddell, Scott K. 2003. *Grammar, Gesture, and Meaning in American Sign Language*. Cambridge and New York, NY: Cambridge University Press.

Lillo-Martin, Diane. 1986. Two kinds of null arguments in American Sign Language. *Natural Language and Linguistic Theory* 4:415–444.

Lillo-Martin, Diane. 1991. *Universal Grammar and American Sign Language*. Dordrecht: Kluwer.

Lillo-Martin, Diane. 1995. The point of view predicate in american sign language. In K. Emmorey and J. S. Reilly, eds., *Language, Gesture, and Space*, pages 155–170. Hillsdale, NJ: Lawrence Erlbaum.

Lillo-Martin, Diane and Edward S. Klima. 1990. Pointing Out Differences: ASL Pronouns in Syntactic Theory. In *Theoretical Issues in Sign Language Research, Volume 1: Linguistics*, pages 191–210. Chicago, IL: The University of Chicago Press.

MacLaughlin, Dawn. 1997. *The Structure of Determiner Phrases: Evidence from American Sign Language*. Ph.D. thesis, Boston University, Boston, MA.

MacLaughlin, Dawn, Carol Neidle, Benjamin Bahan, and Robert G. Lee. 2000. Morphological inflections and syntactic representations of person and number in ASL. *Recherches Linguistiques de Vincennes 29: Langage et Surdité* .

Meier, Richard P. 1990. Person deixis in American Sign Language. In S. D. Fischer and P. Siple, eds., *Theoretical Issues in Sign Language Research, Volume 1: Linguistics*, pages 175–190. Chicago, IL: The University of Chicago Press.

Miljan, Merilin. 2003. Number in Estonian Sign Language. *Trames* 7(57/52):202–223.

Neidle, Carol. 2003. Language across modalities: ASL focus and question constructions. *Linguistic Variation Yearbook* 2:71–98.

Neidle, Carol, Benjamin Bahan, Dawn MacLaughlin, Robert G. Lee, and Judy Kegl. 1998. Realizations of syntactic agreement in American Sign Language: Similarities between the clause and the noun phrase. *Studia Linguistica* 52:191–226.

Neidle, Carol, Judy Kegl, Dawn MacLaughlin, Benjamin Bahan, and Robert G. Lee. 2000. *The Syntax of American Sign Language: Functional Categories and Hierarchical Structure*. Cambridge, MA: MIT.

Neidle, Carol and Robert G. Lee. 2006. Syntactic agreement across language modalities. In J. Costa and M. C. Figueiredo Silva, eds., *Studies on Agreement*. Amsterdam: John Benjamins.

Neidle, Carol and Dawn MacLaughlin. 2002. The distribution of functional projections in ASL: Evidence from overt expressions of syntactic features. In G. Cinque, ed., *Functional Structure in the DP and IP: The Cartography of Syntactic Structures*. Oxford: Oxford University Press.

Padden, Carol A. 1983. *Interaction of Morphology and Syntax in American Sign Language*. Ph.D. thesis, University of California, San Diego.

Padden, Carol A. 1988. *Interaction of Morphology and Syntax in American Sign Language*. New York, NY: Garland Publishing.

Padden, Carol A. 1990. The relation between space and grammar in ASL verb morphology. In C. Lucas, ed., *Sign Language Research: Theoretical Issues*, pages 118–132. Washington, DC: Gallaudet University Press.

Perry, D. 2005. The Use of Reduplication in ASL Plurals. MA project, Boston University, Boston, MA.

Pfau, Roland and Markus Steinbach. 2006. Pluralization in sign and in speech: A crossmodal typological study. *Linguistic Typology* 10:135–182.

Stokoe, William C., Dorothy C. Casterline, and Carl G. Croneberg. 1965. *A Dictionary of American Sign Language on Linguistic Principles*. Silver Spring, MD: Linstok Press.

Supalla, S. J. 1986. The classifier system in American Sign Language. In C. Craig, ed., *Noun Classes and Categorization*, pages 181–214. Amsterdam: John Benjamins.

Supalla, Ted and Elissa L. Newport. 1978. How many seats in a chair? The derivation of nouns and verbs in ASL. In P. Siple, ed., *Understanding Language Through Sign Language Research*. New York, NY: Academic Press.

Sutton-Spence, Rachel and Bencie Woll. 1999. *The Linguistics of British Sign Language*. Cambridge: Cambridge University Press.

Thompson, Robin, Karen Emmorey, and Robert Kluender. 2006. The relationship between eye gaze and verb agreement in American Sign Language: An eye-tracking study. *Natural Language and Linguistics Theory* 24:571–604.

Wilbur, Ronnie B. 1987. *American Sign Language: Linguistic and Applied Dimensions*. Boston, MA: College-Hill Press.

25

Prioritizing Constraint Sets in the Grammar of Carnatic Music

K.G. VIJAYAKRISHNAN

25.1 Introduction

Carnatic music, the classical music of South India, requires a ranked, prioritized approach to output wellformedness requirements. This model of grammar is inspired by Optimality Theory as outlined in Prince and Smolensky (1993) and McCarthy and Prince (1993) and subsequent literature.[1] Like the model of language in OT, the model proposed for Carnatic music too requires markedness constraints to be ranked with respect to the Faithfulness constraints specific to notes, sequences, phrases listed in the Lexicon of Carnatic music which I term Faith.Lex constraints. However, the model proposed for Carnatic music is different from that of language in OT in several, significant respects (sections 25.2 and 25.3 below). This prioritized approach to output wellformedness is best suited for Carnatic music for two major reasons. Firstly, Carnatic music cannot be adequately described using a bottom-up, derivational model as the concerns at lower levels may be overridden by higher ranked concerns of higher level requirements. For instance, a constraint at the level of the musical sequence prohibits the sequence 'ri ma' (D F)[2] for the *raagam* Bhairavi. However, constraints at the levels of the musical

[1] The ideas outlined in this paper are discussed in detail in Vijayakrishnan (2007).

[2] The Carnatic music equivalent of the notes *do, re, mi, fa, so, la, ti* of Western music are *sa, ri, ga, ma, pa, da, ni* when sung. The Carnatic music system interprets the twelve notes of the Western scale as a sixteen note octave and the notes D, E flat, A and B flat receive dual interpretation. For lack of space I am unable to account for the logic of labeling the notes 'xa', 'xi' and 'xu' where 'x' stands for the designated note i.e., 'r', 'g', 'd', 'n' etc. Thus the notes 'r',

Reality Exploration and Discovery: Pattern Interaction in Language and Life.
Linda Uyechi and Lian-Hee Wee (eds.).

phrase and musical line overlook this violation in the musical phrase [ri má *gi, ri] (D F E flat: D) with 'gi' (E flat) receiving prominence at the phrasal level (and emphatic prominence '*' at the level of the line).[3] The constraints at the levels of the line and phrase are higher ranked than the constraints at the level of the sequence and they do not detect any violations at higher levels. Thus the line is tolerated. Compared to this phrase, the phrases [ri má, gi ri], [rí ma gi ri,] and several other possibilities would have incurred violations at the levels of the sequence, phrase and musical line as well making the phrase ungrammaticality as a musical phrase in the *raagam* Bhairavi. Notice I said 'tolerated'. When asked to introspect, many musicians would, in fact, notate the phrase as [gi ma *gí, ri] which would emerge the optimal candidate without any violation at any of the levels. But the physical fact is that the frequency of the initial note is 'ri' (D) and nowhere near 'gi' (E flat) for many users (there are several recordings of this phrase which may be subjected to empirical verification). The point I am trying to make is that the evaluation procedure required for Carnatic music may have to be fine tuned to capture these shades of grammaticality. [4]

Secondly, like language, Carnatic music is characterized by variation across time and across users and is therefore inherently variationistic. Thus like language, Carnatic music benefits from a ranking approach to output wellformedness requirements as different varieties can be shown to be related through demotion of specific Faith.Lex constraints in the same constraint hierarchy[5].

The aim of this paper is to show that the grammar of Carnatic music is different from that of language in yet another significant respect in allowing sets of constraints specific to grammaticality to be downgraded and rendered violable/invisible under certain conditions. In the main part of the paper, section 25.4, I show that the grammar of Carnatic music must prioritize style/stylistic requirements above grammaticality requirements allowing style and stylistic

'g' and 'd' and 'n' have three variants each but 'm' has only two as in the Western F and F sharp. Since the Western equivalents are always specified along with the Carnatic notation, I hope the reader will not be unduly inconvenienced.

[3]The underlined notes are in tempo 2 and a comma stands for a mora (unit of timing). This is the way many musicians of standing render the opening phrase of the composer Tyaagaraajaa's (1767-1847) composition 'Upacaaramu' in Bhairavi, Ruupaka Taaḷam.

[4]Personally, I take it that the phrase under discussion is perfectly grammatical. We will see how the delimitation condition of the constraint hierarchy (CH) discussed in section 25.2 below can account for the grammaticality of this line. I offer a solution along these lines in the context of re-prioritization of constraint sets in section 25.4.

[5]Or conversely, the introduction of a new Faith.Lex constraint in the lexicon of the artist. Thus, as in language change, we have instances of 'simplification' as well as spontaneous emergence of complexity accounted for in terms of demotion of Faith.Lex constraints or introduction of high ranked new Faith.Lex constraints respectively in the constraint hierarchy. (I am grateful to Paul Kiparsky (pc)for bringing this to my notice.).

considerations to overrule violations of grammaticality under strictly controlled circumstances.

25.2 Background

Carnatic music, the classical music of South India, has fairly complex systems of rules for interpreting pitch values which may be specific to *raagas*[6] and rules for regulating the rhythm (the *taaḷas* or beats). In this paper, since I will be looking exclusively at issues pertaining to pitch and interpretation of tone, by the grammar of Carnatic music I mean the complex system of rules of interpretation of pitch values in Carnatic music. Like language, Carnatic music too exhibits structure dependence at minimally two levels namely, that of the pitch and the phrase. The Carnatic system allows notes to be interpreted as steady pitch, pitch wave, pitch curve, or pitch spike specific to *raagas*.[7] For example, whereas in the *raagam* Tooḍi[8], the note 'gi' (E flat) may be interpreted as any of the above mentioned possibilities (traversing pitch ranges from as low as the 'sa' or the fundamental C going up to as high as the notes 'ma' (F) or even higher to 'pa' (G)) depending on the context and the style of the performer, in the *raagam* Hindooḷam the same note 'gi' (E flat) can be interpreted only as the steady value of E flat or a pitch wave traversing E flat from a pitch value slightly lower than that of E flat. In this context of a range of pitch values for notes, the notion note itself is interpretable only in context; it is structure dependent. In other words, a pitch value, say x, in the pitch curve may be interpreted as note Y in the context of one *raagam* and as note Z in the context of another *raagam* just like the way the flap in American English may be interpreted as *t* in the word 'latter' and as *d* in 'ladder' depending on the context (the length of the preceding vowel) though the physical realisation of the flap may be the same in both words.

The second instance of structure dependence in Carnatic music comes from musical phrasing. The same sequence of notes e.g., 'sa ri gu ma' (C D E F) may be interpreted as the *raagam* Harikaamboodi if the phrasing is [sa ri gu ma] (phrasal boundary being indicated by brackets) but may be interpreted as the *raagam* Sahaanaa if the phrasing is [sa] [ri gu ma]. The placement of phrasal boundary (realisation may vary widely) is crucial to the interpretation

[6]The notion of *raagam* (in the singular) is notoriously difficult to define. Each *raagam* has an arbitrary name and may be defined by the selection of notes in an octave with sometimes strict prohibition on certain linear sequencing of notes, many idiosyncratic phrases using the specified notes and sometimes accidental notes. The *raagam* emerges when these stipulations are subject to melodic explorations.

[7]The exploitation of intertonal frequency is by no means unique to the musical system of South India. But perhaps, the range of intertonal pitch variations attested in Carnatic music may not be equalled in other systems of music.

[8]Names of *raagas* are transcribed according to the Tamil pronunciation (with aspiration thrown in when I am aware of it). Specifically, they are not Sanskrit based.

of a *raagam* and therefore central to the grammar of Carnatic music. Thus the former phrasing as an input for the the *raagam* Sahaanaa will be assigned a violation mark by the Faith.Lex.Sahaanaa constraint *[sa⇒ma] which says, informally, that a phrase initiated by the note 'sa' cannot contain the note 'ma' as the final note for the *raagam* Sahaanaa. As it cannot be saved by higher ranked constraints at the same level or higher levels, it will constitute a case of pure ungrammaticality and will be rejected by the grammar.

At the heart of the grammar of Carnatic music is the Lexicon of Carnatic music which is a compilation of constraints at the levels of the note, sequence and phrase de-composed from musical corpora. This lexicon must assume a networked system of *raagas* as, it will have been noticed, issues of interpretation and grammaticality examine an input in the context of two factors: namely, the idiosyncratic features listed in the lexicon of a particular *raagam* e.g., the pitch values for the note 'gi' (E flat) in the *raagam* Tooḍi and also evaluate one *raagam* in the context of a cluster of *raagas* requiring many of these *raagas* to be distinct from one another e.g., the note 'gi' (E flat) in the *raagas* Tooḍi and Hindooḷam (and several other *raagas* as well). While the former *raagam* belongs to the small set of *raagas* which I call the Idiosyncratic Set (I Set for short) which admit specific interpretation of notes, specific sequences and specialised phrases, the latter belongs to the Scalar Set (S Set for short) to which the large majority of *raagas* belong which do not require constraints specific to notes, or phrases. While the I Set *raagas* should be normally disambiguated with all other *raagas* at all levels, the latter *raagas* require the establishment of their identity at the level of the musical line.[9] I call the requirement that a *raagam* must be differentiated from other *raagas* *Ambiguous (*Amb for short).

Further, there is is a major difference between the Lexicon of Carnatic music and that of language. In the latter, the usual thinking is that all words (however they are defined) are listed in the lexicon and the templates for word formation step in only when new words have to be coined. Therefore, when we refer to Faithfulness in the grammar of language, we mean faithfulness to the input taken from the lexicon (with the assumption Richness of the Base allowing us to import all the predictable details along with the unpredictable ones to form the lexicon). In Carnatic music, however, this definition of the input is not maintainable most of the time. A large part of the phrasal output in a performance of *aalaapanai*, *taanam* and *kalpanaaswaram*[10] will admit phrases which do not have the psychological permanence of words in a language or even in Carnatic music compositions. Further, for most artists, the same notated phrase may admit more than one way of rendering, depend-

[9] See Vijayakrishnan (2007) chapter 8 for details.

[10] These three forms are impromptu, free renderings (non-rhythmic, semi-rhythmic and rhythmic respectively) which are supposed to be unrehearsed and spontaneous.

ing on factors like the range of interpretation of pitch allowed in the lexicon, matters of style signaling a school of music, signaling an individual, and/or stylistic factors, e.g., emotive factors. To assume that each of the possible interpretations is an actual entry in the Carnatic music lexicon is misguided for at least two reasons. Firstly, an actual output may be attributed randomly to any one of the possible 'entries' if the user is asked to introspect. Further, a user may not even be aware which of the possible entries he/she produces. More importantly, the multiple entries merely reflect the specific constraints pertaining to tone, sequence, phrase already listed in the lexicon for this particular *raagam*. This is why I assume that we require Faith.Lex constraints for Carnatic music rather than or in addition to the IdentIO constraints invoked for language. If a phrase is taken from the lexicon, it can then be subject to IdentIO constraints (if necessary). But in the large majority of cases, the function of the grammar of Carnatic music is to examine a line of structured pitch sequence and evaluate it for grammaticality in the context of the constraints specific to tones, sequences and phrases listed in the lexicon (Faith.Lex constraints) which are ranked with respect to markedness constraints in the individual user's grammar.

25.3 The Model of Grammar for Carnatic Music

As I explained earlier, there are two major arguments against a deterministic, derivational model and in favour of an output oriented, nonderivational model like OT for Carnatic music. The first argument pertains to the ranking of higher and lower level concerns of output wellformedness. The second argument is based on the fact that, like language, Carnatic music exhibits variation across time and users, and that this variation can best be captured typologically as instances of reranking of the same set of constraints.

25.3.1 Evaluation of the input in the grammar of Carnatic music

The first argument pertaining to the higher priority accorded to higher level constraints was earlier explained with an example from a musical phrase from the *raagam* Bhairavi. Let me now present a more detailed argument pertaining to the execution of a single note. As already mentioned, Carnatic music has strict rules for the interpretation of notes of a *raagam* set out in its Lexicon. Let us call them rules of Tone construal. In an output oriented constraint based approach, the grammar is an interaction of Markedness constraints and these lexically specified Faith.Lex constraints. In the case of the note 'gi' (E flat)[11] the least marked of the Markedness constraints in question is the requirement that a note be rendered as a steady pitch at the pitch value of the note in a twelve tone system to be called Render as Scale or RenScale for short. The

[11] Or any other note for that matter.

fact that Tooḍi allows a deep pitch curve on the note 'gi' (E flat) implies that Faith.Lex.Pitch.Curve 'gi' is high ranked in the constraint hierarchy (CH) of this *raagam*. However, notice that since the requirement that a note be rendered as a scalar note with steady pitch is the least marked among the realisations of the note, it can, in principle, never be banned in the lexicon of any *raagam*. It can only be banned in specified contexts. Continuing with the case of the *raagam* Tooḍi, RenScale 'gi' (steady pitch E flat) is prohibited in a sequence like [sa ra gi ma] (C D flat E flat F) rendered in the normal tempo, referred to here as Tempo 1. Let us formalise this context sensitive markedness constraint as *RenScalegi [.ra_ma.]. Thus the constraint set for the note 'gi' can be summarized as in (1) below.

(1) Faith.Lex Constraint and Markedness Constraints for 'gi' in Tooḍi

Faith.Lex.Pitch.Curve 'gi' tempo 1, Faith.Lex.Pitch.Wave 'gi' tempo 1

$\gg$

*RenScalegi [.ra_ma.] (context sensitive)

$\gg$

*Pitch.Curve 'gi' $\gg$ *Pitch.Wave 'gi' $\gg$ *RenScale 'gi' (context free)

In normal tempo (tempo 1) the ranking Faith.Lex.Pitch.Curve 'gi', Faith.Lex.Pitch.Wave 'gi' $\gg$ *RenScalegi [.ra_ma.] accounts for the absence of RenScale 'gi' in this context. But notice that the potential candidates for the phrase [ra gi ma] are at least (i) [ra Pitch Curve gi ma], (ii) [ra Pitch Wave gi ma] and (iii) [ra RenScale gi ma]. The last candidate is, of course, suboptimal given the CH in (1) above. However, both candidates (ii) and (iii) will be equally optimal. And that is the way it should be given the intra/inter-user variability in Carnatic music. This is one of the reasons why I assume that the model I am proposing for Carnatic music is not a generative one unlike that of language. It takes a single input and evaluates it for grammaticality/style/stylistic criteria simultaneously.[12] Another point worth noting is that invoking Faith.Lex instead of an IdentIO constraint allows us the freedom to take it that the input to be evaluated is extracted from the lexicon or composed online with the help of the specific Faith.Lex constraints in the lexicon with the help of the templates for constructing musical phrases listed in the Lexicon. However, given the CH in (1) above, comparing candidates (i) and (ii), the latter will always emerge optimal as *PitchWave 'gi' is lower ranked than *PitchCurve 'gi'. This is the reason that I propose that the entire CH does not evaluate an input in the grammar of Carnatic music, unlike the grammar of language. I assume that the constraint set is **delimited** in the grammar of Carnatic music to include constraints only up to the context sensitive markedness

[12]Another reason for assuming a non-generative model for Carnatic music is that, unlike language, general structural principles that allow one to generate multiple candidates (possibly infinite) have not yet been worked out for music.

constraint and no further down in the full CH. But as we will see, this needs to be slightly revised. I will state the delimitation condition of the CH in the grammar of Carnatic music in a short while. If the lower ranked context free markedness constraints are rendered invisible, both inputs (ii) and (iii) will be considered optimal as they would not have been assigned any violation marks by the active CH. Thus candidates (i) and (ii) can be considered to be equally grammatical.

At a faster tempo, say tempo 2, as pitch curve renderings will be ruled out by the difficulty in executing pitch curves at higher tempo, we have the new superordinate context free markedness constraint *PitchCurve 'gi' tempo 2. With this new context free markedness constraint ranked above the set in (1), a pitch curve interpretation for 'gi' will be ruled out and only a pitch wave interpretation will be possible. At an even faster tempo, say tempo 3, even pitch wave interpretations will be difficult and so, with both pitch curve and pitch wave interpretations being rendered more marked and higher ranked, the lowly RenScale 'gi' emerges as the optimal candidate in spite of the specific context sensitive markedness constraint. Thus we get the expected result of the 'emergence of the unmarked' in Carnatic music, as in language, as the CH in (2) illustrates.

(2) Constraint Hierarchy for 'gi' in Tooḍi

*PitchCurve 'gi' tempo 2, *PitchWave 'gi' tempo 3, 2

≫

Faith.Lex.Pitch.Curve/Wave 'gi' tempo 1

≫

*RenScalegi [.ra_ma.] (context sensitive)

≫

*Pitch.Curve 'gi' ≫ *Pitch.Wave 'gi' ≫ *RenScale 'gi' (context free)

But notice that in the earlier case when we wanted to consider both pitch curve and pitch wave interpretations as equally optimal, I had suggested that the CH is delimited to include only those constraints ranked above the context sensitive constraints to allow multiple, optimal inputs. But when we have specific references made to the context free markedness constraints ranked higher than the Faith.Lex constraints, we are forced to consider the entire CH. Therefore we are now in a position to revise our delimitation condition as in (3) below.

(3) Delimitation Condition for the CH in the Grammar of Carnatic Music

Only constraints up to and including the context sensitive constraints are considered for evaluation purposes in the grammar of Carnatic music normally. The constraints ranked below the context sensitive markedness constraint are delimited to play no role in the evaluation process.

If specific context free markedness constraints are higher ranked than Faith.Lex constraints, then the full Constraint Hierarchy including all the context free markedness constraints may be considered for evaluation purposes.

25.3.2 Accounting for variation in the grammar of Carnatic music

The second argument for a ranked output wellformedness oriented model of grammar for Carnatic music comes from variation in Carnatic music. Carnatic music is essentially variationist oriented as it exhibits variation across time and across users. I shall give a simple example of the rendering of a note in two different styles on a commercial recording featuring a vocalist accompanied by violin. [13] The vocalist has the constraint *RenScale nu [pa __: Sa]; informally stated, the steady pitch rendering of B is prohibited when the note is in the ascent in the sequence G_(upper) C and is long for the *raagam* Janaranjani (and in fact, the actual pitch rendering is a starting pitch value hovering between A and B flat – the last being a note not selected by the *raagam* at all). Therefore for the vocalist the ranking is Faith.LexPitch Curve reduced.nu (the lexical information that the 'nu' is reduced and rendered as a pitch curve for the *raagam*) ≫ *Renscale 'nu'. However, the violinist happily uses RenScale 'nu' in the same context time and again. Thus while the ranking for the vocalist is Faith.LexPitch Curve reduced.nu ≫ *Renscale 'nu', the accompanying violinist has the ranking *Pitch Curve reduced.nu, *Pitch wave reduced.nu ≫ *RenScale 'nu' ≫ Faith.LexPitch Curve reduced.nu, making the Faith.Lex constraint invisible in his CH . At times one wonders whether the two are rendering the same *raagam* at all. Let me quickly add that the violinist is not ungrammatical; it is just that the vocalist accesses a different, presumably, earlier grammar and the violinist a later version of the grammar which has generally replaced the earlier one for many users now.[14] One can see that *raagam* change like language change is from marked to less marked or unmarked structures.[15] We are now ready to examine the unique character-

[13] To avoid controversy, the names of the performers have been withheld.

[14] Needless to say that I hold onto the more orthodox, presumably older version of the *raagam* and it was my mother, my music guru, who first brought this to my notice. These two rankings are not the only possible types of change that the *raagam* Janaranjani can undergo. Yet another 21st century artist exhibits a twist in the change that the *raagam* has undergone. Like the violinist in the commercial recording described above, she is uncomfortable with the pitch curve rendering on reduced 'nu' in Janaranjani when the note is long and in the ascent. But she is equally uncomfortable with replacing it with RenScale 'nu'. So she adopts the avoidance strategy. Her phrase [pa nu : Sa] is rendered in such a way that the 'pa' is prolonged and the pitch curve on 'nu' is made a passing glide to the 'Sa'.

[15] In the golden age of Carnatic music between the mid-18th to mid-19th century one finds many examples of composers forging their individual grammars of *raagas* by incorporating several Faith.Lex constraints at the level of the tone, sequence and even phrase. Being part of the idiolect of a single composer and being distinct from other contemporary composers, one can

istic of prioritized constraint sets in Carnatic music.

25.4 Prioritized Constraint Sets in the Grammar of Carnatic Music

In this, the main section of the paper, I show how the grammar of Carnatic music is different from the grammar of language in yet another crucial respect. I assume without discussion that two factors, namely style and stylistic conventions, are largely responsible for elevating a Carnatic music discourse to an art form.[16] It is these two factors which constitute constraint sets which are prioritized over grammaticality requirements in the grammar of Carnatic music. I shall advance an argument based on the style of a performer to show how the set of constraints pertaining to style may override the constraint set evaluating grammaticality in section 1.4.1. Apart from style, Carnatic music, being an art form, has evolved certain stylistic conventions which once again may overrule grammaticality requirements. I shall put forward an argument based on one such stylistic convention practised in Carnatic music where constraints specific to this convention may overrule the constraints determining the grammaticality described in section 1.4.2.

25.4.1 Style prioritized above grammaticality in Carnatic music

It is reasonable to assume that the onus of creating a distinct style is on the performer in Carnatic music. We need to explore the factors which go into the making of this style, this dialect. The uniqueness of this style/dialect lies not so much in the originality of the ideas expressed but in the medium.[17] The 'voice' of the user must be unique. By voice I mean all that goes into defining the user as a unique artist to be reckoned with. Among many possible ones, some of the characteristics signaling such individuality may be the physical voice (or properties of the instrument), the personality of the user, or the expectation of the user.

Let me elaborate the characteristics a little. Take the voice. It could be nasal, the person could have an inadequate lung capacity, the voice could be

---

assume that the effort was to stem the tide of 'simplification'. But the post-golden age phase has been one of extended rule bound (scalar) behaviour, even attempting to rewrite earlier rules to conform to certain 'strict' notions of grammaticality.

[16] I am deliberately side stepping the contentious issue of the distinction between a composer and a performer in the context of Carnatic music for lack of space. Suffice it to say that the dividing line is, to say the least, difficult to define and sometimes non-existent. The 'composition' is not something performers handle with kid gloves and is as much subject to the individual's grammar as the rest of the impromptu discourse known as *manoodharma sangeetam*, roughly translated as creative music.

[17] In the context of the oral traditions of culture in south Asia and elsewhere, the canons of art are not governed by copyright considerations and the need to strike a distinct path to set oneself against a tradition, as is the expectation in the West. For instance, imitation is a form of tribute that an artist pays a greater artist (in other words, plagiarism is acceptable).

low/high pitched, recalcitrant, loud, soft, or any of a number of other characteristics. If one looks at the range of Carnatic music performers of standing then one sees that many of them have attained recognition by working with their disability rather than against it. The person with a small lung capacity forges a style with short musical lines, a style characterised by quick brush strokes, so to speak. Then take the personality. If one is of an emotional bent of mind, religious bent of mind, or a mind which revels in abstract musical ideas, the music is informed by these traits. By expectation of the performer I mean what the performer wants from the audience; for example, whether she/he desperately wants a large, unthinking following or is satisfied with a committed group of listeners.

I shall take up one particular example of style to illustrate the central idea of this paper namely, how style factors can be prioritized over grammaticality factors in the grammar of Carnatic music. The style I have in mind is that of an acclaimed, male vocalist of the last half of the 20th century, who was much admired by fellow musicians and a few knowledgeable music lovers.[18] He had a resonant low pitched voice. But the voice was not highly maneuverable as pitch manipulations and fast tempo passages were not easy to handle with this voice. Given this voice profile, the artist had to define his style by restricting pitch curves and pitch spikes and maintaining a steady, slow tempo. Had the artist merely done this, he would have achieved a sober, perhaps, careful style, nothing more. But what he did achieve was nothing short of a miracle; he was an innovator and at the heart of his innovative approach was this simple idea of taking RenScale values of notes and exploring the relationships among steady pitch values of notes in scales of *raagas*. The central style statement of this artist was then 'Explore RenScale relations of notes in a scale'. When one is exploring the relations that hold between notes in a scale, the criteria that are put to work are the following :

(4) Style Set for RenScale Relations in Scales
  a. explore steady pitch contrasts of non-linear notes (Informally, consider notes which are not linear adjacent in the scale, e.g sa- di/ pa Gu; sa gu pa/ ma di Sa)
  b. look for symmetry
  c. look for patterning
  d. look for unusual sequences of notes

Let me explain briefly how these construals work in the grammar of Carnatic music. They are not unworkable, abstract concepts of art but concrete principles which are at the heart of the grammar of Carnatic music. Taking

[18]Since I have not said anything uncomplimentary about the artist, respecting the reviewer's point of view (and going against my general practice), let me reveal that the artist in question here is the late M.D.Ramanathan.

up construal (4a), if non-adjacent notes are sequenced in phrases, then what one looks for is the distance between notes on the scale. For instance, 'sa' (C) and 'di' (A) are five notes apart and so are 'pa' (G) and 'Gu' (upper E). Construal (4b) pertains to notions of symmetry, a notion central to music. Dividing the scale into two parts 'sa – pa' (C – G), 'pa – Sa' (G – upper C) or 'sa – ma' (C – F) and 'ma/mi – ni/nu' (F/F sharp – B flat/B) one gets two easily accessible and definable measures of symmetry between notes in the lower and upper parts of the octave. For instance, in the *raagam* Tooḍi the notes 'ra' (D flat) and 'da' (A flat) are symmetrical and so are 'gi' (E flat) and 'ni' (B flat). Further, the lexically specified pitch manipulations on the latter pair of notes are identical, another example of symmetry. Like symmetry, patterns are at the core of melody and rhythm in music. One can look for patterns by finding identical phrase-making templates and/or finding the same distribution of short and long notes across phrases e.g. [ta taa ta ta ta] is a frequently used six mora phrase with a long second note. The patterns can and do get very complex with complex combinations of patterns employed very frequently. Finally, the last construal, (4d), is not really an undefinable concept at all. In the context of Carnatic music, keeping in mind that performers do not perform with notes in front of them, phrases culled over a life time, common and usually heard phrases, enter the lexicon as entries. Going over the listed phrases allows us to recognise novel sequences. It is not very different from speakers recognising new coinages or nonce words in spoken and written discourse.

One can list more specific strategies. But for our purposes, these would more than suffice. Armed with this style constraint set, he set out to explore the world of musical ideas in Carnatic music. The result was great music but certain issues of grammaticality were the casualty. The style set can and does override many constraints specific to the grammaticality set. I base this discussion of this artist on his rendering of *aalaapanai* and *taanam* in the *raagam* Shankaraabharaṇam.[19] Like other I Set *raagas*, Shankaraabharaṇam has several notes which admit complex pitch movements. For instance, the *raagam* selects the scale [sa ri gu ma pa di nu] (the major scale of Western music) and the notes 'ri' (D), 'ma' (F) and 'di' (A), specifically admit a range of pitch interpretations.[20] As in other *raagas* there are context sensitive *RenScale constraints specific to these notes prohibiting RenScale rendering of these notes in the lexicon of Shankaraabharaṇam. These grammaticality

[19]The music discourse I have in mind was broadcast on the music channel Worldspace I assume it may be available commercially.

[20]The pitch specifications on 'ri' and 'di' is another instance of symmetry. If one considers the scale, another interpretation of symmetry emerges; alternating notes in the scale i.e., 'ri', 'ma' and 'di' admit identical pitch manipulations (though the inter-note intervals may not be identical).

constraints are deliberately violated when the artist launches his RenScale explorations time and again in both the *aalaapanai* and *taanam*.[21]

As mentioned earlier, in addition to determining the grammaticality of notes in the scale there are grammaticality issues pertaining to note sequences governed by the overarching constraint *Amb that requires each *raagam* (specifically I Set *raagas*) to be distinct from every other *raagam* at the level of the sequence, or musical phrase. Shankaraabharaṇam, too, has several such *AmbSeq constraints (avoid ambiguous sequences of notes) e.g., avoid *[sa gu pa] (C E G), *[gu pa nu] (E G B) (as that would point to another *raagam*, namely Hamsadhvani) because they will result in Shankaraabharaṇam being mistaken for some other *raagam*. The exploration of RenScale relation by the artist results in violations of constraints pertaining to *AmbSeq. Thus we see that the constraint ranking pertinent for the artist has the set ranking as shown in (5). The higher ranked style set overrules violations at the lower levels of notes and sequences.

(5) Set Ranking for the Style Set for RenScale Relations in Scales

a. explore steady pitch contrasts of non-linear notes
b. look for symmetry
c. look for patterning
d. look for unusual sequences of notes

$\gg$

Context sensitive *RenScale constraints specific to several notes, *AmbSeq constraints specific to sequences and musical phrases

The question that arises is 'if all constraints which define the grammar of the *raagam* can be violated, how is the discourse perceived as Shankaraabharaṇam?' Naturally, irrespective of style, if ALL constraints defining grammaticality may be violated, there is no question of the discourse being perceived as Shankaraabharaṇam. It will not be Shankaraabharaṇam. For the discourse to be recognised as Shankaraabharaṇam it should be possible to partition the grammaticality constraints into a violable and an inviolable set with the latter working to maintain the identity of the *raagam*. One natural place to look for this partitioning is the note and sequence within the musical phrase in one set and the musical line in the other set. In fact, this seems to be the required partitioning that explains why each musical line is unambiguously assigned to Shankaraabharaṇam even though there are violations at lower levels which are tolerated. If every musical line is taken as the domain for evaluation, then we see that constraints at the level of the musical line, such as interpretation of emphatic prominence or checking to see that all the notes listed in the

[21]This style, at its best, can be very moving, expressing an austere, expansive grandeur. But it can also degenerate into empty rhetoric resembling the incoherence of a drunk.

scale are satisfied, allow us to verify that the grammar of Shankaraabharaṇam is not jeopardised. Thus the overall constraint ranking for the artist (for this discourse) is as captured below.

(6) Set Ranking for Style

Grammaticality Set 1

Construals pertaining to the musical line:

Construals for emphatic prominence,

Checking for presence vs absence of notes in the scale

≫

Set for RenScale Relations in Scales

a. explore steady pitch contrasts of non-linear notes

b. look for symmetry

c. look for patterning

d. look for unusual sequences of notes

≫

Delimited Set __________

Grammaticality Set 2

Context sensitive *RenScale constraints specific to all notes,

*AmbSeq constraints specific to sequences and musical phrases

Thus, specifically, the two major areas where violations are tolerated are with respect to individual notes and sequences in musical phrases. This results in a delayed satisfaction of grammaticality concerns, creating a kind of tension which is resolved at the level of the musical line. The two issues that this discussion leads to are regarding this delay in the satisfaction of grammaticality concerns and whether even higher order grammaticality concerns can be set aside, even temporarily.

As for the first issue, I would like to submit that the delayed satisfaction of grammaticality concerns is a stylistic convention in Carnatic music which I call 'wit' (see next section). As for the second possibility namely, whether the entire set of grammaticality constraints can be set aside temporarily, we will see in the next section how this is done when the stylistic convention called *ʃruti bheedam* (modal shift) is invoked.

Turning back to our earlier discussion of the 'tolerated' musical phrase in the *raagam* Bhairavi in section 25.1, it will now be clear that the phrase under discussion can be considered fully grammatical, if construals at the level of sequence, one of them being the construal which bans the sequence *[..ri ma..] (..D F..) for the *raagam* Bhairavi, are 'temporarily' demoted and the CH appropriately delimited.[22]

[22]As one of the reviewers correctly observed, my attempts here and in Vijayakrishnan (2007) could be taken as exploratory attempts at laying the ground rules for a detailed, fine grained

25.4.2 Prioritization controlled by stylistic conventions

I next turn to stylistic factors in Carnatic music. By stylistic factors I mean those conventions of musical discourse and musical meaning making that are at the disposal of the artist. For instance, devices like imagery, the matching of the language and the musical note, wit and *ʃruti bheedam* or modal shift are some that readily come to mindy.

Musical imagery is bound by the conventions of the system (like onomatopoeia being bound by the phonotactics of the language) e.g., the scale 'sa ra gu pa da Sa- Sa nu da pa gu ra sa' (C, D flat, E, G, A flat, upper C-, upper C, B, A flat, G, E, D flat, C) of the *raagam* Bauḷi is considered to evoke sunrise for the Carnatic music fraternity. Further, imagery can be the transfer of spatial relations to that of pitch. For instance, to convey the concept of vastness of space the pitch glide may range over the entire octave. Imagery can also be highly stylised. For example, the Sanskritic tradition has conventions for capturing the meandering of a river or the shape of the cow's tail which are used fairly frequently in Carnatic music. The matching of the syllables of language with the solfa notation is much appreciated in Carnatic music.

Turning next to wit, I define wit in Carnatic music as an instance of a musical discourse where the elaboration of the *raagam* leads to the brink of an *Amb violation but is rescued just in time, sometimes barely so, but within the musical line. Some popular artists of the past were known to render a few phrases which are deliberately ambiguous between two *raagas* and after the violinist made bold to assume that it was one of the *raagas* to go on to the other *raagam* to the discomfiture of the accompanying violist. Of course, this is not a very good example of wit as it violates the basic convention to be followed in a public recital – the principle of mutual cooperation. However, there are good examples of wit in Carnatic music where composers have created this tension in the first few musical phrases of a musical line to go on to resolve the tension later on in the musical line. It should now be clear why I compared the style of the artist in the previous section to the stylistic device 'wit'. The artist also revels in taking the *raagam* to the brink of *Amb violations at the levels of the note and the phrase but rescuing it finally at the level of the musical line.

I turn next to the stylistic device *ʃruti bheedam* or modal shift. I will show that this device allows the artist to temporarily violate ALL the constraints pertaining to grammaticality. *ʃruti bheedam* is a device which shifts the fundamental from C to any other note of the scale in the middle of a discourse without changing the designated notes of the original scale; only their rela-

grammar of Carnatic music. This is the reason that the eminent musicologist the late Harold Powers (p.c) commented that a better title for my book would have been "A Grammar for Carnatic Music" rather than the current title. But his suggestion came too late to be carried out.

tions are redefined. This results in the scale of a different *raagam*.

For example, if one takes the scale of Shankaraabharaṇam – the major scale 'sa, ri, gu, ma, pa, di, nu, Sa' (C, D, E, F, G, A, B) and shifts thc fundamental to D then the relation that obtains in the scale 'sa, ri, gi, ma, pa, di, ni, Sa' (C, D, E flat, F, G, A, B flat, upper C) the minor scale of Western music or the scale of the *raagam* Karahapriyaa. If *ʃruti bheedam* is undertaken in a Carnatic music recital, it is usually done while rendering the *aalaapanai* of the main *raagam*, towards the end of the *aalaapanai*. Typically, when *ʃruti bheedam* is undertaken, then all the constraints defining the base *raagam* are set aside when the fundamental shifts to some other note of the scale. In the example quoted above, if an artist were to do *ʃruti bheedam* on Shankaraabharaṇam on 'ri' then she/he has to set aside all the constraints for interpreting the notes, sequences, phrases of Shankaraabharaṇam and replace them with those for Karahapriyaa. There is no question of interpreting the discourse as Shankaraabharaṇam as long as the *ʃruti bheedam* is on (often the vocalist signals the violinist to keep bowing the shifted fundamental). The ranking that would account for this stylistic convention then is as shown below:

(7) Ranking Convention for *ʃruti bheedam*

Constraints specific to *Raagam* Y at the level of note, phrase, line,
The fundamental note of *Raagam* Y is a RenScale note_n of *Raagam* X

$\gg$

Delimited ___________
Constraints specific to *Raagam* X at the level of note, phrase, line,
Constraints specific to note_n of *Raagam* X
The fundamental note C of *Raagam* X

The stylistic device of *ʃruti bheedam* sanctions this set prioritization. However, not all performers/theoreticians accept this type of *ʃruti bheedam*. Let me outline a more subtle approach to *ʃruti bheedam* which may be acceptable to more performers/theoreticians, in principle, though it is much more difficult to execute and perceive. This approach demands that all the lexical pitch specifications of the parent *raagam* be kept inviolable and RenScale pitch value be sanctioned for the selected note of the original *raagam* which is to be taken as the changed fundamental note of *ʃruti bheedam*. Thus, for example, the note 'ri' (D) would no longer be an appropriate note for undertaking *ʃruti bheedam* in the *raagam* Shankaraabharaṇam as this note has many Faith.Lex Pitch specifications. More appropriate notes would be 'gu' (E) or 'pa' (G). But the former note would be problematic as its third note 'pa' (G), the 'gi' (E flat) of the new scale, would never admit any pitch maneuvers at all, resulting in a fixed E flat which is only sparingly used in Carnatic music as a RenScale note. Under *ʃruti bheedam*, only the lexical pitch specifications or phrase requirements of the new *raagam* which match those of the original *raagam* are selected for rendering the new *raagam*. This approach requires partitioning the constraint sets of the original *raagam* (*Raagam*$_a$) and the new *raagam* (*Raagam*$_b$) such that there exists a partition (Partition$_{sx}$) of each *raagam* where there are no mutually conflicting pitch/phrasal requirements which are to be exclusively utilized under *ʃruti bheedam*.[23] The set prioritization required is then as in (8) below.

(8) Ranking Convention for *ʃruti bheedam* (Revised)

Partition$_{sa/x}$ = Partition$_{sb/x}$, *Partition$_{\text{-}sb/y}$,
Fundamental note$_n$

$\gg$

Delimited ___________
Fundamental note$_c$,
[Partition$_{\text{-}sa/y}$]

The overlapping constraint partition sets of the two *raagas* are exclusively to be used and are therefore inviolable. The residue partition set of the new *raagam* is negatively stipulated and the change in fundamental note is also ranked above the original fundamental note. This kind of *ʃruti bheeedam* is not only more difficult to render, it is also more difficult to perceive. However it is done, *ʃruti bheedam* as a stylistic device requires reprioritization of the constraint set defining grammaticality.

25.5 Conclusion

In this paper I showed that it is desirable to adopt a non-derivational, ranked output wellformedness approach to Carnatic music. Under two strictly definable conditions of style and stylistic requirements, sets of constraints defining grammaticality may be rendered violable by lowering their prioritization in the overall constraint hierarchy of the *raagam*. Further, we saw that while styles may require the prioritization of grammaticality constraints at the level of the musical line ranked above lower levels, namely note and phrase, rendering the latter violable (and delimited), the stylistic device of *ʃruti bheedam* may keep the grammaticality considerations of the original *raagam* on temporary hold while *ʃruti bheedam* is in progress. It is assumed that such radical set re-ranking becomes possible in the grammar of Carnatic music because it is an art form requiring the individual to craft her/his dialect consciously, and it admits stylistic devices which allow grammaticality issues to be set aside under precisely definable conditions.

---

[23]The perfect *ʃruti bheedam* i.e., according to (6) is the one done on the note 'ma' (F) in the *raagam* Yadukulakaamboodi where one gets the same *raagam* (RR Ayyangar p.c.). Even here it will be seen that the partitioning of constraints must be done, though the mapping is not between two *raagas* but between different notes of the same *raagam*.

Acknowledgement

I am grateful to the editorial board of this volume for including my contribution. That I dared to creatively interpret and apply the principles of modern linguistics to Carnatic music is certainly owing to the fact that K.P. Mohanan and Tara Mohanan took me – a raw graduate – under their wing and led me into the intricacies of phonological theory building with tremendous patience and affection way back in 1976. I am grateful to the anonymous reviewers for bringing my attention to areas of unclarity in the earlier draft of the paper. Of course, I am solely responsible for the remaining inconsistencies, if any, in this version of the paper.

References

McCarthy, John and Alan Prince. 1993. Prosodic Morphology : constraint interaction and satisfaction. Ms., University of Massachusetts and Rutgers.

Prince, Alan and Paul Smolensky. 1993. Optimality Theory. Ms., Rutgers University.

Vijayakrishnan, K. G. 2007. The Grammar of Carnatic Music. Mouton de Gruyter, Germany.

Part IV

Bibliography of K.P. Mohanan's Work (1981–2009)

26

Works by K.P. Mohanan

1981. Pronouns in Malayalam. *Studies in Linguistic Sciences* 11:67–75.

1982a. Grammatical relations and anaphora in Malayalam. In A. Marantz and T. Stowell, eds., *Papers in Syntax*. Cambridge, Mass.: MIT Press.

1982b. Grammatical relations and clause structure in Malayalam. In J. Bresnan, ed., *The Mental Representation of Grammatical Relations*. Cambridge, Mass.: MIT Press.

1982c. Infinitival subjects, government and abstract case. *Linguistic Inquiry* 13:323–327.

1982d. Issues in lexical phonology. University of Montreal, Montreal, Canada (Invited Talk).

1982e. On syllabicity. In K. Safir, ed., *Papers in Syllable Structure, Metrical Structure and Harmony Processes*. Cambridge, Mass.: MIT Press.

1982f. What is lexical phonology? McGill University, Montreal, Canada (Invited Talk).

1983a. Functional and anaphoric control. *Linguistic Inquiry* 14:641–674.

1983b. Move NP or lexical rules? In M. Rappaport and A. Zaenen, eds., *Papers in LFG*. Indiana: Indiana University Press.

1983c. The structure of the melody. MIT and the National University of Singapore.

1984a. Lexical and configurational structures. *Linguistic Review* 3:113–139.

1984b. Lexical phonology. Australian Linguistic Society Conference, Alice Springs, Australia (Keynote Address).

1984c. On locally bound anaphora. *Linguistic Analysis* 13:329–331.

1984d. Operator binding and the path containment condition. *Natural Language and Linguistic Theory* 2:357–396.

1985a. Remarks on control and control theory. *Linguistic Inquiry* 16:637–648.

1985b. Syllable structure and lexical strata in English. *Phonology Yearbook* 2:139–155.

1985c. Vowel epenthesis in Malayalam: Schwa or u? *Indian Linguistics*:97–101.

1985d. What the literary critics know about verse: Towards a theory of cadence. In C. Nicholson and R. Chatterjee, eds., *Tropic Crucible*. Singapore: NUS Press.

1986a. Introduction to lexical phonology. New Ways of Analyzing Variation. Stanford University, Stanford, California (Invited Talk).

1986b. *The Theory of Lexical Phonology*. Dordrecht, Holland: Reidel Publishing.

1987a. The bases of lexical phonology. University of Arizona, Tucson, Arizona (Invited Talk).

1987b. Morphological and syntactic features. University of Southern California, Los Angeles, California (Invited Talk).

1988. Naturalness in phonological alternation. University of California, Los Angeles, California (Invited Talk).

1989a. The bases of underspecification. Kyung Hee University, Seoul, Korea (Invited Talk).

1989b. Universal archetypes of phonological alternation. Forum Lecture. Kyung Hee University, Seoul, Korea (Invited Talk).

1989c. Universal attractors in phonology. Berkeley Workshop on Rules and Constraints. University of California, Berkeley, California. Later published as 1993b.

1991a. Malayalam. In B. Comrie, W. Bright, and D. Crystal, eds., *Oxford Encyclopaedia of Linguistics*. Oxford: Oxford University Press.

1991b. On the bases of radical underspecification. *Natural Language and Linguistic Theory* 9:285–325.

1992a. Describing the phonology of non-native varieties. *World Englishes* 11:111–128.

1992b. Emergence of complexity in phonological development. In C. Ferguson, L. Menn, and C. Stoel-Gammon, eds., *Child Phonological Development*, pages 635–662. Maryland: Timonium.

1992c. Why should we care about word order in South Asian languages? South Asian Languages Analysis XIV. Stanford University, Stanford, California (Keynote Address).

1993a. Conflict resolution in phonology and syntax. University of Konstanz, Konstanz, Germany (Invited Talk).

1993b. Fields of attraction in phonology. In J. Goldsmith, ed., *The Last Phonological Rule*, pages 61–116. Chicago: Chicago University Press.

1993c. The formal interpretation of robustness: Storage or processing? The Robustness of the Language Faculty: Coping with Incomplete Information. Utrecht University, Utrecht, The Netherlands.

1993d. Patterns and pattern interaction. University of Konstanz, Konstanz, Germany (Invited Talk).

1993e. Self organization in linguistic systems. Stanford University, Stanford, California (Invited Talk).

1995a. Argumentation as invitation and demonstration. Meaning as Production: The Role of the Unwritten. Dept. of English Language and Literature, National University of Singapore, Singapore.

1995b. Inculcating critical and creative thinking. Dept. of Biochemistry, Faculty of Medicine, National University of Singapore.

1995c. Malayalam writing. In P. Daniels and W. Bright, eds., *World's Writing Systems*, pages 420–425. Oxford: Oxford University Press.

1995d. Open book exams to discourage regurgitation. Workshop on Open Book Exams. Faculty of Arts and Social Sciences, National University of Singapore, Singapore.

1995e. The organization of the grammar. In J. Goldsmith, ed., *The Handbook of Phonological Theory*, pages 24–69. USA: Basil Blackwell.

1996a. Critical and creative thinking in science. Workshop on Critical and Creative Thinking. Department of Civil Engineering, National University of Singapore, Singapore (Invited Talk).

1996b. Encouraging interactive learning in large group teaching. Workshop on Large Group Teaching. Center for Development of Teaching and Learning, National University of Singapore, Singapore (Invited Talk).

1996c. Indoctrination in pedagogical texts in linguistics. Language and Knowledge: The Unpacking of "Text", Department of English Language and Literature, National University of Singapore, Singapore.

1996d. Types of incommensurability. Workshop in Honour of Thomas Kuhn. National University of Singapore, Singapore (Invited Talk).

1996e. Where does allomorphy begin? In R. Singh, ed., *Trubetzkoy's Orphan*, pages 32–42. Amsterdam: John Benjamins Publishing Co.

1996f. Where does morphophonology belong? In R. Singh, ed., *Trubetzkoy's Orphan*, pages 140–154. Amsterdam: John Benjamins Publishing Co.

1997a. Falsifiability in OT. Linguist List 8.575.

1997b. How does education paralyze independent thinking? 7th International Conference on Thinking. National University of Singapore, Singapore.

1997c. Open book examinations and educational goals. Seminar on the Conduct of Open Book Examinations, National University of Singapore, Singapore (Invited Talk).

1998a. Crosslinguistic variability of linguistic patterns: Paramenter setting or constraint priorization. GLOW Workshop on Verb Typology, CIEFL, Hyderabad, India.

1998b. Non-monotonicity in linguistics: Transformations, constraint ranking, and weighted laws. PACILIC 12 (Keynote Address).

1998c. On the bases of optimality theory. South Asian Language Analysis Roundtable, York University, UK.

1998d. Unpacking opimality theory: Non-monotonicity as transformations, rule ordering and constraint ranking. Australian Linguistics Society Conference. Brisbane, Australia (Plenary Talk).

1999a. Feature network. University of California, Irvine, California (Invited Talk).

1999b. Morphosemantics of deverbal adjectives in Malayalam. 25th Annual Meeting of Berkeley Linguistics Society, University of California, Berkeley, California (Invited Talk).

1999c. On the bases of optimality theory. The University of Hong Kong, Hong Kong (Invited Lecture).

1999d. Postmodernism and science: A critical assessment from a linguist's persepective. The University of Hong Kong (Invited Lecture).

1999e. Problems of dialogue across domains. CAS Research Papers Launch. National University of Singapore, Singapore (Invited Talk).

1999f. What is wrong with undergraduate linguistic education today. New Zealand Linguistic Society Conference, Massey University, Palmerston North, New Zealand.

2000a. Evidence-based and inquiry-based learning in linguistics education. The University of Hong Kong, Hong Kong (Invited Lecture).

2000b. Postmodernism and scientific inquiry. City University of Hong Kong, Hong Kong (Invited Lecture).

2000c. Quality of teaching in higher education. Center for Development of Teaching and Learning, The University of Hong Kong, Hong Kong (Invited Lecture).

2000d. The theoretical substance of the optimality formalism. *Linguistic Review* 17:143–166.

2001. Peer review at NUS: Rationale and implementation. Dialogue Session on Peer Review. Center for Development of Teaching and Learning, National University Singapore, Singapore.

2002. Applied epistemology in pedagogical theory and practice. Teaching and Learning in Higher Education. Center for Development of Teaching and Learning, National University Singapore, Singapore.

2003a. Objects of inquiry, theory, data, and methodology in linguistics. Stanford University, Stanford, California (Invited Talk).

2003b. Reflections on language, grammar, and society: Connecting generative linguistics and sociolinguistics. Sociorap. Stanford University, Stanford, CA.

2004a. Assessing and improving quality of education: A multi-leveled integrated approach. Teaching and Learning in Higher Education. Center for Development of Teaching and Learning, National University of Singapore, Singapore.

2004b. Assessing and improving quality of education: The NUS experience. Teaching and Learning in Higher Education. Center for Development of Teaching and Learning, National University of Singapore, Singapore.

2004c. Self assessment in higher education. Teaching and Learning in Higher Education. Center for Development of Teaching and Learning, National University of Singapore, Singapore (Pre-Conference Workshop).

2005a. Critical thinking and inquiry in science education: Science as a body of knowledge vs. science as paradigm of knowing. National Seminar on Science Education. Vidya Bhavan Education Resource Centre, Udaipur, India.

2005b. The place of student feedback in teaching evaluation. CDTL (Center for Development of Teaching and Learning, NUS, Singapore) website.

2006a. Many cultures of academic inquiry. World Knowledge Dialogue Symposium. First edition. Crans-Montana, Switzerland.

2006b. A selective report on graduate education. IARU Symposium on Graduate Education. Copenhagen, Denmark.

2006c. Teaching to learn: The what and how of higher education. 50th Anniversary Special Series of Seminars on Language and Language Teaching. Hong Kong Baptist University, Hong Kong (Invited Talk).

2006d. Thinking about undergraduate education: Convergences, divergences, and challenge. IARU Symposium on Undergraduate Education: The Transforming Power of Undergraduate Education. The University of Copenhagen, Denmark.

2007. What is a proof? Towards a general theory of soundness in justification. Department of Philosophy, National University of Singapore, Singapore.

2008a. Methodology and justification in academic inquiry. Indian Institute of Science, Bangalore, India (Invited Talk).

2008b. Reflections. Roundtable on Communication and Cooperation: Conditions for a Dialogue Addressing the Fundamental Problems of our Time. World Knowledge Dialogue Symposium. Second edition. Crans-Montana, Switzerland.

2009a. Inquiry-based pedagogy and problem-based pedagogy. Second International PBL Symposium. Republic Polytechnic, Singapore.

2009b. Instilling the habits of academic inquiry among the young. Second International PBL Symposium. Pre-symposium workshop. Republic Polytechnic, Singapore.

27

Co-Authored Works by K.P. Mohanan

Alsina, Alex, K.P. Mohanan, and Tara Mohanan. 1996. On COMP. Submission to the LFG list, 1 October 1996.

Alsina, Alex, K.P. Mohanan, and Tara Mohanan. 2005. How to get rid of COMP. 10th International Lexical-Functional Grammar Conference. University of Bergen, Bergen, Norway.

Halle, Morris and K.P. Mohanan. 1985. Segmental phonology of Modern English. *Linguistic Inquiry* 16:57–116.

Mohanan, K.P. and Tara Mohanan. 1984. Lexical phonology of the consonant system in Malayalam. *Linguistic Inquiry* 15:575–602.

Mohanan, K.P. and Tara Mohanan. 1988. Dative subjects in Malayalam. 17th Annual Conference on South Asia: Symposium on Experiencer Subjects in South Asian Languages. University of Wisconsin, Madison, Wisconsin.

Mohanan, K.P. and Tara Mohanan. 1991. Dative subjects in Malayalam: Semantic information in syntax. In M. K. Verma and K. Mohanan, eds., *Experiencer Subjects in South Asian Languages*. Stanford, CA: CSLI.

Mohanan, K.P. and Tara Mohanan. 1993. Conflict resolution in South Asian syntax. Symposium on South and East Asian Languages.

Mohanan, K.P. and Tara Mohanan. 1994. Issues in word order in South Asian languages: Enriched phrase structure or multidimensionality? In M. Butt, T. H. King, and G. Ramchand, eds., *Theoretical Perspectives on Word Order in South Asian Languages*, pages 153–184. Stanford, CA: CSLI.

Mohanan, K.P. and Tara Mohanan. 1996. Semantic representation in the architecture of LFG. In M. Butt and T. H. King, eds., *Proceedings of the First LFG Conference*, pages 293–310. Grenoble: Rank Xerox Research Centre.

Mohanan, K.P. and Tara Mohanan. 1997. On morphology, morphemes, and words. In M. Hariprasad, H. Nagarajan, P. Madhavan, and K. Vijayakrishnan, eds., *Phases and Interfaces in Morphology*, pages 1–35. Hyderabad: CIEFL.

Mohanan, K.P. and Tara Mohanan. 1998a. Lexical logical form and verb typology: A case study from Malayalam. GLOW Workshop on Verb Typology. Central Institute of English and Foreign Languages, Hyderabad, India.

Mohanan, K.P. and Tara Mohanan. 1998b. Strong and weak projection: Lexical reflexives and reciprocals. In M. Butt and W. Geuder, eds., *Projection of Arguments: Lexical and Syntactic Constraints*, pages 165–194. Stanford, CA: CSLI.

Mohanan, K.P. and Tara Mohanan. 1999a. Representing presuppositions. In T. Mohanan and L. Wee, eds., *Grammatical Semantics: Evidence for Structure in Meaning*, pages 217–260. Stanford, CA: CSLI and NUS.

Mohanan, K.P. and Tara Mohanan. 2000a. Modes on inquiry in academic disciplines: A prolegomena to comparative epistemology. Available on GE Website, http://www.cdtl.nus.edu.sg/gem/articles.htm.

Mohanan, K.P. and Tara Mohanan. 2000b. Parameters of modes of inquiry. Workshop on Modes of Inquiry. Center for Development of Teaching and Learning, National University of Singapore, Singapore.

Mohanan, K.P. and Tara Mohanan. 2003a. The logical structure of OT constraints. Stanford Linguistic Colloquium. Stanford University.

Mohanan, K.P. and Tara Mohanan. 2003b. On deriving constraints and constraint ranking. Trilateral Phonology Weekend. University of California, Santa Cruz, California.

Mohanan, K.P. and Tara Mohanan. 2003c. Universal and language particular constraints in OT-LFG. In T. H. King and M. Butt, eds., *Eighth International Lexical-Functional Grammar Conference*. Stanford, CA.

Mohanan, K.P. and Tara Mohanan. 2005a. Indoctrination in linguistics education. Departmental Seminar, Universitat Pompeu Fabra, Barcelona, Spain.

Mohanan, K.P. and Tara Mohanan. 2006. A trek through Malayalam verb morphology. In S. Inkelas and K. Hansen, eds., *The Nature of the Word: Essays in Honour of Paul Kiparsky*. Cambridge, Massachusetts: MIT Press.

Mohanan, K.P. and Tara Mohanan. 2009a. Linguistics education and cognitive liberation. *The EFL Journal* 1. Hyderabad: The English and Foreign Languages University.

Mohanan, K.P., Tara Mohanan, and Alex Alsina. 1996a. Responses to the discussion on COMP in LFG. Submission to the LFG list, 6 September 1996.

Mohanan, K.P., Tara Mohanan, and Lionel H. A. Wee. 1999. On grammatical semantics: An introduction. In T. Mohanan and L. Wee, eds., *Grammatical Semantics: Evidence for Structure in Meaning*, pages 1–21. Stanford, CA: CSLI and NUS.

Mohanan, Tara, Alex Alsina, and K.P. Mohanan. 1996b. Untitled. Submission to the LFG list, 3 September 1996.

Mohanan, Tara and K.P. Mohanan. 1999b. On representations in grammatical semantics. In T. Mohanan and L. Wee, eds., *Grammatical Semantics: Evidence for Structure in Meaning*, pages 23–76. Stanford, CA: CSLI and NUS.

Mohanan, Tara and K.P. Mohanan. 1999c. Two forms of BE in Malayalam. In M. Butt and T. H. King, eds., *Proceedings of the LFG99 Conference*. Stanford, CA: CSLI.

Mohanan, Tara and K.P. Mohanan. 2003d. Conditionals in Malayalam and Hindi: A theoretical-typological perspective. Conditionals and Counterfactuals. Department of Linguistics, University of California, Berkeley, California.

Mohanan, Tara and K.P. Mohanan. 2003e. Emergence of structure in Malayalee English. Stanford Linguistics Colloquium. Stanford University, Stanford, California.

Mohanan, Tara and K.P. Mohanan. 2003f. Input, output candidates, markedness constraints, and ineffability in OT-LGF. In T. H. King and M. Butt, eds., *Eighth International Lexical-Functional Grammar Conference*. Stanford, CA.

Mohanan, Tara and K.P. Mohanan. 2005b. Constructions in linguistic theory. Colloquium Department of Translation and Philology. Universitat Pompeu Fabra, Barcelona, Spain.

Mohanan, Tara and K.P. Mohanan. 2005c. Universal grammar, constructions, and South Asian languages. The 25th South Asian Language Analysis Roundtable. University of Illinois at Urbana-Champagne. (Plenary talk).

Mohanan, Tara and K.P. Mohanan. 2008. Multiple tenses in the Malayalam verb. In S. Inkelas and K. Hansen, eds., *The Nature of the Word: Essays in Honor of Paul Kiparsky*. Cambridge, Mass.: MIT Press.

Mohanan, Tara and K.P. Mohanan. 2009b. Education and cognitive liberation. *The EFL Journal* 1. Hyderabad: The English and Foreign Languages University.

Singh, Rajendra, Jean D'souza, K.P. Mohanan, and N. S. Prabhu. 1995. On "new/non-native" Englishes: A quartet. *Journal of Pragmatics* 24:283–294.

Velayudhan, S. and K.P. Mohanan. 1974. *Introduction to Phonetics and Structure of English*. Bombay. Macmillan India.

Verma, Manindra K. and K.P. Mohanan, eds. 1991a. *Experiencer Subjects in South Asian Languages*. Stanford, CA: CSLI.

Verma, Manindra K. and K.P. Mohanan. 1991b. Introduction to the experiencer subject construction. In M. K. Verma and K. Mohanan, eds., *Experiencer Subjects in South Asian Languages*. Stanford, CA: CSLI.

Wang, C.M., K.P. Mohanan, A. Christudason, and D. Pan. 2000a. Teacher appraisal: How to measure. In *Proceedings of the First Symposium in Teaching and Learning in Higher Education*, pages 87–92. Singapore: CDTL, NUS.

Wang, C.M., K.P. Mohanan, D. Pan, and Y.S. Chee, eds. 2000b. *Proceedings of the First Symposium on Teaching and Learning in Higher Education*. Singapore: CDTL. 500 pp. (Conference Proceedings).

Index